BLACK NATIONALISM STILL ALIVE AND WELL

FREDERICK MONDERSON

SUMON PUBLISHERS

SuMon Publishers
PO Box 160586
Brooklyn, New York 11216

fredsegypt.com@fredsegypt.com
sumonpublishers.com@sumonpublishers.com
blackfolksbooks.com@blackfolksbooks.com
blackegyptbooks.com@blackegyptbooks.com

Copyright Frederick Monderson/ SuMon Publishers, 2016 All Rights Reserved.

No part of this book may be reproduced, stored in a retrieval system, or transmitted by any means without the written permission of the author.

ISBN – 978-1610230537
LCCN - 2016900808

In the "Tribute to Professor George Simmonds," 'Unsung Hero,' Dr. Fred Monderson sat at the feet of his heroes, Brother X, Michael Carter, Dr. Leonard Jeffries, El Hombre Brath, Dr. Lewis, Prof. George Simmonds, Dr. ben-Jochannan, Sister Camille Yarbrough, Etc.

ABOUT THE AUTHOR

Frederick Monderson is a retired college professor and school teacher who taught African History in the City University of New York and American History and Government in the New York public schools. He has written more than 1000 articles in the New York Black Press, *Daily Challenge*, *Afro Times* and *New American* newspapers. In this venture, Monderson lends his expertise as a historian, Egyptologist, journalist and author of several books including *Black Nationalism: Alive and Well*; *Michael Jackson: The Last Dance*; *50 on Point*; *Barack Obama: Ready, Fit to Lead*; *Barack Obama: Master of Washington, D.C.*; *Obama: Master and Commander*; *Sonny Carson: The Final Triumph*; and on ancient Egypt *Seven Letters to Mike Tyson on Egyptian Temples*; *10 Poems Praising Great Blacks for Mike Tyson*; *Research Essays on Ancient Egypt*; *Temple of Karnak: The Majestic Architecture of Ancient Kemet*; *Where are the Kamite Kings?*; *Abydos and Osiris*; *Temple of Luxor*; *Medinet Habu: Mortuary Temple of Rameses III*; *The Quintessential Book on Ancient Egypt*: "*Holy Land*" *(*A Novel on Egypt); *Hatshepsut's Temple at Deir el-Bahari*; *The Majesty of Egyptian Gods and Temples* (a book of Egyptian Poems); *Egypt Essays on Ancient Kemet*; *The Ramesseum: Mortuary Temple of Rameses II*; *The Colonnade: Then and Now*; *Reflections on Ancient Kemet*; *Grassroots View of Ancient Egypt*; *Glory of the Ancestors: 19 Letters to O.J. Simpson on Ancient African History*; and *Celebrating Dr. Ben-Jochannan*. A student of the esteemed Dr. Yosef ben-Jochannan, Dr. Monderson conducts tours to Egypt.

For Tour information, Please contact Orleane Brooks-Williams at Nostrand Travel, 730 Nostrand Avenue, Brooklyn, New York 11216. Phone Number 718-756-5300. **Next Tour of Egypt** is **August 3-August 17, 2016**

BN PHOTO - The image of the person on the pinnacle of the Capitol Building and Elombe Brathe, "Ultimate Nationalist Warrior" makes a point standing before the nationalist Red, Black and Green.

BLACK NATIONALISM STILL ALIVE AND WELL

TABLE OF CONTENTS

1. DR. ADELAIDE SANFORD — 5
2. MILLION MAN MARCH - Substance and Significance — 32
3. MARCUS GARVEY REFLECTIONS TODAY — 51
4. ERIC GARNER ONE YEAR LATER — 64
5. SALVATION THROUGH PAN-AFRICANISM — 77
6. BETTY DOPSON - "WARRIOR QUEEN" — 91
7. THE BLACK WOMAN — 107
8. SALUTING THE BLACK WOMAN — 138
9. MOOD OF THE COUNTRY — 171
10. THAT MISSOURI COMPROMISE — 177
11. SLAVES, MASTERS AND SECURITY — 184
12. "LYNCHING AS RACIAL TERROR" — 190
13. MARCH ON WASHINGTON — 203
14. SHARPTON, TODAY — 208
15. THE WHITE HOUSE CONTRADICTION — 216

FREDERICK MONDERSON

16.	FRANKLIN AVENUE SHUTTLE: SHUTTLE INTO THE MILLENNIUM	227
17.	BLACK SOLIDARITY DAY: HISTORY AND VISION	242
18.	ARC OF THE MORAL UNIVERSE	250
19.	Dr. YOSEF A. A. BEN JOCHANNAN: A TRIBUTE	259
20.	ELOMBE BRATH: ULTIMATE NATIONALIST SOLDIER"	288
21.	"HEAVEN IN AN UPROAR"	294
22.	THE UNBELIEVERS	310
23	OBAMA: WORSE PRESIDENT? PHOOEY!	323
24.	WHEN RUBY MEETS OSSIE!	337
25.	NEWT! RUNNING DOWN THE MAN!	344
26.	OBAMA: "A BAD YEAR? NO!"	355
27.	THE MUMMY MYSTIQUE	369
28.	JITU WEUSI "MOUNTAIN OF A MAN"	380
29.	HAPPY MOTHERS' DAY	389
30.	THE POWER OF WOMAN!	399
31.	OBAMA: UNEASY LIES THE HEAD	410
32.	HONORING A GIANT	420
33.	A. PHILIP RANDOLPH "MARCH	427

BLACK NATIONALISM STILL ALIVE AND WELL

	ON WASHINGTON, D.C. 1941"	
34.	TALKING POINTS OR COGNITIVE DISSONANCE?	441
35.	"FOOLS" ON "ERRANDS"	447
36.	DEFENDING A MYTH!	454
37.	PUTTING THEM AWAY NICELY	470
38.	"UNITY MARCH FOR GRANGER!"	476
39.	"PLAYING THE JAGAN CARD!"	484
40.	WHEN MCCONNELL MEETS OBAMA!	496
41.	CALLING OUT OBAMA!	504
42.	OBAMA AND LEADERSHIP	511
43.	HOME GROWN RACIAL TERRORISM	527
44.	THE SCOURGE OF RACIAL HATRED	536
45.	THE ILLUSTRIOUS QUEEN MOTHER	543
46.	QUEEN OF SHEBA IN RACIAL PORTRAIT AS HISTORICAL DISTORTION	553
47.	THE POWER OF ECONOMIC BOYCOTT	566
48.	SONNY CARSON: MAKING OF A REVOLUTIONARY	573

49.	PERSPECTIVES ON SONNY (AB) CARSON	588
50.	ROSA PARKS	596
51.	"CHICKEN COMING HOME TO ROOST"	598
52.	THE "SOUTHERN FIREWALL"	603
53.	THE TRIPARTITE PAN-AFRICANISTS	616
54.	"WE BE MARCHING"	623
55.	PRESIDENT OBAMA IN AFRICA I	686
56.	PRESIDENT OBAMA IN AFRICA II	709
57.	BOATING ON THE NILE	723
58.	PO BEN CARSON!	731
59.	THAT OBAMA LEGACY	737
60.	RALLY AROUND BARACK!	740
61.	DIVIDING THE COUNTRY	749
62.	BARACK OBAMA - RHETORIC AND REALITY	755

BLACK NATIONALISM STILL ALIVE AND WELL

BN PHOTO - Her Majesty, "Intellectual Queen Mother" Adelaide L. Sanford, in all her regal splendor.

1. DR. ADELAIDE SANFORD
By
Dr. Fred Monderson

The intellectual nationalist community in New York gathered in Harlem on Saturday, November 21, 2015, to celebrate the 90th Birthday of Dr. Adelaide Sanford, a resolute and venerated scholar and "Queen Mother" of educational, social and Africanist activism who constantly pursued constructive pleasures in exercise of the mind while exhibiting charm and fortitude with a tenacity of unbelievable expression. "Beloved" as she has so often greeted her constituency in the most thoughtful and eloquent addresses, Dr. Adelaide Livonia Sanford not simply achieved the venerable age of

FREDERICK MONDERSON

90 but has still masterfully retained the full-compliment of her intellectual faculties and while able to hold the attention of her audience she continues to artfully speaks truth about and to power. Even more important, this iconic genius and beautiful soul, a lady of impeccable grace and fashion, one of the finest women in the African universe, not simply possesses an unmatched command of intellectual communication finesse, but as a role-model offers much to the young, women especially, who must wonder at the "benefits of staying the course" as she has, whether it be health-wise, academically, even symbolically as humanistic and nationalist spokesperson whose elegance, reverence and courageousness has helped galvanize and emboldens a thinking constituency committed to uplifting and advancing African people's aspirations and empowerment especially through consistent and constructively demonstrated educational effort.

BN PHOTO - Dr. Adelaide Luvenia Hines Sanford "Holding Court" at her 90th Birthday Celebration in Harlem on Saturday, November 21, 2015.

Dr. Sanford, a thinking, talented woman created in a divine mold, possessed tenacity and extraordinary leadership skills and push and while espousing "excellence without excuses," she emerged from being a local efficient and effective school administrator and principal; who, through the force of constructive ideas and effort

BLACK NATIONALISM
STILL ALIVE AND WELL

emerged as Vice-Chancellor of New York State Board of Regents, a powerful body that sets policies, principles and standards for education in the state. However, from this lofty academic citadel, uncompromising in principle and humanistic practice, her role as an activist administrator and educator helped cultivate a cadre of dedicated activists pursuing the **Curriculum of Inclusion** struggle which helped advance the cause of Africans seeking knowledge of self, esteem and academic and social advancement. As such, her vision and well-deserved recognition became inspirational and international in scope and often coupled with **CEMOTAP's** Co-Chairs "Warrior Queen" Betty Dopson and the deep-thinking Dr. James McIntosh she achieved remarkable progress across this nation and abroad in furthering the African intellectual ideal. Thus, it can be said of Dr. Adelaide Sanford, "She knows what the best purpose of education is" not simply for African people but humanity in general, and so has constantly emphasized pleasurable educational pursuits in the exercise of the mind to advance self in benefit of community.

Possessing nobility of spirit and elegance of mind as well as an educational philosophy grounded in African cultural norms, she consistently demonstrated a masterful command of an "intellectual gift of gab." In this and constantly exploring, cultivating and insistently emphasizing the goals, objectives and function of education, Dr. Sanford often mesmerized as a guest on Gil Noble's **Like It Is** program on ABC TV, New York. There, she often critiqued New York State's educational curricula and the nature of its teaching techniques and exam formats while offering thoughtful and provocative corrective suggestions for improving the learning process with an aim to elevating African-American students, and all students. Her goal has been to move students from the dull and encumbering negative objects of history to being empowered positive subjects actively involved in impacting their world through creative strategies for educational advancement that benefit all in search of truth. A tireless education champion, Dr. Sanford endeavored to banish the drudgery of ignorance through involving both parents and students in cultivating creative ideas exploring and

FREDERICK MONDERSON

pursuing efforts to move her constituency beyond mediocrity towards excellence. Serving 21 years as a New York State Regent, her guiding philosophy underscored, "When you have low expectations you have nothing." So she endeavored to identify and focus students on their potential while accentuating what they can accomplish. Fertilizing their minds.

BN PHOTO - Mr. David Sanford, son of the "Honoree" as he thanks the organizers and audience for the celebration in praise of his mother. He spoke of "reversal of roles," for as a young man his mother often stayed awake waiting for him to return home at night and now as elderly as she is, he stays awake waiting up for her to come home from speaking engagements from near and far.

BLACK NATIONALISM STILL ALIVE AND WELL

BN PHOTO - Dr. Adelaide Sanford in a family photographic portrait with Emma Merneith-Mitta under her loving, motherly embrace and goodwill.

FREDERICK MONDERSON

BN PHOTO - An Africa Cake Celebrating Dr. Adelaide Sanford's 90th Birthday.

It needs be emphasized, while the educational mastermind Jitu Weusi recognized in Dr. Sanford a master-teacher, enlightener, social-uplifter and uncompromising academic and intellectual fighter committed to challenging distortions, misrepresentations and stigmatism of African people in media and educational systems dedicated to degradation to hold their aspirations; his counterpart Sonny Carson, himself an avid educational activist, early recognized Dr. Sanford's role as educational leader and always stood ready to "back her play." Thus, in the case of Dr. Sanford, Mr. Carson would have similarly echoed the sentiments of Seymour St. John, Headmaster, Choate School under "Hard Education or Soft" published in *Vogue*, January 15, 1958 that, "In education the closeness of students to a good and great man or woman is the finest we can offer our children." Thus, this insight reflected Dr. Sanford's mindset and proximity to her constituency and mission when as a New York City Principal; she achieved such remarkable success empowering her student body.

BLACK NATIONALISM STILL ALIVE AND WELL

BN PHOTO - As "Beautiful as the Rainbow," these Ladies were nothing short of "Belles of the Ball" on a night honoring an equally elegant and audacious Lady, the intellectual giant, Dr. Adelaide Luvenia Hines Sanford.

A linchpin in establishment and sustainability support of Dr. Clarke's House in Harlem, that veritable home of the **Board of Education of People of African Ancestry (BEPAA)** and Elders Home in Selma, Alabama, as Wordsworth described "a perfect woman, nobly planned," Dr. Sanford was fortunate to know, work with and support the vision of Dr. John Henrik Clarke and his brother and companion in the struggle Dr. Yosef ben-Jochannan in their life-long dedication to the betterment of the status of African people. In that quest, the great educators, teachers, activists as Dr. Sanford, Jitu Weusi, Sonny Carson, Dr. John H. Clarke, Dr. Leonard James, Rev. Herbert Oliver of Montgomery economic boycott fame, Dr. Leonard Jeffries, Dr. Yosef ben-Jochannan and so many others marching in the footsteps of Mary McLeod Bethune, Dr. Carter G. Woodson and Claude McKay, could borrow a phrase and express the

FREDERICK MONDERSON

sentiments Adlai E. Stevenson presented in an address to United Parents Association published in *The New York Times* on April 6, 1958 wherein these heroes all worked unending to assure, "Respect for intellectual excellence, the restoration of vigor and discipline to our ideas of study, curricula which aims at strengthening intellectual fiber and stretching the power of young minds, personal commitment and responsibility - these are the preconditions of educational recovery in America today; and I believe they have always been the precondition of happiness and sanity for the human race."

Nonetheless, the above educational icons who struggled in the vineyards alongside Dr. Sanford have consistently insisted on positive inclusion of African-American contributions in the curriculum embodied in a status on par with every other group. However and concurrently they have equally insisted the African-American youth must liberate themselves through available means and cultivate the knowledge to realize such freedoms and associated power are never given but are possible, attainable through unending commitment and unending dedication for betterment. These young minds must understand further, educational effort and intellectual achievement is a life-long pursuit and treasure and to achieve such, they must cultivate genius with a vision to helping self and community as they challenge the possibilities of the future, for as Aristotle once expressed, "education is the best provision for old age." Nevertheless, given that Nile Valley Africans were original in originating all forms of knowledge; they must have as this writer takes all branches of such mental treasures of the mind to be my province.

BLACK NATIONALISM
STILL ALIVE AND WELL

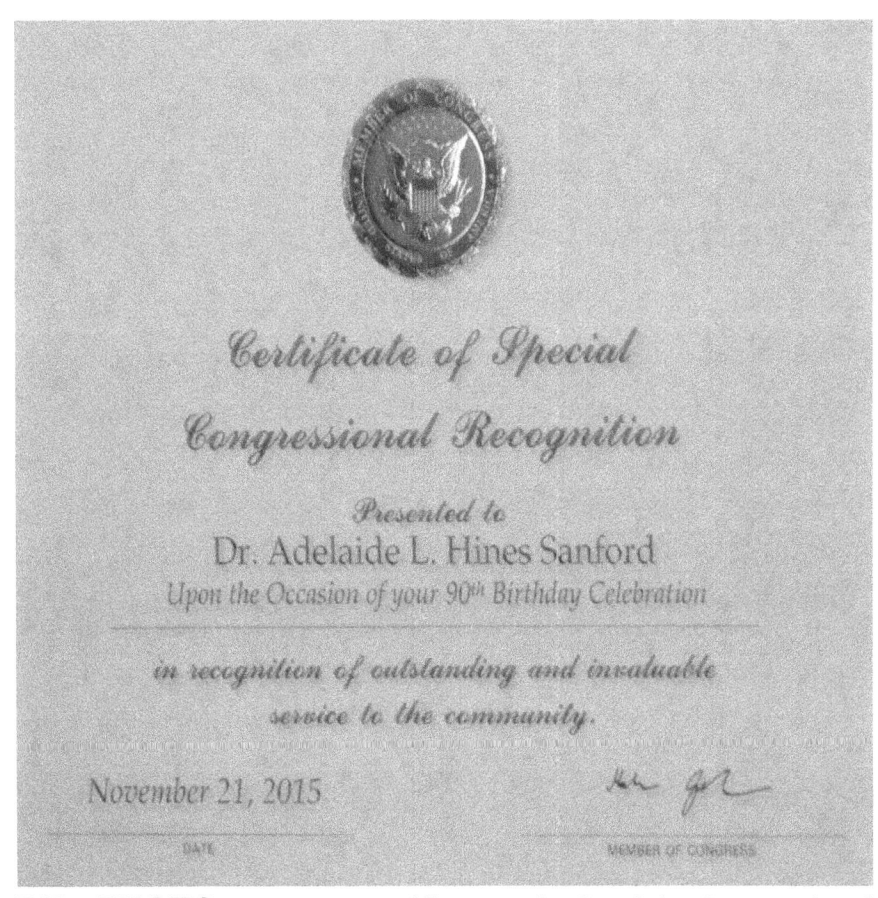

BN PHOTO - "A Certificate of Special Congressional Recognition Presented to Dr. Adelaide L. Hines Sanford Upon the Occasion of your 90th Birthday Celebration."

FREDERICK MONDERSON

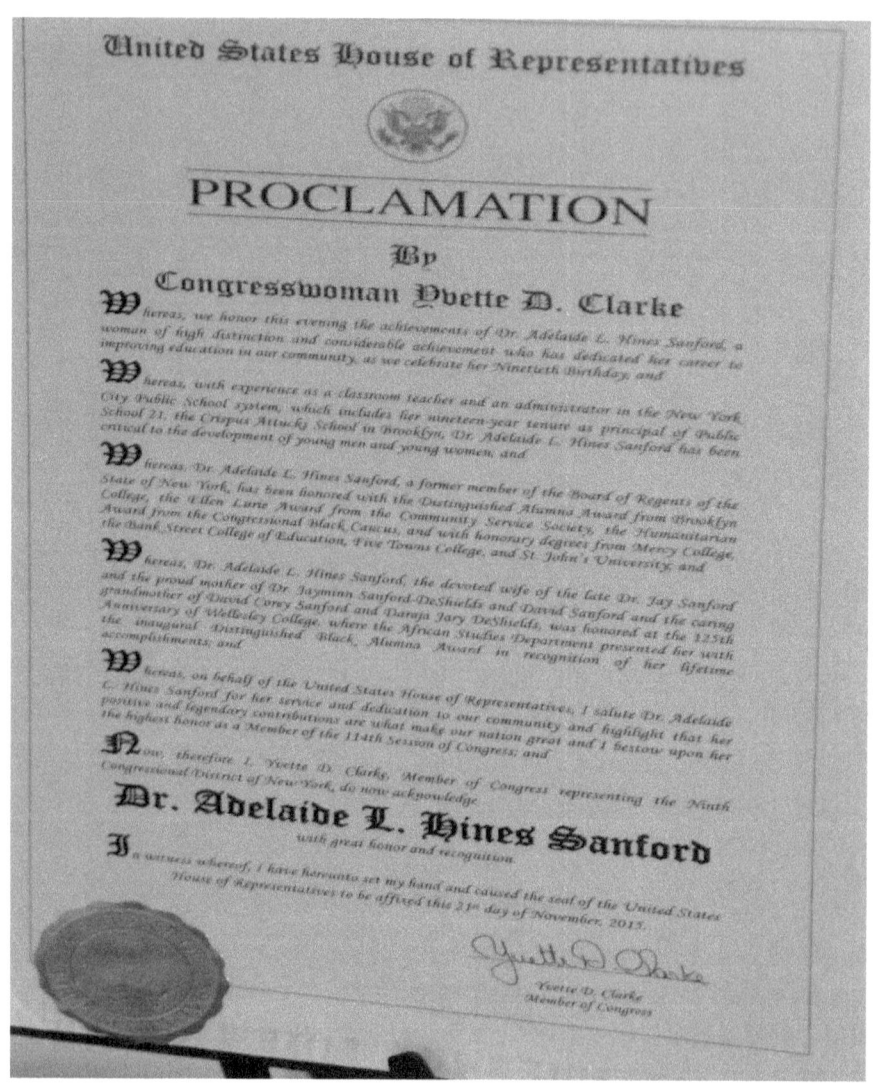

BN PHOTO - United States House of Representatives Proclamation Presented to Dr. Adelaide L. Hines Sanford sponsored by Congresswoman Yvette Clarke that recognizes her life's work on behalf of African people.

BLACK NATIONALISM STILL ALIVE AND WELL

BN PHOTO - New York City Council Proclamation "Presented to Dr. Adelaide L. Hines Sanford on Celebration of her 90th Birthday."

FREDERICK MONDERSON

BN PHOTO - New York State Senate Proclamation Presented by Senator Velmanette Montgomery "To Dr. Adelaide L. Hines Sanford on the Occasion of her 90th Birthday Celebration."

BLACK NATIONALISM STILL ALIVE AND WELL

BN PHOTO - Part of the gathering of well-wishers, with Dr. Young standing, who came to wish Dr. Sanford the very best on her 90th Birthday.

This and more the visionary Dr. Adelaide Sandford unselfishly dedicated her life's work towards achieving. That is, the recognition of self worth and construction of a plan of action focused on the elevation and empowering of young minds to help the lot and condition of society.

As the program unfolded after the "Jazz Prelude by the Doug Harris Quartet," "Honoree's Processional with African Drummers," "Opening Remarks" and "Introduction of Masters of Ceremonies," in his "Prayer of Thankfulness and Hope," Rev. Joel R. Youngblood, Assistant to the Pastor, Mount Pisgah Baptist Church, spoke of the "Spirit of the Creator" guiding the "perpetual pleasure and performance" of Dr. Sanford for "she partnered with humanity for the restoration of the soul of African people." She showed "tenacity" in recognizing the significance of the "Serenity Prayer" trying to

FREDERICK MONDERSON

"feed the lambs" while advocating her philosophy of "perform or perish." Characterizing Dr. Sanford's lengthy life of 90 years, much in constructive service, his mathematical breakdown showed it consisted of 1080 months, 4680 weeks, 32,870 days, 788,412 hours, 47,000, 304 minutes, and 2,000,240,834 seconds, and then he donated a "Check for $25,000!"

In the Libation, Nana Camille Yarbrough recognized this is a "very special day" and reminded "African culture will come to get you!" "African culture is deep inside you." She pointed out, "Houses are rising all over the country" in a reference to Dr. John H. Clarke's House in Harlem and Elders House in Selma, Alabama. She insisted, "We thank the Mighty One, the Great Creator who goes by many names" for "we are the parents of humanity" who have been "Bad, tenacious ancestors." Then she elicited the Roll Call of Illustrious Ancestors and the litany of names included Sister Khefer, Langston Hughes, Frederick Douglass, Malcolm X, Dr. John Clarke, Dr. ben-Jochannan, Adam Clayton Powell, Rosa Parks, Nat Turner, Jitu Weusi, Sonny Carson, Elombe Brath, James Baldwin, Josephine Baker, Nina Simone, Mitta Monderson, Cherise Preville, Major Owens, and a whole lot more.

BN PHOTO - Dr. and Mrs. James McIntosh (left) and Luis and a friend from **Roots Revisited** (right).

BLACK NATIONALISM STILL ALIVE AND WELL

BN PHOTO - Former Councilman Al Vann and a guest (left) and two nationalist persons and members of **CEMOTAP** (right), very much involved in challenging issues and affairs facing the African-American community.

BN PHOTO - Assemblyman Charles Baron and his wife Councilwoman Inez Baron (left); and Dr. Shabaka Segun and a friend, all out to ensure Dr. Sanford's Birthday Celebration was as good as it gets!

FREDERICK MONDERSON

BN PHOTO - African Ladies at Work - Nana Camille Yarbrough doing the Libation Ceremony and Sister Gayle Turner doing her Musical Tribute - "If I can Help Somebody," all for Dr. Adelaide Sanford.

BN PHOTO - "Let's Get the Drummers On, Get the Drummers on;" well, here they are in the Honoree's Processional "Getting On."

BLACK NATIONALISM
STILL ALIVE AND WELL

BN PHOTO - Sister Nana Camille Yarbrough pouring the Libation and asking the Ancestors to bless this wonderful Celebration of Dr. Adelaide Sanford's 90th Birthday.

FREDERICK MONDERSON

BN PHOTO - Councilman Robert Cornegy was also in attendance to pay his respects to the "Queen Mother" Dr. Adelaide L. Hines Sanford.

BN PHOTO - Two Beautiful Ladies, Carmen Monderson and a Sister from the Event's Planning Committee.

BLACK NATIONALISM STILL ALIVE AND WELL

BN PHOTO - Young Erik mugs before the White House fence.

FREDERICK MONDERSON

BN PHOTO - Carmen and Emma along with Assistant Principal Williams.

BLACK NATIONALISM STILL ALIVE AND WELL

BN PHOTO - Former Councilwoman and now Assemblywoman Annette Robinson came to pay respects to Dr. Adelaide Sanford.

Echoing Dr. Sanford's life-work Sister Gayle Turner sang **A Musical Selection** entitled "If I can Help Somebody" while the MC MichelleLindaBaron, thought such was food for the Spirit, Soul and Mind. The other MC, Brian Favors, a Penn State graduate motivated by Dr. Sanford also thanked Michael Hooper and Charles Baron in attendance with his First Lady, Inez.

Betty Dopson, Co-Chair of **CEMOTAP** explained, if you want something, "Work for it; claim it; work and it happens." She praised the Honoree as "adorable and gorgeous." She added, "I was proud to be part of her journey. She [Betty] added value and focus to my life." Addressing the audience, she extolled, "Take a page out of Dr. Sanford's life and get busy." Betty's Co-Chair, Dr. James McIntosh reminded, Dr. Sanford, "You are precious, resilient, courageous, audacious and resourceful." Commenting on her work as Principal of PS 20, **Crispus Attucks School**, he pointed to her education philosophy and methodology that allowed her to take the "lowest performing school in the District and transformed it into the highest performing school in the state." As a Regent, she was attacked viciously because "She was dancing with the real devil." Yet, she brilliantly articulated African intellectual aspirations to liberate the mind, body and soul. Thus, her education philosophy was appropriate and liberating." Finally, he reminded the Good Doctor, "You will live forever in the minds and hearts of the children and people you educated."

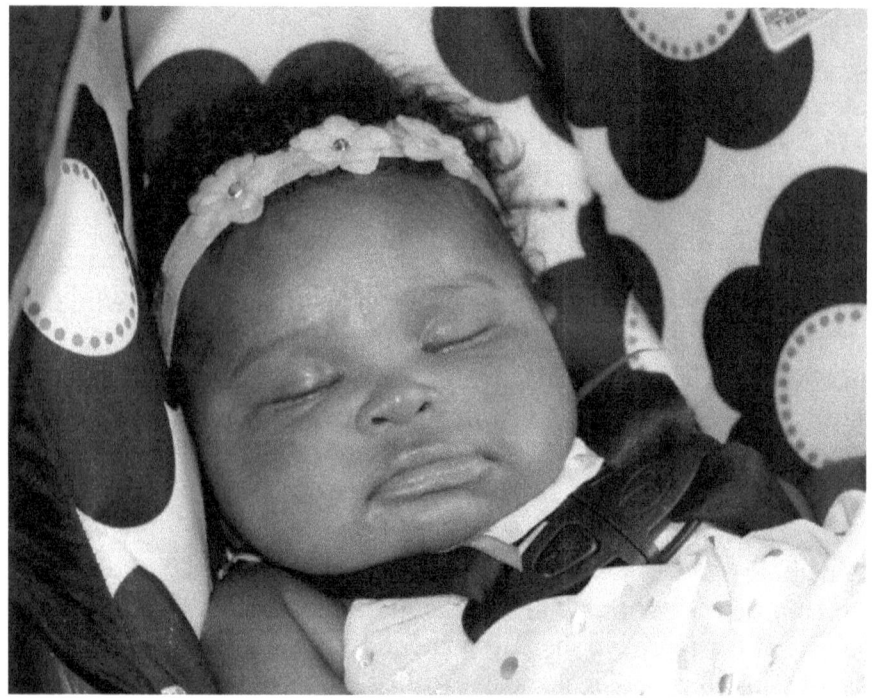

BN PHOTO - Oh, to be so "New Born in America!"

BLACK NATIONALISM STILL ALIVE AND WELL

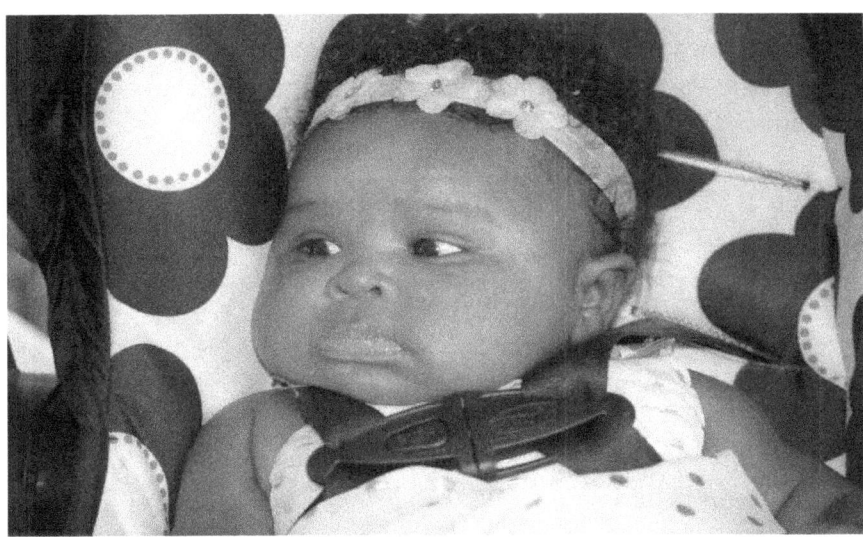

BN PHOTO - Well, bright eyed and bushy-tailed, but still, perhaps, one day we can say, Madam President!

BN PHOTO - "Warrior Queen" Sister Betty Dopson, Co-Chair of **CEMOTAP** and Professor James Blake, Chairman of the **Queens Million March Committee**, both in a happy mood.

Dr. Lester Young, a protégée and associate of Dr. Sanford and now at Adelaide L. Sanford Institute expressed, "When policy makers develop bad policies, it is a real leader who calls them out. This Dr.

FREDERICK MONDERSON

Sanford did, too many of our leaders are afraid to speak out!" He reflected on comparing his work and association with Dr. Sanford to a question once asked of Dizzy Gillespie, "What was it like to play with Charlie Parker," to which Dr. Young, seemingly choked, calmly responded, "You just had to be there."

BN PHOTO – Two beautiful persons at table alongside Dr. Blake and Sister Betty Dopson of **CEMOTAP** came out for Dr. Sanford.

Chief Judge Gonzalez of the Women in Prison Committee praised Dr. Sanford for "She enriched all of our lives. She took one grain of sand and an oyster then made us all pearls." Her associate, also on the Committee, Appellate Judge Priscilla Hall, calling Dr. Sanford exquisite, beautiful, brilliant, profound who awes; and pointed out, on March 7, 2015, in a wheel-chair Queen Mother of African consciousness appeared with President Obama on the Edmund Pettis Bridge is a historian and history maker who taught us, "If you would be immortal, you must write your name in the hearts of the people."

Susan Taylor, echoing similar sentiments offered, "I have the mike but I don't have the words," and explained, the Isis Sisters "never

BLACK NATIONALISM STILL ALIVE AND WELL

fully understood the depth of the crisis facing our youth, our people." This realization "makes us focus on what we take for granted. We're not organized, we don't have a plan. We've got to do better on our watch. What's the Plan? We must stand in strategic unity. Let's get busy. Let's get started."

BN PHOTO - Reverend Herbert L. Oliver of "Birmingham, Alabama Economic Boycott" fame sits alongside two sisters busy in conversation.

FREDERICK MONDERSON

BN PHOTO - MCs for the Night, Brian Favors and Linda Michelle Baron.

BN PHOTO - Dr. James McIntosh, Co-Chair of **CEMOTAP**, spoke glaringly about the ideas, strength and impact Dr. Sanford generated among all she came into contact with, especially the young, as well as her "Beloved strategy" that floored so many.

BLACK NATIONALISM STILL ALIVE AND WELL

BN PHOTO - Brother Barclay of Roots Revisited and Sister Rev. Dr. Sheila Evans Tranumn doing the "Closing Prayer."

BN PHOTO - "Moods" of the **International African Arts Festival** designed to most constructively "Repair and Remake the World" through art celebration!

FREDERICK MONDERSON

2. MILLION MAN MARCH - Substance and Significance
By
Dr. Fred Monderson

Riding in a DC cab the day after the **March**, the driver wanted to know the "**Numbers! - A Million or so**," I responded, "Two million or more," based on my own unscientific observations looking out at the stretched out masses of people within the barricades lining the **Great Lawn**, on adjacent streets, and the continuing streams entering from north and south conduits. Equally significant, even when leaving early, the late throngs of people pouring in and heading to the Mall certainly adds to an elevated assessment of how many people were there. I'm reminded 20 years ago of the controversy over the number of people who attended that first March. While Minister Farrakhan called for, and acknowledged, a million in attendance the government downplayed this number offering no more than 400,000 to 500,000. On the other hand, others gave a figure of more than a million! However, while some folks may have arrived late, such as my daughter Keisha traveling with her family, who incidentally were in attendance at the **Million Family March** in 2000, the 2,000,000 number seems a real possibility.

Continuing the dialogue with the driver, he remarked, "I have been in this town 40 years. This town belonged to African Americans but this has changed." I did observe a fair amount of destitute people on the streets and made contributions. On Sunday morning at McDonalds, to several of the persons nearby I asked, and answered the question, "Did you have your coffee this morning, brother?" To which several resounding "Thank yous" were heartfelt responses.

BLACK NATIONALISM STILL ALIVE AND WELL

BN PHOTO - To be part of that number once, twice, was a remarkable experience.

FREDERICK MONDERSON

BN PHOTO - These folks are among the many groups of people who came to Washington for the **Million Man March's** 20th Anniversary and made that Millionth Marcher above.

Notwithstanding, as the driver said, my mind reflected on a photograph at the Meridian Park, now renamed Malcolm X Park, showing a tremendous gathering of "Marching African Americans" streaming out onto the street on **Black Solidarity Day** in 1972. Gathered in what appeared a military formation, an individual in "fatigues" led and directed persons in prominent Afro hairstyles and wearing dashiki shirts. This was a classic **Black Nationalism moment**! Perhaps this was the "golden age" the driver referred to. Nevertheless, though the "stomach may appear a bit soft," the stalwarts at the far reaches of the "Empire" are "no ways tired," because the "substance and significance" of the gathering inherent in the ideology of the March attracting the numbers in attendance as reflected in the many who announced their presence two decades ago, broadening of the marching ethnic flavor of the gathering to include Whites, Native Americans, Asians, Latinos, LGBTs, in addition to those Black stalwarts who brought their sons and daughters, even wives, those who brought youngsters and those

BLACK NATIONALISM STILL ALIVE AND WELL

returning to assert their manhood in support of the call, the need for, and the demands for "Justice or Else" going forward. Such is the essence of "Substance and Significance" behind this most potent idea of Million March in DC.

BN PHOTO - Two "Brothers Long in the Struggle," Brother Wakilli and Brother Michael Hooper of **Roots Revisited**.

Thus, and without question, we must give praise and thanks to Minister Louis Farrakhan of the Nation of Islam for conceiving, executing and contributing to the "Million idea!" We know there are "forty something" million African Americans in this country. They spend one million million (Trillion) dollars annually and there are perhaps a million Brothers and Sisters incarcerated, but Farrakhan's idea is different, tremendously revolutionary, and with continuous tweaking will remain a potent beacon of consciousness, soul searching with demands on government, all ripe for activism in nationalist assertion. Its crystal clear, in the most vital organ of the American system, Washington, DC, this genius planted a profound idea whose time has not only come but will endure for eons because of the power, substance and significance contained in the message.

The numbers, quality and receptivity of those who answered the call and as they return to their widespread areas of operation, "the trees

FREDERICK MONDERSON

of this forest" will in turn generate forests of their own who will creatively experiment with, carry forward, and sustain the message of Justice or Else, while making their own significant contributions not simply to advance the "cause of Blackness" but equally continue to make America a better place for all.

BN PHOTO - For a century the **NAACP** has been emphasizing the message of this couple's shirt, "We Must Be United" which is a profound message of the 20th Anniversary of the **Million Man March**.

BLACK NATIONALISM STILL ALIVE AND WELL

BN PHOTO - Essentially the above is what the Present Occupants of the White House Michelle and Barack do all the time.

FREDERICK MONDERSON

Living the legacy decades later, when One Million will become Twenty and Minister Farrakhan finally joins the revered ancestral pantheon; that is, among Jitu Weusi, Sonny Carson, Reverend Jones, Elombe Brathe, Dr. Ben-Jochannan, Professor John Henrik Clarke, Bill Lynch, and the oldsters Malcolm X, Martin Luther King, Mary McLeod Bethune, Fannie Lou Hamer, Reverend Shuttlesworth, Dorothy Height, W.E.B. Dubois, Marcus Garvey, Elijah Mohammed, Kwame Ture, Herman Ferguson, Queen Mother Moore, Nelson Mandela, Langston Hughes, Claude McKay, Forbes Burnham, Mitta Monderson, Ollie McClean, on the fiftieth anniversary and after, these will rejoice over the success of their efforts added to the Million Man March ideology and program's harvest of fruitful outcomes.

Naturally much was said, but a most powerful theme Mr. Farrakhan evoked was the call for an economic boycott especially at holiday time especially to send a message. Remember Birmingham! Investing in **Black Enterprise** is always an equally potent idea. However, for the longest our leaders have emphasized the importance of the economic boycott. They cite the successes of the **Montgomery Bus Boycott** and concurrent **Boycott of Birmingham Stores** that brought that city's white supremacy to its knees! Equally, many features of early **Black Solidarity Day Boycott** were successful but for whatever reason that movement lost its way, as only a few groups across the country see the need for and continue the tradition, especially **Roots Revisited**.

When Sean Bell, on the eve of his wedding, was shot many times in Queens, New York, Reverend Al Sharpton called for an economic march along Fifth Ave on December 16th of that year, entering 50th Street in Manhattan and passing through the "Heart of Christmas," the intent was to "Shop for Justice." The theme was, "Hold your money, Don't Shop this holiday!" That was an equally significant theme Minister Farrakhan emphasized on this 20th Anniversary of

BLACK NATIONALISM STILL ALIVE AND WELL

the **Million Man March** under the shibboleth "**Justice or Else**!"

BN PHOTO - The 20th Anniversary of the **Million Man March** with its agenda, "Justice or Else" "By Any Means Necessary" on October 10, 2015.

Again, Bob Law and Reverend Calvin Butts in New York have proposed and are currently pursuing a national economic boycott to redirect the One Trillion Dollars African Americans spends annually. Echoing Adam Clayton Powell's "Don't shop where you can't work" boycott dictum, "What's in your hands," One Trillion dollars! Down through the ages leaders have emphasized the same idea. Thus, Bob Law, also emphasizing the prevalence of "fast food" establishments in the Black community and the implications for long-term health concerns, has advised "redirect your burger and fries money," not necessarily your big spending habits. He emphasized, in these "fast food joint! that don't hire Blacks or support any nationalist initiatives that concern African Americans, they should not shop there. However, when shopping, they should also ask proprietors of such establishments, "Where are the Black people who work here since we're shopping in your place of business?" Without question, "our dollars represent the margin of profit" for these businesses as Bob Law expressed, particularly so the big chains with their ubiquitous presence in or serving the Black Community. More specific, only about "8 percent of Blacks" need to withhold such spending to make a difference and these enterprises will recognize Black aspirations because **Black Lives Matter** in all of its manifestations! One sign at the march even advocated, "Make the Black Dollar circulate more in the Black Community!"

BN PHOTO - Bringing the Children was a great idea for they must carry on the tradition of the **Million Man March** just as the elders did 20 years ago. As such, the Youth must always remain in the forefront of the struggle ... and

BN PHOTO - Black men must continue to stand strong and we will do so for long, long time.

BLACK NATIONALISM STILL ALIVE AND WELL

BN PHOTO - Black men united is a dangerous idea to bigots and racists who win only when we give up the struggle. Jesse Jackson always emphasized, "We win when we are involved!"

BN PHOTO - The Brothers came in all sizes, shapes and persuasions to make the statement, "**Justice or Else**!"

FREDERICK MONDERSON

BN PHOTO - "Stop the Violence" because "**Black Lives Matter**" is a real issue.

A classic case was once observed in Maryland, famous for crabs. One Asian establishment selling crabs but not employing Blacks was servicing a line that stretched around the corner, "Because they make good crabs!" How foolish and counterproductive!

More importantly, however, in his two hour presentation one pointedly important assertion Minister Farrakhan posed, "I know you all think I killed Malcolm! If I killed Malcolm, do you think I would be here? See who was giving him mouth to mouth resuscitation? It was an FBI agent!" The idea elicits a Hollywood analogy in the movie **Shooter** starring Mark Walberg and Danny Glover. When the hero and the FBI agent went seeking "Wisdom" from the old shooting expert, to the question, "Who killed Kennedy?" he responded, "Those boys on the grassy knoll were dead within hours." The FBI agent responded, "You know this for sure?" To which the expert responded, "I still have the shovels in the back!" This sort of lends credence to the Minister's denial. Notwithstanding, Sonny Carson and Herman Ferguson both thought he did it!

BLACK NATIONALISM STILL ALIVE AND WELL

However, he may not have been at the Audubon to pull the trigger but to feign ignorance of the "climate around Malcolm" and "the hit going down" is not a tenable position!

BN PHOTO - The Elders came 20 years ago and paved the way for the young to continue the idea of "Million Expression" for social, political and economic "Justice or Else."

Nevertheless, in regard to the prominent idea then prevalent, the Minister pointed out the Honorable Gentleman had married the ladies and took care of his children, "not like some of you players out there." He equally criticized the many women who "let the players play" and not hold them accountable for their behaviors. He also made special note of black-on-black crime and killings as well police killing of blacks. Others gave a litany of names of victims of such violence. Nonetheless, with these issues and the substance and significance of the March recognized in the numbers who came and the seeds they will plant to creatively organize and continue to demand Justice or Else then return at this idea of anniversary in five years to the **Million Family** in 2020; all the while the **Million Woman** in 2018 and **Million Youth** anniversaries in Harlem and Brooklyn remain on deck, certainly underscores the significance of the idea of the Black Community thinking in the millions as a tool of social and nationalist activism.

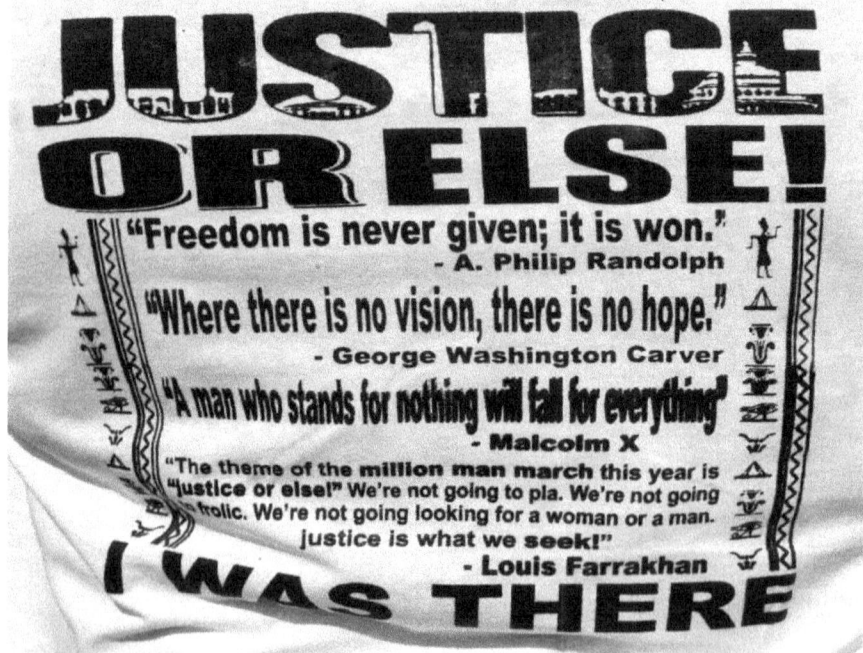

BN PHOTO - Freedom is never given, it is won; Where there is no vision, the people perish; a man who stands for nothing fill fall for everything; **I was there**!

BLACK NATIONALISM STILL ALIVE AND WELL

BN PHOTO - Young and committed to sustain the **Million Man March** "Substance and Significance" idea well into the future, these Brothers are making a statement.

Whatever, we must still acknowledge, praise and give thanks for Minister Farrakhan's vision in seeing the need, inspiring Millions to think in such mega proportions while participating in structured recurring like decimal anniversaries to encourage future youth to build on the multifaceted platforms of social activism he bequeathed them. Thus, the **Million Man March** idea, its history as ultimately will materialize in creative epic proportions is a self-help movement to uplift African people here and abroad; and, we have Minister Louis Farrakhan and his cadre to thank for the creatively brilliant concept. Most important, they will keep sending the message, "Blacks Vote" because **Black Lives Matter**.

FREDERICK MONDERSON

BN PHOTO - Yes, "**Black Lives Matter**" and there is "Power" in its realization.

BLACK NATIONALISM STILL ALIVE AND WELL

BN PHOTO - More important, they came by throngs, in the millions, echoing one voice, "**Black Lives Matter, Justice or Else**."

BN Photo – "No space on the lawn," well, we're here!

FREDERICK MONDERSON

BN PHOTO - When all is said and done, it was truly a **Million Man March** for "**Justice or Else**."

BN PHOTO - However, you take this, to bring these many people to DC means a powerful idea is at work.

BLACK NATIONALISM STILL ALIVE AND WELL

BN PHOTO - And so, they "Kept Coming" in the millions, to fulfill the Mission!

BN PHOTO - Yes, they "Kept Coming" in the millions, to fulfill the Mission of the powerful idea Minister Farrakhan developed!

FREDERICK MONDERSON

BN PHOTO - "Yes, they came Answering the call;" "They came in every Hue and Persuasion."

BN PHOTO - The "Sisters" were there to give support, aid in security and express their heart-felt concern about where we are heading as a people on this 20th Anniversary of the **Million Man March**.

BLACK NATIONALISM STILL ALIVE AND WELL

BN PHOTO - Yes, "Men, Women and Everyone else," all within the shadow of the Washington Monument standing tall in the Nation's Capital, for **Justice or Else**, because **Black Lives Matter**.

3. MARCUS GARVEY REFLECTIONS TODAY
By
Dr. Fred Monderson

Reflecting on the life's work and influence of Marcus Garvey (August 17, 1887-March 12, 1940), who preached "One God, One Aim, One Destiny" and that "Economics is the key," **CEMOTAP** sponsored another of its enormously intellectually stimulating presentations as we enter a new year. Held on January 16, 2016, on the Martin Luther King holiday weekend, the architects of this important program held to the old nationalist admonition this is a serious time, not to be confused with "Sales" and "Shopping."

FREDERICK MONDERSON

Equally, that we must remain committed to African nationalist activism and thought provoking engagements realizing, people of African ancestry are perennially challenged in every field of endeavor, viz., education, economics, jobs, the technology field, politics, the sanctity of being in church, life itself; and especially on the streets where senseless violence is taking a heavy toll. So, we must remain intellectually and consciously vigilant in defense of civil and human rights and family and cultural values. We must also build and circulate wealth to defend ourselves. We must practice ownership, pursue business practices, for as Dr. John Clarke advised, "Buy, don't sell property." This is underscoring Garvey and the UNIA boast of owning this property, this store, this vehicle, this ship, and so on.

The significance of this weekend not simply links the "Great Ms" - viz., Marcus, Martin, Malcolm and Mandela, some say Monderson, men of substance, vision, tenacity, fortitude and effectiveness, whose names have and can galvanize activists across a wide spectrum of ethnic and generational philosophies and ideologies committed to challenge injustice and wickedness in high and low places, but most important, continue to challenge and speak truth to power. Arguably, over the last decade or two, African-Americans can point to gains made in many fields across the American political and social landscape, but even these areas of accomplishments need to be viewed within the overall context of where we were consigned and have come from relative to where we are today, with a view towards the direction we are heading in now. We must also recognize the forces arrayed against and actively seeking to rollback those gains in politics, economics, housing and even education. Thus, the need for unity and vigilance. For example, in 1994, Black South Africans turned out in tumultuous multitudes to vote and ended apartheid thanks to the galvanizing symbolism of Nelson Mandela, who as Dr. Len Jeffries and Bob Law emphasized, represented "a tree in the forest of South African nationalist activism;" but unmistakably those Africans now control their nation, fate and destiny.

BLACK NATIONALISM STILL ALIVE AND WELL

BN PHOTO - Chairman of **CEMOTAP** Dr. James McIntosh about to Introduce Dr. Raymond Dugay (left) and Dr. Tyrene Wright (right) to discuss the influences of Marcus Garvey and the **UNIA**.

In 2008, ending "the long night of their captivity," African-Americans in conjunction with people of goodwill across the conscious and activist, some say nationalist, spectrums, mobilized and in a consorted super-human organizational and strategic effort, helped win the Presidency for Barack Obama. As the thousands gathered on a cold day on January 20th, 2009, Jesse Jackson, that resolute and iconic activist remarked, "Barack Obama represents the best the Civil Right Movement has to offer." Then, with an ebullient confidence President Obama took the reins of government mired in a near-failed-state morass; recognizing the economy in shambles with Wall Street in disarray; banks and financial institutions failing; the auto industry on the brink of collapse with foreclosures escalating in downward spirals putting homeowners chest-deep in water; failing educational practices that mis-educate our young, while "first responders" stood precariously on the proverbial "chopping block"

FREDERICK MONDERSON

as all around the physical infrastructure of the nation's roads, bridges, tunnels, rails, ports, schools and much more were crumbling. Still, as he sought to stop the hemorrhaging, tend the patient and chart a futuristic course, Mr. Obama encountered the "Party of No's" calculated strategy of obstructionism. It is interesting how, Dr. Wright (below) indicated one hundred years ago a prevailing ideological sentiment held: "Black progress in this country would mean white oppression." Strange that this mindset, viz., escalating militia voices of discontent rhetoric and from within the highest echelons of government; there have been purposely fueled opposition to President Obama's persona, ethnicity, responsibilities and intent.

Nevertheless, delving into the ditch in which the nation had slid, with sleeves rolled up, President Obama and his team of dedicated and brilliant minds set about salvaging the ship-of-state adrift in the cataclysmic global waters particularly disturbed by two wars raging in Iraq and Afghanistan that were vacuuming untold resources in a recession-depression international environment in which many blamed the previous Republican administration for contributing to significantly.

In this mix and busy cleaning the manure behind "Door Number One," then "Door Number Two," and secretly behind "Door Number Three" a treasonous gathering was busy formulating a chaotic strategy to deny Barack Obama the right and legitimacy to govern effectively. That is to say, it was Ok to clean up the mess Republicans bequeathed the new administration, but under orchestrated duress the new President was to be vigorously challenged and obstructed every foot of the way. Driving this misguided mindset, the unspoken strategy held, not only must resistance and opposition come from private interests, in the highest echelons of government where flames of racial hatred and disrespect of Mr. Obama were vigorously kindled; and encouraging an alarming increase in militia activity fueled by gun lobby rhetoric such as "Obama will change the Constitution," "Obama wants your guns," "Obama must be defeated;" "Let's make Obama a one-term President;" resist and repeal Obamacare (ACA); and say "No to his

BLACK NATIONALISM STILL ALIVE AND WELL

every legislative initiative." In this day and age, one has to wonder at such pandering, prognostication and provocation. Equally, working in consort with the Obama opposition, former South Carolina Senator Jim DeMint predicted this galvanized effort will become Obama's "Waterloo!" Notwithstanding, the brilliance of Obama's thinking cap; the efficient and effectiveness of his work ethic; the enormous commitment to his responsibility as Chief Executive, Commander-In-Chief, and Chief Diplomat contributed to his registering significant achievements on the world stage and at home. Yet, despite the deep opposition, the reality of his successes has caused economic Noble prize winner Paul Krugman to characterize Mr. Obama as "the greatest American president ever!"

Whether this is because of his visionary Lilly Ledbetter Equal Pay for Equal Work initiative; his championing same sex marriage; the brilliant auto industry, Wall Street and bank bailouts; his tweaking the immigration issue within existing laws; ending two wars in Iraq and Afghanistan, never mind their simmering embers; securing the Asian Economic Trade Pact; renouncing the Cuban Embargo and establishing Embassies here and there; successful pursuit of Osama bin Laden and Alaki in Yemen; passing Dodd-Frank financial reform; brilliantly securing consensus and commitment at the recent Global Climate Change Conference; and even the concerted Iran Nuclear Deal; these successes force objective thinkers to realize, Mr. Obama's legacy; yet a work in progress that still promises even more significant achievements.

Nonetheless, as the **Black Lives Matter** movement has argued, indiscriminate police killing of Black men keeps escalating at an alarming rate; despite Wall Street tripling its portfolio from c. 6500 to c. 18,000 during Mr. Obama's tenure and the national unemployment rate dropping to historic lows of 5%; this important accomplishment in economic activity has essentially by-passed the Black Community. It has doubled among Black adults and rising to nearly 40%-50% among Black teenagers. Yet, undaunted and amidst his many challenges, the President has emphasized education as

FREDERICK MONDERSON

important for Black advancement, encouraging "My Brothers' Keeper" initiatives, and "Race to the Top;" encouraging Community College enrollment as a viable option; pushed for creative research and development in clean energy research to sustain American scientific leadership and help save the environment; all this while encouraging young Black men and women to learn a skill to capitalize on the changing nature of the American economy in the fast emerging clean energy fields that fuel research and development and any and all such creative enterprises. Thus, with all these dynamics manifesting **CEMOTAP** sponsored this new reflection on Marcus Garvey and his impact, held to determine where do we go from here?, on this Martin Luther King Weekend, January 2016.

BN PHOTO - More close-up of the audience attentively listening to one of the presenters on Garvey and his influence and life's work.

Two presenters, Dr. Tyrene Wright and Dr. Raymond Dugay were excellent in their characterization of Marcus Garvey revealing many unknown facts about the man. However, Ms. Wright, in her own right, was able to connect Garvey with Booker T. Washington, showing Garvey's enormous respect for the creator of Tuskegee Institute, which in its own right was more profound than most give it credit for. This iconic creation of Mr. Washington, according to Ms. Wright, the "Tuskegee model" was in itself a "social system," a totally sustainable successful model that Mr. Washington intended to

BLACK NATIONALISM STILL ALIVE AND WELL

export throughout the African World making him one of the earliest proponents of Pan-Africanism. The successes of this social and economic construct is what influenced Mr. Garvey, for having read Washington's autobiography, *Up From Slavery*, along with knowledge of Toussaint L'Ouverture and Dessalines of Haiti and Bookman of Jamaica, Garvey was impressed and wanted to create a similar model in his home state, Jamaica. However, there were other factors in play at the time, such as the political, social and economic condition of Africans globally; the "African Exclusion Measure" that sought to deny Africans entry into America and though passed in the US Senate failed in the House especially because Washington was able to mobilize opposition to the measure; the contemporary "Congress of Race and Race Equality" held at Oxford University; and the "1912 Conference on the Negro," held at Tuskegee, where early African men of vision and tenacity, DuBois, Washington, Garvey, Duse Mohammed, Caseley Hayford, Sylvester Williams, Edward Wilmot Blyden, Carter G. Woodson, Thomas Fortune, Dr. Robert J. Love, Sandy Cox, Bishop Henry McNeil Turner, John E. Bruce, J.A. Rogers, Arthur Schomberg, even Malcolm X's parents, Earl and Louise Little, etc., all coalescing at an important time in history, came to strategize on how to effectively challenge the exploitation and oppression directed against Africa and the Africans coming to America. The "Exclusionary Measure" was designed to exclude Africans coming from Africa and the Diaspora; the "Klansman's" Thomas Dixon articulation of the "Doctrine of Separation and Independence" and Arthur Evans' assessment that Tuskegee was "not simply a school, a city in itself, but an institution that was truly self-sustaining, and as such, a threat to the American system" were measures actively pursued and protested vigorously by Washington. More important, however, all were impressed by the concepts Washington practiced at the Tuskegee school itself being "a nation building model" of making and creating, and however strange, everything they consumed from socks and underwear to buildings and foodstuffs. Again, this sustainable model, that Washington wanted to export, in its multi-faceted creativity is what gave Garvey the idea to build such a school in Jamaica and emphasize economics as the cornerstone of all nation building strategies. Thus, Dr. Wright saw Booker T. Washington as "the concrete model of Black Power." In this way, she was able to link the two great Africans for creating the "sustainable model" as physical structure and the UNIA as an intellectual idea, a philosophy that has withstood the test of time and remains a viable institutional concept with a credible history and a methodology that can, in fact, help bring about nation building through orchestrated organization for economic independence.

What Dr. Wright made known foremost is that Marcus Garvey was the first to organize the **Black World** under a single organization and this was done primarily through his newspaper *The Negro World*, espoused in a communication skill he learned from the printer Alfred Burroughs, which in fact, spread the word, linking Africans globally. He was also able to achieve economic independence by mobilizing and harnessing stock money from the masses to create the economy of independence and power his organization generated. His newspaper, a mechanism to educate and uplift Black people, also ingrained in the minds of disparate Africans the true meaning of the idea of nationhood, nation building, under Black management primarily through economic organization fueling commerce.

According to Dr. Dugay, this economic concept of independence was attained after a historical concepts, perhaps encouraged from Garvey's contact with Duse Mohammed the Egyptian who instructed him on the greatness of the ancient Africans of Egypt. Accordingly, Garvey looked at the Pyramids, and wondered: "Not how they were built, but how they were paid for!" It was through creation of a surplus economy to encourage independent and sustainable growth.

BLACK NATIONALISM STILL ALIVE AND WELL

> **CEMOTAP EXECUTIVE COMMITTEE**
> **1994**
> BETTY J. DOPSON
> JAMES C. McINTOSH, M.D.
> Co-Chairs
> EDWIN WARD
> Treasurer
> PHYLLIS B. CANNON
> Secretary
> KWESI ALI DANLADI
> SARAH MACKEY
> WINSTON GREENE
> YVONNE HILL
> WILLIAM MORGAN
> JOHN POUNDS
> GLENNIE M. PORTER
> SUZANNE WILLIAMS

BN PHOTO - CEMOTAP's Executive Committee under the leadership of Sister Betty Dopson and Dr. James McIntosh and the people who support their unending efforts of intellectual enlightenment and defending African-Americans from the misrepresentation and viciousness of Media portrayal.

Dr. Dugay, equally, saw significance in honoring Marcus Garvey on Dr. King's weekend, for in June 1965, Dr. King, while in Jamaica, recognized, "Marcus Garvey was the first man of color to lead and develop a mass movement. He was the first man to give millions of Negroes a sense of dignity." This mindset was essentially enshrined in "The Declaration of the Right of the Negro Peoples of the World" formulated after he arrived in the United States in March 1916, some five months after "Booker T." had died. From Preamble thorough its

FREDERICK MONDERSON

12 complaints and 53 assertions, declarations, condemnation, demands, protests, etc., are summed up in the following.

"In order to encourage our race all over the world and to stimulate it to overcome the handicaps and difficulties surrounding it, and to push forward to a higher and grander destiny, we demand and insist on the following Declaration of Rights." "These rights we believe to be justly ours and proper for the protection of the Negro race at large, and because of this we believe, on behalf of the four hundred million Negroes of the world, do pledge herein the sacred blood of the race in defense, and we hereby subscribe our names as a guarantee of the truthfulness and faithfulness thereof, in the presence of Almighty God, on this 13th Day of August, in the year of our Lord one thousand nine hundred and twenty."

BN PHOTO - Dr. McIntosh about to introduce Dr. Raymond Dugay to discuss Marcus Garvey, the man, his vision and his history.

Here then is an example, of a few verses from the Declaration…

BLACK NATIONALISM
STILL ALIVE AND WELL

"(4) We declare that Negroes, where-so-ever they form a community among themselves should be given the right to elect their own representatives to represent them in Legislatures, courts of law, or such institutions as may exercise control over that particular community;

BN PHOTO - Dr. Raymond Dugay explaining the moral and economic significance of the ship in the slide Marcus Garvey purchased to further his international commerce within the African world.

"(30) We demand the right of an unlimited and unprejudiced education for ourselves and our posterity forever;

"(39) That the colors, Red, Black and Green, be the colors of the Negro race.

"(40) Resolved, that the anthem "Ethiopia, Thou Land of Our Fathers," shall be the anthem of the Negro race ....

"(41) We believe that any limited liberty which deprives one of the complete rights and prerogatives of full citizenship is but a modified form of slavery."

There were even more important revelations made about Marcus Garvey by Dr. Dugay such as:

FREDERICK MONDERSON

Looking at the pyramids Garvey asked, not how were they built but 'How were they paid for?' The answer was through an economic system grounded in surplus produce which in turn had the capacity to generate the resources to provide the military might to guarantee the stability of a political system that respects liberty and equality. That is, "A strong economic system will give you military power." Yet, "We have let this memory and tradition slip from our hands." However, while economics is the key, "Education is the lifeblood of the nation" and this has been echoed not simply by Marcus Garvey and Booker T. Washington but also President Obama as well as Mary McLeod Bethune, Jitu Weusi, Queen Mother Moore, and Sonny Carson, even Kwame Nkrumah, who were all tremendously influenced by Garvey. Thus, Garvey recognized skill and economic organization is how the pyramids were built, because "A great civilization must have a great economy" and as such, we African people are the "regulators of wealth." After all, the "fertile Crescent" begins in Egypt. Egypt was always been considered the "bread basket" not Mesopotamia! That is, this is so despite distorted presentation of how this historic phenomenon was formed. However, while "it's all about economics," in the United States where African Americans spend $1.1T annually, "this is not an economic and independent economic base."

BN PHOTO - Dr. James McIntosh in full effect as "he helps fill the basket" with generous gifts for the wonderful knowledge presented this time around.

BLACK NATIONALISM STILL ALIVE AND WELL

The money comes and goes. Spanish speakers, Chinese, Koreans, Arabs, even Jews embed themselves in the Black community and remove much of those dollars and do not employ locals, nor contribute to any social program uplift. We have money but no economy! Looking for a significant factor in this malady, consider African-Americans comprise 13% of the US population yet they purchase 85.8% of hair and skin products. This points to their lack of self-confidence and this questions their blackness. Dr. Dugay explained, according to Marcus Garvey, "The world is run on bluff." That is, we were brainwashed to "hate what we love and love what we hate. We hate our blackness and love the white skin." This is not normal, "we have to be trained to be ignorant, because we lack self-confidence. Your history is you! It is in your genes. It is the missing page of history."

Therefore, Garveyism as grounded in economic sustainability and independence was and still is, and can be the solution to the Black man's woes. In this insistence Marcus Garvey gave the Black man confidence, an economic *modus operandi* to operationalize and the requisite motifs viz. religious icons, a flag, "men of big affairs," and much, much more, for which to create and celebrate cultural pride and to make and love one's history.

BN PHOTO - CEMOTAP art that appeals to the inner aesthetic consciousness that sets African people apart.

4. ERIC GARNER ONE YEAR LATER!
By
Dr. Fred Monderson

Echoing sentiments heard from Staten Island to Brooklyn, a huge cry for "Justice for Eric Garner" was raised Saturday July 18, 2015 in Cadman Plaza Park beside the Federal Courthouse off Tillary Street, in Brooklyn. That is one year after Garner's death and on the birthday of Nelson Mandela, his wife thanked the crowd and reassured them their presence and efforts have invigorated her and strengthened her resolve to fight for justice. There, a number of powerful voices in labor, religion, politics, community activism and the legislature were raised, but one of the loudest was made in Congressman Hakeem Jeffries' turn at the podium. As Reverend Al Sharpton said earlier in the year when he called for the "March on Washington," "We are not against the Police, we're against Police Brutality;" now, Mr. Jeffries, in citing deaths at the hands of police in Cleveland, St. Louis, Baltimore and in New York, was quick to point out, "We have a Police problem in New York City." Citing Diallo in the Bronx; Sean Bell in Queens; Akai Gurley in Brooklyn; Dorismond in Manhattan; and now we have Eric Garner in Staten Island, he insisted lawmakers make the "chokehold" a federal offense throughout the entire country. He explained that though the Medical Examiner ruled Garner's death a homicide; it was illegal by New York Police Department standards and policy; and the young man who video the crime is in jail; yet no charges have been filed against the officers who are still on the police payroll. There is thus something wrong with this picture. Fortunately not this picture below!

BLACK NATIONALISM STILL ALIVE AND WELL

BN PHOTO - Reverend Al Sharpton addressing the rally seeking **Justice for Eric Garner**, in Brooklyn, Saturday July 18, 2015.

But, the Congressman was not the only speaker who made a significant contribution. In fact, a litany of speakers wowed the crowd in the hundreds, with their impassioned deliveries. Starting with Kirstin Foy, MC; Rev. Al Sharpton; Rev. Herbert Daughtry; Assemblyman Nick Perry; Comptroller Scott Stringer; Representatives from 1199 SEIU; HHC Nurses Association; the NYC Justice League; and other community activists all echoed the same message, "Only through marching and activism will justice be had." "We must have Justice for Eric Garner."

Rev. Sharpton insisted, "The North needs to catch up with the South. The South indicted an officer for a killing but the North lags behind." He noted; the purpose for the Rally this close to the Federal Courthouse will bring attention to the need for federal indictments in killings by police. Only then will this madness cease. Rev. Daughtry pointed out he has been in the struggle for so long he hardly remembers how long; but he does remember Arthur Miller being killed in a chokehold on Nostrand Avenue in Brooklyn in the 1970s. He praised Governor Cuomo for empowering a Special Prosecutor

FREDERICK MONDERSON

and involving the Attorney General to look into these matters but reminded the gathering, together with a number of others he had met with the governor's father Mario Cuomo, then governor, nearly fifty years ago raising the same issue but for a permanent prosecutor's office to investigate and prosecute these behaviors. He also reminded the crowd, he is "No ways near tired" and he will have to be "carried out" protesting; and even when he gets to heaven and these activists also get there, he will be there to welcome them for a job well done!

BN PHOTO - Reverend Herbert Daughtry of the House of the Lord Church, "still standing," in search of "Justice for Humanity and Eric Garner."

Assemblyman Nick Perry began by counting 11 "I Can't Breathe" pronouncements. Then the newly elected Chairman of the Black and Puerto Rican Legislative Caucus called upon his colleagues in the legislature to be more vigilant and proactive in investigating and helping to prosecute police misconduct, especially when it involves loss of life. There were many other speakers whose names are not here mentioned but their impassioned pleas and their unquestioned commitment not simply for justice but equally to make New York City and the nation a better place for all, were resoundingly recognized by a grateful but motivated crowd.

BLACK NATIONALISM STILL ALIVE AND WELL

A number of banners and slogans expressed the sentiments of the rally that "Black Lives Matter." "Yes," one speaker echoed, "Black Lives Matter, Hispanic Lives Matter, Asian Lives Matter, White Lives Matter, but its Black Lives that are being slaughtered."

Then we saw this movement for change and equality insist on "Justice for Eric Garner;" "This Stops Today;" "White People Against White Supremacy;" "Justice for Freddie Gray, Walter Scott, Eric Garner, Rekia Boyd, Tamir Rice, Akai Gurley, Michael Brown, Tanisha Anderson, Trayvon Martin, Ramarley Graham, Malissa Williams, Sean Bell, Yvette Smith and too many others," so say 1199 SEIU. One of the speakers mentioned Anthony BAEZ, one of the first to die in a chokehold. "Housing Works" were there. So too, "If you are neutral in situations of injustice, you have chosen the side of the oppressor;" "Community Control over Police Now" and "NYC Stands with Charleston against Hate." There were "Keeping the Dream Alive;" "Convict Corrupt Cops;" "When will the In-Just-Us end;" "Balance the Scales of Justice;" "32 BJ SEIU;" "Respect Human Rights;" "Never Forget I Can't Breathe;" "Justice 4 All;" "Justice Champion: Justice League;" "No Justice, No Peace;" "The Black Institute;" "Let Us Breathe;" "Trump You Didn't Build That;" "We Can't Breathe;" and even the "Tuskegee Airmen, 1941," were there.

FREDERICK MONDERSON

BN PHOTO - Housing Works advocates were there in support of Eric Garner.

BN PHOTO - Young people, "White People Against White Supremacy," were there for Eric Garner, equally emphasizing "Black Lives Matter."

BLACK NATIONALISM STILL ALIVE AND WELL

BN PHOTO - The Sign says it all, "Justice for Eric Garner."

FREDERICK MONDERSON

BN PHOTO - "Tricolor" left and right, how Marcus Garvey must be pleased to see his idea of "Red, Black and Green" staying the course.

BN PHOTO - The "Perennial Photographer," always seen in a professional mood.

BLACK NATIONALISM
STILL ALIVE AND WELL

Along with the mother and wife of Eric Garner who pledged to remain front and center in the struggle and that this is not about the **SETTLEMENT**, there were a number of mothers who lost their children. Trayvon Martin's mother was there; Michael Brown's mother was there; Tamir Rice's mother was there; and several other close relatives of these martyred legends. When Eric Garner's mother said "This club of Women" needs no other members, it is closed; there was a resounding **AMEN** from the other mothers and from the fired up crowd.

BN PHOTO - Sure, "**All Lives Matter** but it's the **Black Lives** that are being killed across the nation."

While Rev. Daughtry had gotten the crowd riled up with, "I'm fired up and won't take it no more; No Justice, No Peace;" some of the women activists received resounding receptions for their commitment and grassroots leadership efforts which has been long and sustained.

FREDERICK MONDERSON

BN PHOTO - New York State Assemblyman Nick Perry who led the "16 I-Can't-Breathe" countdown is flanked (left) by Rev. Al Sharpton and Eric Garner's mother and Mr. Kirstin Foy (above) and a woman activist and a Brother among others (below).

BLACK NATIONALISM STILL ALIVE AND WELL

BN PHOTO - That "Awesome Club" of "Mothers whose sons were killed in senseless violence" was joined by Reverend Al Sharpton and Kirstin Foy at the Mike to demand "Justice for Eric Garner."

BN PHOTO - Public Advocate Letitia James is flanked by Kirstin Foy and others on stage demanding for "Justice for Eric Garner."

FREDERICK MONDERSON

BN PHOTO - "Everyone is aboard" in "Justice for Eric Garner."

A number of familiar faces were there including public Advocate Leticia James, Attorney Michael Hardy, "Black Panther" Shepherd, Minister Hafez, and especially Black Muslim representatives in their sharp and tailored outfits.

All in all, the sentiments were that the powers that be hear the voices in protest and especially that Federal representatives must now make meaningful efforts to address the problem of police brutality. This is particularly so especially when local prosecutors balk at prosecuting individuals such as Officer Panatela at whose hands Eric Garner perished because of an illegal chokehold that was against policy and this among other variables, resulted in Garner's death being ruled a homicide.

BLACK NATIONALISM STILL ALIVE AND WELL

BN PHOTO - Congressman Hakeem Jeffries was there to lend his support in calls for "Justice for Eric Garner." Insightfully he called names and explained there were police killings in Manhattan, Brooklyn, Queens, Staten Island and the Bronx. That, the Congressman pointed out, meant there is a "Police Problem in New York City!"

BN PHOTO - National Action Network "Legal Eagle" Michael Hardy was there lending his support calling for "Justice for Eric Garner."

FREDERICK MONDERSON

BN PHOTO - Congressman Hakeem Jeffries and State Assemblyman Nick Perry are flanked by two gentlemen on the stage for Eric Garner.

BN PHOTO - "Oppressor, I Can't Breathe!" Because, "If you are neutral in situations of **INJUSTICE**, you have chosen the side of the **OPPRESSOR**.

BLACK NATIONALISM STILL ALIVE AND WELL

BN PHOTO - Garner garnered an enormous crowd to send a message to the Feds "Justice!"

5. SALVATION THROUGH PAN-AFRICANISM
BY
DR. FRED MONDERSON

Across the globe, the African World is in disarray! Forces in opposition are escalating sentiments of division to suppress and control the aspirations of African people whether in Guyana where racial division is a fact; across the African continent tribalism creates suspicion and division; and in local communities here racists of all hues including militias, skinheads, even "Tea Party" types and associates racially stereotype as powerful an individual as President Obama. Gentrification is not only displacing many long in residence of local areas but a pejorative mentality pervades the behavior of some new residents fed by divisive elements emanating from across the nation; even in the highest levels of government and in the highest ranks of the political and private sector. Significantly, as many greats in Black perennial struggle for salvation through economic, political and social empowerment join the pantheon of revered ancestors because they came early, viz., Rev. Shutlesworth,

FREDERICK MONDERSON

Sonny Carson, Jitu Weusi, Bill Lynch, Ossie Davis, Elombe Brath, Maya Angelou, Ruby Dee, Ollie McClean, Representative Major Owens, Rev. Clarence Norman, Sr., Et. Al., there is an ever-present need for a continued cadre of vibrant young leadership motivated by an active and effective philosophic orientation and *modus operandi* that will remain committed and unite and advance the cause of African peoples' salvation. Pan-Africanism is a viable philosophic ideology and way of life that can help in the process. Pan-Africanism was born and nurtured in the cauldron of African people's struggles across chattel slavery, colonialism and imperialism's exploitation and racism. It also gave birth to nationalist risings in order to assert and secure equality and dignity for African people across the globe.

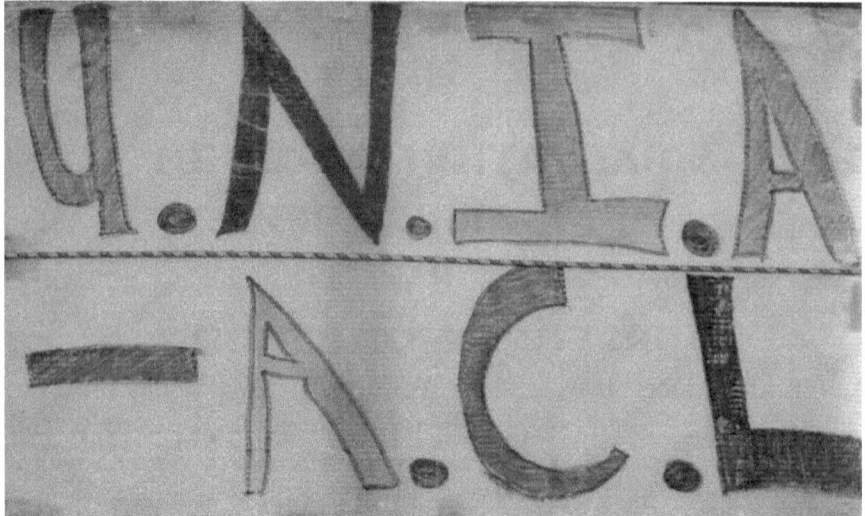

BN PHOTO - The undying, Marcus Garvey's "Universal Negro Improvement Association" - and the "African Communities League."

Viewing the 2014 Soccer World Championship in Brazil, it was clearly evident, that once European elitist sport has "gone African," where such soccer powerhouses as England, France, Germany, Netherlands, and especially South American teams, are manned by players who are descendants of the African continent. Thus, the unmistakable fact is: those teams' striking thrusts and threats are significantly African in representation!

BLACK NATIONALISM
STILL ALIVE AND WELL

BN PHOTO - Part of the 2013 Marchers who came to celebrate the 50th Anniversary of the "1963 March on Washington."

FREDERICK MONDERSON

BN PHOTO - "Eliminate Student Loan Debt" and "For Jobs and Freedom" and with demands to "Support Trayvon's Law" and "We March for **JOBS** and Freedom."

Nevertheless, oftentimes viewing contemporary developments we see a unique phenomenon represented in map displays highlighting significant occurrences. In football, the various stadiums across the host nation Brazil stood out on a representative map. In that nation, there may possibly be 120 million people of African ancestry. This is the largest single number outside of the African continent. As such, it would be an important first-step if many Brazilians root for

BLACK NATIONALISM STILL ALIVE AND WELL

African teams taking the field to qualify as top contenders. Of course, we do not mean when their nation is playing, for then we saw the stands full of symbolic yellow and green Brazilian colors. After all, and notwithstanding, enlightened Brazilian intellectuals have insisted that their people learn more about and appreciate their African heritage.

The notion of Pan-African consciousness was first articulated and championed by W.E.B. DuBois and Sylvester Williams in 1900 although it dates back to the efforts of Paul Cuffe, Martin Delaney, Henry Highland Garnett, Frederick Douglass, Sojourner Truth and Harriet Tubman; most notqbl4 Booker T. Washington and his "Tuskegee Model," among many others. In the early decades of the 20th Century, Marcus Garvey was an ardent advocate for the unity of African people, at home and abroad, and thus founded the Universal Negro Improvement Association (**UNIA**) to advocate such a goal.

Garvey came to America to meet Booker T. Washington who died just before his arrival in 1916, yet he continued the task of mobilizing and unifying African people under the shibboleth of **"One People, One God, and One Destiny**!" However, he was not alone in that era for Washington's Tuskegee Institute and the birth of the National Association for Advancement of Colored People as well as the National Urban League proved active and today enduring institutions and testaments of constructive African unity for uplift. Then in 1919, DuBois convened the First Pan-African Conference in Paris contemporary with the Versailles Peace Conference concluding World War One. To contest the negative reaction to the conference from America and Great Britain especially, the latter quintessential imperialist and colonialist nation; DuBois appealed to Blaise Diagne, a Senegalese Delegate to the French Assembly during the tenure of Prime Minister Georges Clemenceau government.

During the war, as the German military hammer pounded France, Clemenceau dispatched Diagne to West Africa to recruit Africans to

FREDERICK MONDERSON

fight France's German enemy. He successfully recruited some 120,000 Africans who helped stem the German onslaught thereby rescuing France. In payback, Clemenceau simply said, "Go ahead, have the Conference, but keep it low key!" So once the go-ahead was given and venue secured, DuBois invited delegates from Europe, Africa, North and South America and the Caribbean. There the flames of a unifying global African consciousness had been lit! During the inter-war years (1919-1939) three such conferences were held as DuBois, aided by George Padmore and others remained active in the struggle. This struggle espoused the networking intent and philosophic benefits of a Pan-African consciousness to combat the many years of systematic assaults upon the humanity and integrity of the African persona, long oppressed, at home and abroad.

BN PHOTO - "Dreaming" "We are Everywhere" "Empowered" because "My Voice Matters."

Africans from all over, particularly the colonial possessions on the continent and in the New World, fought to check German World War Two rampage in Europe, North Africa and the Atlantic Ocean states. At war's end in 1945, then an elder and somewhat tired DuBois turned over leadership of the Pan-African Movement to a younger and more vigorous Kwame Nkrumah of Ghana who chaired the Fifth Pan-African Conference at Manchester. In that city, the

BLACK NATIONALISM STILL ALIVE AND WELL

Socialist Fredrick Engels championed the Labor Movement, and so reception to the conference was more favored there. This time, the Pan-African Movement had come of age, and so the next generation of leadership charted the movement with a mandate to decolonize Africa and the other colonial areas in the Caribbean. In America, desegregation of the Armed Forces following World War II coupled with the on-going activism of such persons as A. Philip Randolph, Rev. Shuttlesworth, Harry Belafonte, and legal eagles such as Thurgood Marshall, kept the flame burning in the desire that African people be seriously free and equal!

With the Conference over and marching orders spelled out, as these delegates returned to their respective countries and began organizing their people to become more knowledgeable about colonial administration and politics, the one unifying and effective idea pursued was that of Pan-Africanism. The philosophy of Pan-Africanism essentially expressed: African people globally have been the victims of European and American political expansion, exploitation, racism and all solely for the furtherance of these nations' interests and privileges. In this climate, as people's consciousness evolved further encouraged by activism and unionization, the colonial powers began incarcerating leaders of the new movement seeking to free their land. Nevertheless, within just over a decade of the **5th Pan-African Congress** of 1945, Kwame Nkrumah led Ghana to independence on March 6, 1957. With the colonial powers weakened by the war and the people united under a vibrant group of leaders, viz., Sekou Toure of Guinea; Namdi Azikwi of Nigeria; Jomo Kenyatta of Kenya; Gamal Abdel Nasser of Egypt; Tafawa Balewa of Nigeria; Et. Al., all espousing an equally vibrant strategies, dominoes began to fall and African nations became independent enmasse; thereby also becoming members of the United Nations simultaneously. In America, reaction against Blacks in general, nationalists, the Black Panthers, the Student Non-violent Coordinating Committee, the Republic of New Africa and the Southern Christian Leadership Council under Rev. Joseph Lowery who pressed their case, protested, marched, sit-

FREDERICK MONDERSON

ins, and encouraged economic boycotts while seeking political rights and educational and social advancement drew condemnation on the world stage. All this occurred against a heightened and vehement backlash from persons seeking to "hold back the dawn" of civil rights. We are told the South Carolina Confederate flag emerged in opposition to such Civil Rights struggles. This group was represented especially by Southern racists, foremost among who were the segregationist George Wallace of Alabama, "Bull Connors," including the KKK, White Citizens' Council, etc., and other nefarious allies in the North.

BN PHOTO - Beautiful Art of the Black Woman on display at the International African Arts Festival.

The success of African and Latin American nations in winning their independence and being seated at the United Nations in the 1950s and 1960s emboldened the Civil Rights Movement in this country. So much so, the reactionaries of "Bull Connors," the "White Citizens Council" and "Ku Klux Klan" demonstrated their inhumanity and unabashed racism against protesting African American men, women and children who simply expressed rights guaranteed by the U.S. Constitution, especially the Bill of rights. As all this played out, the

BLACK NATIONALISM
STILL ALIVE AND WELL

nation continued to be embarrassed on the world stage. The climate gave birth to a "push and pull," emergence of young and persistent leadership in Jesse Jackson, John Lewis, Stokely Carmichael (Kwame Ture) and Rev. Abernathy. Then there was the official and unofficial backlash resulting in the assassination of key figures in the struggle; and, government complicity in unscrupulous behaviors against its citizens; nevertheless, hard won gains were accomplished. Just as the 1960s was the decade of African independence, concerted African American struggles in coalition with progressives and sympathetic activists in that decade and in the 1970s, men of goodwill in and out of government, especially the Kennedy brothers, and their successor Lyndon B. Johnson brought about important gains in voting, housing, education and solidarity with Africa.

BN PHOTO - The Doug Harris Quartet entertaining at Adelaide Sanford's 90th Birthday Bash.

FREDERICK MONDERSON

BN PHOTO - "Blow that Sax, Sir, Blow!" accompanied by the Doug Harris Quartet so we Celebrate Adelaide Sanford's 90th Birthday.

The struggle to achieve success in the historic 1954 *Brown v. Board of Education of Topeka, Kansas* laid the foundation to desegregate the nation's school system, and the election of John Kennedy in 1960 started America down a "no-turn back" road. The new philosophy and energy Mr. Kennedy brought to the office was designed to transform the nation while looking to encourage its people to outdistance others in science and the various areas that measure global leadership. The president was naturally impressed with Dr. Martin Luther King's poor people's "March on Washington" in August 1963 that was actually the brainchild of A.

BLACK NATIONALISM STILL ALIVE AND WELL

Philip Randolph, longtime worker in the vineyards of social activism. There Dr. King delivered his famous "I Have a Dream" speech which was really about jobs and the poor! However, within months President Kennedy was assassinated and his successor, Lyndon B. Johnson, in the interest of "continuity," launched his "Great Society Program" which was actually Kennedy's brainchild.

Surprisingly, this master politician, Lyndon Johnson, a Southerner from Texas, was able to cajole, "push and pull," "give and take" and his efforts emerged successful in passage of the 1964 Civil Rights Bill. The next year, the Voting Rights Act was passed and then Malcolm X was assassinated. This was a major blow to Black American nationalism. The Vietnam War was also a factor. Nevertheless, the struggle continued and by the end of the decade, Medgar Evers and Martin Luther King were also assassinated. Throughout, several acts of brutality were committed against the African-American community including more than 100 civil rights murders for which no one was brought to justice! Of course, in the southern "lynching states," for nearly a century after passage of the 13th Amendment outlawing slavery; these, by today's definitions, terrorists, lynched, killed, tarred and feathered, terrorized, bombed and burned churches, and intimidated African people and deprived them of society's protections of equal, human and civil rights in this nation. Meanwhile, the Africans continued to express concern at the United Nations regarding the condition of their brothers and sisters here in America.

FREDERICK MONDERSON

BN PHOTO - The "Empowered" message is clear, "We Demand Equality for All!"

It is believed, that such behaviors continue today, often in clandestine actions and coded statements. Nevertheless, as once said, "There are no permanent enemies, only permanent interests," Blacks continued to push their agenda Malcolm X, on the other hand, declared "History is a great teacher" and instructed we must learn about how others addressed and solved their problems. As for example, without question, America was at war with Germany in World Wars One and Two. In these conflicts, untold numbers of American citizens were killed. Yet, as of today, June 22, 2014, on Fareed Zakaria's Sunday Program on CNN, in an interview with the German Minister of Defense, and in response to a question, she is quoted as saying, "We share the same values as America." Therefore, that being so, and despite the war dead, the unmistakable fact is, if the above is true, then Africans worldwide, at home and abroad, should unite under the ideological philosophy of Pan-Africanism for this is a potent formula, ideology and philosophic

BLACK NATIONALISM STILL ALIVE AND WELL

shibboleth to strengthen African resolve and the only way the world will respect each and every one of Africa's sons and daughters!

BN PHOTO – "Only a bag of skillets and a can of tea…I am Trayvon. We can change this … Realize the Dream." Leaders Martin Luther King and Barack Obama - **NAACP**.

FREDERICK MONDERSON

BN PHOTO - Justice for Trayvon Martin and "What do we Want, JOBS, when do we want them NOW.

BLACK NATIONALISM STILL ALIVE AND WELL

BN PHOTO - Malcolm, Mandela and Martin, even Monderson would say "Justice for Trayvon Martin;" "What do we want ... **JOBS**, When do we want them ... **NOW**;" "Protect the Vote!! Rock the Vote at the Polls;" "Against Anti-Worker Laws and Voter Suppression."

6. BETTY DOPSON - "WARRIOR QUEEN"
By
Dr. Fred Monderson

In a splendid and colorful turnout members and friends of **CEMOTAP** came to the Robert Johnson Lite Center in Queens, New York, on May 31, 2015, to recognize, complement, praise, honor and offer a heartfelt **Thank You and Farewell to Betty Dopson at her Going Away Party**! More importantly, however, these people came out not simply to celebrate Betty Dopson, Co-Chair of **CEMOTAP** along with Dr. James McIntosh but to give thanks for their unrelenting, uncompromising and steadfast nurturing of an organization brought to adult manhood/womanhood while standing unflinching in the face of misdirected, pernicious and deplorable depiction of African people in the various modes of media, whether TV, print or radio. They

FREDERICK MONDERSON

came to praise a movement nurtured in an oasis of intellectuality and activist daring that challenged false representation of African people.

BN PHOTO - Dr. Adelaide Sanford and Reverend Herbert L. Oliver paying tribute to Betty Dopson on her "Going Away Party."

BN PHOTO - Dr. James McIntosh, Co-Chair of **CEMOTAP** (left); Professor James Smalls (center); and Attorney Dr. Mack (right).

BLACK NATIONALISM STILL ALIVE AND WELL

BN PHOTO – At the Dais, from Prof. James Blake (left), Betty Dopson, Mr. and Mrs. White, and Reverend Norris, Sr.

BN PHOTO – Father Laurence Lucas, Sister Viola Plummer and Mr. Bernard White, present a Proclamation to Betty Dopson.

FREDERICK MONDERSON

This courageous leader of men and women, Betty Dopson, standing next to her Co-Chair, Dr. James McIntosh, for some three decades demonstrated and spoke truth to power! Their message was clear! Stop mischaracterizing our people in your presentation or we will use every strategy in our arsenal, whether to boycott you and your sponsors, picket your place of establishment to shine the light of truth and correction; or, write and publish exposure of your malicious depiction of African people. This message remained consistent and has not let up!

While **CEMOTAP** simultaneously educated its members by inviting and presenting, in enriching discussion, untold numbers of trained and effective professionals and activists baptized in the arena of fire made enemies of African people stand up and take notice. Appearing on TV, whether "**Like It Is**" or other programs, on the radio or presenting carefully crafted position papers, conducting college tours to expose young people to this higher form of liberation, holding forums, sponsoring activist outings, etc., **CEMOTAP** enshrined its image and stature in the annals of African American activism and education with a resolve designed to achieve success in every endeavor to promote African upliftment and mental liberation.

In the Opening Prayer, Rev. Simmons characterized Betty Dopson as possessing tenacity, courage, stick-to-it-ive-ness while emphasizing "Faith without works is dead." Recognizing that she is a gem he asked the Creator to sustain and bless her, insisting we give thanks for Betty Dopson. He thanked the Lord for filling our time with joy, peace, hope and his unending love for us and the world. That "Your blessing is food for us and the mingling of our spirits is a testament of how great a Creator you are."

Dignitaries on the Dais included: (1) Professor James Blake, Chairman of **Queens Million Man March**; (2) Sister Betty; (3) Mr. and Mr. John White 'who stood up for blackness!' (4) Reverend Charles Norris, Spiritual father of the **CEMOTAP** movement; (5) The People's Chancellor "Intellectual Warrior Queen

BLACK NATIONALISM STILL ALIVE AND WELL

Mother" Adelaide Sanford; (6) Reverend Herbert Oliver; and (7) Sister Frederika Bey. Those in attendance, easily recognized, included Dr. Arthur Lewis and Wife; Dr. Jack Felder and son; Michael Grey of "100 Blacks in Law Enforcement Who Care;" Attorney Dr. Joseph Mack; Prof. James Smalls; Pam Africa; Sister Viola Plummer; Omowale Clay and others too many to mention. Such persons as Brother Fuller, Razakhan Shaheen, Father Lawrence Lucas, Brother Harold, Brother Bryan, Sister Penny, Olmeda and Shazanne Williams and Ed Ward, original **CEMOTAP** members were also there.

BN PHOTO - The Brothers speaking their piece to and about "Power" at Betty's "Going Away Party!"

BN PHOTO - "Sisters in the Struggle" alongside Betty Dopson, Co-Chair of **CEMOTAP**.

There was the New Jersey crew with Sister Frederika Bey including Brother Ladine Calibah as well as Radio personality Bernard White, NAKO representative Bokim, Shadini, Broca, Richadena Theodore

FREDERICK MONDERSON

and Molefi, among the "Sons of **CEMOTAP**." Artist Brother Lucian Pinckney was in the house!

Throughout Stephanie Juneau and Shawn Broughata sang "Love Train," "Just My Imagination Running Away with Me;" "My Girl" and many other old sentimental favorites that had people dancing while others clapped hands and even tapped their feet.

BN PHOTO - Father Lawrence Lucas, "The Priest of the Revolution," would never be absent at Betty's "Going Away Party."

Dr. Adelaide Sanford began with her customary "Beloved," and acknowledged the opportunity to be with Sister Betty all over the world. She pointed out; Betty Dopson brought a lightening rod spirit to activism. Equally, as Co-Chair of **BEPAA (Board of Education of People of African Ancestry**) at Dr. Clarke Elders' House she strove to promote liberation through education for our people. She established policies to achieve "education for liberation." On a lighter note, "She makes fantastic biscuits. You must taste those famous Betty Dobson biscuits."

BLACK NATIONALISM STILL ALIVE AND WELL

BN PHOTO - Reverend Herbert L. Oliver, of "Birmingham, Alabama Economic Boycott Fame!"

Reverend Oliver was happy to celebrate this wonderful occasion. He classed Betty Dopson as "mediating on young, gifted and black! She is educated and black! A community activist and black! A woman of character, a woman of integrity, compassion and beautifully black! Personable and black! Black, proud and happily Black!"

The St. Albans Church congregation offered a heartfelt "Thank you for blessing us in a wonderful way. Yours is a foundation of faith!"

Rev. Norris praised the Beacon School, IS 8, affiliated with **CEMOTAP**, and offered his continued praise, support and elicited a wonderful blessing. Jokingly he mused that his "Teeth are like the stars that come out at night!"

Mr. John White offered a praise that Betty Dopson and **CEMOTAP** were "There when we needed them. They supported so many groups there and then." His wife classed Betty as gorgeous, a warrior

FREDERICK MONDERSON

woman. She is a giant alongside people who appreciate freedom. More especially, 'You look beautiful. Happy Birthday Betty!'"

Prof. James Blake thought, "Jitu even made this event. Give me my flowers while I'm alive." Speaking of Betty, he insisted "She is a flower. She pollinates. She challenged Mayor Koch. She closed strip joints and racist merchants. She closed drug dens. She organized college tours after the Million Man March. She has tenacity, continuity and consistency. 'God brought you into this world to help our people,'" he reminded the beautiful lady.

BN PHOTO - Assemblyman Charles Baron and his wife Councilwoman Ines Baron flank Father Lawrence Lucas, "The Priest of the Revolution."

Inez Baron thought Betty Dobson the complete, thoughtful package, being bold, innovative and on the battlefield in all our struggles. She was fortunate to work with Charles Baron, Chukwu Lumumba, Sonny Carson, Jitu Weusi, Dr. Ben Jochannan and Dr. Clarke. Viola Plummer of the New York 8 and the December 12 Movement insisted Betty "Keep it going!"

BLACK NATIONALISM STILL ALIVE AND WELL

Mr. Bernard White characterized Betty Dopson with Dr. McIntosh as a "Tag Team." He confessed, "They recognized I was worthy of support." Father Lucas in paying tribute to "Our warrior sister" explained "The wives are known by their wisdom but the great are known by their actions and work. And in this Betty Dopson was supreme!"

Sister Shahid offered "Asante Sana" and thought it was an honor and privilege to know and work with Betty. Molefi McIntosh recounted "She took care of me" and that "Betty the Belly Dancer" is a beautiful lady.

BN PHOTO - Brother Yusuf Salaam praises Betty Dopson for an outstanding career in African intellectual activism.

Yusuf Salaam-Hanlon reflected, "They were moving people who were intellectuals while depicting filthy images of our people and **CEMOTAP** stood up." Professor James Smalls reminded, "Betty you are a goddess having a human experience. We make a pact with god. You have done your duty."

FREDERICK MONDERSON

BN PHOTO - Michael Greys recognized the role Betty played alongside Dr. McIntosh to make the "powers that be," stand up and take notice!

Michael Greys of "100 Blacks in Law Enforcement Who Care" confessed, "I am because we are. **CEMOTAP** is like home. Once there is a need, **CEMOTAP** is there. God speed sister!" Attorney Mack insisted, "Great women are known by what they do and leave behind. We must do and continue the work of Betty!" While her brother reminded, "We made Betty fight boys not girls!" and Dr. Arthur Lewis mentioning "Africans Helping Africans" offered, "We Love You Betty!"

BLACK NATIONALISM STILL ALIVE AND WELL

BN PHOTO - Dr. Arthur Lewis, the Harlem Ophthalmologist representing "Africans Helping Africans" came to pay his respects to Betty.

BN PHOTO - Lenora, a young and beautiful sister nurtured in the Intellectual Activist mold, speaks her piece to and for Sister Betty Dopson.

The artist classed Betty Dopson as among "People who bring light to everything." She was connected to her African-ness. She cracks the

FREDERICK MONDERSON

whip and makes people stand at attention. On her own behalf, Betty offered a promise and that the "Remarks are so remarkable and reassuring, of which I am very appreciative. I thank you from the bottom of my heart where Betty Dopson was a mere 81 years old, you made me feel good."

In total, all wished Betty Dopson the very best in the future and she promised to be back in New York at every opportunity time and circumstance permitted.

BN PHOTO - Omowale Clay and Bernard White, "Brothers long in the Struggle!"

BLACK NATIONALISM STILL ALIVE AND WELL

BN PHOTO - Sisters Viola Plummer and Pam Africa, the "Indomitable Twins."

FREDERICK MONDERSON

BN PHOTO - Mr. Greys, Prof. Smalls, and Eric and Luis were there for Sister Betty.

BLACK NATIONALISM STILL ALIVE AND WELL

BN PHOTO - Dr. Jack Felder and the "Boys" are joined by a hard working "Sister in the Struggle."

BN PHOTO - Dr. Adelaide Luvenia Hines Sanford "Queen Mother" of the "Intellectual Activist Elite."

FREDERICK MONDERSON

BN PHOTO - Professor James Smalls speaks of Betty "Having a divine experience in human form."

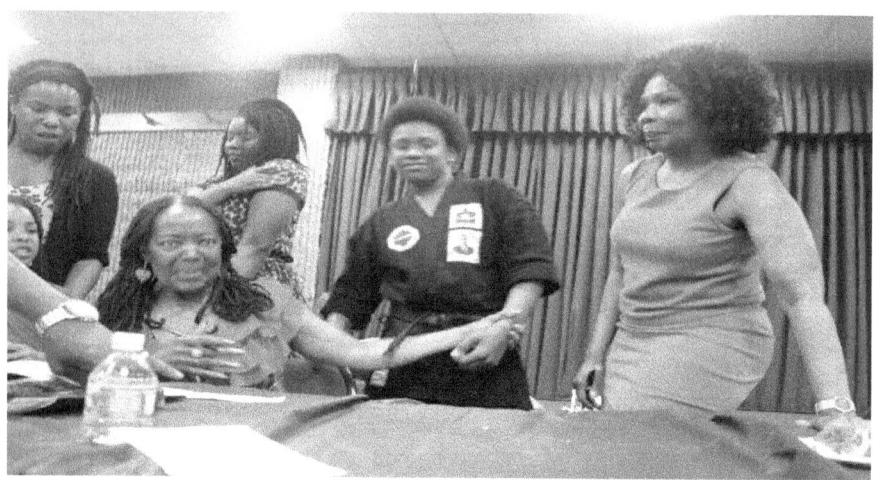

BN PHOTO - Betty Dopson, Co-Chair of **CEMOTAP** is all "eyes" among the young people being nurtured in correct civil activism.

BLACK NATIONALISM STILL ALIVE AND WELL

7. THE BLACK WOMAN
By
Dr. Fred Monderson

The Black Woman is a unique specimen in all facets of the human experience. While admired for her intellect, charm, beauty and supportive motherly sensitivities, she has been the most maligned and abused of all persons down through history. Tremendously physically attractive, she has been admired for these gifts by the male species across all races and concomitantly resented by the opposite sex of the same groups. As such, that paradoxical situation visited upon the Black Woman has manifested in thought and action in both ancient and modern times and the psycho-cultural scars, visible and invisible, testify to this assertion; yet, her quintessential role as mother, wife, companion, and intellectual icon is heralded.

The first Black Woman we know of in the human record was a young female discovered in the Hadar Region of Ethiopia and dated to be some 5 million years old. The contradiction in this wonderful "find" by the anthropologist Johansson was calling the beauty out of her name! Listening to a song playing on the radio by the British rock group "The Beatles" entitled "Lucy in the Sky with Diamonds,"

Mr. Johansson named the Black Beauty "Lucy." The venerated importantly well-respected anthropologist and African historian Dr. Yosef A.A. ben-Jochannan said no! Call her by her African name, *Denk Nesh*!

FREDERICK MONDERSON

BN PHOTO - "Sisters in Embrace" as the work and symbolism of Betty Dopson is finally recognized in this "Going Away Party."

In Ancient Egypt in North-east Africa, as the legend goes, the wife of an Old Kingdom priest was visited by the Sun God and promised her progeny who would become kings in that ancient land. The fourth Dynasty kings Khufu, Khafra and Menkaura whom the Greeks renamed Chufu, Cheops, and Mycerinus issued forth from her loins comprising successive generations. The Great Pyramid builder Khufu buried his mother Hetepheres with great pomp and splendor. Her tomb was discovered early in the twentieth century by George Reisner on an Expedition for the Boston Museum of Fine Arts which exhibited some of the wonderful funerary furniture buried with the beautiful lady. Unfortunately, grave robbers had disturbed the Queen's resting place, perhaps defiled the body which was never found since they robbed the tomb. However, four wonderful alabaster Canopic jars were found indicating the missing deceased was mummified at that early date. Fearful that Khufu would be enraged to know that his mother's tomb was desecrated, the priests simply reburied the remains without telling him.

BLACK NATIONALISM
STILL ALIVE AND WELL

Neithhotep was the last pharaoh of the Old Kingdom but scholars dismiss her reign, whether short or otherwise, perhaps it was because she was a woman who dared to rule this early in time. Nevertheless, the Calypsonian Black Stalin sang, "The more Africans they gun down, the more Africans keep coming!"

After the Old Kingdom, Egypt entered a state of serious instability through the Seventh to the Tenth Dynasty and it was not until the Eleventh Dynasty that order and stability was restored by Theban dynasts. Behind these kings were strong Black women, the mothers of Intef and Mentuhotep, for example, whose rationality and influence enabled these kings to "unite rather than fight." Consolidating their power, they won back the country, and found the Eleventh Dynasty ushering in the Middle Kingdom.

BN PHOTO - International African Arts Festival - "Welcome to the Ancestral Shrine!"

FREDERICK MONDERSON

BN PHOTO - The celebrated Jitu Weusi and Mzee Moya, original founders of the **International African Arts Festival** beginning on Claver Place in Brooklyn, are highlighted in this memorial board.

BLACK NATIONALISM STILL ALIVE AND WELL

BN PHOTO - Hathor takes the hand of Nefertari, wife of Rameses II, from a mural in her tomb in the Valley of the Queens, at Thebes.

FREDERICK MONDERSON

Mentuhotep II built an enormous and attractive temple at Deir el Bahari, the oldest surviving Middle Kingdom temple at Thebes and the best preserved structure of that age. It proved to be a transitional architectural form linking the Old and New Kingdoms in Egyptian building practices. This temple also proved to be a tomb for female members of the King's household. However, one lady Kemsit, because she was painted black as opposed to several servants painted red, scholars argued she was Negro, Negroid, etc. Nevertheless, while the king's statue was painted black and dressed in Heb Sed attire wearing the Red Crown of Lower Egypt was discovered nearby, a line of argument developed stating he was "so painted for the funeral ceremony." Seriously, she was painted Black as a Negro but he was painted Black for the funeral ceremony! What a ridiculous proposition in itself. What a contradiction! This false line of reasoning was also applied to the two statues later discovered guarding Tutankhamon's burial chamber. We must understand; the black pitch placed over the mummy is a preservative that actually covers the brown and black skin of the mummy shown distinctly beneath. Again, the mummy is "pitched" not the statue.

As the Middle Kingdom waned, unable to field strong leadership, the nation weakened disintegrated and foreign invaders; Hyksos, seized the land and founded the fifteenth and sixteenth dynasties. Their insolence motivated Theban princes of the Seventeenth dynasty" from Nubia and holding Thebes as its capital to challenge these occupiers and so waged a protracted 50-year struggle to oust them. While these early African nationalists were up north waging the battle, a Theban opportunist named "Tety the Handsome" sought to seize the throne in a palace coup and so fermented a rebellion. However, Tety underestimated the resolve of the Dynasty's matriarch Aahotep and her daughter Tetisheri who rallied the faithful and put-down the revolt. Her son, Aahmes later immortalized her with a stele in Karnak temple, praising her tenacity and revolutionary fervor. He also donated lucrative utensils and jewelry to the temple in her name establishing a hereditary title and endowment for female members of the family.

BLACK NATIONALISM
STILL ALIVE AND WELL

His wife and sister Aahmes-Nefertari, not simply beautiful but also astute as Queen-mother was later deified along with her son Amenhotep I in the Theban necropolis and a temple was erected there in their honor. One modern commentator argued she was only painted Black by workers in Ptolemaic times but not really so in her time! Of course, Heinrich Brugsch-Bey in *History of Egypt Under the Pharaohs* described her as Ethiopian! Her painted image is in the British Museum! This continues the 17th Dynasty connection.

BN PHOTO - Before a "Table of Offerings" Nefertari offers two ointment jars to enthroned Hathor in horns and disk with hanging uraeus and the Goddess holding ankh and scepter.

No woman was more vilified in the ancient world than Hatshepsut because she dared to seize the throne of power and rule a nation state at the apogee of its power. An assertive woman whom destiny placed among Thutmose I, II, and III, Hatshepsut proved tremendously astute and resourceful in the "art of the possible" contending against

FREDERICK MONDERSON

stiff opposition. "Alliances with strong men in the kingdom," not only empowered her politically but also enabled her artistic and creative abilities to impact heavily on Egyptian society and history. She was thus able to initiate many cultural innovations that became standard pharaonic practices down through dynastic times, particularly giving new impetus to the ancient Heb Sed festival. The anger and hatred of her successors is evident in treatment of her remains once removed from the helm of the state.

Her successor, Thutmose III's adherents attacked her mortuary temple at Deir el Bahari, smashing her statues; he enclosed her Karnak obelisks in a manner hiding it from general view; her tomb in the Valley of the Kings was firebombed; the "Red Chapel" Bark Sanctuary in Karnak she built was smashed and buried. Wherever these fanatics found the Queen's name they were expunged to erase her memory from history. In apartments adjacent to the replaced sanctuary at Karnak her image in association with Amon/Min and being baptized by Thoth and Horus, was walled in and chiseled out neatly. Her mummy was displaced and remained unknown until recently positively identified through scientific and dental sleuthing and now we know her true identity! Fortunately some of her cartouches escaped the destroyer's eyes and hands.

BLACK NATIONALISM
STILL ALIVE AND WELL

BN PHOTO - What a wonderful way to remember the ancestors who mattered in the struggle to advance the cause of African people during challenging times.

FREDERICK MONDERSON

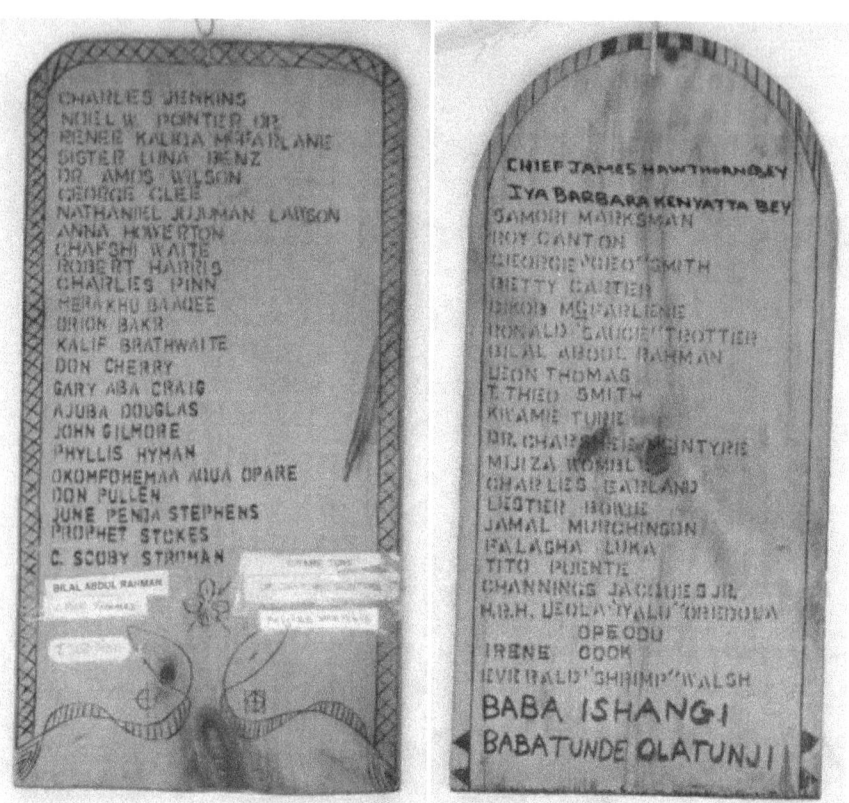

BN PHOTO - The names and deeds of "Soldiers in Struggle" should never be forgotten and *Black Nationalism - Still Alive and Well* is doings its part.

The dastardly deeds notwithstanding, same as that angelic, phenomenal woman Maya Angelo who penned the words, "Still I Rise," the Queen's name, instead of being forgotten by history, resounds well with modern art and architecture lovers, in "after years" as she declared.

BLACK NATIONALISM
STILL ALIVE AND WELL

BN PHOTO - Anubis embraces Hathor's shoulder while she grabs that of Osiris as he, the "God of the Dead," holds scepter and flail.

Rameses II in the next dynasty, the nineteenth, completed his father Seti I's temple at Abydos. Perhaps it was Seti himself who created the **Abydos Tablet** depicting 76 kings in cartouche from Menes to that deified monarch and he was unkind to the queen. Five of the cartouche names were left blank. Four of these names, Amenhotep IV or Ikhnaton, Akhenaton, and Smenkare, Tutankhamon and Aye, associated with the "Amarna Heresy" at the end of the eighteenth dynasty, were never inscribed in the sacred oval.

Hatshepsut, whose reign was much earlier, was proscribed because as a woman she sat on the throne of Egypt claiming to be "Son of the Sun God." That she wore male attire; a false beard and constructed a temple at Deir el Bahari greater than that of her ancestor Mentuhotep II nearby; generated much enmity. Though she had a tomb built in the Valley of the Queens while a young princess, she had another hewn in the Valley of the Kings which Seti probably thought was heresy. Even more revolutionary, while New Kingdom monarchs

FREDERICK MONDERSON

had their mortuary temples distant from their tombs, Hatshepsut planned and began constructing a tunnel linking her Deir el Bahari temple and tomb in the Valley. She intended to be taken directly from the temple's funeral ceremony to the tomb's eternal resting place in the Valley of the Kings. Unfortunately, the ground halfway through the mountain was unstable and not able to support the enterprise, thus it was abandoned.

Nevertheless, despite all the adversity, the Queen's name lives today through her temple, a gem of architectural construction. Her obelisks at Karnak, while one still stands in its original place, another lies broken near the Sacred Lake, were significant logistical and artistic accomplishments. We know from Deir el Bahari she erected four obelisks altogether but the whereabouts and location of the other two are unknown. Labib Habachi mentions an Aswan inscription referring to six obelisks. In addition, she did repair work on temples and other structures throughout the country following Hyksos occupation and destruction. Much more significant, however, the depicted images in her temple of transporting two obelisks on the Nile; the expedition to the "Land of Punt" on the Somali Coast in East Africa; and the revolutionary conception of her divine birth underscores her household name today encouraging many young women wanting to be like "the first queen."

Need it be said, Hatshepsut took great pride in being a Black Woman! When challenged she underscored her relationship and descent from her father Thutmose I's relationship with Aahmes-Nefertari, the Black-skinned Queen and divinity.

BLACK NATIONALISM
STILL ALIVE AND WELL

BN PHOTO - More of the Groundbreakers and stalwarts of the African Movement for emancipation, advancement and economic justice.

The next great Black Woman of history was Queen-Tiy, wife of Amenhotep III and mother of Amenhotep IV. She was well-liked by the king, wielded a great deal of influence in; beside, around and from behind, the throne. Many scholars credit her with initiating the concept of Aten worship. Dr. John Clarke spoke glowingly about this Black Beauty but more poignantly about her response to those critical about her son's Aten revolutionary movement.

She is stated to inform all such, "You may criticize my son's beliefs and actions as much as you want, but if you harm one hair on his

FREDERICK MONDERSON

head, I will send you to the infernal regions;" or words to that effect. Naturally and not surprising, modern critics of Egypt and Black influence therein sought to link her to Syria; this "So Nubian" queen! Her tomb was discovered in the Valley of the Kings in 1905 and revealed resplendent artifacts and jewelry attesting to her status at burial. Of note, she was buried in the Valley of the Kings!

Though Queen Tiy was the principal wife of Amenhotep III; Nefertiti, a Syrian princess came to Egypt to marry the old king in a political marriage, but ended up marrying his son Amenhotep IV, Akhnaton, Akhenaten, the religious reformer. Certainly with Queen-Tiy as a mother-in-law, Nefertiti needed big shoes to fulfill her mission. This she accomplished admirably-well, being seen participating in Aten worship festivities, being in her husband's company on festival and formal occasions and bearing him five daughters. All this is contrary to modern critics questioning her husband's manliness and virility that essentially impugned her integrity and character as a dutiful, faithful and loving wife.

BLACK NATIONALISM
STILL ALIVE AND WELL

BN PHOTO - Hathor (left) and Isis (right) with Nefertari in her tomb in the "Valley of the Queens."

FREDERICK MONDERSON

In the 19th and 20th Century German assault on Egypt, thousands upon thousands of artifacts were unethically removed from the antique land. In one swipe Auguste Mariette shipped 16,500 pieces of artifacts to Berlin. Add to this the great numbers that understandably belonged to Brugsch, Brugsch-Bey, Erman, Liebliz, etc., and multiply this by the thousands of adventurers, explorers, consuls, archaeologists and antiquity lovers who collected untold artifacts. Theodore Davis unloaded hundreds of boxes in California for the University of California. To this we may add collections in England, Italy, France, Turkey, and the United States, among others. Collectively, this is simply a part of what Brian Fagan called the "Rape of the Nile." One significant piece in Berlin, the Nefertiti head, is important for a number of reasons. It is a prized piece coming from an artist's workshop from the time of an important era in the history of Egypt and also since she was the wife of the great reformer. It was removed from Egypt at a time when there were no restrictions against such an important piece being taken out of Egypt. The queen looks "so Caucasian," some pointed out but this is simply because she was Syrian, Even more important she fits the false-razzle-dazzle notion that the "Egyptians were Caucasian."

A modern Egyptian official familiar with the contemporary negotiations on behalf of the Egyptian government seeking return of this valued piece, among others, informed of the complex and frustrating experience in the process, still to no avail. A similar situation occurred in getting the Sphinx's beard back from the British Museum. Consider that Mariette sent 16,500 pieces to Berlin and that Theodore Davis sent some 400 boxes to the University of California, then multiply such by the thousands who excavated and collected, the adventurers who worked for private collections in addition to themselves, museums, governments etc. To return any such piece as the Nefertiti bust would open the "flood gates" demanding that all such artifacts be returned. So the British returned the Sphinx beard on a "permanent loan" basis. So much for diplomacy and its languages in negotiations.

We know Rameses II's most favorite wife Nefertari was Nubian. They always choose the best and brightest! But he himself was a

BLACK NATIONALISM STILL ALIVE AND WELL

serial polygamist. They tried to tell us he was Syrian, but his skin was "brown" with black splotches from the mummification.

BN PHOTO - Nefertari, with hands empty and raised, stands before the "Four Sons of Horus."

FREDERICK MONDERSON

Al Sharpton dances with young ones at NAN's 25th Anniversary.

BLACK NATIONALISM
STILL ALIVE AND WELL

BN PHOTO - Papyrus depiction shows Hathor grasping the hand of Nefertari in their wonderful blue Galiebas or dresses.

Cleopatra, the seventh queen so named, is another African woman confronted with changing realities, at the end of the Ptolemaic

FREDERICK MONDERSON

dynasty. She was the only one in her line who understood hieroglyphics and spoke the native language. Confronted with the geo-political and military dynamics of a changing era and in the Harriet Tubman tradition she chose to "**Live Free or Die**!" So she killed herself rather than become the love toy of Octavian, the future Roman Emperor Augustus! Two respected African scholars, Dr. Yosef ben-Jochannan and Dr. John Henrik Clarke offered different perspectives on the Queen. Dr. Ben argued she was the last of a line of hated Ptolemaic dynasts. While Dr. Clarke explained, she was an astute African Queen faced with the realities of her time and acted in the best interest of the African state with dignity and uncompromising determination. Critics also contest her image at the rear of Hathor's Temple at Dendera while others contend the artists of her time certainly knew more about the Queen than speculative theorists two millennia removed.

The many acrimonious assaults visited upon the Egyptian, African, queen chronicled above in no way compares to the extant defacement and destruction evident on the walls of temples in Egypt. Art lovers around the world will attest that Egyptian art is probably the greatest in its genre for its originality, longevity and abundance. Many may speculate divine inspiration and guidance was foundation in creating such masterpieces that continues to excite and amaze, whether the expert or novice who travels from far and wide to appreciate and wonder about their majestic and timeless creative beauty, they remain breath-taking and awe-inspiring.

A valid question, therefore, is "Why would anyone want to deface and destroy such splendid works of art?" "Would an art lover stoop so low?"

BLACK NATIONALISM STILL ALIVE AND WELL

BN PHOTO - Papyrus depicts Tutankhamon and his wife Ankhsapaten in a relaxing mood.

Visit any Egyptian temple or tomb that can be reached today and behold practically every image of the beautiful Black Woman has been defaced or destroyed. Again, why would anyone want to disfigure the face of a beautiful woman represented in art? In India rejected suitors throw acid in a woman's face disfiguring nature's art. Many consider such actions sinful, full of hatred, spiteful and certainly illegal. In Egypt, however, hateful, spiteful, most certainly illegal may also apply. But, there may be an even more sinister motive behind such actions. In fact, it may very well be part of the "Conspiracy Against ancient Egypt!" Let us admit, "There are experts and there are experts" and even when that first expert points to his discovered observation, we ask, why should the other experts continue to deny that immutable truth. Thus, this action in itself raises more far reaching questions particularly about the ethnicity of the ancient Egyptians and what was the principal role of Africans in the Nile Valley?

The pertinent causal independent psycho/cultural variable is the white supremacy ideology. "Egyptians must be Caucasian!"

BLACK NATIONALISM STILL ALIVE AND WELL

BN PHOTO - The "Architect of this Movement" insisted he wanted these "Ancestors' Memories" to be remembered and we lend our assistance to the effort.

For example, several commentators had observed and commented, all Egyptian art, certainly her human figures are created in an African mold! Yet, many continue to deny this observed fact. Perhaps it is because the images of females on the walls of Egyptian temples and tombs, be they wives, mothers, sisters, daughters, are all created in the African mold projecting African features and therefore challenges and defeats the false notion of a Caucasian dynastic Egyptian. They were certainly created in the most meaningful periods of Egyptian history when Egypt excelled in art, architecture, science, medicine, government, militarism and religion. This existential element of African History is denied by European scholars because primarily it refutes the myth of the "Hamitic hypothesis," set forth by European scholars.

Perhaps then, this outlook is generated out of envy and in hatred to hold fast the waning and false belief and view of white supremacy that is continuously being challenged by the human record. The sad part of all this is, practically every statue or wall image has had its nose or mouth attacked and disfigured. To wit, another one of these lame excuses reads as follows: "Well, the brains of the mummy were extracted through the nostrils!" How pathetic! Presently two mummies repose in glass cases in the Luxor Museum where one is thought to be Rameses I. The face is not broken! The nose is still intact. There are many beautiful statues in the same Luxor Museum under tight security, and their noses are not disfigured. However, in foreign museums, in Britain, Brooklyn, the Met, statues "after being dressed" have their noses broken. The question is why?

Still, this assault on the Black Woman is not unique to Egypt. The Ethiopian Queen of Sheba has also been a victim of equally nefarious assaults.

One of the supposed great love stories of history is that of Solomon and Sheba, though the king had some 600 women in his harem! Of course, she was included but he never married the Queen in order to legitimize his relationship with this Black Beauty. Some have argued that her kingdom was ten times the size of his and his "love play" was really an opportunistic gambit for political opportunistic consolidation.

BLACK NATIONALISM STILL ALIVE AND WELL

BN PHOTO - Papyrus depiction of Lady Musicians, flutist, banjo and harp.

Though often shown in contemporary times as a White Woman, we know the Queen of Sheba boasted "I'm Black *and* comely!" More

FREDERICK MONDERSON

importantly, however, perhaps it was one of the six hundred disaffected women or racist commentators who began saying the Queen of Sheba said instead, "I am Black *but* comely!" Then a further disaffected descendant picked up the falsehood and continued into contemporary times, in itself a contradiction considering extant archaeological evidence. Thus, this negativity in perception of the Black Woman, buttressed by the daily observed defacement and destruction of the facial images evident in the Egyptian temples and elsewhere, should lead thinking people to wonder, 'why would anyone injure such beautiful masterpieces of art created by nature and also by human hands?' The saddest thing about all this is, it has been done; and it remains constant reminders of the inhumanity and envy of man to man. It also seeks to totally divorce from the role of the Black African, man, woman and child in formation, creation and perpetuation of the grandeur and permanence of the Nile Valley Civilization and its general human achievements.

In the Medieval period, Islamic scholars arriving in West Africa commented positively on the friendliness, beauty and good nature of African Women who greeted travelers crossing the desert. The hospitality they extended was superb, but within a few centuries the same women were dragged off to the New World in a horrendous system called the Atlantic Slave Trade. The horrors of that Middle Passage psychologically scarred the Black Woman in unimaginable ways through the trauma of personal abuse; inhuman conditions of trans-shipment; and the laviscious behaviors of many sailors on board such vessels or slave ships often called "sailing coffins."

BLACK NATIONALISM STILL ALIVE AND WELL

BN PHOTO - The "Table of Offerings" that celebrates the lives and work of these illustrious "Ancestors."

BN PHOTO - Again, "Illustrious Ancestors" on display at the International African Arts Festival.

FREDERICK MONDERSON

BN PHOTO - RETIRED SLAVE. There's been a wide diversity of "Ancestors" who stood up and fought for African people in challenging and dangerous times for African survival.

Arriving in the New World, in the Caribbean and North, South and Central America, for centuries, the Black Woman was mercilessly dehumanized. *Roots, Twelve Years a Slave, Django Unchained* and Ruby Dee's narration of *The Fight Against Slavery* graphically depict the inhumanity meted out to the Black Woman. When in 1808 the American Congress outlawed the Slave Trade, the Black Woman

BLACK NATIONALISM
STILL ALIVE AND WELL

was still consigned to the beastly behavior of "slave-breeding" practiced on Southern "Slave Farms" designed to produce off-springs to enrich the slave holding assets of the owners. Clearly there was a difference in the stature and treatment between the Black Woman as "house servant" and the Black Woman as "field hand." Still there was also a difference between the Black as a kept woman and the young woman as "fair game to the owner and overseer's desires." Sure Phyllis Wheatley may have had it a little better, able to write poetry; but Sally Hemmings was not freed by President Jefferson upon his death even though he fathered several of her children. The story is told of one Black Woman from "slave farm" days who was promised freedom if she made so many children; yet she died a slave having produced 36 children. This was the act of a white "Civilized" European Christian in America!

Harriet Tubman would not have any of this and insisted "I must live free or die!" In the 19th Century days of southern white terrorism the Black Woman suffered tremendously as young sexually exploited and beautiful but also as wife and mother of lynched and terrorized husband and son. In the 20th Century, a young man was lynched and his mother protested. That day the racist mob lynched both mother and son. This murderous reality was part of the daily life of African people living in 20th Century America!

During the Civil Rights Struggles of the 1960s, 4 little Black girls were killed by a bomb in a Birmingham church. Significantly, however, Malcolm X railed against the police officers "sicking dogs" on men, women and children protesting for human and civil rights. Malcolm X, "Our Shining Black Prince," also singled out the police officer who planted his knees in the chest of a Black Woman lying prostrate on the ground as he assaulted her and the FBI stood nearby taking notes!

FREDERICK MONDERSON

BN PHOTO - Hatshepsut, in full stride, on a wall in her Deir el Bahari Temple, Thebes.

We can therefore reasonably argue that the Black Woman down through history has remained a unique and original specimen of God's creation! Importantly, she has been blessed with physical beauty and attractiveness; ingeniously demonstrated intellect and knowledged assertiveness; exhibited love, compassion and sensitivity; and has been courageous, supportive and faithfully loving while simultaneously rising above the challenges of greed, malice, the lust of white males, and envy. Still more significantly, as mother, wife, sister, aunt and friend, the world must be thankful and is a better place because of the forgiving nature, wisdom, tenderness and loving companionship of that wonderfully created, divine spirit, the Black Woman!

BLACK NATIONALISM
STILL ALIVE AND WELL

BN PHOTO - Raised Relief of Goddess Mut of the Theban Triad wearing the red and white Double Crown.

FREDERICK MONDERSON

8. SALUTING THE BLACK WOMAN 4 By
Dr. Fred Monderson

+The Black woman has been instrumental in defining the parameters of our struggle, our being, and our existence.

BN PHOTO - A woman of dubious identity, often regarded as Rameses II's daughter and also as Rameses III's daughter named after the Syrian goddess Banta Anta, this colossal image stands in the Great Court at Karnak Temple, just before the Second Pylon.

BLACK NATIONALISM STILL ALIVE AND WELL

Through the evolution of the dynamic change man and humanity have undergone in Africa, in the long march of cultural, religious, spiritual, scientific and technological transition, she has held her own! In step and never lagging, supportive, watchful, comforting, nurturing, she has been the object of joy and desire, forward ever, backward never.

From then to now, roaming the savannas of East Africa, within the palaces of Egypt/Kemet, across the glory days of the Western Sudan, through the "door of no return" in West Africa, into the bowels of the floating coffins, singing work songs on the plantations in America, amidst whippings between the big house and the field shack, playing the game with Massa, while comforting the black man, raising his children, assertively in the civil struggle then standing in the halls of power, she has defined the destiny as a proud heroine, daughter of "Mother Africa."

BN PHOTO - Mut in disk stands beside Ra-Horakhty also in disk on a Karnak Temple wall.

FREDERICK MONDERSON

Science, utilizing DNA reconstruction, has demonstrated that the earliest surviving progenitor of the human race has been a woman who roamed the plains of East Africa over two hundred and fifty thousand years ago. Earlier, a palaeo-anthropologist named Johanson discovered the most complete human fossil. It was of a woman in the Hadar region of Ethiopia, who was subsequently, nicknamed "Lucy," and dated to more than five million years old.

Emerging fully formed in radiant splendor she was a prized jewel of praise and adoration, in the next great flowering of African womanhood that occurred in the Nile Valley. As a result, in this unfolding drama, the role of women in ancient Egypt/Kemet earliest showcase of Africa's cultural excellence she has been essential, appreciated, respected and necessary.

From the earliest times the indispensable position of Egyptian women has been depicted in the graves of the prehistoric period and in the tombs of deceased nobles. Their roles as goddesses, queens, princesses, mothers, and plain old folks, were demonstrated and the impact on numerous pharaohs as well as Egyptian society has been recounted in successful continuity.

Many women have ruled as queens of Egypt but Hatshepsut of the Eighteenth Dynasty has been the only woman bold enough to rule as King or Pharaoh of this ancient land. This was certainly against stiff male opposition.

The female principle in Egypt, as in Africa, is divine in nature. In Egyptian cosmogony and religious beliefs, female divinities have played important roles. They have featured prominently in divine triads, and in a number of instances females were a part of pharaonic triads.

BLACK NATIONALISM STILL ALIVE AND WELL

BN PHOTO - One of the most interesting images on this wall depicts the Queen of Rameses II as goddess leading bound prisoners at Karnak Temple.

The goddess Nuit or Nut was from the earliest times a water goddess who formed part of a divine company of eight. The males were Nu, Hehu, Keku and Kerh. The females were Kerhet, Keruit, Hehut and Nut. Not much is known about the other goddesses in the earliest time but, in the New Empire, Nut was represented as a woman and as a cow.

According to the *Book of the Dead* or the Hieratic Transcript of the *Papyrus of Ani*, translated by E.A. Wallis Budge, there were a number of female deities in the Egyptian religious drama. Among the earliest, the male Shu and the female Tefnut were children of Ra, the Sun God. Tefnut formed the third member of the company of gods of Anu. Tefnut is sometimes represented as moisture and at other times as sunlight. This goddess originated in the Nubian Desert. She had a lion head and wore a disk or uraeus or both. She drank her enemies' blood and had fire in her eyes.

The next female divinity of importance was Isis or Auset. She was the seventh member of the company of Anu, sister and wife of Osiris and mother of Horus. She is usually depicted as a woman with a headdress in the shape of a seat. One of her surviving temples is located at Philae, now transferred to Agilka Island. Some early names ascribed to her are "the great goddess, the divine mother, the mistress of words of power and enchantment." In later times she is called mother of the gods and the living one. Isis is sometimes shown as a cow and has a solar disk between her horns with a throne or seat, and she also has plumes or feathers. Her most famous depiction is as the mother suckling her child Horus. The original "Madonna and Child" concept is based on this depiction. Naturally, she was Black like the sky, hence, the Black Madonna.

BN PHOTO - Backed by wife in the Temple of Khonsu at Karnak, Rameses III offers two bouquets to God Horakhty and Goddess Mut of the "Theban Triad" whom we do not see.

Nephthys was Isis' sister and wife of the evil god Seth. "When the sun rose at the creation of the primeval waters Nephthys occupied a place in his boat with Isis and other deities; as a nature goddess she either represented day before sunrise or after sunset, but was not associated with night. Her hieroglyphic name means "lady of the house." Plutarch tells of a legend that said she was the mother of Anubis by Osiris, who later became judge of the dead. She is shown as the companion of Isis and was grieved during Osiris' murder.

BLACK NATIONALISM STILL ALIVE AND WELL

The next female divinity was Ma'at, the female counterpart of Thoth. The Heliopolitan tradition makes her a daughter of Ra. She was the wife of Thoth, the god of writing. A feather symbolizes her name and she also holds a scepter in one hand and an ankh in another. The name Maat means straight, right, genuine, righteous, just, real, truth, balance, order, steadfast, unalterable, etc.

Hathor, the "House of Horus," was the goddess of the sun where the sun god rose and set. Hathor is depicted as a woman with a disk and horns on her head. She is also shown as a cow with a disk between her horns. The daughter of Ra, her temple is at Dendera, but she was worshipped throughout Egypt, oftentimes doubling as Isis.

SALUTE: THE BLACK WOMAN. PART II.

Whereas today imperialism and balkanization of colonialism has left political boundaries in Africa, in that proto-typical age of African consciousness formation, when the gods roamed freely, there was no such division; certainly not as pronounced as today. As such, then, regarding Hathor, Budge notes that as a "Cow-goddess she is probably of Sudani origin." That is Africa proper, to the south of Egypt.

FREDERICK MONDERSON

BN PHOTO - Hathor as Mut does her, "I got your back" Ra-Horakhty routine in temple of Khonsu at Karnak. This frieze follows the previous image.

Neith has been called "the divine mother, the lady of heaven, even mistress of the gods." She is mentioned in the *Pyramid Texts* as the mother of Sobek, the crocodile god. Neith was believed to be self-produced and an ancient Saite tradition made her to be the mother of Ra, the Sun God. She is depicted in the form of a woman, having upon her head a shuttle or arrows, or she wears the Red Crown and holds arrows, a bow and a scepter in her left hand.

Sekhmet was the wife of Ptah, and the mother of Nefer-Temu and of I-Em-hetep. She personified the terrible heat of the desert. "When Ra determined to punish mankind with death, because they scoffed at him, he sent Sekhment, his 'Eye' to perform the work of vengeance; illustrative of this aspect of her is a figure wherein she is depicted with the sun's eye for a head." Bast was a sort of opposite to Sekhmet. She personified the gently and fructifying heat of the sun. She is usually pictured as cat-headed.

BLACK NATIONALISM
STILL ALIVE AND WELL

BN PHOTO - Standing at his rear, the queen in horns and disk mounted on a mortar with uraeus, watches Rameses III's back in a presentation.

Neheb-ka is the name of a goddess represented by a serpent. Uatchit and Nekhebt were very special goddesses. They personified Upper and Lower Egypt respectively and comprised the Pharaoh's "Two Ladies" name. Uatchit, a form of Hathor, is depicted as a woman with the crown of the north and a scepter. Nekhabit was the vulture goddess, tutelary deity of Upper Egypt from the city of Hekheb. Mut the earth goddess was wife of Amon Ra the Sun god and mother of Khonsu the moon god. She was an essential part of the Theban triad, comprising Amon Ra, Mut and Khonsu. She too is sometimes shown as a vulture.

FREDERICK MONDERSON

As a result, female roles in the divine cosmogony and religious drama of the Egyptians, people of Kemet, gave them a special place in the social fabric of the society. Whether wife, mother or sister, females were respected, cared for, and had equal statues before the law. They could inherit property, become literate and were able to conduct business. Oftentimes they were spokesperson for their husband's business.

The graves of the Badarian, Amratian and Naqada I burials show much evidence of some association between the dead and women. What we call female paraphernalia can be found in many graves of the time. These include combs, rings, bracelets, studs for the nose, jewelry of shells, carnelian and coral around the neck. There, earrings and dresses are also included. These ancient Africans utilized dyes with green malachite and castor oil for cleansing and softening the skin.

By the time of the Gerzean culture or Naqada I and II period, figurines of the fertility goddess are found in graves. Carved bone and ivory figurines of women are also found in graves. They were designed to accompany deceased men into eternity for purposes of companionship and pleasure.

Female jewelry was made from a wide variety of materials including amethyst, button-pearl, and amber, agate, onyx, and glass. The jewelry included necklaces, girdles, bracelets, and a circlet or diadem for the head, bracelets, arm-bands, and ankle-bands were also worn. Therefore, in the pre-dynastic time, before 3200 B.C., the role of women was considered important enough to receive the attention indicated in the graves.

BLACK NATIONALISM STILL ALIVE AND WELL

BN PHOTO - Wearing the Double Crown Rameses III faces Hathor in Horns and Sun-disk.

From the First Dynasty, 3200 B.C. onwards, the position of women seems advanced and appreciated. On the Narmer Macehead the king is shown under a pavilion. His wife, Queen Neithhotep is shown also seated and facing him. Some feel this is probably a marriage ceremony. However, it clearly shows an elevated position for his wife. They had a son named Aha, who succeeded his father to the throne.

While Narmer was buried in a regular sized mastaba tomb at Abydos, Aha built an elaborate tomb for his mother, Queen Neithhotep. The indications of this are that the husband and son, in ancient Egypt, loved and respected the wife and or mother. The same care and concern could be found for the daughter and for the sister.

In this respect, the basis for the love, respect and proper consideration of women or females in Egypt is clear. This treatment is evidence by the roles of and respect for the goddesses, queens, mothers and princesses. It stands to reason that the ordinary woman also enjoyed some of this special attention. However, it must also be pointed out, there were women who held positions as household help and slaves, as in many societies in the ancient world.

The significance of women in Egypt is further indicated by their statues before the law. The "Supreme Court," according to an inscription on the walls of a tomb at Sakkara, upheld a certain woman's right to inheritance. Schafik Allam's *Everyday Life in Ancient Egypt*, argues that women could "inherit moveable things, house and landed property."

Even more, women were held accountable for their actions in the society. They could also engage in business or represent their husbands in business transactions. They could receive loans, mediate between two parties and were allowed to bear witness in many judicial proceedings. Women had the legal right to conduct legal affairs without the prior authorization of their husbands.

BLACK NATIONALISM
STILL ALIVE AND WELL

BN PHOTO - "Beauty in the Grass" beside Rameses II's "Girdle Wall" in the rear at Karnak Temple of Amon.

FREDERICK MONDERSON

The inscription at Sakkara tells of a woman named Ornero, who was "designated by the courts as representative for a group of heirs and who consequently had to administer on trust all the property in question." Women could sue in court. Many wives of officials were "responsible for regulating their husbands' affairs and looking after their husbands' interests." Many were authorized to act in his absence. Therefore it is clear how such liberality has enabled a number of dynamic African women to have impact on three thousand years of socio-political-religious cultural expression in dynastic Egypt. This is well in keeping with Diop's notion of African matriarchy that encouraged female creativity, and the wielding of influence and exercise of power. As well as transmitting the divine genes into pharaoh. As opposed to the European and Asiatic patriarchal system which debunks the Caucasian, Egypt myth. That is, more African queens played active roles in their society than in other ancient states.

While women in general enjoyed these freedoms the power of royal women was inherent in their family connection and can be gleaned from the titles they bore through association with their fathers, husbands, sons and brothers. Some royal women held the title of Regent, in charge of young protégées who would succeed to the throne. Not all of them walked away from the glory of exercising that power. The first such regent was Merneith, an Ist Dynasty Queen. As Narmer's wife was Neithhotep, Djer's wife Herneith, and now Merneith, this shows the Goddess Neith fashionable during the First Dynasty at the head of 3000 years of Black women's glory. The sisters holding it down today enjoy an illustrious tradition. Van Sertima's *Black Women in Antiquity* deals with: The African Eve; The Great Queens of Ethiopia; The Female Horuses and Great Wives of Kemet; Tiye: Nubian Queen of Egypt; Egypt's Isis: The Original Black Madonna; African Goddesses: Mothers of Civilization; Female Styles of Beauty in Ancient Africa; The Image of Woman in African Cave Art; African Warrior Queens; and African Women in Early Europe. Gay Robbins *Women in Ancient Egypt* and Margaret Bunson's *The Encyclopedia of Ancient Egypt* are useful sources on the role of women in that society.

BLACK NATIONALISM
STILL ALIVE AND WELL

BN PHOTO - Holding scepter at Karnak Temple, Mut, wife of Amon, wears the "Double Crown" of a United Egypt.

The Step Pyramid at Sakkara marks the start of significant African architectural construction. The Archaic Period or First and Second Dynasty kings built tombs at the holy city of Abydos, the world's first city of pilgrimage. They also built a second tomb at Sakkara, burial place of the city of Memphis. By building a second tomb, they were reinforcing the dual nature of their power as kings of Upper and Lower Egypt/Kemet. Many scholars are still not sure which was the real tomb or a cenotaph or dummy. Consensus seems to favor Abydos, because it's religious significance in connection with the gods of the dead, first Wepwawet and then Osiris. Seti I's 19th Dynasty temple at Abydos, dedicated to seven gods faces the desert and believed to honor the archaic kings buried there. This lends greatly that Abydos is the site of the real burials.

These burial structures were mastabas, called "benches" by the modern Arabs. They were subterranean with one-storied superstructures. The Step-Pyramid was built in this necropolis by Imhotep, the world's first multi-genius for his pharaoh Zoser of the Third Dynasty, c. 2600 BC. This Step-Pyramid, a great seven step-mastaba in decreasing size, and the great mastaba tombs became prototypes for the true pyramids of the Fourth Dynasty. Hapynma'at was the mother of Zoser. Zoser, because of his renowned architect and administrator, Imhotep, was able to construct the Step-Pyramid. We can only wonder at the magic and majesty of Hapynma'at and what influence she had on her son Zoser. He was married to Heterphenebty. Clearly he was influenced by one of these Black African women.

The Third Dynasty began the first golden age in Egypt. It also began the Old Empire.

The accomplishments of the preceding Pre-dynastic and Archaic periods set the stage for the new era. The Step-Pyramids and the great mastaba tombs became prototype for the true pyramids of the Fourth Dynasty. The next woman of significance here is Meresankh I, wife of Huni and mother of Sneferu.

The architectural erections of this age became symbols of early African engineering and technological genius. Coupled with the sphinx, they typify resolute and defiant challenges to time as they face eternity, being testaments to the greatness of the African spirit.

The pharaohs who dominated the Fourth Dynasty were Sneferu, Khufu, Khafre and Menkaure. The first built two pyramids at Dashur and Meydum. The other three built the famous Giza group.

BLACK NATIONALISM
STILL ALIVE AND WELL

What is significant, however, is the role Queen Hetep-Heres played in influencing these four great African kings. There is divine prophesy connected with her, in that it was predicted three of her sons would become kings of Egypt, not the "Disney" type. Thus, Queen Hetep-Heres was the wife of Pharaoh Sneferu, mother of Khufu, grandmother of Khafre and great-grandmother of Menkaure. What a progeny! She must have been a powerful African woman.

In 1925, excavators in an expedition from Harvard University worked at Giza. Behind the pyramid of Khufu, they discovered the "only intact tomb chamber from the Old Kingdom" found up to that time. According to J.E. Manchip White's *Ancient Egypt: Its Culture and History*, a "wonderful collection was unearthed."

BN PHOTO - Truly a "Warrior Queen," this beauty grasps the enemy by a string as she follows her king on a wall south of the Hypostyle Hall at Karnak.

FREDERICK MONDERSON

BN PHOTO - Close-up of a queen holding Ankh and Mace in right hand and Bow and Arrow in left, as she leads prisoners on a string.

Archaeologists found, "there was a canopy, a bed, two chairs and a carrying chair, all sheeted in gold. There were alabaster vessels, a copper and gold manicure instrument. There was a toilet box with cosmetics contained in eight little alabaster pots, and a jewel case with twenty silver anklets inlaid with lapis lazuli, carnelian and

BLACK NATIONALISM STILL ALIVE AND WELL

malachite. Inlaid gold hieroglyphs on the ebony panels of the carrying chair carried the fourfold inscription: 'Mother of the King of Upper and Lower Egypt, follower of Horus, guide of the Ruler, favorite whose every command is carried out for her, daughter of the god (born) of his body Hetepheres.'"

In the tradition of powerful African women, Hetepheres was one of the greatest. The bust of Pharaoh Khufu is so African with his broad nose and thick lips; one can only wonder what his beautiful mother and father looked like. Diop's argument for the blackness of Egypt, states the fundamentals elements of the civilization, viz., architecture, religion, writing, governmental structure, navigation, medicine, etc., were thought out, functional and in place, put there by Black men and women, before whites ventured into Egypt. They were filterings of whites who came to Egypt during this time but their role was inconsequential at this time. It was millennia before great numbers of whites came to Egypt with the Hyksos and they were only able to gain significant inroads when there was a breakdown of strong leadership. Was it because of the lack of Black woman input?

Still, before this fateful development we could envision that strong Black woman, Hetepheres, the mistress, mom, grand-ma, great grandmother about her palace, perhaps baking cookies, and even engaging in a little mischief. But what an influential woman she was. She was also one of the earliest surviving examples of the art of mummification, a craft that would become so refined more than a thousand years later.

The strength, power and majesty of the IV, and V, petered out in the VIth Dynasty. As Egypt stumbled into the First Intermediate Period, Dynasties VII-X (7-10), we see a decline in strong leadership. Can we surmise that they lost touch with their women, stopped cultivating their genius, no longer used their intellectual insights, abrogated the partnerships that worked so well. The record is silent.

FREDERICK MONDERSON

It does show disruptions, warfare, famine, breakdown in the centralized system of government and we could well imagine religion and spirituality suffering. We know African people are religious. God first appeared to man in Africa, and since, his greatest adherents, in the minds of many, has been African.

This writer was in Egypt with Dr. Ben-Jochannan in 1989. Then he planned the First Nubian Festival for the next year. When we returned in 1990 the Festival was a flop. He had been betrayed, but, in 1989, he held the First and only *Panel Discussion*. The Panel consisted of a practicing minister, an ex-minister, then a counselor, a young couple, a ten-year old brother and a fiery sister from California.

The topic of discussion was: "Now you have come to Egypt after what you have seen, how has it affected you? What are you going to do with this knowledge?"

It was a beautiful Panel discussion. In the Question and Answer period, the young sister said to the practicing minister: "Rev. McNair after what you have seen, can you go back to Philadelphia and teach the same sermon?" The old doctor looked at her real sternly and said: "I cannot tell my people there is no god, I can only show them where god comes from." I still think this the most sincere and revolutionary statement ever.

BLACK NATIONALISM STILL ALIVE AND WELL

BN PHOTO - Mut stands before Khonsu who wears a super necklace in Karnak Temple.

The XIth (11th) Dynasty marks the beginning of the Middle Kingdom when Theban princes began a process of unification, organization and consolidation. During the First Intermediate Period, the country was again split into North and South, the dual kingdoms before Narmer had united the lands to begin Dynastic rule and the First Dynasty. In this period of disruptions and breakdown of centralized authority, Assuit noblemen were pivotal middlemen between the Upper and Lower Kingdoms. The important city of Abydos became the "gate to the South." With the emergence of powerful Theban princes as Intefs and Mentuhoteps, embodying strong leadership, a strategy emerged to retake the North and reunite the country. Abydos then became the "door to the north."

In one of the family squabbles among the Thebans, Intef took the field against Mentuhotep. When he came out from the pass and entered the Plains of Thebes, he encountered a stronger army waiting for him. Intef had his mother queen Achtothes intercede with Queen Aam, mother of Mentuhotep, to broker a peace between the two

FREDERICK MONDERSON

armies. They then united to face the common enemy of disorganization, the order of the day, but successfully united the two lands.

As with the First Intermediate Period, following the XIIth (12) Dynasty or Middle Kingdom, the Second Intermediate Period again saw breakdown in centralized authority. An alien people, Hyksos, invaded and held the northern kingdom. The south was nominally free. They accepted the suzerainty of the north, paying tribute to their kings.

However, who's better than the greatest? The answer is Teti-sheri!
The Eighteenth Dynasty was the most remarkable of all others. This was so because of the females who provided the progeny and inspiration for this greatest golden period. Teti-sheri was the wife of Sekenenra II of the Seventeenth Dynasty. Flinders Petrie writes, "They came from Nubia." In *Temples, Tombs and Hieroglyphs*, Barbara Mertz wrote: "Teti-sheri survived him; she lived to see her daughter marry her own brother, Sekenenra the Brave. Her granddaughter Aahmose-Nefertari also married her brother, Ahmose …. Ahmose's queen was a lovely woman, and a great lady, who was deified in later times." Sekenenra-Tao was killed with an axe-blow to the head in the war of liberation against the Hyksos, or Asiatic invaders.

BLACK NATIONALISM STILL ALIVE AND WELL

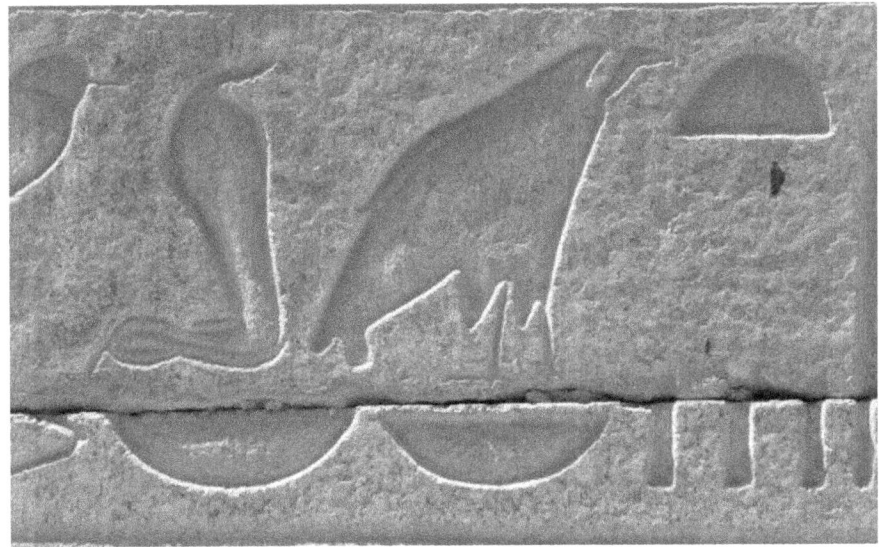

BN PHOTO - The "Two Ladies," *Nekhabit* and *Wadjit*, of Upper and Lower Egypt, also one of the five titles of the king.

The family relationship of Teti-Sheri's progeny is important for it clearly establishes the Blackness of the Eighteenth Dynasty. In *The Splendor That Was Egypt* Margaret Murray describes Ahmose, the founder of the dynasty as a "strongly built man, broad-shouldered, and with curly brown hair; he was not good-looking for he had projecting front teeth, and his portraiture suggests an admixture of Negro blood."

From her portrait in the British Museum the beautiful Aahmes-Nefertari leaves no doubt about her Black Ethiopian origin. Her grand-daughter Queen Hatshepsut had to contend with the fact of her "Ethiopian blood" as the heiress to the throne after her father Thutmose I's death. This equally remarkable woman challenged male dominance and ruled for two decades. Her personal circle was headed by Senmut, her favorite and architect who built the magnificent Deir el-Bahari temple at Thebes.

FREDERICK MONDERSON

Senmut also quarried and erected two obelisks for the queen. Another architect, Amenhotep, erected two others. Two have disappeared and one still stands at Karnak while another remains beside the Sacred Lake. The standing obelisk measures 105 feet and is the tallest in Egypt. This queen, who described her-self as "beautiful to look at above all things; her voice was that of a god; her frame that of a god; her spirit was like a god," maintained the prosperity of her nation but succumbed to male rage and dominance. Her name still ranks as one of the most beautiful and powerful of African heroines.

Queen Tiye was the wife of Amenhotep III and the mother of Amenhotep IV. Her husband ruled Egypt at the height of the New Kingdom's "Golden Age." She played a prominent role in events of her time. Amenhotep III built a palace called Malcata for his beautiful Black Queen Tiye. She had a significant impact on her son Amenhotep IV. He changed his name to Akhenaten and ushered in a new religious movement. Also, the art of the time was probably influenced by his ideas. Critics have credited her with influencing the rebellion her son introduced.

BN PHOTO - Ma'at in Cartouche name of Rameses II, *Usr-Ma'at-Ra*, in Karnak Temple.

BLACK NATIONALISM
STILL ALIVE AND WELL

BN PHOTO - Wearing a long flowing Gallibea on the Tenth Pylon, Rameses II presents a plant to Mut wearing the "Queen Mother Crown," a vulture headdress, surmounted by a "White Crown" with feathers.

Nefertiti, Dushrata's daughter Thadukippa, was a Mitanni princess who came to Egypt and married Queen Tiye's son Akhenaton or Ikhnaton. She came into a powerful family and played a significant role in her husband's rule. She bore him five daughters and visibly displayed her love for him in a number of representations.

In the Nineteenth Dynasty Rameses II, the great builder and warrior Pharaoh built the Abu Simbel temple in Nubia. He married Nefertari, a Nubian princess and built her a temple next to his at Abu Simbel. This was the supreme test of love, which clearly indicates the power of this African woman.

This selection seeks to highlight the majesty, power, beauty and everlasting testimony of the greatness of African and African American womanhood. Clearly, no nation on earth can boast such a splendid line of outstanding women as did Egypt for they influenced their states and the world. They remain to be admired and serve as role models of integrity and accomplishment for an entire race of people. These were indeed great African women and they set powerful examples for progeny of the African race.

BLACK NATIONALISM STILL ALIVE AND WELL

BN PHOTO - Image of Goddess Mut in the likeness of Tutankhamon's wife, placed before the Sanctuary by Tutankhamon as part of the "Restoration of Amon" to power following the "Amarna Heresy."

Queen Amenardis, sister of Piankhy of the Twenty Fifth Dynasty was a beautiful woman who became God's wife to Amon-Ra at Thebes following the Ethiopian conquest of Egypt.

FREDERICK MONDERSON

Queen Cleopatra was beautiful and had to contend with the changing realities thrust upon her nation and she rose to the occasion. Ethiopia produced a strong line of queens called Candace who were warrior Queens and represented their nation and people with distinction. These followed in the tradition of the Queen of Sheba, who while not a warrior, was Black and beautiful and a lover.

In West Africa the role of Queen and Queen Mother was very significant contributing much to that culture cluster in the Ghana, Mali and Songhay empires. The descendants of these women were later dragged off to be slaves in the New World. One of the first of those was Angela who disembarked from the Dutch Man O' War in 1691 and Isabela who in 1624 gave birth to the first Black African child born in the New World. Tonya Bolden in *The Book of African American Women* mentions 150 crusaders, creators and up-lifters of Black men in America. These women were in every walk of life, from slave to plantation owner. Some were entrepreneurs, preachers, abolitionists, activist-lecturers, thinkers, conductors of the Underground Railroad, writers, singers, mothers, nurses, spies, real estate investors, playwrights, cooks, poets, journalists, educators, civil rights activists, doctors, pharmacists, aviators, army officers, judges, lawyers, anthropologists, historians, dancers, psychologists, politicians, athletes, mathematicians, slaves and even more. Some were lynched and there were the "Four Little Girls," victims in a Birmingham Church bombing.

In looking at James Allen's exhibit on "Lynching across America" a grandmother in the line said: "I must get my grandchild to come over to look at this," as she viewed the Black woman Laura Nelson who was lynched in Oklahoma in 1911. That day both mother and son were lynched! Interestingly enough, there is no question that in the more than one hundred slave rebellions Herbert Aptheker chronicled in this hemisphere, women played a significant role, and we can add to this Angela Davis and Assata Shakur.

BLACK NATIONALISM STILL ALIVE AND WELL

BN PHOTO - Statue of Hatshepsut just before the Sanctuary at Karnak Temple.

FREDERICK MONDERSON

BN PHOTO - Native Egyptian Guide Showgi Abd el Rady points to Goddess Sekhmet enthroned at the entrance to Rameses III's Mortuary Temple at Medinet Habu, Thebes.

Recognition is due the dignity and accomplishments of the ancient "sheroes" mirrored in the struggles and untiring efforts of many modern women. Today, Queen Mother Moore, Joyce Dinkins, Adelaide Sandford, Winnie Mandela, Coretta Scott King, Ollie McClean, and Mrs. Jessie L. Jackson stand for the same principles of

BLACK NATIONALISM STILL ALIVE AND WELL

African achievement. We should also not forget Phyllis Wheatley, Harriet Tubman, Sojourner Truth, Mrs. David Walker, Mrs. Henry Highland Garner, Mrs. Frederick Douglass, Mrs. Booker T. Washington, Mrs. W.E.B. Dubois, Mrs. Marcus Garvey, Priscilla Dunjee, Mrs. Carter G. Woodson, Mary McLeod Bethune, Fannie Lou Hamer, Septima Poingette Clarke, Gemma Grigsby and Anna Arnold Hedgemon. Miriam Wright Elderman founded the Children Defense Fund. Lets also mention Dorothy Height, Barbara Jordan, Patricia Harris, Cybil Holmes, Juliet Plummer Cobb, biologist, Alice Walker and Zora Neal Hurston, writers, Johnnetta Cole, educator and Rev. Elizabeth Lott, mother and member of the CME Church. Then there is Jean Leon, Marjorie Matthews, Kathie Rones, Mrs. Benjamin, Jacqueline Lennon, Kadiatou Diallo, Audrey Phillips-Caesar, Mrs. Steil, Gloria Thomas, Germaine Burger-Gaskin, Debra Tyndale, Mrs. Parris, the Auxiliary Ladies at Kings County Hospital Center, and Betsy Youman, Katie Harrell, Renee Morgan, Mrs. Mock, Josephine Brathwaite, Renee Smoke, Marilyn Washington, Marisela Alcantara, Ruth Green and Carmen Rudder.

Betty Dopson, Ella Fitzgerald, Carmen McRae, Vonetta Price, Bessie Smith, Aretha Franklin, and Philippa Duke Schuyler and Cybil Williams Clarke and Gertrude ben-Jochannan, Numsa Brath, Dr. Adelaide L. Hines Sanford, Mrs. Lewis, wife of the Ophthalmologist, Mrs. Mae Sonny Carson, Shirley Chisholm and Una Clarke are only some of the names.

FREDERICK MONDERSON

BN PHOTO - Papyrus depiction of Rameses II, Usr-Ma'at-Ra presenting two bouquets to enthroned Hathor in Horns and Disk.

Then there's "Moms Mabley." "Me Moms" Mitta Monderson, "Me grand-Moms" Cherise Preville, "Me Sister" Cherise Maloney, "Me Wife" Carmen Monderson, Enid Graham, Mavis Hill and we could add contemporary woman educators, Rhonda Hurdle, Mrs. Purdie, Hyacinth Rowe, Lucille Lang, Mrs. Ilene Loncke, Hessel Woolcock, Mrs. Harper, Mrs. Elizabeth Buckman Jones, Suhail Pena, Yvette

BLACK NATIONALISM STILL ALIVE AND WELL

Hall, Mrs. Virginia Jackson, Mrs. Jane Roberts, Estelle, Valma and Lorna Browne, Rhonda Mormon Harris, Merimba Ani Richards, Mrs. Winna Allette, Sophie Williams, Ethel Foy, Melinda Melbourne, Mrs. Murray, Bernice Wiley, Evelyn Castro, Debra Brathwaite, Mrs. Angela Jitu Weusi, and so many more. Still, we can't forget Kiatdou Diallo, Agnes Green, Mrs. Haggler, Linda Bascombe, Osela McCarty, philanthropist, Sarah J. Hale, humanitarian, Annette Robinson and Mary Pinkett, City Councilwomen, Andre Pennix Smith, Lois and Ruth Goring and Gwendolyn Harmon community minded women. Choyice Diane Robinson, mother and concerned citizen. Deanna Corbett, woman of insight; Marcia Melbourne, Toni Morrison, Madame C. J. Walker, Mary Church Terrell, Ava Stagger, Pura Belpre, writer, Bessie Coleman, Aviator, and other women in music, Pearl Bailey, Mariam Anderson, Marlon Williams, Sarah Vaughn, and Lena Horne, Rosetta Dunning, Veronica Corbett, Doris Alexander and Priscilla Maddox, Bernice Green, Holly Fuchs, Njoni Granville, Madame Marie Rene Pologne, Connie Lesold, and Viola Sanders, all the School Nurses.

The African American male is therefore fortunate to have such powerful women to stand with, beside and behind him to help guide his endeavors. This tribute to these women is well deserved. There are conduits in the tradition of strong Black women bequeathing the strong yet tender and ferocious African womanism in the American experience. Black men, make your women proud!

FREDERICK MONDERSON

BN PHOTO - Face of the Goddess Hathor with "Cow's Ears" in the Court of her temple at Dendera in Upper Egypt. Notice her necklace halter.

BN PHOTO - Isis in her many moods, in Presenting an "eye of Horus" and "White Crown" (left); and backed by Thoth (right) as he records.

BLACK NATIONALISM STILL ALIVE AND WELL

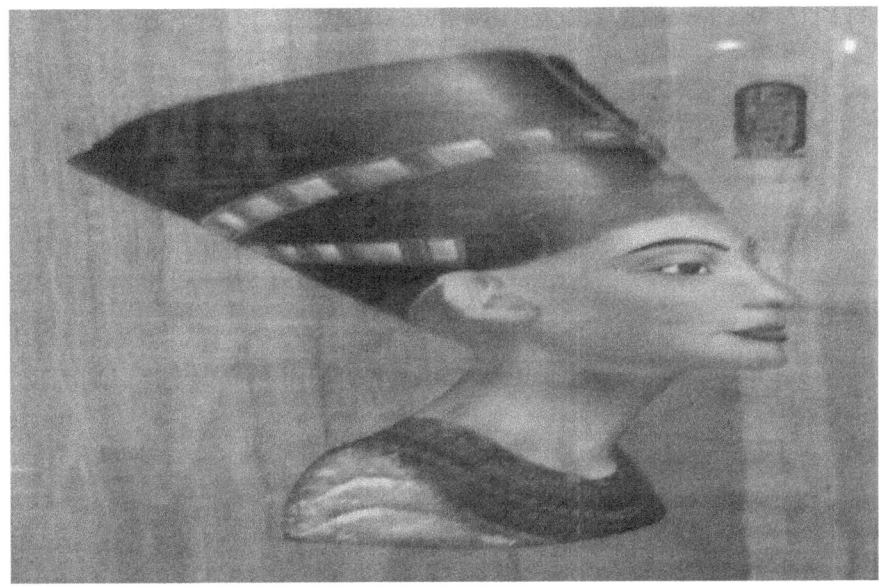

BN PHOTO - Papyrus depiction of the famous "Nefertari Bust" in Berlin.

9. MOOD OF THE COUNTRY
By
Dr. Fred Monderson

The mood of America is at an important crossroad, which means turning left at the fork promises encounter with a simmering cauldron of inequality of wealth and inequity before the law that will not bode well for this country. The right turn will go far in pursuing the very best for this country, the clear skies, smooth sailing, respect and equality in person and opportunity that will make all Americans stand proudly against every thought, action and deed that contravenes and threatens the American way of life, the fundamental principles the nation seeks to perfect, whether such is from foreign or domestic threats. But, we must remember, a threat to justice, equality and freedom anywhere in America is a threat to justice,

FREDERICK MONDERSON

equality and freedom of person or expression everywhere in America!

Revisiting President George Walker Bush's Inauguration Address 10 years ago in 2005, he insisted racism as practiced in this new century is not in the nation's best interest and all must work to eradicate this scourge which has festered since the foundation of the nation. Three years later Barack Hussein Obama, an African-American dared to declare for the Presidency. He waged a well-orchestrated campaign in the most unbelievable and relentless fashion finally winning the day and becoming the 44th President of the United States.

BN PHOTO - The Name of Malcolm X is legendary, iconic, having demonstrated his Black Nationalist outlook.

At the 2009 Inauguration of this first African American President, the civil rights icon Reverend Jesse Jackson remarked, "Barack Obama represents the very best the **Civil Rights Movement** has to offer." In addition, the then Mayor of Newark, New Jersey, Cory Booker expressed an emerging and prevailing view, "We have now entered a post-racial period in our nation's history." As time and events have shown since then, the level of respect and protections for Black men plummeted with the reported deaths of Trayvon Martin, Michael Brown, Eric Garner, Gurley, Reece, etc. New York City Police Commissioner Bratton introduced a "Broken Windows" program to replace "Stop and Frisk" because crimes were rampant in Black and minority communities!

BLACK NATIONALISM STILL ALIVE AND WELL

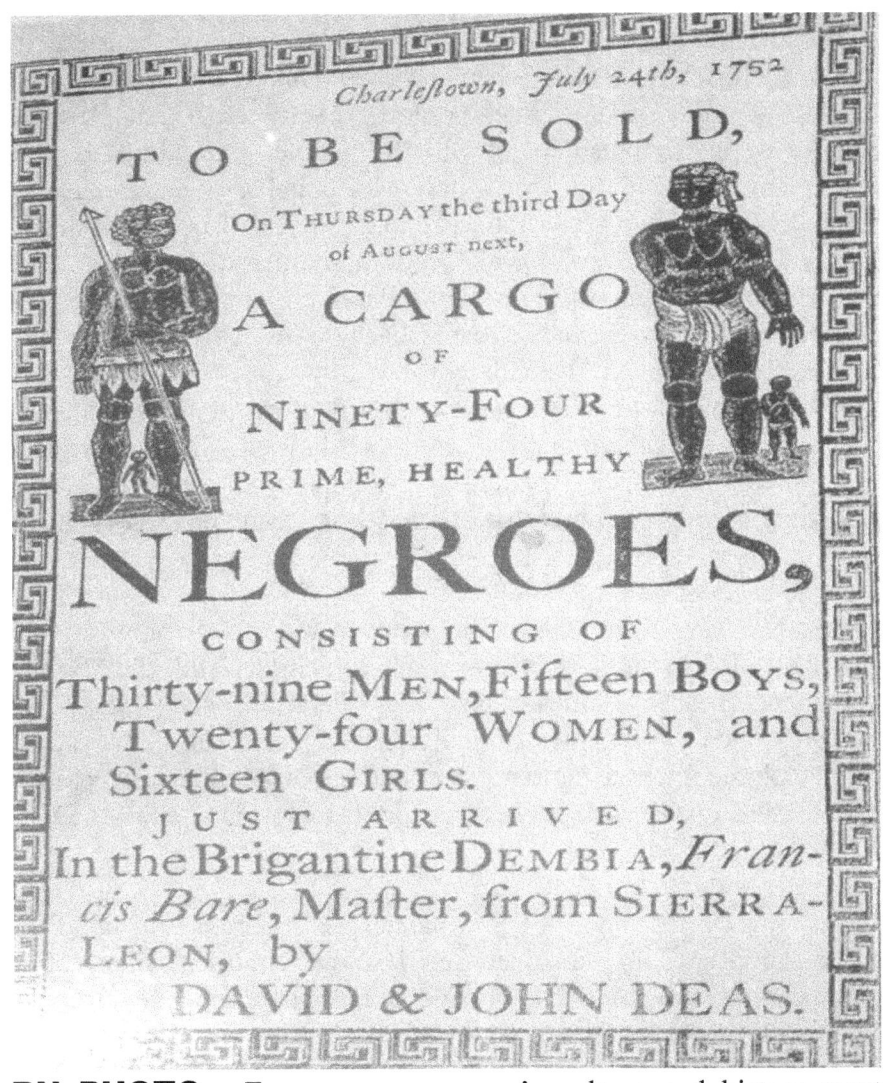

BN PHOTO - Everyone agrees one's culture and history must never be forgotten.

From the inception, this latter behavior has been characterized first by militias propagating false information about Mr. Obama's initial intent, significantly arming their groups and conducting military drills in preparation for a race-war they falsely envision. The

FREDERICK MONDERSON

"Birther" movement, Congressional disrespect, perennial sabotage of every Presidential legislative initiative by the "Party of No," and every time the issue of race as a discussion topic, the answer is "Let's not discuss such!" When the President injects a statement about a seeming racial issue, commentary states he should not because he is the president of "all the people." Yes, but "all the people say nothing" to the Mitch McConnells, John Boehners, Michelle Bachmanns, Marco Rubios, Joe Wilsons, DeMints, Grassleys, "Black Protester with Guns" and "men of the cloth" like his pastor praying for the President's death and even "Papa Cruzs" who want to "Send Barack Obama back to Kenya!" Guess what; perhaps he has taken that advice and going back to Kenya, his father's homeland, only this time as President of the United States. The Africans over there clarified an important point. They indicated they welcomed Barack Obama as President of the United States, first; then as one of their own. This is not the reverse and that is important for the "Birthers."

Today, *The New York Times*, "the paper of record," is reporting on Campbell Robertson's "History of Lynchings In the South Documents nearly 4000 Deaths" that identified and intends to publish some 3,959 names of individuals lynched in 12 Southern states with the intent to further place markers on each location where such dastard deeds were perpetrated in an inglorious history of this nation from 1877 to 1950.

About two years ago, CBS Channel 2 reported on an FBI investigation of an unsolved civil rights murder where the perpetrator is still alive but no one is talking except the victim's family. The report mentioned more than "100 unsolved civil rights era murders" and that many persons who ran for office in associated areas had either to belong to or espouse racist and "Klan Ideology" especially while running in "White Primaries." Clearly, there is a connection between such requirements and activities in the "Lynching States" and their metamorphic descendants now commanding state houses and national political forums. These are the people who threatened voters' abilities to cast this cherished American right to elect their leaders.

BLACK NATIONALISM STILL ALIVE AND WELL

BN PHOTO - Legba and Gye Nyame (Guardian of the Crossroads and Supremacy of God) are spiritual forces that guide and protect African people.

Without a doubt, the national groundswell of protest and demonstrations following the Trayvon Martin murder, the Ferguson Rebellion, the Eric Garner protest movement at home and abroad by young and old members of all races, sends a powerful message people want change in the way this nation "regards and does business" towards its citizens, particularly the most vulnerable. They certainly don't want "new wine in old wineskins."

In addition and most important, published in 1944, Gunnar Myrdal did a study entitled "An American Dilemma" in which he showed how the "Southern Prisons," especially, part of today's "Prison Industrial Complex" were used to keep Blacks in line, having them inform on others and exerted control over their communities. Some years ago Jesse Jackson railed against the state of South Carolina that had some 36 state prisons and 1 state college! Fact is, as former Assemblyman Roger Green said some years ago in his fight against

FREDERICK MONDERSON

governor Pataki, it costs some $70,000 to keep a youth in prison; $35,000 for an adult; and only $12,000 to keep a student in college. At that time a jail cell cost $110,000 to build and another $110,000 interest for a total of $220,000. Now we see and could understand the saintliness of the Charleston Emanuel Church congregation counteracting the historical "heritage" of South Carolina.

While today we recognize the psychological and social emasculation a rampant prison system is having on Black men and women and their impact on families at home, the report on lynching also identified this mechanism as a replacement tool during the Depression Era when lynching was ruled "Illegal!" Question is, at what point was lynching legal?

Fact is, slave trade, slavery, Jim Crow, Segregation, racism, the Prison Industrial Complex, lynching, tar and feathering, share-cropping, terror as intimidation, denial of the right to run for office and to vote, redlining, and all such odious practices are simply terror tactics waged against African-American citizens because of their race and it is not only wrong, ungodly but certainly illegal under law and perpetrators should be punished!

BN PHOTO - ASASE YE DURU (Divinity of Mother Earth) and HYE WON HYE (Imperishability and Endurance).

BLACK NATIONALISM STILL ALIVE AND WELL

10. THAT MISSOURI COMPROMISE
By
Dr. Fred Monderson

Contrasting the actions of the Chief Executive when Missouri first became an item of significance and how President Obama responded to the current situation says much about how each view of the issue differed and though things change how very much they remain the same. James Monroe was president when the Missouri Compromise became an issue of historical, political and moral significance and his impact seemed minimal. On the other hand, after Ferguson exploded, President Obama directly intervened by sending a high level delegation to investigate and act. Now, as the community in Ferguson, Missouri await the Grand Jury decision on whether to indict officer Darren Wilson for the killing of the unarmed teenager Michael Brown and in anticipation Governor Nixon declared a state of emergency in readiness of unlawful behavior; a young rapper and activist remarked to CNN Anchor Don Lemon, covering developments, "The racism of white supremacy is in the DNA of this state." This belief, therefore, forces a look at some aspects of the state's history particularly from the inception of the Missouri Compromise of 1820; a significant milestone in the question of slavery and subsequently inequality of Blacks in that now famous or infamous state of Missouri, the "Show Me State!"

FREDERICK MONDERSON

BN PHOTO - LATIN CROSS (symbol of the Christian Faith) and ANKH (Egyptian Symbol of Life).

The Missouri Compromise was an important development in the legislative history of the New American Republic coming as it did in aftermath of the War of 1812 which ended in 1815 and the beginning of Internal Improvements as the Industrial Revolution began to take hold in America. That year of 1820, with the Compromise of 1787 or "Three-fifths Clause" as a backdrop designed to appease the slave holding South efforts to occupy and exploit the vast tracts of new land acquired in the Louisiana Purchase, the future of enslaved Blacks in America was bleak at best! The dynamics unleashed in the Cotton Gin revolution of 1793 conflicted with the shortcomings stemming from outlawing the slave Trade in 1808. Then the labor demands and wealth aspirations of plantation owners mounted and they demanded much from legislatures and protective forces. In Florida, generally under Spanish rule, the Seminole nation (Native Americans) had long been a place of refuge for runaway Blacks that were a source of irritation for slave-holding elements. So General Andrew Jackson was dispatched with a force to cross over to Florida to punish Seminoles for their acts of mercy in aiding runaways. This occurred in 1818 and if you add the creation of horrendous "slave farms" producing dreaded coffles of slaves chained and restrained in

BLACK NATIONALISM
STILL ALIVE AND WELL

the most barbaric manner, this signaled Black lives within and outside the United States was not worth much, except as a commodity to a heartless, get rich slave owner class. After all, the entire "New World" seemed an enormous plantation where professing Christian White men, guided by the Bible, practiced the most inhuman crime against humanity lasting for centuries; and all with the sanction of the church, Catholic and all denominations.

BN PHOTO - MEDICINE WHEEL (Native American Circle of Life); and TANIT (Islamic Faith).

Thus, the Missouri Compromise of 1820 was accepted to achieve political balance by admitting into the Union one Slave State, Missouri; and one Free State, Maine. Harold G. Syrell in *American Historical Documents* (New York: Barnes and Noble, (1960) 1965: 177) explained it best in the following statement. "Missouri, part of the Louisiana Purchase, applied for admission to the union as a slave state in 1819. At the time there was an equal number of Slave and Free states, and neither wished the balance to be changed in favor of the other. James Tallmadge, a representative from New York, offered an amendment to the enabling act that would have gradually eliminated slavery in Missouri. The act as amended passed in the

FREDERICK MONDERSON

House but failed in the Senate. Meanwhile in December, 1819, Maine applied for admission as a free state. In the Senate the two admission bills were combined and were finally accepted by the house after the addition of a compromise amendment, introduced by Senator Jesse B. Thomas of Illinois. In November, 1820, when Missouri's constitution was submitted to Congress, it contained a clause unacceptable to the antislavery groups. Henry Clay, then, formulated a satisfactory compromise proposal, which was adopted on March 2, 1821."

Constance Baker Motley, in an Introduction to "The Legal Status of the Negro in the United States" in John P. Davis' *The American Negro Reference Book* (Englewood Cliffs, New Jersey: Prentice Hall, Inc., 1964: 484) discussed the case involving Dred Scott and its impact on the status of enslaved Africans in America languishing on the altar of the **Missouri Compromise of 1820** and the unfinished Constitution of that Age. Ms. Motley wrote: "In 1857 in the momentous Dred Scott case, nine members of the Supreme Court reviewed, at length, the prior and then current legal status of Negroes in the United States. At that time, most Negroes were slaves. Some had been freed by their masters in accordance with the legal procedures established by the law of the slaveholding states; others had likewise purchased their freedom. Dred Scott had been a slave in Missouri. In 1834 he had been taken by his master, an army surgeon, into the free state of Illinois. Subsequently, he was taken to the territory which is now Minnesota. There slavery was prohibited by the **Missouri Compromise of 1820**. In 1838 Scott was returned to Missouri and later sold to another army surgeon. In 1853 Scott brought suit in a Federal Court in Missouri claiming to be a free man. His claim was that he had become free upon being taken into free territory and consequently remained free upon his return to Missouri." It is to be noted, the many years he was languishing as a slave in an institution where untold millions were supplying free labor generating a significant portion of the nation's wealth! Equally too, the heartless system "sold" him and so many more. This, then is what chattel slavery meant.

BLACK NATIONALISM STILL ALIVE AND WELL

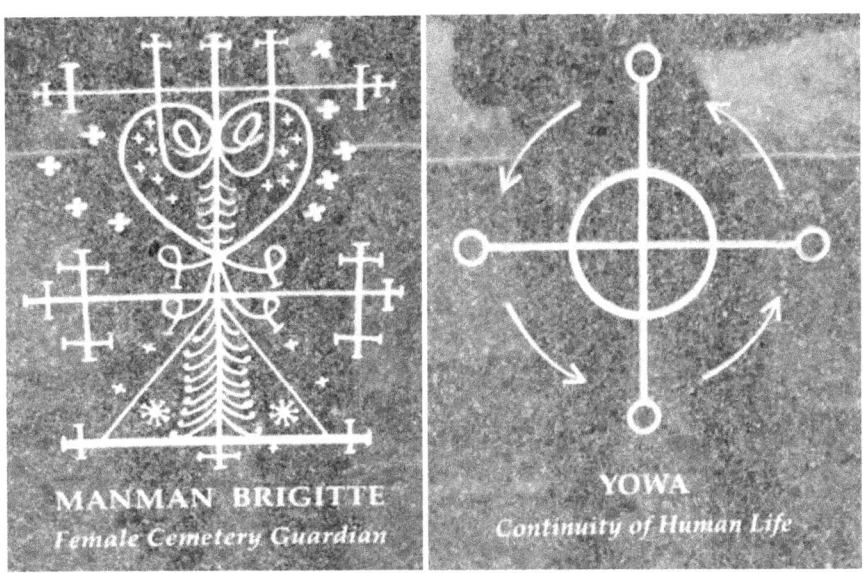

BN PHOTO - MANMAN BRIGITTE (Female Cemetery Guardian); and YOWA (Continuity of Human Life).

However, as this courageous writer and activist continued, she noted: "The New York citizen who claimed to be his master defended on the ground, among others, that Scott could not bring suit in a Federal court because he was not a citizen of Missouri. Scott had just lost a suit on his claim to freedom in Missouri courts. The New York master asserted the Federal court would have jurisdiction of the suit only if Scott could show diversity jurisdiction, i.e., a suit by a citizen of one state against a citizen of another. Thus two questions required resolution: first, whether Scott was a citizen of Missouri, and second, whether Scott had been freed by being taken into free territory. The latter question involved a determination whether Congress had the power under the constitution to prohibit slavery in the territories, thus making Scott a free man in Minnesota. Chief Justice Taney's adverse conclusions on these questions were concurred in by the majority. He held Congress did not have power to prohibit slavery and consequently the Missouri Compromise was unconstitutional. He held Scott was still a slave because the highest court of the state of Missouri had held in Scott's case when it was before it that under the law of that state a master did not lose his property right in his slave by taking him to a free state like Illinois." Which, as stated above, "the legal procedures established by the law of the slave holding states" would have prevented Scott from being free and thus having no rights?

The tipping point in that famous Supreme Court case of *Dred Scott v. Sandford* of 1857, Chief Justice Taney ruled: "Can a negro [sic] whose ancestors were imported into this country, and sold as slaves, become a member of the political community formed and brought into existence by the Constitution of the United States, and as such become entitled to all rights, privileges, and immunities, guaranteed by that instrument to the citizens? One of which rights is the privilege of suing in a court of the United States in the cases specified in the Constitution .... The only matter in issue before the Court therefore, is, whether the descendants of such slaves, when they shall be emancipated, or who are born of parents who had become free before their birth, are citizens of a State, in the sense in which the word 'citizen' is used in the Constitution of the United States.'"

Ms. Motley rightly concluded, "Taney ruled that Negroes were not citizens within the contemplation of the Constitution. He based this on what he claimed to be the Negro's legal status throughout the civilized world at the time of the adoption of the Constitution. This status was a non-citizenship status, and he said, 'so far inferior, that they [the Negroes] had no rights which a white man was bound to respect.'" Given that the civilized world created and perpetuated a barbaric system of inhumanity of man towards man; yet, being born within the boundaries of the nation ought to have been enough. Such a situation later became law under the 14th Amendment to the Constitution, but the Court seemed to be favoring the planter class who benefitted from denying Africans those protections citizenship conferred. Notwithstanding, even when the Civil War Amendments conferred this right, it was often ignored and denied. In some respects, the oppressor tends to bend the law, and to ignore and

BLACK NATIONALISM STILL ALIVE AND WELL

suppress these rights guaranteed by the constitution, the "supreme law of the land!".

Nevertheless, it goes to show, "This view of the Negro's legal status at the time of the adoption of the Constitution was disputed by the dissenting justices. One dissenting justice found that: 'At the time of the ratification of the Articles of Confederation [which preceded the Constitution], all free native born inhabitants of the states of New Hampshire, Massachusetts, New York, New Jersey, and North Carolina, though descended from African slaves, were not only citizens of those States, but such of them as had the other necessary qualifications possessed the franchise of electors on equal terms with other citizens."

Given what is stated, does the Roger Taney, planter class mentality still pervade in its many guises? After all, "Jim Crow, Jr., Esq. seems to have evolved from "Jim Crow."

BN PHOTO - Map of Africa and African burials as depicted on the marble floor in the well.

President Obama speaks at "Sharpton's Affair" as Obama visits New York for the "Affair" honoring Dr. Martin Luther King.

FREDERICK MONDERSON

11. SLAVES, MASTERS AND SECURITY
By
Dr. Fred Monderson

Sure, there is a police organization in New York called "100 Blacks in Law Enforcement Who Care" and there may very well be similar groups across the country, but they are few. Most Black Police officers who fill this category function with a sense of community in pursuing their calling as police officers committed to protecting their respective then respective community but also caring about how they go about such business. One such policeman confessed in twenty years of service, not once did he pull his service revolver. However, across the country, for the most part, Black Police Officers serve as minorities ethnically and numerically, but are yet constrained within a "Blue Wall of Silence." Yet, strange enough, when they are in forefront of vigorously policing, in contradiction, they resolutely brutalize!

Notwithstanding, the great many officers mostly white who serve consciously are also constrained by the "few bad apples" who spoil their barrel disregarding the fact "**Black Lives Matter**." Nevertheless, all function within psychological mindsets sanctioned by legal precedence created and held over under ante-bellum legislation that held the Black Man in contempt. *Ipso Facto*, and in service to the ante-bellum cultural norm the false claim of Blacks being inferior in both the natural and social order seems, for the most part the operational definition. As such, law enforcement functionality that grew out of an empowered "slave catchers" ideology and operationalization was designed to protect property at all costs and so viewed Black Men especially as chattel and so disregarded their humanity in serving the interests of the "business class" who not only subjugated the unfortunates but when they

BLACK NATIONALISM STILL ALIVE AND WELL

revolted or ran away, these "rough riders" ran roughshod over them disregarding whether they were enslaved or free.

When the recent saga of Ferguson unfolded a young Missouri activist declared "Slavery is in the DNA of this state!" Equally, it can be argued, the ideology, personality and make-up of the slave catchers' DNA seem transmitted into the vein of current law enforcement as evident in the wanton police killing of unarmed Black men from the recent Trayvon Martin through Freddie Gray. To understand how we got here, however, history provides a clear road map from the brutality of the overseer, through the rapaciousness of the slave catcher in service to the planter class and supporting the need for law and order that disregarded the humanity of the Black person in executing the need to protect property even though the Black was regarded as property under the system of chattel slavery.

Regardless of arguments for origins and dynamics of New World Slave Trade and Slavery unmistakably Europeans morphing into Americans removed and all caused Africa to lose some "100 Million" souls depopulating the continent to engineer the transformation of the New World through a system of plantation slavery. In response to an old adage, "You can take the horse to water but you can't make him drink!" to this Teddy Cubia responded, "If you work that beast unending he will get thirsty and must drink!" Thus, in the reversal of science undergone by the African from a "Happy-go-Lucky-Freeman" to a "captured and degraded piece of property" engineered through legally sanctioned chattel slavery, was born an enforcement mechanism of cruelty designed to reduce into subservience and forced into unpaid labor, an African spirit dehumanized by god-fearing Christian white men who orchestrated a regimen "To make them stand in fear!" of the white man, that is!

FREDERICK MONDERSON

BN PHOTO - MATE MASIE (Wisdom and Prudence); and AKOMA NTOSO (Understanding).

Now, having suffered through the "long night" of the first two centuries of that inhuman ordeal of captivity, the promised light of the American Declaration of Independence and the freedoms of the US Constitution were nothing but dim candles flickering in a windswept storm "unable to see the humanity in the enslaved." While the art of compromise for political appeasement elevated the enslaved African from the depths of the "animal kingdom" to "three-fifths" of a man; the demands of cotton fueling economic progress, unconscionable "southern gentlemen" were confronted with the contradiction of freedom's aspirations to slavery's hopelessness. So repression in *de jure* and *de facto* garb, having enlisted the nation's slickest legal minds who crafted Black Codes that empowered an enforcement mechanism of slave catching along the nation's by-ways. Such actions work well in conjunction with the overseer mentality on the plantation sanctioned by the planter and his son's desires and appetites.

As the slave world turned, protection of the African spirit, his family and his future were a far cry from the ears of government responsibility. Thus, the Willie Smiths and terror groups with the

BLACK NATIONALISM STILL ALIVE AND WELL

same objective in mind evolved a disregard for Black lives patterned on the slave catchers' strategies and tactics and much of this undergirded emerging law enforcement practices. In the mix of a lynching mentality, disregard for the humanity of Blacks, envy toward his humaneness despite his trials and tribulations and when you flavor all this in a law to Jim Crowism, add a little "separate but equal," push racist white supremacy ideology, create lack of jobs, poor housing and inadequate education, their lack of protection opens doors to inequality before the law that translate into injustice towards the fly in buttermilk.

Interestingly enough, though liberal elements may protest mildly, the "old money" and their progeny sanction the protection apparatus for fear of Black uprising in the form of Denmark Vesey and Nat Turner even moderns Malcolm X and Martin Luther King that would threaten a social order in itself tottering under a yoke of inequality on the verge of vigorous social challenge. In a nation that has fought many wars at home and abroad and knowing the consequences of such destruction has nevertheless empowered domestic law enforcement with the most devastating armaments ostensibly to keep the peace, a la Ferguson. Yet, the citizenry, not being fully apprised of this machinery is left to feel the brunt of its culpability.

Again, when an event such as Ferguson unfolded and local government deployed this war machine to face down its citizenry, observers are forced to ask who really is the enemy!

Recall the TV glimpse of Koreans firing their weapons from roof tops into rioting looters after the Rodney King verdict. In Baltimore, after the now infamous night of looting and burning, the next day another glimpse after the governor had declared a state of emergency, a line of military Humvees backed by several thousand national guardsmen and other law enforcement personnel now took center stage to maintain law and order. The opposite, in a more human realization after Katrina, when General Honore was sent in,

FREDERICK MONDERSON

he instructed his men, "Turn down those weapons, this is America not Iraq!"

BN PHOTO - DWENNIMMEN (Humility and Strength); and DENKYEM (Adaptability).

In decoding the American social environment, a latent disregard for Black lives has led to many deaths; Jesse Jackson gave a number of 100, at the hands of law enforcement, White and Black police officers. The "party line" justification for such killings or deaths is that the "officers were in fear of their lives" from "Negroes with Guns" even though these young men, were, for the most part, unarmed. This behavior, scrutinized through the benefits of technology that is, the video, the camera, the cell phone has moved the people to a new sense of conscious realization and activism because contrary to denial and false justification of wrongful police action, there is a "third eye" looking.

One such recording made known the Rodney King beating; Eric Garner homicide; execution of Tamir Rice; shooting of Michael Brown; and who knows what happened to Freddie Gray! Unfortunately George Zimmerman got a pass in killing Trayvon Martin but we later see his deeper pathological maladies in run in

BLACK NATIONALISM STILL ALIVE AND WELL

with the law. Let us not go into Eleanor Bumpers, Dorismond, Amadou Diallo, but Jesse Jackson's reminder is that there were at least 100 such incidents of fatalities.

BN PHOTO - FUNTUNFUNEEU (Unity in Diversity); and AKOMA (Endurance).

As familiar as a "Ladies man" Michael Hooper of **Roots Revisited** is at it again.

FREDERICK MONDERSON

12. "LYNCHING AS RACIAL TERROR"
By
Dr. Fred Monderson

For decades scholars have taught and activists labeled 19th century Southern white behavior towards African-Americans as terrorism. Equally, in a serious but humorous manner a popular "T-Shirt" depicts images of Native-Americans as "Fighting Terrorism since 1492." However, as "radical Islam" began attacking American personnel and interests, the issue of terrorism, brought home this reality and it has now become a household word. More important, an article published in *The New York Times* and dated Tuesday, February 10, 2015, p. A-11 and written by Campbell Robertson is entitled "History of Lynchings In the South Documents Nearly 4000 Deaths." Essentially the article focuses upon the work of an organization entitled **Equal Justice Initiative** under the praise-worthy leadership of civil rights attorney Mr. Bryan Stevenson and his group who chronicled and identified some "3,959 victims of racial terror lynchings in 12 southern states from 1877 to 1950." Equally significant, the year 1877 is very important in American history for many characterize it as a "betrayal" in which Rutherford B. Hayes, a Southerner, was spuriously placed into the Presidency to succeed Ulysses S. Grant. This artificial installation of the new President removed the protections of federal troops from the South, ended Reconstruction and opened the doors of ascendency to a more vigorous "white supremacy" that began to unleash unspeakable horrors against the freed, African-American, peoples.

Campbell Robertson's article notes that while the states of Texas through Louisiana, Mississippi, Alabama, Florida, Georgia, South Carolina, North Carolina, Tennessee, Arkansas, Kentucky, and Virginia were numbered, Arkansas, Louisiana and Mississippi, often called "The Deep South," had the most such killings. In Phillips County, Arkansas, for example, 237 people were lynched in 1919 during the Elaine race riot alone for a total of 243 listed deaths for that year. Next in position came Louisiana with Caddo Parish (54),

BLACK NATIONALISM
STILL ALIVE AND WELL

Lafourche Parish (50), Tensas Parish (4) and Ouachita Parish (35). In "73 Years of Lynchings" the article continues, "The most recent data on lynching, compiled by the **Equal Justice Initiative** shows premeditated murders carried out by at least 3 people from 1870-1950. The killers claimed to be enforcing some form of social justice. The alleged offenses that prompted the lynchings included political activism and testifying in court." These are fundamental rights guaranteed by the Constitution and required for good citizenship; yet such were systematically and forcefully denied African American citizens. However, what Mr. Stevenson intends to do in his project is to erect markers on every possible lynching site to identify the place where each gory crime was committed. Naturally, pulling back the covers of this vicious part of this nation's history and exposing the involvement of families, farms and personnel in these racial tragedies do not sit well with current white property owners, politicians and ideologues who may subscribe to "white supremacy" views and the implications they present.

BN PHOTO - NSIBIDI SYMBOL (Love and Unity).

FREDERICK MONDERSON

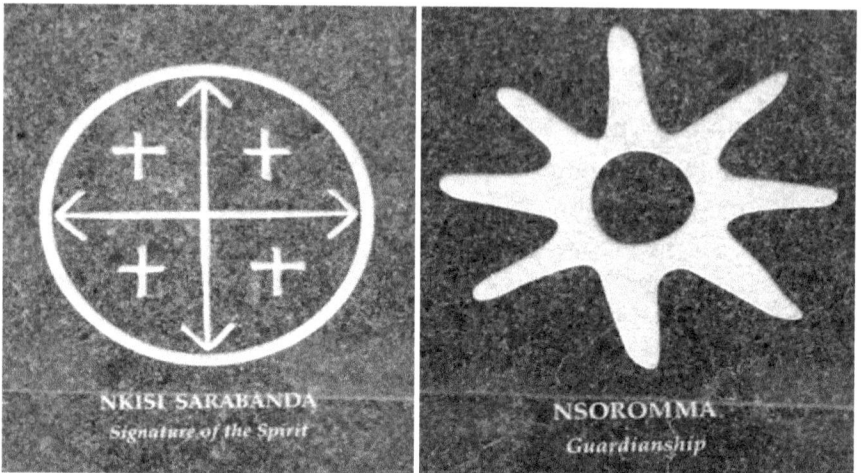

BN PHOTO - Nkisi Sarabanda and Nsoromma (Signature of the Spirit and Guardianship) are spiritual protective forces that serve the Community.

A good example of this "denial" is reminiscent in the 2012 Republican campaign to deny Barack Obama a second term as President. It came out Governor Rick Perry of Texas is the owner of a piece of land named "Nigger Head Mountain." He claimed some time previously his father had "painted over the sign" that was prominently displayed. Naturally, then, concerned citizens had wondered whether on that site, a famous memorial had been erected to an equally famous Black man who had benefitted that community or whether that was a killing site where many a "Nigger Heads" rolled! Now, persons can see the inherent implication of marking such sites for the embarrassment this silent yet deadly legacy presents.

The history books have taught that American heritage is traceable mainly to British colonists who settled the land. In their brightest moments Presidents such as Ronald Reagan and Jimmy Carter traced their family heritage to illustrious individuals and proudly boasted of this connected badge of honor. One wonders how many will willingly allow such markers on their property and be publicly associated with those murderous packs Ms. Constance Baker-Motley and others experienced and wrote about from the time of the "1877

BLACK NATIONALISM
STILL ALIVE AND WELL

betrayal," when federal troops, removed from the South, enabled and resulted in formation of the Ku Klux Klan, White Citizens Council, Knights of the White Camelia, Jim Crow legislation and practices particularly aided by the Dred Scott historic Supreme Court decision of 1857, in which Chief Justice Roger Taney ruled that "A Black man has no rights a White man is bound to respect." During Jim Crow times, such practices weighed heavily to influence the 1896 *Plessey V. Ferguson* ruling that in fact formally established *de jure* and *de facto* segregation as "Separate but Equal" which was actually "Separate and Unequal." That ruling was finally struck down in *Brown v. Board of Education of Topeka, Kansas* in 1954.

In this "hell on earth," lynching was not the only tool in the repertoire of the racist who perpetrated these heinous crimes against African-American citizens finally granted America's momentous protections under the 13th, 14th, and 15th Amendments enshrined in the United States Constitution. That is, after two centuries of horrendous chattel slavery, that fundamental and hard won right to vote was denied through orchestrated chicanery, intimidation, threats, tar and feathering, killings and economic peonage perpetuated through "share cropping" and crop lien as part of agricultural tyranny. But, most brutal was lynching which became a spectator sport entertaining whole families such as the image depicted in the *Black Book* showing "a Black man on as bed of coal-fire being roasted." This was an extremely agonizing death much more different than the "Roasting" Whoopi Goldberg's boyfriend gave her on television. This was indeed a horrifying experience to see and smell a human being burnt to the delight of pictured White men, young children and old people, gleefully enjoying the ghastly spectacle. This is the history partially hidden that needs to be told and the markers can begin to help!

Importantly, seldom is an article in *The New York Times*, "the paper of record," followed by a lead Editorial the next day, but this story was so compelling that it did under the title "Lynching as Racial Terrorism." For sure, many persons of all political and social

FREDERICK MONDERSON

persuasions across the country have criticized *The New York Times* for being a vehicle of liberal bias. However, even though persons have a problem with such quality reporting, *The Times* serves as an agent of the social conscience of this nation, raising significant and deep-rooted human concerns while the greater political leaders and ethical champions turn a blind eye and deaf ear to the plight of these and other victims of social, economic and even political injustice, constantly crying out for relief.

The lead paragraph of *The Times* Editorial stated, "It is important to remember that the hangings, burnings and dismemberments of black American men, women and children that were relatively common in this country between the Civil War and World War II were often public events. They were sometimes advertised in newspapers and drew hundreds and even thousands of white spectators, including elected officials and leading citizens who were so swept up in the carnivals of death that they posed with their children for keepsake photographs within arm's length of mutilated black corpses." Even further, the article states, "These episodes of horrific, communitywide violence have been erased from civic memory in lynching-belt states like Louisiana, Georgia, Alabama, Florida and Mississippi. But that will change if Bryan Stevenson, a civil right attorney, succeeds in his mission to build markers and memorials at lynching sites throughout the country to confront an era of racial terror directly and recognize the role that it played in shaping the current racial landscape."

Seldom, if any whites at all were held accountable for such unspeakably horrific behaviors. President Nelson Mandela after 27 years of unjust incarceration empowered a "Truth and Reconciliation Committee" to record, chronicle and forgive the ghastly behaviors of some 85 years of Apartheid South Africa. Yet, it is unthinkable for such a panel to be empanelled in this country in order to officially look into and record, then to seek the forgiveness of the victimized and their descendants. Perhaps it is because the victimizers past and present time memories are too horrendous to forget and remains so to this day.

BLACK NATIONALISM STILL ALIVE AND WELL

BN PHOTO - The "Door of No Return" as seen from within and the map of Africa.

As Mr. Stevenson argued, "Lynching declined as a mechanism of social control as the southern states shifted to a capital punishment strategy, in which blacks began more frequently to be executed after expedited trials. The legacy of lynching was apparent in that public

FREDERICK MONDERSON

executions were still used to mollify mobs in the 1930s even after such executions were legally banned." Recognizing the powerful role lynching played in shaping Southern society, the report continued, "Most Southern terror lynching victims were killed on sites that remain unmarked and unrecognized." Nevertheless, in contradictory and wicked irony, the Southern landscape is cluttered with plaques, statues and monuments that record, celebrate and lionize generations of American defenders of white supremacy, including public officials and private citizens who perpetuated violent crimes against black citizens during the era of racial terror."

That is to say, the heroes of the "Rebel South" are known and their memories perpetuated while the memories of associated terroristic horrors must not be. Or, put another way, we know of them in "Glory" but we should not know of them in "Savagery!"

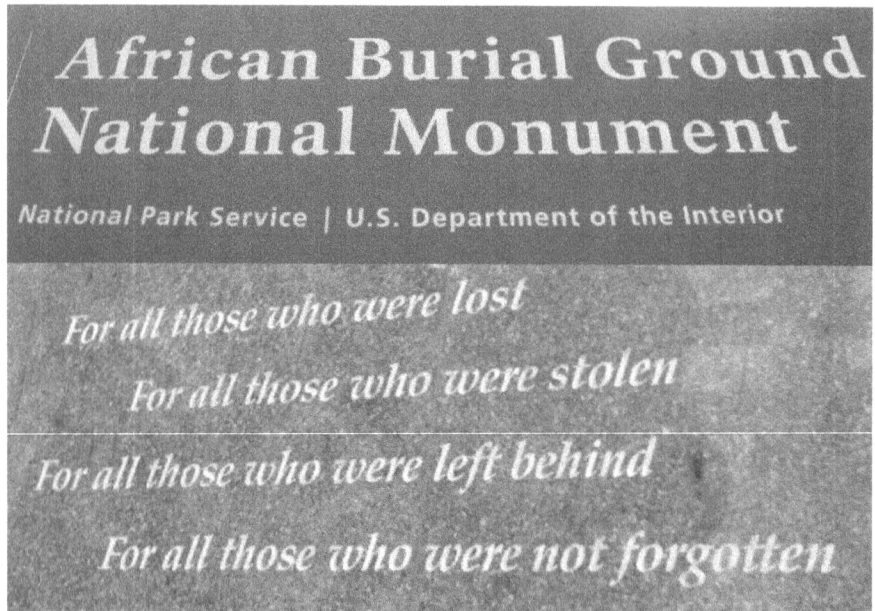

BN PHOTO - Marble expressing one of the purposes behind the memorial paying tribute to the African American ancestors buried beneath downtown New York City.

BLACK NATIONALISM STILL ALIVE AND WELL

"For all those who were lost
For all those who were stolen
For all those who were left behind
For all those who were not forgotten."

BN PHOTO - *Daily Challenge* Weekend Edition, August 14-16, 1998, pp. 12-13.

FREDERICK MONDERSON

The Ghana Dance Company enacts a play depicting how the ancestors were kidnapped into slavery.

Thousands of Ghanaians and African Americans came together recently in Accra to reminisce the dehumanizing system of chattel slavery during the pre-colonial and colonial era as they welcomed the remains of runaway slave Samuel Carson and Crystal, a Jamaican slave prior to burial of the remains in Assin Manso. The burial, which was depicted in the Wednesday Daily Challenge centerfold, was preceded by a series of rituals and festivities, including a dramatic and emotion-filled slave walk portrayed by the Ghana Actors Guild.

On Monday at 5 p.m. film footage of the historic event will be shown during a birthday tribute to late nationalist leader Marcus Mosiah Garvey at the Billie Holiday Theater, located at 1360 Fulton Street at the Bed-Stuy Restoration Center in Brooklyn. Speakers will include Sonny Abubadika Carson, great-great nephew of the runaway slave; Professors Leonard Jeffries, James Smalls and Brooklyn educator, Michael Hooper.

(Photos: SYLVESTER CRAWFORD)

BN PHOTO - *Daily Challenge* Weekend Edition, August 14-16, 1998, pp. 12-13.

(L-R) Dhoruba Bin Wahad, director of the Institute for the Development of Pan-African Policy, Carson and Minister of Cultural Affairs Nana Akwuaku Sarpong.

Visitors in the dungeon of the Slave Castle at Elmina file past an altar in honor of the millions of ancestors who were victims of the most inhumane system of slavery in the history of mankind.

BN PHOTO - *Daily Challenge* Weekend Edition, August 14-16, 1998, pp. 12-13.

BLACK NATIONALISM STILL ALIVE AND WELL

Members of Marie Brooks Dance Troupe of Brooklyn, Jeremiah Gaffney (foreground), owner of Gaffney's Funeral Home in Queens and Carson.

Performer Rita Marley

(From left) New York Professors James Smalls and Leonard Jeffries and Ghanian Ambassador to Benin Akuoko Sarpong.

Elmira Slave Castle

BN PHOTO - *Daily Challenge* Weekend Edition, August 14-16, 1998, pp. 12-13.

FREDERICK MONDERSON

Special Sankofa Section

The Final Journey

Procession of Chiefs lead off Emancipation ceremony.

Part of tumultuous welcoming committee greets an

Boats display flags of colonial powers and ports to which Africans were taken at height of slave trade.

BN PHOTO - *Afro Times* Saturday, August 22, 1998, pp. 12-13.

Africans from the Americas and Motherland carry the bones of an elder.

Honor guard escorts bones to final destination.

BN PHOTO - *Afro Times* Saturday, August 22, 1998, pp. 12-13.

BLACK NATIONALISM STILL ALIVE AND WELL

Ghana's Ambassador to Benin makes a point, as (left to right) Professor James Smalls, Sonny Carson, Jeremiah Gaffey and Rev. Warren Shivers listens. Ilyasha Shivers is seen in the background.

Mike Gizo, Ghanaian Minister of Tourism, speaks during a ceremony supported by Prof. Leonard Jeffries, Minnie Simpson, owner of Minnie's Vergetarian and Seafood Restaurant and Lounge (Ocho Rios, Jamaica) and Professor James Smalls.

Thousands of Ghanaians turned to welcome home the remains of two slaves who made their final journey home as the highlight of this year's Emancipation Week celebration. Samuel Carson, a runaway slave who ran away from a South Carolina plantation and became a U.S. Navy veteran, and Crystal, a Jamaican slave, were both re-interred at Assin Manso, Ghana last week.

Photo: Sylvester Crawford

Sonny Carson, right, listens intently to Chief Linguist. Chief of Chiefs speaks during ceremony.

BN PHOTO - *Afro Times* Saturday, August 22, 1998, pp. 12-13.

Gloria Stokes holds a wreath at service accompanied by Sonny Carson and Reverend Chivers.

It was cleansing process that in the end was difficult to not be emotional during the funeral service.

BN PHOTO - *Afro Times* Saturday, August 22, 1998, pp. 12-13.

FREDERICK MONDERSON

BN PHOTO - Young people, who came to the 50th Anniversary of the "March on Washington," are 'Wading in the Water' of the "Reflecting Pool."

BLACK NATIONALISM STILL ALIVE AND WELL

BN PHOTO - Red, Black and Green, the African Nationalist Flag, given by Marcus Garvey in 1920 and still going strong and symbolic.

13. MARCH ON WASHINGTON
By
Dr. Fred Monderson

Joining the Reverend at the rally and in an Academy Award presentation, legal eagle Attorney Benjamin Crump eloquently made the case of "Why we are going to March on Washington!" Mr. Crump first of all thanked and congratulated Rev. Al Sharpton for "always answering the bell, whether the camera is there or not, he is there when it is not popular." Praising his fellow lawyers Jonathan Moore and Michael Hardy for their stalwart role in quest of justice, he praised "Young people who stood up!" and indicated the National Bar Association, the largest African-American organization of lawyers, stands behind Rev. Sharpton and this movement. Then he recognized "Eric Garner inspired and galvanized young people who crafted their own slogans," which the marchers chanted: "Hands Up, Don't Shoot" and "I Can't breathe;" "Black Lives Matter," "I am Michael Brown" and "Justice for Michael Brown!"

FREDERICK MONDERSON

BN PHOTO - Two sisters as Egyptian Goddesses bears their two ankhs.

BN PHOTO - Nkisi Sarabanda and Nsoromma (Signature of the Spirit and Guardianship) are spiritual protective forces that serve the Community.

BLACK NATIONALISM STILL ALIVE AND WELL

BN PHOTO - Another of the "Black Icons," Red Foxx is pictured on this Brother's chest at the International African Arts Festival.

BN PHOTO - Mural depicts Malcolm X and Harriet Tubman on a wall at Boys and Girls High School in Bedford-Stuyvesant, Brooklyn. Interesting that this image is also at the intersection where Malcolm X Boulevard and Harriet Tubman Avenue intersect.

FREDERICK MONDERSON

Next Mr. Crump explained his "Theory of the case!" because "the system needs to be indicted!" He insisted, "The system is what breaks our hearts." He decried the "closeness in time" of the killings of Eric Garner, Michael Brown, and Tamir Rice and pointed to the symbolism and seemingly inherent conflict of interest, "Even Stevie Wonder could see," when a local Prosecutor must investigate a local police officer. Calling Ferguson "a fraud" he advised, "We must be specific. It's about chess not checkers!"

BN PHOTO - A colorfully attired Lady came out to pay her respects to the Great One, Dr. Yosef A.A. Ben-Jochannan.

He then proposed a precedence by which he questioned Ferguson! That is, for 30 years the Prosecutor has been presenting cases to the Grand Jury. All of a sudden he changed his strategy!

BLACK NATIONALISM STILL ALIVE AND WELL

Mr. Crump insisted the audience see what he termed "attempts to demonize young Black men" because as he pointed out, "Police officers are hired to protect and serve the community," but what you get is "Police protection for police and Police enforcement for Black victims." Searching for precedence he stated, "In 1982 the Supreme Court ruled, 'not to allow a suspect to testify!'" So for 30 years the Ferguson District Attorney presented to the Grand Jury but did not allow any suspects to testify. "All of a sudden he wants to be fair," and in presenting to the Grand Jury, allows the suspect, Darren Wilson, to testify. He therefore asked, "Had he not been fair for 30 years?" His view of "police demonizing young Black men" is seen, first, where Officer Wilson compared his encounter with Michael Brown as "Hulk Hogan to a 5-year old." Then he pointed out how they use the terms "Supporters for Officer Wilson" but "Protesters for Michael Brown and Eric Garner!" Then again, three seconds after the police arrived he shot Tamir Reid, yet he claims he told him to put down the gun three times. With Eric Garner they tried to play up he was arrested previously and that he was selling "loose cigarettes" which he was not doing at that time.

Vowing "Due Process" for Michael Brown, Eric Garner and Tamir Rice, Mr. Crump quoted former Supreme Court Justice Thurgood Marshall that "the Constitution guarantees the same equal rights to a Black, uneducated, poor, mother who gives birth in Mississippi to an affluent, educated, wealthy, white mother born anywhere in the United States. That is what being born in this country means."

Rev. Sharpton reminded all the National Action Network will provide free buses at different locations across the five boroughs but those interested must sign up for a seat. Go to National Action Network.Net or call and add your name. Buses will leave about 5:00 AM Saturday, December 13, 2014, to rendezvous at Pennsylvania Avenue and 13th Street.

FREDERICK MONDERSON

BN PHOTO - W.E.B. DuBois and Frederick Douglass, great intellectuals and activists, and orators, abolitionist and publisher.

14. SHARPTON, TODAY
By
Dr. Fred Monderson

Returning to New York the weekend of August 17, 2014, "A Headline" report indicated "Sharpton Slams Christie" for dancing while Ferguson burns! Sharpton, himself just returning from Ferguson posed the question "Why have men of substance, seeking to become President not spoken out on Ferguson." However, as everyone has seen Rev. Sharpton vilified on TV, in Tabloid articles and "Letters to the Editor," one has to wonder what motivated Sharpton's role in the Tawana Brawley Affair, as part of a lifetime of social activism. The shortsighted and prejudiced view is just that, he was opportunistic but it undervalues the true measure of the man!

BLACK NATIONALISM STILL ALIVE AND WELL

BN PHOTO - Part of the Audience at Abyssinia Baptist Church bidding farewell to Dr. Yosef A.A. Ben-Jochannan, the "Great Teacher."

Luis and Rev. Al Sharpton at NAN's 25th Anniversary, April 16, 2016.

FREDERICK MONDERSON

BN PHOTO - Mural of Nelson Mandela (left) and Oprah Winfrey (right) in Bed-Stuy, Brooklyn.

In this situation, Al Sharpton did what any self-respecting gentleman would have done. He came upon a young Black woman who claimed she was raped by a bunch of White men, one of whom committed suicide shortly afterwards Sharpton fought but was stained by the developments generated by the behemoth of the law.

Today we recognize the word gentleman has lost its true meaning. Once upon a time, for example, the term "Southern Gentlemen" conjured up a mythical individual who even took his hat off when a lady passed. Then he returned to his slave farm and ordered the young female slave to his bed while is son was taking advantage of another. Today, when we see the vitriol directed toward President Obama by "Southern Gentlemen" as Mitch McConnell; "Waterloo" Jim DeMint; "You lie" Joe Wilson; "Stupid" Senator Grassley; this notion is indeed mythical compared to Sharpton's commitment and resilience which is real! His "Damn the Critics" attitude, full-speed-ahead activism, is not inconsistent with Presidential admonitions.

BLACK NATIONALISM STILL ALIVE AND WELL

Let's face it. Whatever the incident, when there's a call for justice, his is oftentimes the only significant voice there; even after the media leaves.

Way back in 1941, after A. Philip Randolph spoke at a White House dinner decrying the practice of excluding Blacks from government job and threatened to "March on Washington!" President Franklin D. Roosevelt listened intently to the message, passed out cigars and after a long pause insisted, "Mr. Randolph, you want change? Go out there and make me do it!" That's the American way.

The problem with the Brawley affair is that Black women have little value in this society. They are, equally, not considered beautiful. White women, on the other hand, are considered the epitome of beauty. Witness her lofty position in the images in the Jefferson Building of the Library of Congress where no Black women are shown. Let us not forget, Thomas Jefferson took advantage of Sally Hemmings, gave her kids, and yet left her a slave. Thus, the Library of Congress is a classic example of the white woman as the symbol of beauty. Still, Michelle Obama can hold her own with the best of them. Remember "Dynasty" days on TV. In one episode, the heroine poisoned the hero at the end, and in the next frame of the TV ad the same woman was shown as a symbol of beauty, pitching a hair product, as she threw her hair back.

Tawana Brawley and Sharpton were vilified for years. In that horrifying experience, the "powers that be" came and smashed the truth. In the "Central Park Jogger Case" they came in with guns blazing and ruined the lives and spirit of five young Black men. Years later these victimized youth, rushed to conviction were judged innocent of the crime and awarded a settlement, too little, too late! Donald Trump said nasty things then and also with the Settlement and the New York *Daily News* front page, in response read JUST-ASS.

FREDERICK MONDERSON

BN PHOTO - Mural in Brooklyn depicting Michael Jordan and Ray Charles.

Again, White over the Black woman dictates, glorify Bonnie with Clyde but vilify Assata Shakur and Joanne Chessamard. Not much of a stretch, but, the reason President Obama engender such racial enmity in his efforts to govern is because his father chose to "Marry not live with" his mother.

BLACK NATIONALISM STILL ALIVE AND WELL

BN PHOTO - Image of Barack Obama, President of the United States of America, in Bed Stuy.

Nevertheless, from Bensonhurst to Brawley and Amadou Diallo to Sean Bell with Garner and Michael Brown in Ferguson along the way, standing and marching to shine the light of truth is a testament to Sharpton's involvement as a civil right leader whose vision has grown tremendously over the years. As such, Sharpton is unique. It was that uniqueness Bishop Washington saw when he began cultivating the boy preacher at 7 years of age. Rev. Jesse Jackson also tapped that youngster to head the Youth Division of Operation Breadbasket of **PUSH**. That is, People United to Save Humanity.

BN PHOTO - Biggie Smalls and Jay-Z Carter, Brooklyn Musical Icons.

This show of early and consistent genius, notwithstanding, in their nefarious criticisms, many enquire, "Where is Rev. Sharpton's church?" Jesus did not have a church. However, he did castigate the hypocrites and money-changers occupying the church! Sharpton's church is in the streets! Like Jesus, he calls out perpetrators of injustice and oppression and has paid a price, not just in words but in blood when he was stabbed in Bensonhurst. Yet, he forgave his assailant. This assault was not unlike that of Dr. King who told of the young white girl who wrote saying she prayed and thanked god the knife wound was inches away from his heart. Sharpton too came

BLACK NATIONALISM
STILL ALIVE AND WELL

within inches of leaving the Civil Rights Movement without a champion of courage, vision, tenacity and resilience who stands irrespective, yet pays a price in vilification.

In the journey that shaped the civil rights icon evident today, Sharpton dared to run for the Senate, Mayor and President, all the while cultivating the greater vision to see and understand the issues from the "bird's eye view." In that Presidential bid, Sharpton, primarily a winner, proved a master of organizational institution building by establishing chapters of the National Action Network throughout the country. This is so evident at the organization's "Keeping the Dream" Convention in April of every year, now it's in its 17th year in 2015, where many boast of the voices they now have thanks to Al Sharpton's activism.

Being human, Sharpton certainly has faults but who is without sin! More important, however, his activism shines light on and keeps the issues on front burners even when the media moves on. Therefore, in lieu of any substantial individual standing up and calling attention to those important issues of Black concerns, Sharpton is the man! When he calls, many come running! In the Diallo protests, many "men of big affairs" lined up to get arrested. In the "Sean Bell shooting" incident he called and some 50,000 came to "Shop for Justice" in Mid-town, Manhattan. Partnering with Martin Luther King III, he spearheaded the 50th anniversary "March on Washington" in 2013. And he continues to speak on the "Central Park Five" issue, the "Tribute to Michael Jackson," "Prison violence at Rikers Island," the deaths of Trayvon Martin and Eric Garner at whose march he presided, and much, much more.

Therefore, in the final analysis, many are praying for God to protect and strengthen Sharpton for him to remain standing until "righteousness rolls down like a mighty stream" and "justice is meted out to all men" in equal measured proportions, irrespective.

FREDERICK MONDERSON

BN PHOTO - Covering both "back and front doors" of the White House, perhaps for a long time before we see another Black man or woman occupy this historic mansion.

15. THE WHITE HOUSE CONTRADICTION
By
Dr. Fred Monderson

I was in D.C. on Sunday, August 17, 2014 about 5:00 pm walking on 15th Street and made the turn at the Treasury Department building to enter the rear "White House Street Plaza." Alongside Lafayette Park, Capitol Police vehicles approached the corner barriers with lights

BLACK NATIONALISM
STILL ALIVE AND WELL

flashing and sirens blaring. Approaching the classic White House viewing location; I saw a Secret Service agent and his dog whiz by. Nearby in the street a Baptist preacher was wailing about "the King of Kings;" the "144,000;" "Preparing for death and heaven and hell;" "Corruption in the American system of government;" and much more could be heard and seen.

As we got closer to the fence for the customary photographs, there stood a compelling contradiction! A white male, naked except for a pair of short-shorts with tattooed writings on his chest and back, was facing the fence and White House. In apparent glee, he stood there jerking his middle finger unendingly. He did seem to have companions nearby. As onlookers gazed in disbelief the fellow continued his weird behavior. This, then, was the contradiction plain and simple! Why? But first!

The law enforcement interest was generated by the appearance and continued behavior of this individual as the Secret Service and Capitol Police observed his shameless behavior. They sent in the "dogs" to detect at least, whether he was on or had drugs in his possession. This was probably the only way to remove this citizen since in expressing his First Amendment "Rights of Free Speech," there was no explosive threat. The police could only stand helpless but vigilantly observing this vivid example of "white trash" jubilantly thrusting his middle finger skyward thereby sending an obscene message to the White House and its occupants.

FREDERICK MONDERSON

BN PHOTO - Plaque commemorating and memorializing Dr. John Henrik Clarke, "Historian of a People," January 1, 1915 - July 16, 1998.

As to why! This is a shameless desecration of the nation's most sacred space. This lower-class behavior is a continuum of the climate of disrespect engendered against President Obama and his family! Now, as to the preacher working up frenzy, this is not unusual. This is "church" in the street! The other protesters, one about nuclear proliferation had been long-standing beside the Lafayette Park with its floral decoration and Jackson and his canon on guard behind. Another gentleman sat in the street playing a recording of former President Jimmy Carter explaining the pros and cons of the Arab-Israeli conflict. Both protests, however, were peaceful and civilized, unlike the other lewd demonstration.

BLACK NATIONALISM STILL ALIVE AND WELL

BN PHOTO - CEMOTAP Co-Hosts, Sister Betty Dopson and Dr. James McIntosh in deep discussion.

Hypothetically speaking, foreign visitors, of whom there were many, observing this "freak show," were amazed that such behavior could be directed towards the White House and its occupants. However, the problem manifesting here today is not with "a roach thinking he is an eagle," or even "minions thinking they're whales." What we have witnessed in recent years is a climate of disrespect for President Obama created by government officials, senators, governors, and important people in private life and some in the press. These supposedly responsible leaders have shamelessly created a climate of hatred for President Obama and his family that we, the people, must never forget. Often we are reminded that a given officer or uniform, philosophically, represents the value of a given social institution. So, for example, when we respect the policeman, we respect both the uniform and the philosophical principle of law and order which they both symbolize.

FREDERICK MONDERSON

BN PHOTO - The "Logo" of **CEMOTAP** (Committee to Eliminate Media Offensive To African People).

Mr. Obama did not inherit his political position. He happened to be the son of an African father who married a white American female from Kansas; both of whom were of modest means and in love. Nevertheless, the hatred for Mr. Obama really stems from the hatred against his father for marrying a white female! Visit the Jefferson Building of the Library of Congress. Notice how images depict the white female as pristine, the epitome of female beauty! That this African chooses to marry, not live unmarried, to the beautiful lady meant nothing to these individuals who by their practice of hatred for others really betray their true pathological selves. Such hatred is also most malignant for persons in interracial marriage; especially if the male partner is Black.

On Mr. Obama's part, through hard work, competence, resilience, fortitude, organizational skills and tenacity, he won the Presidency of the United States. In the history of this nation and considering the millions who have lived and died on these shores, only 43 men previously accomplished this feat. Less than half did it twice and one, four times, because of prevailing circumstances during World War II.

BLACK NATIONALISM STILL ALIVE AND WELL

Most people believe that the Presidency of the United States is a hallowed institution that also makes the individual inhabiting the position and sacred space, special. This, like the Officer and the uniform, both must be respected. As such, any behavior that impugns the man sullies the institution. Therefore, the crass attitudes and behaviors of the mud-slingers at Obama; those who throw stones to break the window; speak volumes not of noble souls' magnanimous actions but men of vile temperaments and questionable character.

BN PHOTO - Images in the "Living Room" of Dr. Clarke House, home of **BEPAA** (**Board of Education for People of African Ancestry**).

In Meridian Park in Washington, DC, a statue sits as a memorial to President John Buchannan with an inscription that reads: "He walked on the mountain tops of the law." Such a tribute says much for this gentleman, certainly attesting to a noble spirit. Today evidence of elegance of mind and nobility of spirit are missing in that "City on the Hill," we know as Washington, DC.

For centuries there has been a certain kind of behavior which was called psychosexual pathology. Today its "intellectual, cultural and ethnic heritage envy," that has become pathological. This behavior involves attacking a work ethic that is creative and successfully superior which generates the venomous hatred we see directed toward Mr. Obama as President heading the most powerful nation on earth. The disgusting behavior of the citizen referenced above was motivated by the behaviors of the many winners of the "Little Man" award who created that climate of contempt.

First and foremost, Mitch McConnell (R. Kentucky). One has to wonder how the people of "The Great State" of Kentucky could countenance the petty behavior. John Boehner, the Speaker of the U.S. House of Representatives who disrespected Mr. Obama; Then we have "Waterloo" Jim De Mint, formerly (R. South Carolina); Donald Trump, seeking a birth certificate and college transcript, as if he did not have such; "You Lie" Wilson (R. South Carolina) who disrespected the President when he gave the State of the Union Address. The next day, Wilson received $1 million dollars in donations. Speaking of pathology!; "Gangster Government," "God told me to run," Michele Bachmann; "a fraud" Senator Ted Cruz; "Poison the Well" Rick Santorum; "Lipstick on a pig" Sarah Palin; "Healthcare is Slavery" Benjamin Carson; and last but not least, John McCain, privy to this and more, yet his open attempts to demean Obama did not preclude him from trying to become President of the United States!

BLACK NATIONALISM STILL ALIVE AND WELL

BN PHOTO - From the Podium of **CEMOTAP** to the attentive Audience, nothing but intellectual vigor and penetrating analytic discussion of contemporary issues can be found in this reservoir of positivity.

Some have accused Senator McCain of milking his "Hero" name for nearly half a century. Yet, comparatively out of nowhere "Po Boy" Obama was elected twice mostly through masterly organizing his assets and relentlessly pursuing his objective.

FREDERICK MONDERSON

We cannot forget malicious psycho/spiritual lepers and powerful commentators like Charles Krauthammer, Michael Goodwin, and other sick minions, particularly Rush Limbaugh and Sean Hannity, all of whom possess and use malevolent vocabularies devoid of any respectful terminology when it comes to their commentary on Mr. Obama. These are classic manifestations of not simply penis, but more particularly intellectual and moral envy. Certainly constructive criticisms are always welcome from honest critics. But destructive malicious commentary and blatant denial of any of Mr. Obama's accomplishments are behaviors unworthy of responsible men in such high positions.

BN PHOTO - The "Movers and Shakers" of **Roots Revisited** at the **International African Arts Festival** in Brooklyn.

Somehow they all manifest a Ron Paul reflection piggy-backing on George W. Bush moment, for when asked, "Can you name one good thing President Obama has done?" That "liberal" paragon of virtue, Ron Paul, thought looong and haaard and honestly confessed, "I can't think of anything good Mr. Obama has done!" Jesse Jackson once insisted, "Stay out of the Bushes!" Mr. Paul did not and stole a

BLACK NATIONALISM STILL ALIVE AND WELL

phrase and mentality from George Bush though Mr. Paul turned that phrase on its head, but with the same meaning!

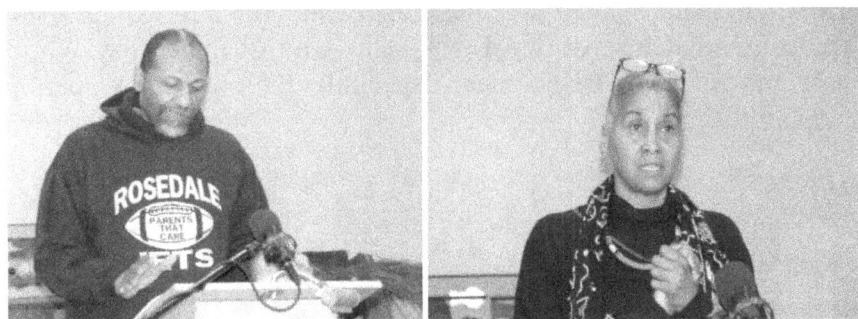

BN PHOTO - Dr. James McIntosh, Co-Chair of **CEMOTAP** introduces one of his invited speakers.

BN PHOTO - CEMOTAP Co-Chair Betty Dopson and one of her invited guests.

Now, if these re-spectable individuals could so disparage Mr. Obama, they certainly provide incentive and justification for bottom of the barrel types to vent as this fellow did in front of the White

FREDERICK MONDERSON

House. Strange that this individual felt justified in his highly disrespectful conduct. Obviously, given Mr. Obama has been subject to more threats, vilification and derision than any other President, a very dangerous climate and in which sinister behaviors including doing bodily harm to the nation's leader by some hate-filled lunatic is a real possibility. Nonetheless, the superior intellect and noble spirit which Mr. Obama embodies impels his critics to expose their deep fear and hatred of the Black man who occupies the White House and all such Black men, especially those with a superior mental attitude.

BN PHOTO - Luis stands guard (above) as Dr. Adelaide Sanford speaks her considered and enlightened piece (below).

BLACK NATIONALISM STILL ALIVE AND WELL

16. FRANKLIN AVENUE SHUTTLE: SHUTTLE INTO THE MILLENNIUM
By
Frederick Monderson

The Franklin Avenue Shuttle is a beauty to behold, a joy to ride, and a symbol of the revitalization possibilities of a community served by this historic rail link. However, in the dismal days when it languished on the termination altar of non-revitalization and its backdraft posed a serious economic and social blow to the Central Brooklyn communities of Bedford Stuyvesant and Crown Heights, a handful of activists and concerned community residents would not let it die. This was similarly tantamount to the Biblical story of the individual who would not let the angel depart until he had blest him.

Some say the fight to **Save the Franklin Avenue Shuttle** is traceable to the days of Fred Richman and Woodrow Lewis, State Assemblymen. Indicative of one person becoming a majority, if he or she vigorously advocates their truths, a small group of activists, realizing the significance of the line to its residents met perennially to strategize on efforts to make revitalization a reality. The Shuttle serves major Brooklyn institutions, including the Brooklyn Museum, Brooklyn Botanic Gardens, Prospect Park, Interfaith Hospital, and the Center for Nursing and Rehabilitation, Prospect Heights High School and Clara Barton High School, the School for the Blind, MS 320, PS 316 and nearby religious institutions, all will be affected by its closure. Students and faculty from Clara Barton and Prospect Heights High Schools played a key role in urging legislators to restore funding for the Shuttle. So too did students from Middle School 61 who wrote MTA urging the reconstruction project but also requesting the adoption of an elevator at Franklin Avenue Station on Eastern Parkway to be accessible to the handicap. The Shuttle links the A and C lines at Franklin and Fulton Streets and the D and Q lines at the Prospect Park Station and offer the only transfer between

FREDERICK MONDERSON

the lines. The shuttle now features stations that are accessible for the disabled persons, and a free walkway between the Shuttle and the 2, 3, 4, and 5 lines at the Botanic Garden Station.

BN PHOTO - Presenters at Dr. Clarke's House in Harlem, where contemporary issues of education and social developments are always the topic of discussion.

Helmut Lesold and Lois Goring, bless their souls, led the efforts at public hearings, Boro Consultation meetings, Transit Advisory Meetings, petitioning of Public officials, educating the community at Community Board Meetings and through and from the pulpit of religious, civic, social, educational and artistic associations. Then Mabel Boston, Chairperson of Community Planning Board 8's Transportation Committee came aboard. She soon realized the task ahead, picked up the mantle of leadership and baptized in the fire of activism, led the charge. Into the citadels of Metropolitan Transit Authority and Transit Authority decision-makers headed by Virgil Conway and the other big boys, the struggle was unrelenting. The banners of "Save the Franklin Avenue Shuttle," "The Community Needs the Franklin Avenue Shuttle" and the *Daily Challenge* newspaper advocacy under the pen of Journalist Fred Monderson writing for the *Daily Challenge* began to mobilize the community.

BLACK NATIONALISM STILL ALIVE AND WELL

BN PHOTO - Guests at **CEMOTAP** and Dr. Clarke's, Houses of "Intellectual Consciousness."

Former Assemblyman Joe Ferris did work on the Shuttle, Tupper Thomas has been a consistent friend of the Shuttle, so too Sophie Johnson of the Brooklyn Museum. Jennie Porter was the first Chairman of Community Board 8's Transportation Committee and Ruth Goring its Manager. Gwen Harmon of the Crown Heights Service Center, Bless Her Soul, kept people informed. Joe Rappaport of NYPIRG's Straphangers Campaign, wrote articles, attended meetings, gave Press Conferences and distributed literature on Subway platforms. Also, the New York City Environmental Justice Alliance was a part of the struggle. Connie Lesold attended meetings, held press conferences and spoke out on behalf of the Franklin Avenue Shuttle and the Franklin Avenue Shuttle Garden. This perennial social activist and garden lover along with her husband, have for decades, been stalwart fixtures advocating social, psychological, transportation and environmental well-being for

FREDERICK MONDERSON

Community Board 8 and therefore Brooklyn and New York City. Touché! Kudos!

BN PHOTO - What great company to keep, "scholar warriors" and mother and son.

BLACK NATIONALISM STILL ALIVE AND WELL

Gloria Briggs was a chief advocate for the Franklin Avenue Shuttle Garden. Bishop Owen Augustine and the Eastern Parkway Coalition were both involved in the struggle. Hatthie Carthan and Magnolia Tree, the Brooklyn NAACP, Sybil Holmes of HPD and 77 New York Avenue rode the Shuttle to school as a teen, would not cooperate with HPD on the Shuttle and its Garden. She organized friends in the struggle. Lars Larmon from Interfaith was the last of a long line of Public Relations Chiefs from 1972 to present who championed the Shuttle, and the Botanic Gardens, Prospect Park, Operation Green Thumb and the Parks Department were key institutions in the fight. When questioned on the Shuttle, Connie Lesold remarked: "People often think transportation is an issue only interesting to men but this has not been true. The Shuttle and many other transportation issues are more women's issues for they certainly get involved."

Mary Pinkett, the social conscience of government and community was at practically every meeting held. After meeting at the Lesold Residence, then the Joe Richards of the Haitian American Day Care Center's summer youths on Bedford Avenue and St. John's Place played a role and the center then became the venue. When the other elected officials were 'busy,' and some sent their representatives, Mary Pinkett was there. In the City Council, she championed the vital economic artery of her community.

Connie Hall, Chairman of Community Board 9's Transportation Committee was a regular fixture at those meetings that emboldened Mabel Boston in her struggles with the Citadel of MTA power. Chief Charles Joshua of the Central Brooklyn Coordinating Council was working, and the ubiquitous Ann Marie Blynn was there also. Despite his avalanche of responsibilities, Robert Matthews, Chairman of Community Board 8, came out too and raised the issue from his pulpit. Former District Manager Al Wright, now District

FREDERICK MONDERSON

Manager, Doris Alexander were in the mix advocating for the Shuttle.

BN PHOTO - Murals in Harlem depict Langston Hughes and Rosa Parks, icons of music and social activism.

BN PHOTO - "Black Alumni," 2001 Group, SIU-C Chapter, Say no more!

As the Community Planning Board 8's steam-roller with its allies in a number of change agencies became mobilized and began to batter the board room of MTA, those 'big boys' responded by saying 'Let's study the issue.' In 1994, they sponsored a Public Hearing at Clara Barton High School in Brooklyn. Boro President Howard Golden sent his representative Jeanette Gadsen, Deputy Boro President. That mountain of a community resident, Jitu Weusi was there. Alice Wengrow and Helmut Lesold, advocates for wheel-chair accessibility in the transit system were there. From the comfort of his wheel-chair, Mr. Lesold addressed the dais of MTA decision-makers. Having traveled the long road of Franklin Avenue Shuttle advocacy he beamed with a smile reminiscent of Jesse Jackson,

BLACK NATIONALISM STILL ALIVE AND WELL

Joseph Lowery, et al, present when George Wallace signed that historic bill moving Alabama forward in the Civil Rights struggle.

BN PHOTO - Sister Santina Peyton and family at the International African Arts Festival.

FREDERICK MONDERSON

BN PHOTO - Sister Carmen Monderson, in her beautiful splendor, at the International African Arts Festival.

Helmut said, "I'm happy to be here. We have come a long way. I may not live to see it, but I am confident the Franklin Avenue Shuttle will be rebuilt. I only hope they preserve the historic station house on the platform of Park Place." For his efforts on behalf of the Franklin Avenue Shuttle and the Reconstruction of Eastern Parkway, some believe, Helmut Lesold's name should be permanent, perhaps in plaque, at the Park Place stop.

Carlos Lezama of the West Indian Day Carnival Association tapped Fred Monderson of the Save the Franklin Avenue Shuttle Coalition to collect signatures to Save the Franklin Avenue Shuttle and Share the name Caribbean Parkway with Eastern Parkway. After 5 years of such an endeavor and more than 10,000 signatures, for whatever reason, Carlos Lezama suddenly stopped pushing Caribbean Parkway. He did not specify whether it was 'Save the Franklin Avenue Shuttle' or 'Caribbean Parkway Now.' The 10,000 signatures are no longer valid for with the Franklin Avenue Shuttle restored 'Caribbean Parkway Now' is no longer an issue, just as vital

BLACK NATIONALISM
STILL ALIVE AND WELL

for the economic, socio-cultural and nascent political well-being and cultural pride of the district, Brooklyn and New York.

BN PHOTO - That Harlem musical sound and the "Tree of Live Entertainment."

BN PHOTO - The "Chamber's" entrance at the African Burial Ground.

FREDERICK MONDERSON

BN PHOTO - The African Family attendees at the **Million Family March** rally in Washington, DC, in 2000.

BLACK NATIONALISM STILL ALIVE AND WELL

BN PHOTO - Marcus Garvey believed, "If you have no confidence in self ... you are twice defeated."

Nevertheless, in customary manner, the MTA promised repairs then balked. Elsewhere in other areas, particularly in the southern end of Brooklyn repairs and refurbishing of subway stations continued at a

FREDERICK MONDERSON

hectic pace. The community and its activist adherents refused to accept MTA's stone wall. The activist juggernaut, experienced in the long struggle mobilized their resources and met at Restoration Center on Fulton Street in Brooklyn. The Regiment, the Brigade, Battalion, Company, Platoon and Squad of Franklin Avenue Shuttle activism, tried and proved, on the battlefield of MTA stonewalling were in full activist regalia. Everyone was there. Community Board 3, Community Board 8's Bob Matthews, Ann Marie Blynn, Doris Alexander, Connie Lesold, Fred Monderson, and Community Board 9's Connie Hall. Joe Rappaport and several others were there.

Assemblyman Al Vann stood up and drew a line in the said. As State Assembly Chairman of Corporations in charge of their budgets he stated flatly: "No Franklin Avenue Shuttle, no Budget." Francis Byrd of Parkway Independent Democrats gave credit to "the leadership of Al Vann, Catherine Noland and Speaker Sheldon Silver for they are the reason our efforts paid off." Gene Russianoff of the NYPIRG Straphangers Campaign pointed out State Assembly Speaker Silver threatened to cut the MTAs 2000-2001 capital budget and remarked: "One lesson of the Franklin Avenue Shuttle is that the Assembly can be a powerful friend because it played a giant role in winning this battle." Mary Pinckett the perennial social activist conscience on the City Council stood beside him. "Tell the monarch of City Hall to let our people have the Franklin Avenue Shuttle." Annette Robinson, Roger Green, Frank Boyland and Velmanette Montgomery championed the cause. Underscoring the power of the vote, Marty Markowitz admonished our people must register and vote. Howard Golden's people were there, so too was Jeanette Gadsen.

In Jubilation the community was rejuvenated. There was a tremendous sense of inevitability this time. This was the final battle! Activists burned their boats. Victory was in sight. Faced with the potential of this experienced battering-ram at its doors, Virgil and his boys acquiesced. 'We were with you all the time' they shouted. 'Work will begin soon.' In typical corporate bureaucratic strategy 'they championed the cause in their public relations spin.'

BLACK NATIONALISM STILL ALIVE AND WELL

BN PHOTO - The quintessential nationalist, iconic, "gone but never forgotten," Malcolm X will always remain close to the hearts of African people.

FREDERICK MONDERSON

Finally, after two years of restructuring, reconstruction and beautification the work was completed. However, not without community and Mary Pinckett's challenging the MTA, about the closing of the Dean Street Station, and the contractor Judlau and all concerned for jobs for local residents, and important participation of local artisans in creating and designing the layout. At the Opening Ceremony and Ribbon Cutting many who had worked hard were in attendance and Mabel Boston was very pleased. She remarked: "This is an exhilarating day because we didn't just stop the MTA from cutting off our community; we won the complete restoration of the subway line for decades to come."

The inevitable local transportation problems had to be coped with. The TA supplied Shuttle Buses to Prospect Park. Arthur Brave, West Indian Restaurant on Franklin Avenue at Fulton Street suffered throughout the reconstruction. Still, he was optimistic and remarked: "I know there must be some inconvenience for the betterment of the community. We all stand to gain from this revitalization and beautification of the community." This notwithstanding, when the *Daily Challenge* contacted Jitu Weusi regarding his views on the newly completed multi-million dollar reconstruction, he stated clearly: "I was infuriated a week ago at Franklin Avenue, the elevator was broken and graffiti scrawled over the station. We will not let this station be treated like a ghetto station. I threatened to write the MTA" he said, "and hope the community is as displeased as I am." Further, he uttered: "I am not finished with the Franklin Avenue Shuttle."

BLACK NATIONALISM STILL ALIVE AND WELL

BN PHOTO - Members in the Audience at Dr. Clarke House listen intently to another of those intellectually inspiring lectures.

BN PHOTO - The message is clear, these Africans must and will always be remembered.

FREDERICK MONDERSON

17. BLACK SOLIDARITY DAY: HISTORY AND VISION
By
Dr. Fred Monderson

(This article was first published in the *Daily Challenge* Tuesday, October 28, 1997, p. 2.)

Black Solidarity Day was first organized in 1969, at the height of those years when Blacks were being killed and jailed all across this society. The U.S. government was in an especially reactionary mood towards Black and poor people, while it tried to wage its war in Viet Nam.

As a result, Black men and women across this nation chose to make a statement. They believed it was possible it was possible that the poor, whites, Blacks, Latinos, and Anti-Viet Nam war groups could make a political statement that we are the huddled victims of a system of racism that was institutionalized.

Yet, there were others who were prepared to seek reform through organizational and electoral politics. Among this group were some persons from New York who thought that it was necessary to impact on society in order to stop the killing of our Black men. At that time, also, Douglas Turner Ward's play, "Day of Absence" was being featured. It concerned a setting in a southern town where Blacks did all the menial work such as garbage collection, shoe shine and all other miserable forms of labor. When all the Blacks were forced to disappear from the town, everything stopped. The town suffered a serious hemorrhage before Whites appealed to Blacks to return.

BLACK NATIONALISM STILL ALIVE AND WELL

BN PHOTO - Dr. Martin Luther King firmly believed freedom is never given; in fact, "It must be demanded" through constructive non-violent action.

FREDERICK MONDERSON

BN PHOTO - View from within the "Well" showing the descent into the historic experience to which African-Americans were subject, all buttressed by snow.

The reappearance of the Black townsfolk was a clear signal of the interdependence of citizens in the nation. Even more far reaching, however, was the significance that if one group wanted to make a statement in protest of some social injustice, then their absence would seriously affect the functioning of the system.

In addition, this was also the decade in which Dr. King had struggled with non-violent protest in the Civil Rights movement. As a result, some nationalists began to see reason and logic in Mahatma

BLACK NATIONALISM STILL ALIVE AND WELL

Gandhi's dictum: "To make change, you must deal with the economic system, in a non-violent manner." The word that symbolized that ideal was *Hartal* (Come together).

The Black minds who spoke on behalf of our people believed that we should come together on one day for spiritual and cultural reawakening. The significance of this was tantamount to a strike. This meant that if Blacks in hotels, schools, banks and other institutions and industries were to stay home on **Black Solidarity Day** - the first Monday in November and the day before the General Elections - then a powerful statement could be made to the powers that be.

The Black family through its physical and spiritual absence would sure make its presence was felt. As a result, **Black Solidarity Day** was to be a **Holy Day**, not a holiday! Therefore, we needed to recognize that the system was arrayed against us, particularly because we are Black. As that thinking went, the Black church, NAACP, Ultra Liberals, Muslims and Catholics all needed to join us in this day of solidarity.

Why did they choose the first Monday in November? In the United States, Election Day is important to show that Democracy works and there is equal justice. The organizers of Black Solidarity Day choose to let people understand the inherent contradictions in the system. If we shut down the city, the problem would be highlighted. And following this, our people would vote their conscience and interests the next day, Election Day.

The elders who thought of this strategy included Dr. Carlos Russell, Philip White, Reggie Watts, Dr. Megan McClassen, Eugene Callender and Hosea Williams.

FREDERICK MONDERSON

BN PHOTO - Minister Clemson Brown and his Guests; and another couple who came to pay respects and tribute to Dr. Yosef A.A. ben-Jochannan at his "Going Home Ceremony."

BN PHOTO - As Brother Barclay, Luis Daniel and Brother Michael Hooper look on, people flock to the **Roots Revisited** table at the **International African Arts Festival**.

The first gathering at the Manhattan Center attracted 15,000 people with speakers including Congressman Charles Rangel and Minister Louis Farrakhan. They all decried the nation's racism, militarism, capitalism and treatment of a significant sector of the population. There were too many of us and if we all decided not to spend or buy anything, we would send a powerful message to the oppressor.

BLACK NATIONALISM STILL ALIVE AND WELL

BN PHOTO - Righteous individuals as Frederick Douglass and Malcolm X will always loom large in the minds and hearts of African people.

Our elders wanted to examine questions regarding the state of the quality of life for the majority of Black people, poor people, Latino people and a host of others who are victimized by inequality and oppression in this country. Therefore, the message should be: "Let there be solidarity in the home, city, and nation and internationally among Black people and their allies. Not one of us should die at the hands of another. We should have positive outlooks. We should stop venting necessary energy and support our communities."

Over the years, particularly in the 1970s, this method of atonement was very effective. Schools were closed, most Blacks did not shop on this day and positive activities were scheduled. Parents demanded that on our Holy Day, schools be closed. This is what the Citywide Black Solidarity Committee is asking this Black Solidarity Day, Monday November 3. They are calling for a citywide march at 12 noon. The marchers will gather at Fulton Street and Malcolm X

FREDERICK MONDERSON

Boulevard and march to the Brooklyn Bridge. They are insisting that voices be heard on such issues as police brutality, schools mis-educating our youth, economic racism, jobs, gang violence and the denial of immigrant rights.

We must stand together or be struck down individually!

The cry is "Show Your Courage." "Show your outrage." "Don't go to work." "Don't go to school." "Don't shop." When the goals of this Black Solidarity Day have been accomplished, then the next day, Election Day, November 5, we must turn out in record numbers and vote.

BN PHOTO – Enthusiastic Brother Wakilli and the Red, Black and Green on Black Solidarity Day, celebrating.

This year, there will be a Pre-Black Solidarity Day Celebration, Sunday, November 3, 2013, 2:00 PM at Fort Green Senior Citizens Center, 966 Fulton Street, Brooklyn, NY 11238. Featured will be Bro. Michael Hooper, the Honorable Inez and Charles Barron and Bro. Bob Law. There will be cultural Presentations, Martial Arts, and performances by Capoeira Angola, the Afrikan Community Drummers and Children of the International Sankofa Academy. This free event is supported by Roots Revisited, NAAKO, CEMOTAP, BEPAA, DECEMBER 12th MOVEMENT, NBUF, SANKOFA INTERNATIONAL SCHOOL, UNIA-ACL, and the African Nationalist Pioneer Movement.

BLACK NATIONALISM STILL ALIVE AND WELL

BN PHOTO - The remarkable "Marble Terrace" on the West entrance of the Capitol Building.

There will also be a 44th Commemoration of **BLACK SOLIDARITY DAY** Monday, November 4th, 2013 at the Adam Clayton Powell, Jr. Harlem State Office Building, 2nd Floor Gallery, 125th and Adam Clayton Powell Jr. Blvd, under a theme of "Fighting for Political Unity, Cultural Identity and the Movement for Reparations." Here a partial listing will include Amadi Ajamu, Gary Byrd, Bob Law, Honorable Charles and Inez Barron, George Edward Tait, Roger Wareham, John "Watusi" Branch, Jah Man, and many more.

FREDERICK MONDERSON

18. ARC OF THE MORAL UNIVERSE
By
Dr. Fred Monderson

Dr. Martin Luther King exhorted, "The arc of the moral universe is long, but it bends towards justice!"

At his 2005 Inaugural, the Republican President George W. Bush decried the prevalence of racism in the country up to that date, one hundred and fifty years after the Emancipation Proclamation and subsequently the Civil War Amendments. Through Jim Crow (1865-1890), *Plessey v. Ferguson* (1896), *Brown v. Board of Education* (1954), the *Civil Rights Acts* (1964) and the *Voting Rights Act* (1965) in response to the Civil Rights Movement activism demonstrated advances in the American social order. The 1965 Voting Rights Act empowered African Americans to gain political representation across the different states, culmination in the 2008 election of Barack Obama as the first African American President. In response, the then Mayor of Newark, New Jersey, Cory Booker characterized Mr. Obama's election victory as ushering in a new "post-racial America." Naturally, there was a difference of opinion on both sides of the issue, Black and White.

Then along came Mr. Mitch McConnell (R. Kentucky), Minority Leader in the Democratic controlled Senate of the United States Congress. First, Mr. McConnell made a publicly advertised statement, "I intend to make Barack Obama a one-term president." This statement, Mr. Morgan Freeman, the actor, on Piers Morgan's CNN program, characterized as "blatantly racist!" Mr. McConnell's next ground-breaking and outrageous statement was, after an important round of negotiations with the president, where bright-eyed and bushy tailed, a smiling Mr. McConnell gave that now infamous "thumbs up" signal to like minded cohorts watching on television who were probably in the treasonous gathering. Observers with penetrating vision saw this for what it was, a signal to his handlers;" that, "I got that Nigger in the White House!" Some five

BLACK NATIONALISM STILL ALIVE AND WELL

years later in October 6, 2013, *The New York Times* newspaper published a "big write-up" indicating in the run-up to the 2012 election, a group of influential Republicans and their backers met and strategized on how to deny Mr. Obama a second term. The article named individuals and some 20 heads of and Republican affiliated non-governmental organizations, many trained or involved in training propaganda programs designed to propagandize falsity and generate opposition to Mr. Obama's Affordable Care Act. Many characterized the gathering as a treasonous conspiracy to subvert the legally elected representative of the United States Government.

BN PHOTO - They kept coming in all sizes and shapes to celebrate 20th Anniversary of the **Million Man March**.

Because Mr. Obama is African American who had the audacity to declare for the presidency, beat back his democratic challengers and be chosen to represent his party, a number of racial cross-currents began to emerge directed at the man and his family. While Blacks accused him of not being Black enough, Whites accused him of being too Black. As a result, a whole flurry of activity mobilized to denounce Mr. Obama's quest. Republican propaganda helped spread

FREDERICK MONDERSON

false notions Mr. Obama would change the Constitution and this motivated right-wing militias to purchase and stock up on enormous armaments for the coming "race riots" which, up to this date, have yet to materialize.

BN PHOTO - Baron (Male Cemetery Guardian).

BLACK NATIONALISM STILL ALIVE AND WELL

An unregistered plumber named "Joe the Plumber" accused Mr. Obama of "promoting socialism" and this garnered him enormous but short lived fame. "I can see Russia from my front porch" "Lipstick on a pig" Sarah Palin accused Mr. Obama of "Palling around with terrorists." Questions of his patriotism, ability to effectively lead and lack of foreign policy experience proved enormous capital for the Anti-Obamites who were rolling, unfortunately, in the wrong direction. Still, Mr. Obama forged ahead with an effective organizational strategy, a tremendous work ethic and an unfailing desire to be successful while not paying much attention to nay-sayers. Along came the "Birther" movement with its queen and king Trump on their fools' errand and while this embolden anti-Obama forces, it also gave birth to the "Tea Party" formation. Through all this, Mitch McConnell's parallel quest remained in full stride. All the while, the "Party of No's" obstructionist agenda blocked practically every legislative effort by Mr. Obama designed to improve the condition and advance the cause of the American people. Meanwhile, Senator McConnell, having issued his charge set about plowing the path of opposition as part of the grand scheme we could come to learn of later.

FREDERICK MONDERSON

BN PHOTO - Well, as it says, "I was there!" for the 20th Anniversary of the **Million Man March**.

Undaunted, President Obama continued to repair the faltering auto industry; lending money to banks and to bail out Wall Street; assessing the nation's crumbling infrastructure and providing for "shovel ready" jobs. Next Mr. Obama sought to overhaul the nation's economic and financial systems through Dodd/Frank; and express concern about the environment, energy supplies and research and development of future energy related resources. Nevertheless, Republicans turned up the heat on the President. As a result, a climate of hatred and disrespect manifested against Mr. Obama. Surprisingly, as Republicans and their allies peppered Mr. Obama, unmindful that Edmund Burke wrote, "The only thing necessary for evil to triumph is for good men to do or say nothing;" among the higher echelon of Republican leadership nothing was said or done against such mis-characterization. Nothing!

Despite their failure to achieve anything but block the President's every move and falsely characterize the man and his work, they

BLACK NATIONALISM STILL ALIVE AND WELL

hood-winked the American people and the Republicans made gains in the 2010 and 2014 mid-tern elections. Despite the vituperative Republican mischief, President Obama continued his efforts to scale down the wars in Iraq and Afghanistan, contend with Somali pirates and pursuit of Osama Bin Laden and Al Qaeda affiliates. As this unfolded, Obama continued his responsibilities as Chief Executive and Commander-in-Chief. Meanwhile the Republicans convened, in a tunnel vision focus on how their new Congressional majority will hamstring Mr. Obama in the incoming Congress and for the umpteenth time Republicans tried to eviscerate and repeal the Affordable Care Act mischaracterized as "Obamacare." Fortunately for the umpteenth time they failed to repeal, twice the Supreme Court voted down challenges to the momentous health care achievement. Today, ACA "is here to stay!" Throughout it all, as Mr. Obama played it cool, in response to unfolding events, several Grand Jury decisions happened and this galvanized protests across cities, the nation and worldwide.

FREDERICK MONDERSON

BN PHOTO - Michael Hooper of **Roots Revisited** sports the Malcolm X "Shining Black Prince" T-shirt.

BLACK NATIONALISM STILL ALIVE AND WELL

BN PHOTO - Legendary photographer Lem Peterkin (left) and the renowned Dr. Jack Felder, biologist and revered Black Nationalist strutting their stuff at the International African Arts Festival 2015.

The Arc of the Moral Universe swung back when people of goodwill, young and old, across all ethnic spectrums took to the streets in city after city. The "Chickens had come home!" Republicans were caught off-guard. They said nothing and had nothing to say as the people staged numerous "Die-Ins" across the various cities and states. They protested and demonstrated and chanted "Justice for Michael Brown," "I am Michael Brown" and "Hands-Up, Don't Shoot!" In New York and as far away as California protesters chanted Eric Garner's last words, "I Can't breathe!" and demanded "Justice for Eric Garner!" as well as "Black

FREDERICK MONDERSON

Lives Matter!" Prominent Athletes in the NFL and NBA joined the fray with "Hands Raised" in a "Hands Up, Don't Shoot" gesture.

Again, Republicans, caught bent over with their pants below the knee and the people at their rear, were in a quandary. The hatred and disrespect they have sowed was now being called into question by young people who want an America with justice for all. If, as some predict, this consciousness may last into next election, then the country may be transformed in more ways than one.

BN PHOTO - It is safe to say, this Gentleman brought his son, even though he seems ready for the revolution, "Spit and Polish" and all.

BLACK NATIONALISM STILL ALIVE AND WELL

BN PHOTO - A little music to go with everything, is not a bad MMM prescription.

19. Dr. YOSEF A. A. BEN-JOCHANNAN: A TRIBUTE
By
Dr. Fred Monderson

It is with great sorrow that I announce the death of my mentor, friend and world renowned African historian, Egyptologist and humanitarian DR. YOSEF ANTONIO ALFREDO BEN-JOCHANNAN. At this time, **AFRICAN PEOPLE HAVE LOST A CHAMPION OF GREAT MAGNITUDE**, wisdom and intellectual fortitude. **LET US WISH HIM A WONDERFUL RECEPTION INTO THE PANTHEON**

FREDERICK MONDERSON

OF GREAT AFRICAN ANCESTORS who have never compromised in quest of the best for African people.

BN PHOTO - Putney Swope spoke of the message of the drums, but James Brown insisted, "Let's get the drummers on!" So they came to provide sweet music and spiritual grounding for our intellectual father, Dr. Yosef A.A. ben-Jochannan, at his "Going Home Party," an extraordinary affair.

Among his many accomplishments, Dr. Ben has placed the Black Woman on the HIGHEST PEDESTAL to be admired and respected in the hope she will continue to do what no Black man can ever do! DR. BEN HAS BEEN A LIGHT and he has shown us the LIGHT!

LET US ALSO HOPE PEOPLE, YOUNG AND OLD, WILL CONTINUE TO READ HIS BOOKS AND FOREVER DRINK FROM THE FOUNT OF HIS ENLIGHTENMENT EFFORTS as Tour Guide, archaeologist and national cultural spokesman whose 97 years on earth have been a tremendously wonderful and enlightening experience. He possessed a vision that looked far into the future. His efforts HAVE

BLACK NATIONALISM STILL ALIVE AND WELL

KNOWN NO LIMITS in quest for the very best for AFRICAN PEOPLE! Again, his books should be introduced into the schools to let young people understand the man and forces at work!

GOD BLESS DR. BEN-JOCHANNAN AND MAY HIS EFFORTS AND MEMORY CONTINUE TO BE AN INSPIRATION AND GUIDE TO US ALL!

Dr. Ben was an extraordinary man of many talents, but principally a man who held the African woman in the highest esteem. He taught us in the beginning was the African woman! Creation came out of the African woman! As the obelisk is a small pyramid on a tall base, this is the pedestal upon which Dr. ben-Jochannan placed the African woman. He honored the Black Woman who is the source of the Black Family! He taught us the Black Woman is a Goddess! He also led the light to the Nile Valley. He "took Egypt to challenge and destroy white supremacy!" It's like Marcus Garvey said, "the cubs are running free out there," and thanks to Dr. Ben, intellectual cubs are challenging the distortions, omissions and putting Africa in its proper place in world civilization history given its accomplishments in Nubia and Egypt, Nile Valley cultures, that gave so much to the world.

FREDERICK MONDERSON

BN PHOTO - Sister Camille Yarbrough seated with mourners and well wishers celebrating Dr. Yosef A. A. Ben-Jochannan's "Transition."

BN PHOTO - Greg Hardy, friend, student and compatriot was visibly shaken by the passing of his teacher and Brother Dr. Ben-Jochannan.

The Twentieth Century has been blessed with great African and African-American writers and historians. These include Dr. W.E.B. Du Bois, Dr. Carter G. Woodson, Dr. Kwame Nkrumah, Dr. Ivan Van Sertima, J.A. Rogers, Cheikh Anta Diop and Dr. Leonard

BLACK NATIONALISM STILL ALIVE AND WELL

James, Emeritus Professor of New York City Technical College of the City University of New York, among others. This enormous collection of brainpower equally extends into the Twenty-First Century. However, none of these giants singularly surpass the literary production, commitment, tirelessness, and sincere dedication of Dr. Yosef Alfredo Antonio ben-Jochannan. Outspoken visionary, iconic symbol and above and ahead of his time; controversial and not afraid to take an iconoclastic and individual if a somewhat idiosyncratic point of view; Dr. Ben was always prepared to defend his positions, irrespective. His friends and students, affectionately call this father, teacher, historian, friend and Egyptologist, "Doc Ben." In fact, back there in the early 1970s when even "Black folks" did not readily accept "Dr. Ben," has anyone ever wonder how he got his name? It was a young man named "Barney" and myself, Fred Monderson, who first started calling him not "Dr. Ben" but "Ben Jo" and the name stuck and finally when a fellow student Curtis Dunmoodie picked it up and said we must be more respectful, we began calling him "Dr. Ben" in defiance of those "feather bedders" who said "Dr. Ben has no PhD!"

FREDERICK MONDERSON

BN PHOTO - "Long in the Struggle," Brothers Michael Hooper and Tariq came to bear witness to the life and work of Dr. Yosef A.A. ben-Jochannan.

BN PHOTO - Herb Boyd (with glasses center) looks towards Dr. Ben in his coffin.

BLACK NATIONALISM STILL ALIVE AND WELL

Ever cried for Dr. Ben? This odious statement once made me cry at New York City (Community) Technical College. I hurriedly took the A Train to 125th Street to their second floor office on Lennox Avenue across from the Choc-Full-O-Nuts Coffee Shop in Harlem, before Prof. George Simmonds calmed me down, showing me Dr. Ben's Doctorate in Anthropology on the wall. That is what some of the "false prophets" still do today in academia to him and others! And so, you ask them to match their literary production with their in-clandestine vituperativeness and they cannot! Period!

Here was a serious scholar, Dr. ben-Jochannan, who spent a lifetime researching, writing, and defending the integrity and intellectual capabilities of African people worldwide. Dr. Ben pioneered in indigenous ancient African terminology. Imagine a European-American scholar discovered the bones of a fossilized African woman in Ethiopia and named her "Lucy" after an Englishman's song "Lucy with Diamonds," then playing on the radio. Dr. Ben said "No! Her name is *Denk Nesh* not Lucy!"

FREDERICK MONDERSON

BN PHOTO - The **Roots Revisited** gang mugging at the African Arts Festival.

In 1989, Doc Ben celebrated fifty years of visiting ancient Kemet, Ta-Merry (Egypt) and the Nile Valley cultures. This prolonged involvement has under-girded the basis of his researches, speeches, writings and educational tours. Equally, he began and for some time maintained archaeological digs on the Island of Elephantine and elsewhere. Alas, these have been discontinued.

BLACK NATIONALISM STILL ALIVE AND WELL

BN PHOTO - Minister Clemson brown greets Dr. Ben's son before the coffin at Abyssinia Baptist Church in Harlem.

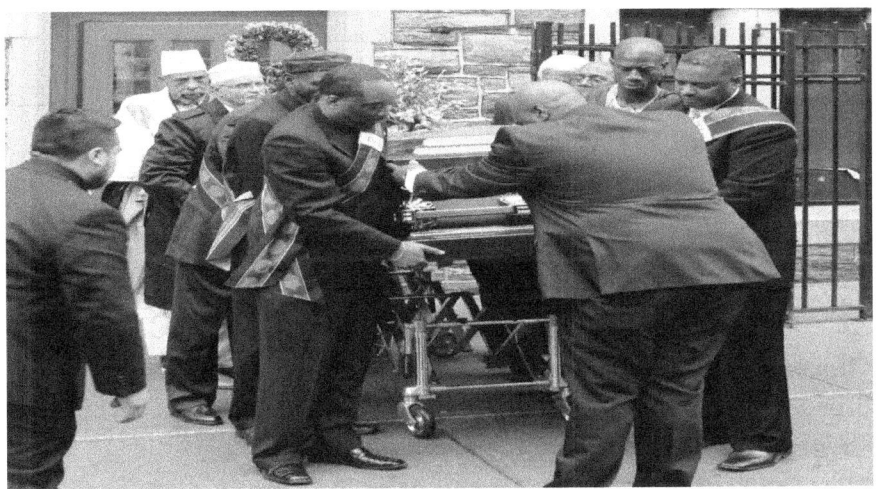

BN PHOTO - "Going Home to Rest" after a lengthy life of intellectually inspiring contributions in praise of Africa and the Black Man and Black Woman, Dr. ben-Jochannan is led out of Abyssinian Baptist Church in Harlem, USA, for his final journey to meet the ancestors.

FREDERICK MONDERSON

BN PHOTO - "Funeral Shroud," a quilt of wonderful expressions covers the coffin before its exit from Abyssinia Baptist Church and he's on his way.

This writer was happy to be a part of that epoch making tour that marked Doc Ben's Fiftieth Anniversary visiting the ancient African "holy-land" and the next year for the First Nubian Festival. More importantly, I met "Doc Ben" in early 1972. This was right after the publication of his seminal "Trilogy" works, *African Origins of the Major Western Religions* (1970), *Africa: Mother of Western Civilization* (1971), and *Black Man of the Nile* (1972), later *Black Man of the Nile and his Family*. The style of his writings, copious nature of referents employed to defend things African, and his Afrocentric pioneering approach made "Doc. Ben," a very well-respected elder, and in his later years a sought after speaking attraction, a man who "tells it like it is!"

Dr. ben-Jochannan has compiled an impressive thirty odd publications that I am intimately familiar with. He helped set the stage for a whole new approach in interpreting Africa's contributions to civilization and its legacy. He lit the fire of intellectual and cultural consciousness in Africans worldwide. The Diasporian style

BLACK NATIONALISM
STILL ALIVE AND WELL

of dress with an Afrocentric flavor is also credited to him. Establishing connections between Africans in America, the Caribbean, Africa, Asia and Europe are all attributed to Dr. ben-Jochannan, a man of vision, a seer, and intellectual giant. Many of his books challenged the distortions of Europeans in writing, publishing and disseminating knowledge about the arts, sciences, religion, etc., of the ancient people today called Egyptians and equally all along the Nile River. Dr. Ben has rightly included omissions and corrected distortions systematically implanted and perpetrated by racist Western, European and American historiography that has falsified the historical past with a prejudiced interpretation against African people. Dr. Ben dared to expose the hypocrisy of western scholarship. He attacked the foundational pillars upon which this false legacy rests. Naturally, he paid a price!

Very early he also expressed the view some scholars are confused because they were taught from a wrong premise. In his own right, and as a result of his teachings, he had no choice but to produce, publish and distribute his works without the aid of major publishing firms. He was thus a pioneer in self-publishing, launching Alkebu-Lan Publishing Company and appealing and winning the support of many upcoming nationalists as "they purchased his books in first edition form!"

Initiating a new approach to history, the end result was an exposition and critical analysis of dynamic forces of Europe and Africa in struggle to claim heritage of the ancient and modern historical record. Dr. Ben addressed professionals, laymen, clergy, students and educators. He stressed vitality, resilience and creative expressions that shaped the modern African personality and worldview. Such an approach found ready ears among a people yearning for enlightening factual information about their illustrious African past in effort to free their minds shackled by the European experience. These young and old minds were enthused by the positive nature and potency of their cultural African heritage as

FREDERICK MONDERSON

"Ben" outlined it. He also took great pains to explain that there were lusterless pages in Africa's past but these must be remembered but discarded. Nevertheless, his concern fueled their emerging aspirations. This outlook brought Dr. Ben the adulation and respect of a grateful people, he for long deserved. They understood and welcomed his contributions among the litany of great African-American literary artists.

BN PHOTO - And they marveled, "Truly he was a great man who represented African people very well."

BN PHOTO - As I watched this Gentleman's performance, I mused, "If Dr. Ben makes it across to join the ancestors, his works notwithstanding, this gentleman should get much credit for his intentions and efforts were tremendously sincere and heart-felt in pushing the esoteric and spiritual forces."

BLACK NATIONALISM STILL ALIVE AND WELL

BN PHOTO - Dr. Yosef ben-Jochannan, the master teacher brought the "Light of Egypt" and liberated many in Africa, America and the Caribbean.

Dr. Ben's writings, lectures and educational tours over the years have stressed two essential themes. The first is that the "emergence of civilization, viz., science, religion, government, architecture, agriculture, philosophy, and the arts, began in Africa." The mouth of these utterances became the conduit of today's Egypt and the Nile Valley. In his approach, Dr. Ben has shown how the structural foundations of western civilization developed from discoveries and scientific applications in this ancient African land. Lastly, he took great pains to show the writing and teaching of modern history has been distorted to elevate Europe and degrade Africa, which is clearly wrong and must be rectified. This fundamental view helped establish the need for African historical reconstruction and interpretation particularly as we navigate this new century and millennium.

BN PHOTO - Speaker about to introduce Dr. Rosalind Jeffries while her husband, Dr. Len Jeffries and Dr. Calvin Butts, Brother Hafiz among others, sit and watch.

The second of Dr. Ben's themes has been that "Africans worldwide should be proud of their ancestors' accomplishments. The arts and sciences that today govern the world are Africa's legacy. African-Americans should show great pride and dignity in their history and heritage." They must respect themselves and carry themselves with dignity and pride. Those who know can and should teach the young

BLACK NATIONALISM STILL ALIVE AND WELL

how to identify with Africa. In so doing, they must form study groups and visit Africa. Yet, they must also be aware of the machinations of cultural imperialism and cultural genocide constantly at work. Further the young must immerse themselves in an African-centric perspective and research, write and teach others in turn. They must study languages such French, German, Swahili, Greek, Latin, Coptic, Arabic and *Medu Netcher* or Hieroglyphics. They must struggle to correct the recent distorted history of Africa's past. In this way, future leaders would help to better the lot of humanity and save the world from its impending moral, spiritual and scientific destruction. To accomplish these objectives the good doctor has supplied a reservoir of information and strategies from his life's researches in the arsenal of published works he has created. Of course, these works must be read, ingested and digested and returned to time and again. This is important for as Dr. John Henrik Clarke once said, "People buy but never read Dr. Ben's books." Herein then is the dilemma!

The author's major thesis of his *African Origins of the Major "Western Religions"* is that African religious practices were denigrated and called "fetishism" and "paganism." In fact, these early thought processes he showed are the fundamental bases of Judaism, Christianity and Islam. He argued that these ideas were first developed and nurtured in Central Africa among indigenous peoples and then migrated and extended throughout the Nile Valley. They found greatest fruition in Kemet (Egypt) and were preserved by its civilization advances and the nature of its geography. The early knowledge was first written down in such selections as the "Book of Gates," "Book of Knowing Ra," "Book of Breathings," "Book of What is in the Underworld," etc. These were part of the earlier "Pyramid Texts" (Old Kingdom); then "Coffin Texts" (Middle Kingdom); and the later *Book of the Dead* or *Book of Going Forth By Day* (New Kingdom); and the "Mysteries of Sais" (Egypt). The fortunes of geography enabled Africa's second cultural daughter, Kemet, to rise to greater prominence than did the eldest,

FREDERICK MONDERSON

Ethiopia, Dr. Ben explained! He stressed and maintained to the day of his death, despite all the "new evidence," that civilization began to the south of Egypt! However, despite modern falsification of history and the insistent propagation of such falsity, his thesis is as credible as ever.

BN PHOTO - Seti I being introduced to Amon-Ra and Goddess Mut in the northern half of the Hypostyle Hall at Karnak temple, and similarely may he (Dr. Ben) have "Health, Dominion, Stability and Life" "like Ra forever!"

BN PHOTO - Dr. Len Jeffries stands at the podium among others with Dr. Butts in purple tie, as all coalesce for the Master Teacher, Dr. Yosef Ben-Jochannan on his way to "Ancestordom."

BLACK NATIONALISM STILL ALIVE AND WELL

Another of Dr. Ben's seminal works is *Africa: Mother of Western Civilization*. Its major thesis holds that the "fundamental laws, principles, philosophies, ideas, arts and crafts that educated the west, are indigenous to Africa through the Nile Valley cultural experience." For critical teachers who face this dilemma he has some advice. As such, he wrote: "The only credentials necessary in the experience of African history, otherwise mis-nomered 'the Black Experience' and 'Black Studies' are the documented proofs and the sources from whence they are taken."

For this reason, *Africa: Mother of Western Civilization* is an enormous compendium of facts, sources, illustrations, and analyses that challenge laymen and scholars alike. It suggests all educators and lay persons alike become involved in reclaiming the stolen heritage of Africa. This *magnum opus* opens new vistas for historical investigation and provides a wide array of references relating to the significance of Africa in world civilization.

Black Man of the Nile and his Family marks the third in the "trilogy of Dr. Ben's seminal works." This particular source represents the maturity of his thoughts and presentations for it focuses on the role Black men and women have played in bequeathing science, religion, arts, metaphysics, agricultural method, quarrying and stone transportation for erection at building site, boat building and Nile River navigation to the world through Africa's conduit in Egypt and Nubia. It also contains a number of objectives the author seeks to accomplish.

FREDERICK MONDERSON

BN PHOTO - "The Ark at Rest" in the Hypostyle Hall at Karnak Temple, may he (Dr. Ben) similarly have "Life, Health, Stability, Dominion!"

BLACK NATIONALISM STILL ALIVE AND WELL

BN PHOTO - Professor James Smalls, the Funeral's MC stands at the Mike to pay tribute to his friend.

The first of these objectives is, "an attempt to create in young African, African-American (Black person), and all other African people, a sense of belonging in the great African heritage." It is, writes Dr. Ben "specifically directed to those who have criminally demasculinized, denuded, and otherwise denigrated the Africans of their CULTURAL, ECONOMIC, POLITICAL, SCIENTIFIC, SPIRITUAL, and all other forms of their heritage and human decency." To this we should add the intellectual heritage as represented in Egypt; that is, through "acquisition methods," and teaching, writing and representation of the artifactual evidence.

It also presents, "AFRICAN ORIGINS OF EUROPEAN CIVILIZATION" in a manner whereby, "scholars can find interesting use for it in their research; as much as the layman can for processing information."

Dr. Ben views his role as gadfly presenting, "pertinent information needed in the African peoples' RE-IDENTIFICATION with their great ancestral heritage." Lastly, he continued, the "major desired accomplishment this volume seeks to achieve, is to provide anthropological evidence in the ancient heritage of the Africans" and their contributions all over the world.

Abu Simbel to Ghizeh: *A Guide Book and Manual* is in itself a useful piece of writing. But, there are other books.

In the acquisition of knowledge, Sir Francis Bacon (1561-1626) told us: "Some books are to be tasted, others to be swallowed, and some few to be chewed and digested." This much can be said of the trilogy of Dr. ben-Jochannan's works, *Black Man of the Nile and his Family*, *Africa*: *Mother of Western Civilization* and *The African Origins of the Major Western Religions*. The others are equally interesting! Everyone must buy and read these books and pass them on to others particularly their sons and daughters.

Finally, as a student of his, and based on observations and analytic critique, this writer would like to add a 15-point summation of how we can view Dr. Yosef Alfredo Antonio ben-Jochannan's contribution as an unselfish and fearless elucidation of the historical record systematically distorted to elevate Europe and denigrate Africa while wrecking psycho-social debasement of the African spirit and persona. Without question, whether through omission, distortion and even false presentation, the urban youth across America have most seriously been victimized in the systematic alienated educational process they have been subjected to. As such, the potent cultural lifeline Dr. Yosef Alfredo Antonio ben-Jochannan has provided is today critical in rescuing these young people adrift in the academic and intellectual cosmos of these modern times going forward. The critical prescription therefore is as follows:

BLACK NATIONALISM STILL ALIVE AND WELL

BN PHOTO - Sister recounts how Dr. Ben-Jochannan influenced her intellectual development and needed to be there for him at this important time.

1.   We must praise and show thankfulness for the man who, for more than half a century challenged the behemoth of western intellectual oppression of Africa and her offspring while enlightening many to the wonders of a creative African cultural heritage.

2.   We must commend Dr. Ben-Jochannan for the humanitarian work he did among the Nubians in Egypt and Sudan, viz., Aswan, Daboud, Wadi Halfa, Dongola Province and Fashoda.

3.   We must recognize his call to action to combat the cultural genocide in the African American studies curriculum predating the Afrocentric insistence on multi-culturalism.

4.   We should continue to emulate his style of critical analysis of contemporary developments, whether it was historical omissions in

FREDERICK MONDERSON

Alex Haley's *Roots*; misrepresentation in King Tut's exhibition that has taken place several times in America; taking to task T. Eric Peet's "The Problem with Akhenaton;" Criticism of Father Temple's *Bantu Philosophy*; challenge to another writer's description that Rameses II had "badly abscessed teeth," and so forth.

5. We can appreciate his identifying "They all look Alike, All," thus linking African peoples across the globe who were victims of racial hatred and cultural aggression.

6. His early clarification of the differences between the *Black Nationalist* and the *Black Marxist* was very timely and inspiring and still is.

7. First to outline the *History of the Bible*, he challenged the *Black Clergy Without a Black Theology* and offered *A Black Bible for Black Spiritual and Religious Consciousness*.

BN PHOTO - Part of the audience at Abyssinia Baptist Church paying tribute to Dr. Ben-Jochannan.

BLACK NATIONALISM STILL ALIVE AND WELL

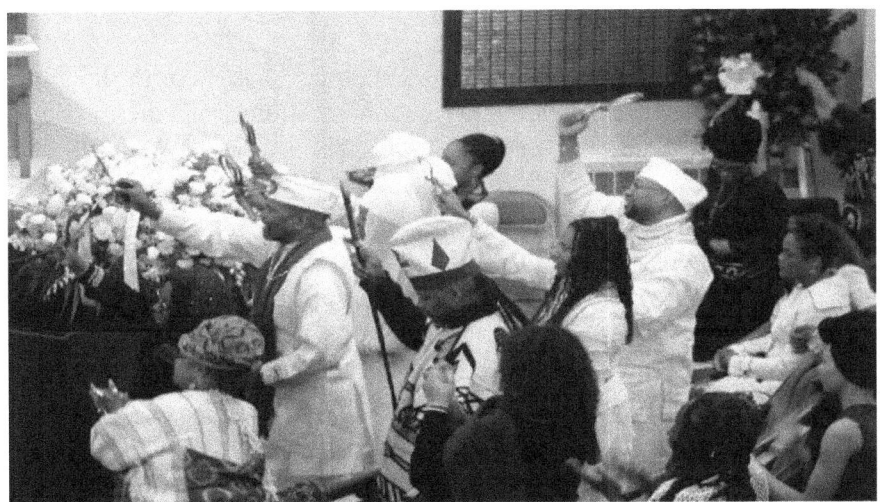

BN PHOTO - This group, often awarding Ankhs, is here making their statement in support of the Master Teacher, Dr. Yosef Alfredo Antonio ben-Jochannan.

8. We must acknowledge as a human he may have made some mistakes; miniscule, as they probably were outweighed the foundational reservoir of ethical, intellectual and cultural Ma'at or fairness he implanted in the consciousness of African people worldwide.

9. His insistence that all African Americans visit the Nile Valley to imbibe in the cultural heritage and grow from the intellectual exposure, but more particularly their dress code and mannerism among the people must not be construed as the "arrogance of Ugly Americans," was and is still timely and insightful.

10. His outspoken nature, love for Marcus Garvey and his *Philosophy and Opinions*, praise of Black women as Goddesses, critique of Academics who are "fifth columns," made him anathema to people with ill-intentions, black and white, in their views toward African people.

FREDERICK MONDERSON

11. Dr. ben-Jochannan had little respect for people in high positions who never promoted the aspirations of their Black subordinates. He pointed to many in academic, business enterprise and even the military.

12. A staunch Pan-Africanist, he aspired to see accomplished sustained and measurable economic, political and educational empowerment for people of African heritage worldwide.

13. He said, "I took Egypt to show our people the proper way" and to challenge its misrepresentation, racism and projected religious bigotry.

14. He insisted we not just read books and do research on Ancient Egypt in Africa, but also form study groups that debate and discuss these important issues raised by him as well as personally critique status quo's positions and most important, Academics "publish or perish."

15. He asked us to standardize our learning and take responsibility for our own history. He stated: "Until African (Black) people are willing, and do write their own experience, past, and present, we will continue being slaves, mentally, physically, and spiritually to Caucasian and Semitic racism and religious bigotry." This latter we must never allow to happen, for as Dr. John Henrik Clarke has admonished, "African people must write their own history." That is because the "People who preached racism colonized history" and as a result, "When Europe colonized the world, it colonized the world's history."

BLACK NATIONALISM STILL ALIVE AND WELL

BN PHOTO - Brother Hafiz, in full effect, praises the Great Master Teacher, Dr. ben-Jochannan.

BN PHOTO - Leader of the group, "Do you think it is easy to walk around dressed like this," praises Dr. Ben-Jochannan, one of the recipients of the Ankh his group awards annually.

FREDERICK MONDERSON

Therefore, we must recognize that Dr. Yosef Alfredo Antonio ben-Jochannan has made a major contribution to African intellectual growth and consciousness. He created a cosmological vision over time that allowed us to see the light! His work has been seminal! In fact, he was our light! He taught us how to persevere to persevere! He asked that we establish and maintain a standard for our behavior, and don't fear, don't fear defeat, don't fear death!

BN PHOTO - "To be immortal, to be remembered, you must write your name and works in the hearts and minds of the people." And so they came to validate this reality as Dr. Ben-Jochannan preached and lived.

BLACK NATIONALISM STILL ALIVE AND WELL

BN PHOTO - Taken to his place of final repose, spiritually and psychologically in his "Beloved Egypt," Dr. Yosef A.A. ben-Jochannan will begin his new life among the blessed ancestors with whom he worked for so long in defense of Africa.

BN PHOTO - Psychostasia or "The Judgment" where Dr. Yosef A.A. ben-Jochannan will be declared "True of Voice," since for decades he spoke to and about truth and power in defense of the Black Man and Woman and in this Professor James Smalls did a wonderful reenactment of the "Opening of the Mouth Ceremony" to empower dr. Ben in the eternal existence.

FREDERICK MONDERSON

BN PHOTO - May the "Tree Goddess" empty "four pitchers" of cool and refreshing waters on Dr. Yosef A.A. ben-Jochannan as he makes his way along the path to Judgment and to become an "Osiris," he so richly deserves after his "Purification."

BN PHOTO - Reverend Dr. Calvin Butts, Pastor Abyssinia Baptist Church, leading the **Service Celebrating the Life of Dr. Yosef A.A. Ben-Jochannan**.

BLACK NATIONALISM STILL ALIVE AND WELL

BN PHOTO - Dr. Greg Carr, Chairman, Howard University African Studies Department, came to pay his respects to the Master Teacher.

BN PHOTO - As I told Prof. Smalls on the phone, "Since I could not be there at this moment as 'Dr. Ben Made his Transition,' I would have no one else perform the requisite functions," as he did while wearing his "Lion-skin" as the High Priest who "Opened the Mouth of the Master Teacher."

FREDERICK MONDERSON

20. ELOMBE BRATH: ULTIMATE NATIONALIST SOLDIER

By
Dr. Fred Monderson

Accomplished "Elombe;" numbered among "one-name-revolutionary-giants" Che, Fidel, Malcolm, Sonny, Jitu, Stokely; we mourn your passing at a time your keen consciousness is sorely needed to fend the ever-present oppressor's machinations, openly and inclandestine.

Immortal Black, proponent of a universal Pan-Africanist philosophic outlook manifested through the **PATRICE LUMUMBA COALITION**; your contributions inspired profound ideals in defense of Africa's sons and daughters' humanity and progress towards empowerment and freedom of mind, body and spirit.

Little African man wielding a powerful pen, professing big creative ideas, consciously and perennially nationalistic, when you spoke people listened, for the wisdom you enunciated earned you unmatched tribute from a grateful people who consistently recognized exemplary leadership in your efforts, decade after decade.

Indomitable Elombe, a name that will live in immortal glory, tasked to replenish the magnificent ancestor Brigade, how fortunate you were to be contemporary with Patrice Lumumba, Kwame Nkrumah, Sekou Toure, Nelson and Winnie Mandela, Carlos Russell, Oliver Thambo and the **African National Congress** as well as the "Freedom Fighter" Sam Njomo. We need not forget Martin L. King, Stokely Carmichael, Malcolm X, Bob Marley, Paul Robeson, Sonny Carson, Jitu Weusi, Bill Lynch, Basil Patterson and Gil Noble; all exemplary nationalist beacons casting powerful rays illuminating the paths of African people's cultural consciousness and freedom quest!

BLACK NATIONALISM STILL ALIVE AND WELL

Resolute Harlemite in nicely fitted Dashiki Shirt-Jac, your memorial fits wonderfully well beside Harriet Tubman, whether statue or school, for your association has been nothing short of spectacular enlightenment, persistent champion of the Red, Black and Green!

Emma stands before new Portrait of Rev. Al Sharpton at NAN's 25th Anniversary celebration at the Sheraton, New York.

Quintessential Son of Queen Mother Moore, Mother Jordan and associate of Betty Shabazz; departing for "ancestor glory," you charged Al Sharpton, Michael Hardy, Wyatt T. Walker and Calvin Butts; as well as Gary Byrd, Herb Boyd, Bob Law, Len Jeffries, Leonard and Marilyn James, Job Mashiriki, Louis Farrakhan,

FREDERICK MONDERSON

Michael Hooper of **ROOTS REVISITED** and **CEMOTAP's** Betty Dobson and James McIntosh; to carry on your work of education and enlightenment to free the minds of African people worldwide as they rise to challenge oppression, in its sustained and many clandestine and inclandestine forms.

BN PHOTO - Three pitchers of life-giving waters are just as effective as four.

BLACK NATIONALISM STILL ALIVE AND WELL

BN PHOTO - Sister Camille Yarbrough at the Podium as Dr. Len Jeffries looks on.

Ingenious Elombe, your name should be enshrined "on street" in that glorious Harlem Community similarly as Dr. John Clarke, W.E.B. DuBois, and A. Philip Randolph; Black nationalist and think tank, valiantly you kept the flame of African consciousness burning brightly while bearing the burdens of leadership Garvey spoke of.

Tireless man of vision, tenacity, courage, resilience and activist sustainability; Visionary who would not let Patrice Lumumba's memory fade; you challenged the oppressors of your people.

Resourceful leader whose visionary thought and deed propelled a movement seeking political, economic and educational empowerment consistent with the Civil Rights Movement's aspirations; you were a master tactician victorious on many fronts.

Mr. Brath, you are the newest star in the Black Pantheon, where "Brother Gods" welcome your presence to further invigorate their

FREDERICK MONDERSON

efforts here and there, as we recognize the struggles must continue for our people's Civil Rights and human dignity worldwide.

Indefatigable Nationalist grandmaster, your flames powered Gil Noble's flood-lights awakening our people's intellectual, cultural and political consciousness through the powerful and educational **LIKE IT IS** TV program! Constructive statesman, theorist, master of strategic activism and blest with an enlightening penmanship, go assist Sonny and Jitu to organize heaven assuring our expected arrival in that blessed existence where ancestors earned their reverence and can still inspire our people as we meet challenges.

BN PHOTO - Professor James Smalls at the Podium wearing his priestly "Leopard Skin" (left); and a Diplomatic Corps representative, perhaps from Namibia, all singing praises to Dr. Ben-Jochannan, the quintessential African Nationalist educator.

BLACK NATIONALISM STILL ALIVE AND WELL

BN PHOTO - A somber time, also a time of joy, happy to have been with Dr. Ben's presence and life's work benefits.

BN PHOTO - Herb Boyd among another part of the crowd in the upper balcony, paying tribute to Dr. Ben-Jochannan as he heads to join the other illustrious ancestors.

Incomparable Elombe Brath, we who are yet to die recognize, praise and salute you for a fulfilling life of creative activism with measured attainments; a rich legacy, accomplished in advancing the cause of Africa and all humanity; recognizing we must stay the course you so eloquently and steadfastly charted in your constructive earthly existence. Good-bye and thank you, Beloved Brother Elombe!

BN PHOTO - Still another part of the crowd with Dr. Rosalind Jeffries (white dress and headwear) at the right.

21. "HEAVEN IN AN UPROAR"
By
Dr. Fred Monderson

From the time the great labor leader and political tactician William ("Bill") Lynch had gone to glory and arrived at the "Pearly Gates" a bee-hive of activity began to unfold regarding his entry into the "Kingdom of Heaven." After the "drums" announced Bill was on his way, not only was there consternation here on earth among those he befriended, worked with, influenced and mentored including such political luminaries as John Liu and Bill DeBlasio; yet, ancestral angels in train of Sonny Carson, "over there," insightful as he has always been, supported his theory, there would be static at the gate where St. Peter was mandated to do his heavenly examination.

BLACK NATIONALISM STILL ALIVE AND WELL

Sonny thereupon called upon associates Jitu Weusi, Afori Payton, Hodari the "Fire man," then sent word to Malcolm X, Dr. John Henrik Clarke, W.E.B. DuBois and Martin Luther King with instructions to call upon the oldsters Paul Robeson, A. Philip Randolph, and Marcus Garvey to meet him at the "Gates" for a show of Black Solidarity and to welcome "Brother Bill" into the majesty of heaven!

Since state of mind has a tremendous impact on well-being, and as much as Bill had been preparing in his journey heavenward, leaving a wife, son and daughter behind; as he approached that revered existence, and sensing some kind of commotion from the people massed in and outside the fence; Mr. Lynch stood up from his chair! He approached the table where sat an elderly but vibrant gentleman with a long white beard. Realizing the consternation unfolding in the opposing gatherings for a "potential war in heaven," St. Peter donned his Inquisition hat and exhorted, "Mr. William Lynch, What are your qualifications for entry into this gloriously hallowed and blissful existence?"

Bill responded, "Pardon!"

"What have you done?"

"Your book is a record!"

"No, you tell me!"

Bill Lynch responded: "I am a Harlemite born to a Long Island potato farmer!"

"I served in the United States Air Force and on the Children Defense Fund."

FREDERICK MONDERSON

BN PHOTO - The golden hawk, a manifestation of Horus, son of Isis and Osiris.

BN PHOTO - Even more of the previous frame with Dr. Rosalind Jeffries at the left (white head-band).

BLACK NATIONALISM STILL ALIVE AND WELL

BN PHOTO - Gye Nyame, "Supremacy of God" richly underscores African religious, philosophical and moral belief systems.

FREDERICK MONDERSON

"I managed David Patterson's campaign for New York State Senator in 1985."

"I was Chief of Staff for David Dinkins when he served as Manhattan Borough President."

"Is that all" responded Saint Peter. "Not at all."

"I helped bring the 1992 Democratic National Convention to New York City and was Bill Clinton's 1992 New York State Campaign Manager."

"I became David Dinkins' Campaign Manager and engineered his victory to become New York City's first Black Mayor in 1989."

"In that administration I served as Deputy Mayor or Inter-Governmental Relations."

"I'm sure you have all this in your records."

"Upon Nelson Mandela's 1990 release from Prison in South Africa, I engineered his visit to New York City, coordinated speaking events in Harlem and Yankee Stadium and arranged a Ticker Tape Parade down the New York City's "'Canyon of Heroes.'"

"I served as Director of Legislation and Political Action for District Council 1701 of AFSCME."

"I was adviser to Jesse Jackson's and Walter Mondale's presidential campaigns.

"I served as advisory Vice-Chairman to the Democratic National Committee in 2004.

"I was also Deputy Campaign Manager to Senator John Kerry's 2004 Presidential Campaign.

BLACK NATIONALISM STILL ALIVE AND WELL

BN PHOTO - As Prof. James Smalls in "Leopard Skin" works out over Dr. Ben, Dr. Calvin Butts, Pastor of Abyssinia looks over, perhaps to learn a thing or two, all preparing the Great man for his "Osirian Journey" after the "Opening the Mouth Ceremony."

"I sat on several Boards to aid the cause of my fellow man. Is all this necessary? What does your book say?"

Turning to his official record, St. Peter realized "I'm dealing with a man of superior mentality, who is courageous with a strong sense of commitment as demonstrated in his fight for civil rights and social and racial justice." He noted former Mayor David Dinkins sorrowfully confessed, his friend Bill Lynch "had a unique capacity to pull together bright young women and men who are dedicated to doing good things." In fact, Mr. Dinkins added: "Over eight years, four as Manhattan borough president and four as mayor, much that was accomplished was because of Bill Lynch. It was he who

FREDERICK MONDERSON

persuaded me, in 1989, to run for Mayor, and I shall be eternally grateful for that which he helped me accomplish. Bill, who was sometimes referred to as the 'rumpled genius,' was the architect of so much that I'm credited with having accomplished during our administration. He had a genius for connecting people of common interests and goals, and for the political game and behind-the-scenes strategy. He was a genius but, more than that, he was a dear friend and I will miss him dearly."

Equally, St. Peter realized many important people had been touched by the meaningful life of this giant in New York politics. Many with similar standings had instantly responded in praise of the genius whose accomplishments changed the New York political landscape. Among those, former President Bill Clinton and his wife Hillary Clinton had pointed out, "Bill Lynch always put people first. He had a heart even bigger than the city he served."

BN PHOTO - Khepre, the "Beetle" represents rebirth and the visible sun in the heavens.

BLACK NATIONALISM STILL ALIVE AND WELL

BN PHOTO - Dr. Leonard and Dr. Rosalind Jeffries at the Podium paying tribute to the Master Teacher, Dr. Yosef A.A. ben-Jochannan.

However, feeling somewhat embarrassed by the "third degree," amidst the clamor of the demonstration and the counter demonstration, St. Peter's further read the Clintons' comments stating, "Bill Lynch was a friend to both of us over many years. We admired his integrity and his generosity, including his support for scores of community organizations. New York has lost a champion!" St. Peter, on the other hand and wanting the best for a tranquil and harmonious heavenly existence thought, "Perhaps Bill could save heaven from foolish people, who put this sacred place in a rage." Further, St. Peter's record showed, New York City Mayor Michael Bloomberg also made the statement that Mr. Lynch, "sought to better our city by bringing people together and served as Deputy Mayor because he wanted to make a difference for New Yorkers. He spent his life passionately pursuing his ideals - civil rights and social justice. Many of the most influential political leaders - here in the city and also on the national level - sought his counsel. He lived a remarkable life, and my thoughts and prayers are with his family."

FREDERICK MONDERSON

BN PHOTO - Many aspects to "The Runaway" story, whether Frederick Douglass or Samuel Carson "Runaway Slave" who opened "The Door of Return" in Ghana, West Africa, August 1, 1998.

City Council Speaker Christine Quinn, expressed, "Today, we mourn the loss of a true champion for progressive causes and one of the sharpest minds that New York government and politics has ever seen. Bill Lynch dedicated his life to making New York City a better place. As a Deputy Mayor under Mayor Dinkins, Bill played a critical role in facilitating Nelson Mandela's historic visit to New York City in 1990. Bill was a fighter for equality and the embodiment of a New Yorker: tough, smart, and fiercely loyal to the

BLACK NATIONALISM
STILL ALIVE AND WELL

City he loved. Bill was my friend - he was a one of a kind New Yorker, and he will be sorely missed."

Former Controller Bill Thompson: "I lost a friend today. And the city lost a giant. Bill Lynch was a brilliant strategist and thinker - that was unmistakable from the moment he entered a room. And his body of work, including his tireless effort to help elect political leaders across New York City, most memorably David Dinkins, tells his powerful story. But Bill always understood that politics is about people. He didn't just help elect leaders full of heart and vision and know-how, Bill served. He had a deep belief that government could be a tool to improve the lives of New Yorkers. Bill Lynch lived by that belief. No matter what the challenge, he persevered. Even though he left us today, Bill and his voice will continue to guide our city and its people to a better place."

BN PHOTO - Attorney at Law, Michael Hardy, representing Rev. Al Sharpton and National Action Network, praising Dr. Ben for his unselfish work.

The Rev. Al Sharpton: "National Action Network and I are heartbroken over the passing of Bill Lynch. We lost a brilliant

FREDERICK MONDERSON

political strategist and the 'Godfather' of the Harlem political establishment. Bill was not only one of the most astute political minds in the country, he was a political father to many and worked with National Action Network for over twenty years on some of the most pertinent issues of our time. Bill believed in mentoring young people and it came easy for him because he believed in putting people and community first and said: 'When you do that, you always win.' Bill Lynch personally mentored countless young strategists who now hold key positions including National Action Network's own National Field Director LaMon Bland. Bill has been a revered advisor to some of the great humanitarians and elected officials of our time."

Hector Figueroa, President, 32BJ/SEIU, "32BJ joins the many others across the country saddened by the passing of our brother, comrade, and friend Bill Lynch. Our movement lost a singular warrior today. Bill's years of visionary work with labor, political leaders and the Black community are unparalleled, and the fruits of his many endeavors will live far beyond him. Bill believed in the transformative powers of democracy and political engagement and was an unwavering champion in the ongoing fight to get unheard voices heard. Our deepest sympathies go out to his family and loved ones. Bill, we will miss you."

BN PHOTO - Dr. Rosalind Jeffries offers the deepest consolation to the Ben-Jochannan family, for having shared the Great Teacher with so many in his life as a Pan-Africanist educator, African Nationalist.

BLACK NATIONALISM STILL ALIVE AND WELL

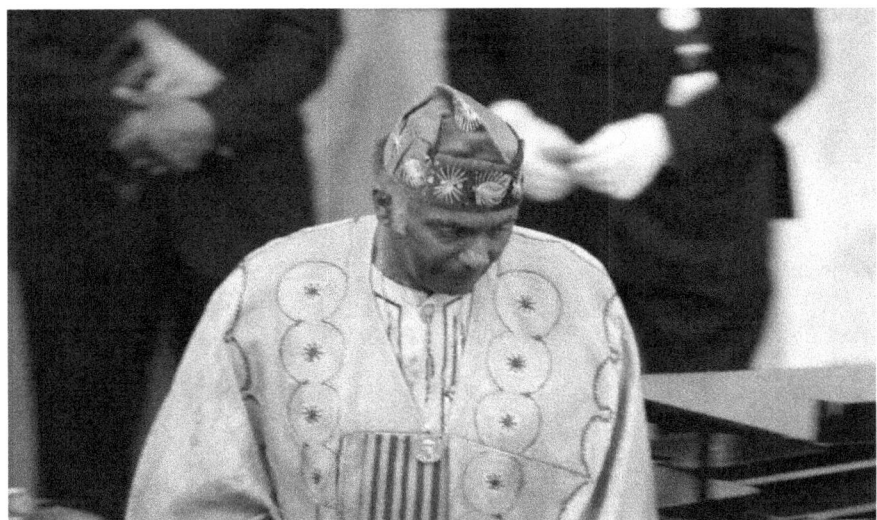

BN PHOTO - Dr. Leonard Jeffries, renowned educator, but a man visibly shaken by the passing of the Legend he knew so well, having walked the same path of intellectually enlightening African people.

Bertha Lewis, President, **The Black Institute**: "I am heartbroken. Today, a great man has passed and I am deeply saddened by the loss of yet another mentor and friend to our community. A lot of what I know about Politics and Organizing, I learned from Bill Lynch. He was undoubtedly one of the greatest political minds of our era, and will forever be known as a giant in politics. He was a legend on the gridiron and on the gritty streets of Harlem and his passing creates a huge chasm in our City and our Nation's political fabric. I am honored to have known, learned and worked with him. Bill was a master political architect who was a key link between the Civil Rights Movement and electoral politics. The effects of his genius touched as far as South Africa and its abolishment of Apartheid and the world mourns his passing. The hearts and minds of **The Black Institute** are with his family and our friends at Bill Lynch Associates."

FREDERICK MONDERSON

Having assessed some such statement, St. Peter then realized humanity had indeed lost a champion, for he had always believed, "Good government is good politics." After that, St. Peter began to ponder his decision!

On Bill's part, awaiting the verdict, he finally turned and affixed his gaze on the group outside the gate who had been most vocal. He could make out a well-dressed gentleman in a white suit with a hood turned backwards over his shoulder. Then he realized, "Heaven is also beset by the great issues of earth!" There were others whose faces he could not make out.

BN PHOTO - Dr. Adelaide Sanford, renowned educator, nationalist and fierce activist in defense of African people's humanity and intellectual capability, speaks her piece in praise of the Great African Dr. Yosef Ben-Jochannan.

Inside, a band of singers comprising Sam Cooke, Baby Huey, Charlie Parker, Michael Jackson, Bob Marley and Luther Vandross were singing "A Change is going to come" and their melodic voices were harmoniously blended with the sweet instrumentation of Louis Armstrong, Dizzy Gillespie, and Hasan Roland Kirk. Just then the Jubilee Singers arrived on a flat-bed truck and joining the others they began singing "When the Saints Go Marching In, when the Saints go

BLACK NATIONALISM
STILL ALIVE AND WELL

marching In, I want to be in that number; when the Saints go marching in." Then hearing these heavenly chimes, Mr. Lynch finally broke into a smile and really noticed the individuals in that group. "All this and heaven too," he thought. The more familiar faces of Carson, Weusi, Malcolm, Marley, Martin, Nkrumah, Sekou and Kwame Toure, and Robeson he easily recognized. Also there in the welcoming crowd were John Brown, William Lloyd Garrison, Charles Sumner, the Kennedy Brothers, and while Betty hugged Malcolm, Coretta grabbed Martin's arm. Bill also recognized Queen Mother Moore, standing beside Mary McCloud Bethune. Much further back and peering over the crown was Booker T. Washington, George Washington Carver, Medgar Evers and Rev. Shillingsworth, all standing behind Yaa Asantewaa, Bottom Belly, Queen Mary, Sojourner Truth, Fannie Lou Hamer and Harriet Tubman. These brothers and sisters were serious about Bill Lynch entering heaven as a member of the great and blessed pantheon of Black hero saints. However, in a note to Sonny, Denmark Vesey, Nat Turner and Samuel Carson had informed, "We can't get there today but we're with you in spirit!"

BN PHOTO - Another well-wisher familiar with the work of Dr. Ben sings him praises as he makes his transition to the revered ancestor pantheon.

FREDERICK MONDERSON

BN PHOTO - Dr. Falu, Biographer and translator of Dr. Ben's works makes a heartbreaking statement of what motivated him about the Great Man and why she spent so many years translating his works into Spanish.

As all this unfolded, Bill was really surprised, that at such short notice Sonny was able to contact so many and organize such a meaningful welcoming committee; all expressing a determination to have him share in the joys of heaven, where the light of righteousness forever shines. Sonny, for his part; and knowing that Bill Lynch was a tireless champion for New York; was thinking, we could really use Bill's organizational and planning expertise, his coalition building acumen and his ability to forge consensus on issues.

Now in a quandary, Saint Peter turned to Bill Lynch and said, "Mr. Lynch you must understand, I have a job to do. My boss, the gentleman with the 'lamb's wool hair,' did insist everyone, no matter whom, must be rigorously examined to enter this eternal realm. You have passed with flying colors, particularly because of your concern for doing good." With that he handed Mr. Lynch the keys of heaven and bid him enter the realm of the sacred and blessed.

BLACK NATIONALISM STILL ALIVE AND WELL

Instantly as the "rumpled genius" entered the realm of spiritual existence, the tactician and strategist that he has always been, immediately forced Mr. Lynch to believe he must contribute to making heaven drowsy with the tranquilizing harmony of love and cooperation. Still, he demanded an assessment of the state of things, to which Mr. Carson instantly handed over a list that included the following demands:

An end to segregation; an end to racial profiling; no more stop and frisk; meaningful programs for seniors; meaningful programs for youth; freedom of expression and freedom from fear; the need for jobs, meaningful jobs, even here in heaven; the need to be more organized; better educational opportunities; and equal compensation for the same work; as well as more concern for the youth.

Just then Mr. Lynch realized his work was cut out for him. Sensing the heavenly waters were not all tranquil, he realized his was a role to bring these blessed souls together through organizational and unifying leadership. He had to help create a new heaven that would lay the ground work for a better earth. Thus, he felt confident with the litany of blessed ancestors present and supportive; his skills will be even more meaningful. Just then he thought, "I have got a lot of work to organize this place. I must continue to work to make all peoples' expectations of heaven a blissful reality!"

FREDERICK MONDERSON

BN PHOTO - Kwesi Ashra, an "Intellectual Cub" of Dr. Ben-Jochannan, speaks his peace in praise of the Great Teacher.

22. THE UNBELIEVERS
By
Dr. Fred Monderson

This is not about "Their Unbelievers" but it is about "Our Unbelievers" whom the columnist Paul Krugman so eloquently and factually identified and critiqued in his piece entitled "Voodoo Time Machine" in *The New York Times* of Friday, January 9, 2015, p. 23. Here is a man, Mr. Krugman, a scholar, an intellectual of the highest order who has not simply sung praises of President Obama, but importantly, over the years has had the vision to recognize and the tenacity to point out the significant accomplishments the Obama Administration has achieved. He equally and rightfully recognized not only have Republicans blocked every meaningful legislative initiative the President proposed but those, through political skill and Presidential pulpit cajoling creatively significant progress was made in furthering the interests of the American people; but, Republicans nevertheless missed these successes. In modern parlance, "They never got those e-mails!"

BLACK NATIONALISM STILL ALIVE AND WELL

Witnesses to the two terms of President Obama's Administration and even "a blind man" can discern the nation has made enormous progress in furthering the best interests of the American Republic, at home and abroad. But Republicans in their "Parallel Universe" understandably deny these accomplishments and where possible still claim responsibility for all that is good and beneficial. Clearly, these "Brothers from Another Planet," like bloodhounds with their noses to the ground, cannot see the clear waters and reflecting blue skies Mr. Obama has sailed the ship of state into in his futuristic vision. Nor have they recognized the fields he plowed with their flowering greenery and prodigious fruitfulness promising many predictable harvests he will reap and bequeath his successors.

Put another way!

A tortoise was ambling along and came upon a giraffe feeding upon the luxurious tall tree greenery amidst the clear skies and fresh air circulating above. Looking skyward and hailing the fortunate ruminant the tortoise asked, "How's it going?" Looking downward the giraffe responded, "Great! It's like Heaven up here! Nothing but luxuriant shrub and clean air amidst a blue sky creating a wonderful view with great promise! How about you?"

The tortoise responded, "It's like hell down here! All I see is garbage. The air is foul and people keep stepping on me!"

"How sad" the giraffe responded, "you should step up a few notches!"

FREDERICK MONDERSON

BN PHOTO - Dr. Tony Browder, educator and author speaks his piece on behalf of the Great Educator, Dr. Yosef A.A. Ben-Jochannan.

BN PHOTO - Dr. Calvin Butts, Pastor of Abyssinia Baptist Church adds the finishing touches to a night of praise and rejoicing, celebrating the life and work of Dr. Ben-Jochannan.

BLACK NATIONALISM STILL ALIVE AND WELL

BN PHOTO - Another student and traveler along the path of intellectual enlightenment, praises the Great Teacher for a life well-lived in defense of and in educating African people in a masterful way.

BN PHOTO - At the Adelaide Sanford's 90th Birthday celebration, one of the speakers offered, "To be remembered, one has to have written their name on the consciousness and spirit of African people." This is what Dr. Ben-Jochannan did in the most memorable fashion for decades in which he enlightened many.

FREDERICK MONDERSON

BN PHOTO - Prof. James Smalls comforts a sister who was heartbroken by the loss of the Great Teacher.

BN PHOTO - To truly sing praises, you can use a Mike with an organ accompaniment, as this sister is doing.

BLACK NATIONALISM STILL ALIVE AND WELL

BN PHOTO - This gentleman sporting the Red, Black and Green colors clutches one of Dr. Ben's books.

Fact is; both parties gave honest appraisals of their situation and view. From his skyward vantage point, the giraffe could see nothing but a positive, clear and refreshingly promising future. Down on earth, the tortoise's vision is clouded and stultified from seeing nothing but trash and wallowing in the foul odor of negativity. Unfortunately these Republicans; as we know, "Leopards cannot change their spots;" while unquestionably having the Obama giraffe towering over their heads, should, to quote Hillary Rodham Clinton, "Get out of the gutter!"

So, Mr. Krugman particularly identified some "bloodhounds" with their noses to the ground, a posture some may call foolish! Fortune has now favored these men, positioning them at the pinnacle of the American political structure, controlling both Houses of one third of

FREDERICK MONDERSON

the American government; but alas a record precedes their ascent and this will influence their future decisions.

Given a fraction of the obstruction Mr. Obama experienced, Mr. Krugman's indictment questions Republicans' ability to govern in a manner beneficial to the broad masses of the American people. Equally too, their misguided determination to roll back Obama's legislative policies and executive actions while also seeking to benefit their wealthy 1% base questions the notion of objective leadership on their part.

BN PHOTO - Gil Noble of **Like It Is** fame prepares to introduce comedian Dick Gregory at **CEMOTAP's** 18th Anniversary Celebration.

Let's look at some features of his indicting critique:

(1)   The author mentions Mitch McConnell is claiming incoming Republican leadership for the nation's economic growth now in process.

BLACK NATIONALISM STILL ALIVE AND WELL

BN PHOTO - Barry Campbell and members of his entourage from Veterans Quality of Life are out in force at the Veterans Parade in November.

BN PHOTO - Barry Campbell and his contingent Veterans Quality of Life Access Network, Inc., in full effect at the Veterans Parade.

FREDERICK MONDERSON

(2) While Republicans chastised "Obamacare" in the Pre and Roll-out stages, particularly the "glitches;" in the positive turn around, some have cried foul, as Senator John Barraso of Wyoming let loose, "They are cooking the books." Can you imagine, President Obama, a leader of impeccable credentials and a clear conscionable view of history, as soon as he steps down, would have to shamefacedly back-peddle, saying, to quote Richard Nixon apologetically, "I am not a crook!"

(3) Paul Ryan, in response to the current successes of the Affordable Care Act, charged, "The law will collapse on its own weight!" The question is will this new Chairman of the House and Ways Committee, after his party has tried nearly four dozen times to gut "Obamacare," will he put his weight behind such efforts "to fix something that works?" Has he not heard of, "If it works don't fix it!" However, "if the law will collapse on its own weight," why after some fifty attempts to overturn Obamacare, why are Republicans in this political campaign season still trumpeting "Overturn Obamacare!" Of course, Mr. Ryan is a "special," and I don't want to say, "Basket" "case." Mr. Krugman wrote, "Speaking of Mr. Ryan: almost four years have passed since he and many others in his party lambasted Ben Bernanke then the Chairman of the Federal Reserve for policies that they claimed would lead to higher inflation and debase the dollar. The inflation never materialized, and the dollar proceeded to strengthen, but Mr. Ryan gave no sign of having been chastened - and many Conservatives including favorite intellectuals like Niall Ferguson of Harvard became 'inflation truthers,' insisting that the government is hiding price rises. Can you do that in an open society? What of the Freedom of Information seekers with their "Hubble-like" intrusion, have they found the price rises? Are they still searching, as the Westerners are probably still looking for "Prester John" in Africa!

BLACK NATIONALISM STILL ALIVE AND WELL

BN PHOTO - Young Dr. Fred Monderson in this old "School Photo" as teacher in NYC.

Next, Mr. Krugman points to "Climate Change" citing 2014 as the hottest year yet! Still, Senator James Inhofe now heading an Environmental Committee thinks, "all the science in this field is a liberal hoax." This "Brother from Another Planet" would not know climate change, if, as E.F. Hutton would say, "It arrived, slapped him on the bottom, and said I'm here!" However and prophetically, Mr. Krugman sounded the alarm, "Congress is now controlled by men who never acknowledge error, let alone learn from their mistakes.'

FREDERICK MONDERSON

Three such mistakes can be referenced here!

(1)   The treasonous conspiracy among high ranking Republicans, and who, while not many names were mentioned in The New York Times article of October 6, 2013, but by virtue of their seniority to hold such Chairmanships today, must have participated in, certainly known of and accented to Mitch McConnell's marching orders, "To make Barack Obama a one-term President!" Instead of Senator McConnell giving that now infamous "Thumbs Up" signal, he should have been doing the "Perp Walk" in front of a Federal Judge for treason or certainly sedition. While Paul Krugman goes on to conclude a brilliant article by stating, "We can't have meaningful cooperation when we can't agree on reality, when even establishment figures in the Republican Party believe that facts have a liberal bias!"

BN PHOTO - Dr. Leonard James and young men he mentored as a "Great Educator."

BLACK NATIONALISM STILL ALIVE AND WELL

BN PHOTO - Rev. Al Sharpton prepares to introduce young Senator Barack Obama at a "Celebrate the King Dream" forum.

One fact among many is that this party's base has not simply been brainwashed, it's been "Republican washed" through misguided propaganda, falsity, juggling and suppressing the facts, listening to Fox News, Rush Limbaugh, Sean Hannity and other such syncopates. It's like these people are in a "Parallel Universe" and their thinking and actions can affect America's future. Fact is, if they remove the plugs Mr. Obama inserted in the leaky ship he inherited, we may end up marooned on some remote island in the stratosphere in their party's fairy tale "Parallel Universe."

FREDERICK MONDERSON

BN PHOTO - Members of the Committee to Honor Black Heroes proudly display the activist and Nationalist Sonny Carson "Bringing the Light."

BLACK NATIONALISM STILL ALIVE AND WELL

23. OBAMA: WORSE PRESIDENT? PHOOEY!
By
Dr. Fred Monderson

In a Quinnipiac University poll, President Obama was named the worse President since World War II! Naturally, skeptics need to query the nature and type of questions asked to arrive at the conclusions stated. Equally, the conscious level of those polled must be taken into consideration. Accordingly, "30% of persons" questioned felt Mr. Obama was the worse President! Apparently, this poll is conducted perennially and the last time it was conducted, in 2006, was two years into President George Walker Bush's second term. At that time, he was voted the worse in this category! Without question, there was "much on his plate." However, many believe what Republicans, especially, are saying about President Obama is what they say about Black people period! Considering his situation, be that as it may, we must remember, even Mr. Obama must remember, Malcolm X said, "You're not catching hell because you're an American. You're catching hell because you're Black!" After all, Vice-President Biden was right in saying, "They're trying to put you back in slavery!" Fact is; assessing contemporary developments; dye-in-the-wool racists cannot comprehend the magnificence of Mr. Obama. He is well educated, very intelligent, compassionate, a humanitarian, far-sighted, historically conscious and cool under fire. So with him on the 20th floor, 1st floor occupants cannot conceive such brilliance in a Black man!

The parallel is simple as T.D. Jakes tells it. A giraffe was feeding at the tree top, enjoying the cool breeze, fresh greenery and staring into the promise of the clear blue skies yonder. Along came a turtle enquiring, "How're you doing?" The giraffe answered, "Great, the view is wonderfully spectacular. And You?" The turtle responded, "Looks like a terrific mess. All I see is garbage and the smell is awful." Fact is; both gave honest answers. However, while Obama grazes in tree top sunlight, his detractors are in turtledom!

BN PHOTO - The first of two volumes of **Sonny Carson: The Final Triumph** by **Frederick Monderson**.

Nevertheless, before we consider the questions, it is interesting to note some factors regarding the state of the nation under Mr. Bush's watch which Mr. Obama inherited and masterfully addressed as President!

First of all, 2006 was five years since the "second attack" on the World Trade Center on 9/11/2001, resulting in the "shock and awe" response visited on the Taliban in Afghanistan! The Taliban harbored Osama bin Laden, leader of Al Qaeda, who was "at war with America," and credited with the attack. The year 2006 was also 3 years into the invasion of Iraq that ultimately toppled Sadam Hussein, resulting in nearly 5,000 American military deaths and thousands more injured. This does not include Coalition forces and Iraqi casualties, military and collateral, and the trillions of dollars

BLACK NATIONALISM STILL ALIVE AND WELL

spent in a war Americans considered useless, wasteful and ill-considered.

The significant players in the Bush Administration included Vice President Dick Chaney, Donald Rumsfeld as Secretary of Defense, Condoleezza Rice as National Security Adviser and ultimately, replacing General Colin Powell as Secretary of State. Based on the information supplied him, Mr. Powell testified to the Security Council of the United Nations that Sadam Hussein possessed weapons of mass destruction (WMD) with a launch capacity that was very rapid. He was even tied to purchasing uranium from Niger in West Africa to make his weaponry more effective. However, while both wars ensued, a number of interesting variables began to surface and in total proving much of this intelligence was considered faulty, if not purposefully deceitful.

Significantly, as it turned out, Mr. Chalaby, an Iraqi national who had written a book on Ancient Egypt was an "American friendly," who fed them inside information about Sadam's armaments. As it turned out, truthfully, "Chalaby had this thing against Sadam," and targeted the Americans at him using purposely faulty intelligence. Notwithstanding, when the "stuff hit the fan," Chalaby fled to Iran, at that time an enemy of Iraq and America.

Apparently and second, evidence indicates, Sadam Hussein had tried to assassinate Mr. Bush's father, President Number 41, in Kuwait; so, Mr. Bush, President Number 43, accordingly was rather eager to get back at Sadam! The crafted web of deceit revealed even more details. Vice-President Dick Chaney was shown to be connected to Halliburton, a contractor company doing business in Iraq with great financial success. Even more important, it was persuasively argued, Iraqi oil would pay for the expense of the war, though this too proved misleading! Equally significant, however, as the occupation unfolded, General Shinseki informed Congress it would require some 500,000 troops to garrison Iraq but he was ridiculed and so, the conflicts revved up in face of Iraqi insurgency and the same happened in Afghanistan, though the deaths were not as numerous but still significant.

BN PHOTO - Volume Three and Four, **Sonny Carson: The Final Triumph** by **Frederick Monderson.**

In as much as the American leadership initially raised the question of Sadam's intentions, the international community remained skeptical and so, Mr. Bush "chose to go it alone." In response, the international community took a dim view of America, thanks to the impetuosity of Mr. Bush, the warlord! This reality stained America's foreign relations image for the rest of Mr. Bush's term! One American woman was overheard saying in the Cairo Museum, saying "It has gotten so we don't want to say we're Americans because all Bush wants is war!"

At home, the economy was in serious disarray. There were bank failures; Wall Street numbers dropped precipitously and the DOW fell to near 6500; high unemployment became the order of the day; the automobile industry was in crisis; the nation's infrastructure had begun to crumble; an energy crisis unfolded; foreclosures were up, new housing starts were down; teachers and first responders' jobs were on the chopping block; and with unemployment up and taxes

BLACK NATIONALISM STILL ALIVE AND WELL

down, state and local governments faced challenging realities. Now, in this bleak moment in America's history, Senator Barack Hussein Obama, from the great state of Illinois, declared his candidacy for the Presidency and the rest is history, literally and figuratively!

After a grueling and well-regulated successful campaign and possessing a beautiful wife, two lovely daughters and a wonderful mother-in-law, like a bright-eyed and bushy-tail knight whose hair was still black, Mr. Obama stepped into the fray to rescue his nation! Just as Jim Santorum would confess after his failure in 2012, "lots of things get said in a campaign;" Mr. Obama felt "the many lights" of this great nation would forget the campaign rhetoric, come together, put their shoulders to the wheel, help to "remove the car from the ditch," and move the country forward. However, this was not to be! Nonetheless, Mr. Obama set about to tackle the myriad foreign and domestic challenges facing the nation, many believed, was in a near failed-state status! Still, rather than condemn his adversaries, Mr. Obama politely but confidently confessed, "Politics is a contact sport" and considered these persons "Good ole boys just acting out!"

Facing the future with a positive attitude, one of the first and significant acts of a new president is to venture abroad, let friends and enemies get a taste of the new executive and lay out a view of the path he intends. This Mr. Obama did wonderfully well. Even more significantly, he astutely "deployed his better half," "Mighty Michelle," who not only wooed the world but provided the cover for him to win allies, put enemies on notice and then address the fundamentals of the two wars. He then dispatched a new envoy to the Middle East and pivoted towards strengthening a foothold in Asia for defense and economic realities manifesting in this new century. All this was very well executed.

FREDERICK MONDERSON

BN PHOTO - Kashida and Cherise (left), Prof Smalls and Chief, join Sonny Carson as he listens to a presentation made for the **"Runaway Samuel Carson"** on his way to internment in Ghana, West Africa.

Next on the domestic front, the president sought to review and strengthen the nation's financial and fiscal policies and practices with a view toward overhauling the monetary system; tackling foreclosure problems and other housing issues; rescuing the auto industry; bailing out the banks; placing a moratorium on impending firing of teachers and first responders such as police officers and firemen; establishing protections for women under the Lilly Ledbetter Act; proposing a more equitable arrangement for student loan debt and easing credit card rates; tackling climate change and global warming; creating incentives for more efficient energy systems and creating initiatives for education excellence. Meanwhile his wife Michelle and Vice-President Joe Biden's wife Jill became active advocates for veteran families faced with the challenges of the two wars.

Unbeknownst to all but a few, the sinisters were at work! While it did not become public until *The New York Times* reported in October 6, 2013, a treasonous group had met and planned a concerted, many pronged campaign designed to sabotage the tenure of the first Black President! Perhaps as the point man, and intoxicated by the glare of

BLACK NATIONALISM STILL ALIVE AND WELL

the cameras, Senator Mitch McConnell laid it bare, as if speaking for his team, "I intend to make Barack Obama a one-term president!" True to his boast and in subsequent negotiations as Senate Minority leader, after an important meeting, the Senator gave his now famous or infamous "Thumbs-up" code symbol signaling to his "people" "I got that Nigger!" However, it's common knowledge, racist hue mentality held, "A Nigger occupies the White House."

BN PHOTO - Bishop Shivers explains he will accompany "The Bones" to Ghana, and will preside over the internment at Assin Manso, the site of burial and place of pilgrimage for African-Americans seeking roots in Africa.

FREDERICK MONDERSON

BN PHOTO - Funeral Director Dr. Gafney explains how he will preside over all undertaking responsibilities in this country and in Africa at the place of burial.

BN PHOTO - Professor James Smalls will accompany the "Burial Party" to Ghana.

It is hard to believe, high up as he is, Speaker Boehner, did not know of the treasonous Republican meeting even if he did not participate. The "conspiracy" existed certainly from 2008 to 2012, so Boehner's

BLACK NATIONALISM
STILL ALIVE AND WELL

denial is considered farcical! Still, he did disrespect Mr. Obama by not returning his phone calls amidst important negotiations. Even more significant, this "representative of the people" held the nation and Mr. Obama hostage in the Debt Ceiling Debate and later symbolically boasted "We got 98% of what we wanted!" This is incredible, for to get 98% of any pie means all others got crumbs!

Today, Mr. Obama's record speaks for itself. He ended and wound down the war in Iraq and Afghanistan. He gets credit for killing and disposing of Osama bin Laden and severely curtailed the aspirations of Somali Pirates. He represented the United States very well at the funeral for Nelson Mandela in South Africa. The economy has rebounded well! Some 9 million new jobs have been added in the private sector so far during Mr. Obama's tenure. Rising from 6500 when he took office in 2008, to 17,000 today, the DOW has experienced a vibrancy unimagined even in "good times," in fact, its historical. The week of July 4, 2014, 300,000 jobs were added. Some even joked, "Knowing Mr. Obama would celebrate Independence Day, Republicans called up Hurricane Arthur to rain on Mr. Obama's parade!" Notwithstanding, on a more serious note, concerted attention is being paid to climate change, a clean air environment and infrastructure repair jobs. Emphasis is also being placed on all aspects of transportation, even creating a high-speed rail system with trains to improve cross-country commute.

Incentives have been offered for innovations in clean energy, better and longer lasting batteries and cars are moving towards cleaner emissions and better gas mileage. Even Black farmers have been paid for their long-standing suit against the government!

FREDERICK MONDERSON

BN PHOTO - Members of the Funeral Director's party prepare to remove "The Bones" to begin the "Journey to Ghana," West Africa, to open "The Door of Return."

In education, Mr. Obama created "Race to the Top" to improve performance; issued incentives for parents to return to college; and he bolstered Community Colleges to lay a foundation for technical education in preparing for the future. Still more seriously important, Mr. Obama conceived of an answer to address the nearly 50 million Americans without health care. He campaigned on this issue in two elections, legislated the **Affordable Care Act** that withstood a Supreme Court challenge amidst acrimonious negative propaganda public debate, and despite technical problems in the health care system roll-out, more than 8 million Americans have signed-up for the insurance protections, so far. With some luck and superb administrative vigilance terrorist attacks on the homeland have been prevented. In fact, a popular T-shirt has a Logo that reads: "Homeland Security: Fighting Terrorism since 1492!" As such, some have considered this nation, the birthplace of terrorism for Ku Klux Klan and Knights of the White Camelia, etc., behaviors towards

BLACK NATIONALISM STILL ALIVE AND WELL

African-Americans during the 19th and 20th Centuries were certainly classic cases of terrorism.

The list enumerated above and much more Mr. Obama achieved despite a Republican "Party of No" actively committed to block-every legislative initiative he proposed. Consider the Affordable Care Act was voted against 43 times (now 50 times) in the House of Representatives controlled by Republicans and not 1 Obama initiated jobs bill got through. Coupled with this subjective campaign *The Times* article named some 20 right-wing groups that were formed and well-financed, also the training of untold numbers of young people to "provide information about Obamacare," which in fact is nothing but efforts to defame Mr. Obama and his work. So much so, Senate Majority Leader Harry Reid decried the exorbitant spending by saying, "They're trying to buy America but it's not for sale!" Sorrowfully, the President confessed, "All they do is talk about me and block my every effort."

The mentality of persons such as the "McConnells" and "Boehners" and their backers believe Mr. Obama is "A Nigger out of place!" Hence, they must and will do everything in their power to defame him and poison the minds of Americans so a negative perception will linger. Important too, Democrats do not stand up for Mr. Obama! Malcolm X called them "Dixiecrats!"

FREDERICK MONDERSON

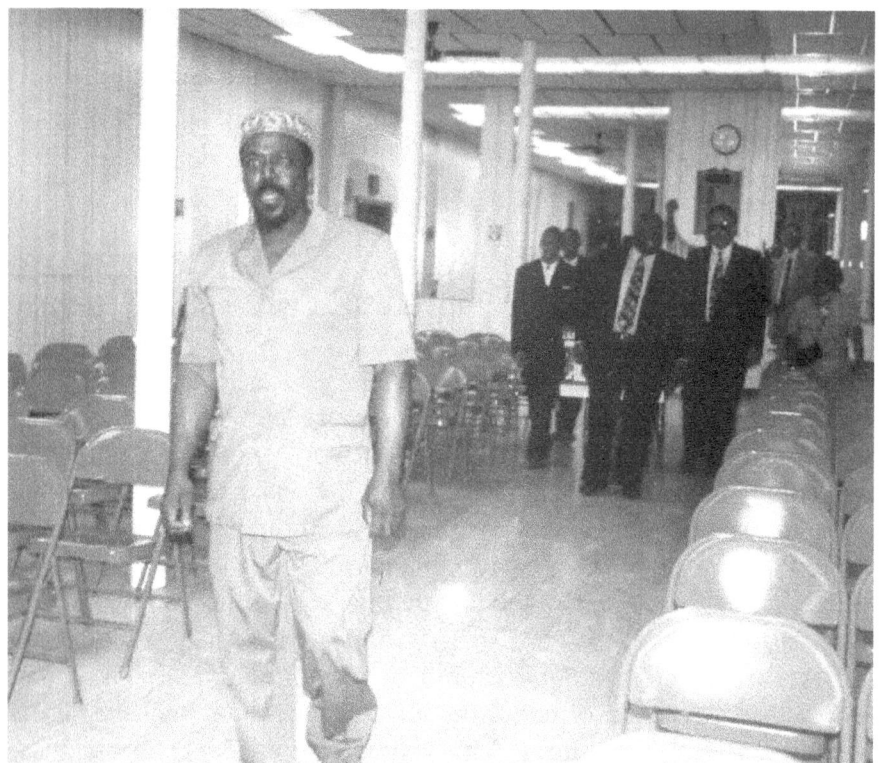

BN PHOTO - Bishop Shivers leads "The Bones" out of the Institutional Church on Adelphi Street in Brooklyn, New York, on its way to Ghana.

Most important, enquiring minds wonder whether the Poll asked did Mr. Obama's race play a role in the negative result. After the "Birther Charade," and the many threats, the fact is in both the 2008 and 2012 election Mr. Obama won by a margin of 53-47 percent of the vote. He lost all the "Lynching States" of the South and thus the 30% number is down from the 47% who would never vote for the man.

Nevertheless, when it comes to the use of Executive Action on part of the President, Mr. Obama was elected to lead the nation. If legislative elements block his every action, he must act on behalf of the people and therefore, Executive Action gets his agenda moving.

BLACK NATIONALISM
STILL ALIVE AND WELL

While the Poll seemed to indicate Mr. Reagan, Bill Clinton and

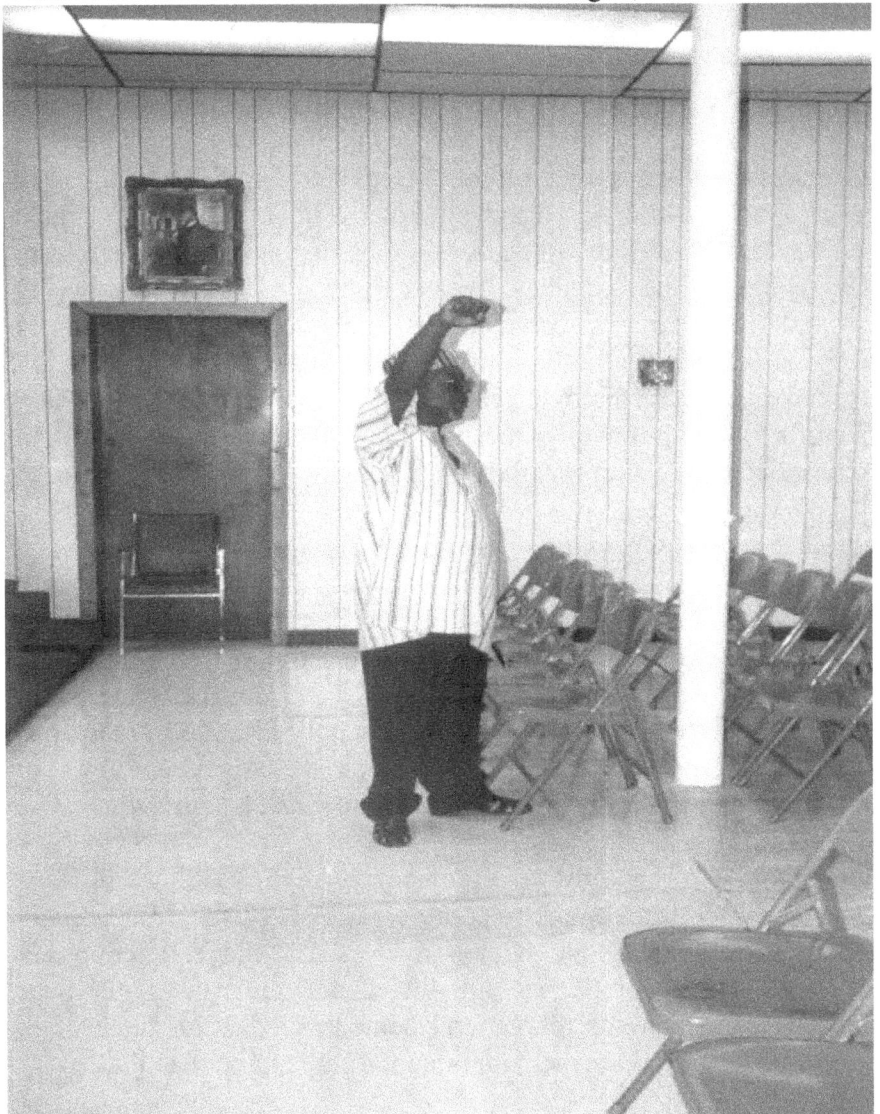

BN PHOTO - Sonny "Abubadika" Carson gives the "Black Power Salute" to send "The Bones" on its way to Ghana, West Africa to open "The Door of Return."

FREDERICK MONDERSON

Richard Nixon scored better than Mr. Obama one has to wonder whether a blind man conducted the poll. History has shown Bill Clinton worked the "Monica Lewinsky matter" in the White House while Hillary was in the next room; Richard Nixon resigned in disgrace after imploring "I am not a crook!" As for Ronal Reagan, for long he was an actor on radio, screen and television shaping his persona in a world of Hollywood many believe is really "make believe." Still, President Reagan, while he deployed "Star Wars" and blew wind at the Russians, their empire was actually tottering, anyway. However, he changed his hairstyle and lied about the Contras! More importantly, however, Mr. Reagan was the master of Executive Action, employing it more times than any other president. Therefore, to significantly question Mr. Obama's use of Executive Action in contrast with Mr. Reagan is actually laughable!

The fact is; Mr. Obama is a humanitarian who put people ahead of politics, has been faithful to his wife and kids and intellectually stands as a Gulliver to his Lilliputian challengers. Nevertheless, all things being equal, objectivity trumps subjectivity, which makes the Poll results questionable at best defaming and destructive at worst. Equally, it is strange how Republicans supply ideas to the terrorists who hate America. These people watch the American news on television. And, Mr. Obama tarries on, for what else is new!

Finally, in a recent press conference on an impending uptick of American involvement in Iraq, the Chairman of the Joint Chiefs, General Dempsey, spoke with a fearlessness and conviction that expresses sheer confidence in his Commander-in-Chief. Such steadfast composure as the general demonstrated in his leader fails the methodology, assessment and intent of the Quinnipiac Poll!

BLACK NATIONALISM STILL ALIVE AND WELL

BN PHOTO - Chief greets the Hearse bearing "The Bones of Runaway Samuel Carson" as it entered Prospect Part to be serenaded in the "Drummers Grove" just before departure from these shores.

24. WHEN RUBY MEETS OSSIE!
By
Dr. FRED MONDERSON

For some time Ossie Davis has been enjoying the "bachelor life," hanging out with his entertainment buddies of screen, stage, song and dance. One night, these icons, Paul Robeson, Mr. Bojangles and Sammy Davis were performing in the "Theater of Heaven." In the audience sat Sam Cooke, Billie Holliday, Ella Fitzgerald, Bessie Smith and Ertha Kitt in the first row and in the next, Hasan Roland Kirk, Charlie "Byrd" Parker, Baby Huey, Miles Davis, Theolonius Monk, and Dizzy Gillespie while George Jefferson, Michael Jackson, Richard Pryor and Redd Foxx couldn't contain themselves

FREDERICK MONDERSON

laughing at the performance. Amidst this illustrious group sat Ossie Davis and as Sam Cooke got up and began singing, "My Baby's Coming Home Tomorrow, Ain't that Good News, Man ain't that News," Ossie's face exploded in a thankful grin rivaling that of Louis "Satchmo" Armstrong, also there.

BN PHOTO - Sonny inspects the coffin in the Hearse before removing it in Prospect Park. Notice the Drummer welcoming "The Bones" to the "Drummer's Grove" in Prospect Park, as part of "Brooklyn Remembers Runaway Slave Samuel Carson."

Queen of the Arts, Ruby Dee, dutiful mother and faithful and loving wife, for her part, had been preparing to take that long awaited journey to meet her beloved, be united and continue that wonderfully blest relationship they enjoyed since being married in 1948, sharing love, acting performances, secrets and advocacy together.

Goddess of Screen and Stage, Lady of Grace and beauty, Ruby Dee you lived an extraordinary life of caring and concern for fellowman.

BLACK NATIONALISM STILL ALIVE AND WELL

Entertainment icon, Ms. Dee your beautiful face graced many an audience in memorable style, yet steadfastly protesting injustice.

Great Black Beauty, from "No Way Out" you became "A Raisin in the Sun" and certainly "Did the Right Thing" in "The Jackie Robinson Story." All the while you were not "Uptight" playing as an "American Gangster." This much you achieved without having any "Jungle Fever," Thespian of excellent performances.

BN PHOTO - Removing "The Bones of Runaway Samuel Carson" from the Hearse to attend "The Drummers Grove" celebration.

FREDERICK MONDERSON

BN PHOTO - Bringing Samuel Carson into the Drummers' Grove. Notice the drummer to the left as he sounds the alarm.

Angelic and talented, Black gemstone, your Civil Rights advocacy broke barriers on stage, screen and television championing opportunities for others to shine, still only pale reflection of your unparalleled talent. Actress of extraordinary note, "Anna Lucasta," from "Boes Man and Lena" to "Roots: The Next Generation," your wonderful smile and exquisite grace under pressure were classic portrayals plying your creative art; and from "St. Louis Blues" to "Checkmates" you were an exquisite talent who inspired others and pressured the powers that be to Let My People Act!

In a tumultuous age of Black assertion to right society's inequities, you proved not just a beautiful Black but a resolute and hard worker whose dedication to your craft spelled trailblazing success.

BLACK NATIONALISM STILL ALIVE AND WELL

BN PHOTO - Chief, Sonny Carson, Dr. Gafney and the drummer working out.

Black Star and "True Apollo Legend," who won an Emmy, Grammy, Screen Actors Guild Award and an Oscar Nomination, President Clinton awarded you the National Medal of Arts and more important, the National Civil Rights Museum Lifetime Achievement Award recognized your unselfish efforts on behalf of others, community activist and woman in the struggle who stood with many.

Active and delightful lady, member of the Congress of Racial Equality, Southern Christian Leadership Council, the Student Non-Violent Coordinating Council and National Association for Advancement of Colored People, your big heart and grace in troubling times inspired and supported many from the Black Panthers to the Anti-Vietnam War Movement.

FREDERICK MONDERSON

BN PHOTO - Chief and Sonny, Bishop Shivers, Dr. Gafney, and the Big Drummer Ashram (in White hat) follow the lead drummer into the Drummers' Grove.

Beautiful soul, you not only acted alongside your darling husband, Ossie Davis; together you championed the causes and symbolism of Martin Luther King and Malcolm X, "Our Shining Black Prince." It's not where you stood in times of "comfort and convenience, but challenge and controversy" that truly defined you and Ossie. Protesting Black Icon, you earned a revered place in ancestral glory.

While you won acclaim at the American Shakespeare Festival for "King Lear" and "The Taming of the Shrew" your performances in "South Pacific" and "Peyton Place" not simply underscored that awesome multi-dimensional talent, but to narrate "The Fight Against Slavery" and be arrested for protesting the murder of Amadou Diallo, the American Negro Theater recognized extraordinary talent "On" and "Off Broadway" embodied in a woman of vision, tenacity, perseverance and artistic excellence.

BLACK NATIONALISM STILL ALIVE AND WELL

When icons as Sidney Poitier, Spike Lee and Michelle Obama can sing praises to a wonderfully departed soul, A grateful community salutes and its people thankfully recognize and commend a committed life of thespian excellence and activism, then in wondrous adoration they bid farewell to a blessed soul, truly a precious gem.

BN PHOTO - Chief Barkin Parker, the "Big Drummer Ashram," Sonny Carson and Atiim Ferguson enter the "Drummers' Grove" in Prospect Park, Brooklyn.

FREDERICK MONDERSON

BN PHOTO - Placing "The Bones" at rest among the crowd who came to appreciate "The Runaway" and what his life will do to "Open the Door of Return."

25. NEWT! RUNNING DOWN THE MAN!
By
Dr. Fred Monderson

Former Republican House Speaker Newt Gingrich wears his "Obama hatred" badge unabashedly. Appearing on Candy Crowley's CNN program "State of the Union," and ignoring all of the current complexities facing President Obama, Mr. Gingrich proclaimed the President's "behavior" is "now cowardly." It is shameful that a few days after the surgical air strike that killed the Al Qaeda-linked Somali Al Shabab leader Ahmed Abdi Godane; Mr. Gingrich would make the above statement rather than rush to compliment the Commander-In-Chief for dispatching one of America's most

BLACK NATIONALISM STILL ALIVE AND WELL

notorious enemies. Consequently, a number of relevant factors involving Mr. Gingrich need be addressed.

First, either Mr. Gingrich did not get the "E-mail" about Mr. Godame's demise because he is out of the loop in such briefings, which the news reported on endlessly; or, he speaks without thinking! Thus, no longer a force in Presidential politics, Mr. Gingrich wants to show that he can still challenge Mr. Obama through his outlandish remarks.

Second, as a presidential candidate, albeit a loser, Newt's fluffy ego was stoked when he was often referred to by his sycophants as "the smartest guy in the room." Now, coming up against President Obama who is demonstrably superior intellectually and politically, Mr. Gingrich demonstrates the envious "fox and the grapes" pathology. Thus, Mr. Gingrich berates everything the President says or does in these challenging times, as his Republican colleagues have and continue to do. As they accentuate their negative posture, they give America's enemies the idea that there is potentially beneficial lack of unity among its leadership.

Third, most career politicians, especially at the Federal level, ultimately aspire to be President. As Speaker of the House of Representatives and by virtue of the line of Presidential Succession, Newt stood "two heartbeats" away from being President. Ever since, Newt Gingrich has sought the Presidency unsuccessfully but he is caught in a contradicting maelstrom. He is a Republican, a member of the "Party of No" and certainly aboard Senator Mitch McConnell's "I intend to make Barack Obama a one-term president" "ship of fools." However, even when doing his best, he falls short.

Fourth, Mr. Gingrich is from Georgia, a southern and "one of the lynching states." Georgia was among the states voting against Mr. Obama in both the 2008 and 2012 presidential elections. It would be nice to know all Georgians are not like Newt!

FREDERICK MONDERSON

BN PHOTO - "The Bones" stand alone before beginning the historic voyage to Ghana, West Africa, to "Open the Door of Return."

BN PHOTO - "The Brothers Stand Guard," part of that Iconic Centerfold, now in the Library of Congress, covering this important event that was never publicized in this country though got published overseas in Germany and the Caribbean.

BLACK NATIONALISM
STILL ALIVE AND WELL

Granted Newt Gingrich is not as smart as Barack Obama, evident in the 2-0 score in the presidential quest. Yet, "Newt is slick, not Vaseline but axle-grease slick." Notwithstanding, while he harbors presidential aspirations he does not want to appear as virulently anti-Obama as McConnell, Palin, Cruz, Trump, etc., who see Mr. Obama as the "Nigger in the White House" and out of his place. This list does not exclude contradictory "Nigger Lover" Jim DeMint who "likes the President" but wants to create his "Waterloo!"

BN PHOTO - Sonny Carson gives the "Salute" and says, "Let's take him home" to Ghana, West Africa to "Open the Door of Return."

FREDERICK MONDERSON

BN PHOTO - "Big Drummer Ashram" leads the "Bones out of Prospect Park" Drummers Grove.

BLACK NATIONALISM STILL ALIVE AND WELL

BN PHOTO - "And, A Child Shall Lead them," represents the long and historic journey of "Runaway Samuel Carson" making his way back to Africa to "Open the Door of Return."

Fifth, former National Security Adviser and Secretary of State Condoleezza Rice once exclaimed, "The view from the Oval Office desk is very different from what many believe." Equally, "Mr. Obama is a decent man doing the best he can for the country." However, smart as Newt is supposed to be, Mr. Gingrich chooses to continuously lambast Mr. Obama because as a member of those who sought the presidency and lost, he seems to follow a puppeteer's agenda. In this charade, he continuously seems to manifest an "antebellum mentality" so characteristic of Southern slave norms that saw the "Negro as inferior to Whites" in the "natural order" and their descendants continue to manifest and reinforce that "white supremacy ideology" in the "social order" today. Mr. Newt Gingrich must also know, unless he is working vigorously and actively to change or remedy that mindset, he continues to reflect and helps to perpetuate that "white supremacy ideology."

FREDERICK MONDERSON

BN PHOTO - Part of the gathered audience who watched the Drummers' Grove tribute as part of "Brooklyn Remembers Runaway Slave Samuel Carson."

BN PHOTO - More of the community audience paying tribute to "Runaway" Samuel Carson in Prospect Park's "Drummers' Grove."

BLACK NATIONALISM STILL ALIVE AND WELL

BN PHOTO - Still more of the community audience honoring Samuel Carson on his way to Ghana.

Sixth, as *The New York Times* reported on October 6, 2013, a number of high-ranking Republican politicians and operatives met contemporary with the 2012 presidential election and strategized on how to obstruct Mr. Obama's re-election and his legislative and Executive Agenda. Big names such as former Attorney General, under Ronald Reagan, Ed Meese as well as nearly 20 Non-Government Organizations were mentioned as planning, training and executing a propaganda campaign under the guise of "educating" but in fact "mis-educating" the public about Affordable Care Act dynamics. Some have examined and characterized this behavior as treason or at least sedition! Given Senator Mitch McConnell's classic racist statement regarding President Obama following events of January 2009, many observers theorized about such a gathering that gave McConnell's his marching orders. However, with no taped recordings it simply remained suspended in thin air. However, in the now famous "Thumbs Up" after that first serious financial standoff,

FREDERICK MONDERSON

many agree Mr. McConnell was signaling his handlers and fellow conspirators. Nevertheless, in the debt-ceiling standoff that closed-down Congress, when Speaker Boehner exclaimed "We got 98 percent of what we wanted," the question is "who were the 'We' interest being served?" However, in as much as *The Times* is the paper of record, its revelation provides the dots linking the 2012 to the 2008 behavior aimed at subverting Mr. Obama's legislative agenda from the beginning as the President's opponents manufactured and sustained a climate of hatred and disrespect for the "Nigger in the White House"

BN PHOTO - Dr. Jack Felder on the Airport Tarmac in Ghana, West Africa as part of the contingent accompanying "Bones of the Runaway Samuel Carson" to open the "Door of Return" for African Americans seeking roots in Africa.

Because he is a significant Republican operative, Mr. Gingrich cannot, even if he did, deny knowledge of and participation in the treasonous behavior. That being the case, Mr. Gingrich and the other plotters should be arrested and put on trial for plotting against the

BLACK NATIONALISM STILL ALIVE AND WELL

legally constituted government of the United States headed by President Obama.

Seventh, those who think like Mr. Gingrich expect Mr. Obama to advise them about his strategies for this or that issue. Unfortunately Mr. Gingrich does not realize Republican behavior towards Mr. Obama locates them in the "enemy camp." So why should he inform them of anything, given that they are obstructionist by conviction and blatantly disrespectful by disposition.

Eighth, when it comes to a strategy for dealing with ISIL, a state of affairs Mr. Obama did not create but inherited, while Mr. Gingrich may claim to know its true ramifications; his denial of participation in its origin also affects his assessment of strategy and tactics to combat it.

Ninth, as complex as the ISIL (ISIS) situation is, it needed the President's comprehensive approach, viz., insistence on a broad-based, multi-ethnic government in a post-Malaki Iraq; move to support, train and strengthen the Iraqi forces, Kurds and others in Syria; creation of a coalition of the willing who will assist in their respective areas of expertise; creation of a regional Middle-Eastern coalition of threatened states dispelling the "Crusader" myth; and with this arrangement satisfied, then requesting Congressional authorization to further pound ISIL in Iraq and Syria consistently insisting no American boots or combat soldiers be placed on the ground, except Special Operations groups to lend their expertise in training and to exploit targets of opportunity, are all complexities Mr. Gingrich missed or chose to conveniently ignore.

FREDERICK MONDERSON

BN PHOTO - The African audience that came to welcome, dance and celebrate the arrival of "Runaway Samuel Carson" opening the "Door of Return."

BN PHOTO - Dr. Len Jeffries, leading the American delegation to bring home "Runaway Samuel Carson" to Ghana, West Africa.

Tenth, perhaps one day, after a refresher course, Mr. Gingrich will come to recognize the dynamic nature of Commander-In-Chief

BLACK NATIONALISM STILL ALIVE AND WELL

President Barack Obama, a thinker and theorist, who keeps besting all of his Republican detractors.

BN PHOTO - Sonny Carson is flanked by well-wishers, thankful he returned his ancestor, Samuel Carson opening the "Door of Return" to create a site of pilgrimage in Ghana.

26. OBAMA: A BAD YEAR? NO!"
By
Dr. Fred Monderson

In *The Washington Post* of Sunday December 14, 2014, Chris Cillizza writer on "The Worse Week in Washington" wrote: "Congrats: President Obama, you had the worst year in Washington, again." Arguably this is another "hatchet job on a good and decent leader swimming in a sea alongside 'gators, barracudas, and piranhas that see only his color, emphasize his failures not his brilliance and refuse to accentuate his accomplishments. Like so many others who see his glass, in contradiction, many see his glass three quarters full.

In his beginning this "hatcheteer" stated: "The year began with Obama proposing a set of reforms to the National Security Agency, a result of on-going National Security leaks and ended with mid-term elections that saw his party lose its majority because of the President's unpopularity! In between were continuing challenges to the Affordable Care Act, America's re-entry into Iraq - a war the President had vowed to exit - and memoirs from former Cabinet officials questioning Obama's decision-making and judgment." This and much more was stated.

Who could forget the famous *Time* Magazine cover that "embellished O.J. Simpson's blackness?" In the same way, Mr. Bingo, the Illustrator for *The Washington Post* emphasized Mr. Obama's color" and traditionally this has been to cast such subjects in a bad light. Why did the artist waiting on No. 45 to shout "Bingo" not color the "White guy" Dan Snyder - "Really Bad Year; the Secret Service men - "Bad Year;" and "Not so good year" Chris Christie! Governor Christie lightened his load by throwing his men under the bus, for after all, "The Buck Stops" with him who is responsible for the wrong-doing notwithstanding!

Naturally, on the next page, both writer and illustrator cast Mitch McConnell as having the "best year." It is said, for McConnell, it was the realization of a life-long dream, a not-insignificant accomplishment for a man who has been around politics since the 1960s. McConnell, like Harry Reid whom he will replace in the Senate's top job is not a flashy politician who surged through the ranks in record time. He is a plotter and strategist of the highest order, a man who always has a plan and executes is relentlessly.

BLACK NATIONALISM STILL ALIVE AND WELL

BN PHOTO - Professor James Smalls greets Sonny Carson, whose ancestor, "Runaway Samuel Carson" is the first African enslaved in America to return to Africa.

FREDERICK MONDERSON

BN PHOTO - Dhuruba bin-Waheed, now resident in Ghana, was among the African-American delegation returning the "Bones of the Runaway."

The "founding fathers" were called "freedom fighters" but today such persons are called "terrorists." Sure Mr. McConnell is not flashy. He did, however, flask that "Thumbs Up" swindlers signal: "I got that Nigger in the White House!" That he is a plotter is no doubt! Too bad *The Washington Post* people don't read *The New York Times*, in particular its article on October 6, 2013, depicting the treasonous or seditious plot by which high ranking Republican operatives and their backers tasked to derail Mr. Obama's Presidency. Nearly 20 NGOs were named as being funded, their operatives trained and deployed to "educate" the public about the evils of Obamacare! Former Attorney General Ed Meese under Ronald Reagan was named as a principal actor in the treasonous plot against the duly elected government of the United States of America under the leadership of President Barrack Hussein Obama. As such, every Legislative or Executive initiative by Mr. Obama was scrutinized by Republicans to determine its legality. Edmund Burke admonished, "The only thing necessary for evil to triumph is for

BLACK NATIONALISM
STILL ALIVE AND WELL

good to do or say nothing." Were there no good Republican men or women when all this transpired emboldening "B and C Actors" who took it upon themselves to pile on the disrespect and generate racial hatred towards Mr. Obama?

An article on former Senator John Thompson was entitled "When Politics Meets Art and Art Meets Politics." Consider this scenario! Given some ingredients, much remains "secret" or hidden, we must conjure the outcome.

BN PHOTO - Professor James Smalls embraces Sonny Carson (left); and a colorful "Sister" on the streets of Ghana at "Bones" returning day.

Mitch McConnell "has been around politics since the 1960s. Who can count the deals he made, the toes he stepped on in his climb to

FREDERICK MONDERSON

accomplish his "lifelong dream of becoming Senate Majority Leader. Did he ever entertain the thought of becoming President? Traveling on the same train he very well could have been a protégé of Ed Meese in his striking days. Now, along comes Barrack Obama, an upstart African American who "Surged through the ranks in record time." This was troubling to Ed Meese and his "knights at table" charged with "stopping Obama," resulting in undermining the Presidency, the well-being of the nation, and the welfare of the American people be damned! "Stop Obama by any means necessary!" Remember the sickening expression of the Naval Commander in "A Few Good Men!"

Possessing seniority in the Club, steeped in intimate knowledge of the workings of politics in Washington, Ed Meese recruited his combatants from the active field of powerful Republican operatives. From his office of high visibility as Senate Minority Leader, nearly 50-years in politics perhaps obligated to Ed Meese for chaperoning him along the way, Mitch McConnell was probably the first chosen for this strategy against the President of the United States because of the color of his skin. Throw in "Waterloo" DeMint; "Stupid" Charles Grassley; add "You lie" Wilson; block Allen West from the inner portals; while we're not sure about John McCain, let the uncontrolled, limelight seeking Sarah Palin earn her stripes, and don't trust "God told me to run" Michele Bachmann because our actions may not set well with her boss, the divine!"

Given McConnell "failed in his famous goal 'to make Obama a one-term President'" the operation evidently began after the 2008 election and by the January 2009 Inauguration though it was revealed in 2013 after the 2012 election. Equally, and given Mr. McConnell is "a plotter and strategist of the highest order, a man who always has a plan and executes it relentlessly," a failure in his primary goal does not preclude a secondary objective. Hence, Mr. McConnell's "Party of No" well choreographed track record of obstruction and blaming the other guy is finally rewarded by a hood-winked America public, aided by some failures on Mr. Obama's part, unrelenting legislative "Lilliputians trying to tie Gulliver" and the confessions of insider foxes who cry sour grapes.

BLACK NATIONALISM STILL ALIVE AND WELL

After Dr. Murray was released from prison, having served time as a responsible party in the death of Michael Jackson, he began making statements about his closeness with the singer even mentioning his "fixing Michael's Catheter." That astute comic and radio and TV personality, Steve Harvey who conceptualizes so readily and well responded, "Hell, he is shopping for a book deal!" Panetta and Gates, it can be argued certainly shopped for book deals. In all likelihood financial gain was their primary objective for they perhaps never donated the proceeds to favorite charities.

BN PHOTO - Dr. Leonard Jeffries amidst the Africans welcoming home the "Runaway Samuel Carson."

FREDERICK MONDERSON

BN PHOTO - Africans lining the street to get a glimpse of the "Runaway Slave Samuel Carson" passing in motorcade to place of internment.

One of Obama's problems was choosing "kiss and tell" guys like Panetta and Gates whose autobiographies were nothing more than insider gossip. So much so, "By the next morning, Republicans were using those lines in TV Ads bashing Democrats as Obama clones." So what's new about Hillary? She started the route down the dusty trail and naturally could have refused the Secretary of State position that gave her the foreign policy credentials to be considered a credible 2016 candidate. Of the three "revealers," she is the only one as a potential candidate and for African-Americans who love this President, the jury is still out! Across the board, many should pay attention to a Biblical expression, "Where were you when they crucified my Lord?"

Notwithstanding, "Sizzling" Chris Cillizza, continued to bash Mr. Obama expressing, "The revelation that the IRS was targeting Tea Party groups for special scrutiny; the Edward Snowden leaks about NSA surveillance and the botched rollout of Healthcare.gov to name

BLACK NATIONALISM STILL ALIVE AND WELL

three that happened in 2013." Equally, "Obama's longtime pledge to 'reset' relations with Russia was exposed as frighteningly naïve when President Vladimir Putin moved into Eastern Ukraine with impunity. Obama's response to Putin's aggression - Sanctions - was derided as using a spray bottle to put out a five-alarm fire." Even further, the "Dumb War in Iraq," the Rise of ISIL, the two turncoats and finally Mr. Obama's confession: "I am not on the Ballot. These policies are on the Ballot. Every single one of them!" Finally, that famous Faulkner's line, "The past is never dead. It is not even past" the author uses to characterize Mr. Obama's political fortunes in 2014, the Past keeps Complicating his Present - and Clouding his Future."

BN PHOTO - Ghanaians marching in celebration to welcome Samuel Carson home in Ghana, West Africa.

FREDERICK MONDERSON

BN PHOTO - The hearse that will carry Samuel Carson to the place of his internment.

Separate rules are constructed for Mr. Obama! Mitch McConnell's racist statements in the past have not complicated his present nor clouded his future. Kentuckians voted for the bacon Mr. McConnell could bring home as Senate Majority Leader as opposed to his fresh opponent and so his life-long dream has become a reality.

Sure "Uneasy lies the head that wears the crown," but Obama's second jeopardy is his color. Sure there is political opposition but political opposition worse than the Ferguson Police initial full-court press response to demonstrators is a low for this country that boasts of being at the apex of the political food chain. Something stinks below.

Perhaps if the article's author had not ended the year before December 15, he would have realized some of the myriad accomplishments of Mr. Obama merit a more positive critique. After all, he gave McConnell nearly 60 years to climb the hill that Obama did in 4!

BLACK NATIONALISM STILL ALIVE AND WELL

By the actual Calendar year's end, the economy is better than good. Unemployment is down 26 percent with some 10,000,000 private sector jobs added even though Republicans refused to pass Mr. Obama's jobs bill. Somewhere in America gas prices may be lower than two dollars and Wall Street is looking good with the DOW nearing 18,000, a height never before reached. That Putin fellow, well he is suffering from Obama's sanctions imposed after the invasion. Boastful as Iran's façade is, it too is hurting from sanctions. Obama's incramentalism has worked. The Presidential historian Doug Brinkley characterized President Obama as one who "doesn't over-react."

A consensus now is that Obama's new book on 'The White House Years,' will perhaps be "Wisdom from My Father" warning to beware of snakes in the grass, or don't trust Washington shadows after noon, or is it 9:00 AM. Still, Mr. Obama is too decent a fellow to wallow in the mud. His opponents have already shown their shallowness.

History must judge Mr. Obama favorably for his climate agreement with China; his new Immigration initiative; and the vision to see and with courage chart a new course in Cuba. This particular act, futuristic in its intent like so many Obama initiatives will realign relations in the American and Western hemisphere. It has been described by the White House Correspondent Jim Acosta as "A major, major step forward." It's a pity the "Sizzle" missed the boat, I mean, did not get that e-mail.

FREDERICK MONDERSON

BN PHOTO - Sonny with the "Chiefs" reflect above the coffin of Samuel Carson.

BLACK NATIONALISM STILL ALIVE AND WELL

BN PHOTO - Dr. Gafney, Funeral Director, with his Bouquet of Flowers, with persons in the background, all excited about the historic situation.

FREDERICK MONDERSON

BN PHOTO - Dr. Jack Felder beside Dr. Gafney and Bishop Shivers and others on the ground in Ghana as part of the American delegation.

BN PHOTO - Again, movement of the "Bones of the Runaway Samuel Carson" at the Drummers" Grove in Prospect Park, Brooklyn, New York.

BLACK NATIONALISM STILL ALIVE AND WELL

BN PHOTO - Professor Patterson (facing the Camera) and Dr. Gafney (backing the camera) (Left); and Dr. Jack Felder on the railway lines in Ghana, West Africa (right).

27. THE MUMMY MYSTIQUE
By
Dr. Fred Monderson

For a great period of his interaction with Egypt, Dr. Yosef ben-Jochannan has criticized how the authorities have treated the mummies of the ancient Egyptians. He has specifically singled out the Cairo Museum of Egyptian Antiquities for their disregard of the sanctity of the sacred and ancient relics. While some consideration can be given to ordinary mummies, the royal mummies are a special matter. While along with others, he advocated for returning the mummies to the sanctity of their tombs, he insisted on providing for security in their resting places. Prior to his death, he was appalled that the Egyptian authorities now put on display with commercialized viewing these sacred and revered royal remains. While not a favorite of his, comparatively he explained, contemporary European royal families would certainly not allow public eyes to view their sacred dead.

The particular archaeological discoveries that shaped Dr. Ben's concern for the Egyptian mummies were essentially three in number. These were; the discovery of the "Deir el Bahari Cache" in 1881-82; the mummies found in the tomb of Amenhotep II in 1898; and the discovery of the tomb of Tutankhamon by Howard Carter in 1922. This latter occurred one hundred years to the date of Champollion's deciphering the Hieroglyphic Code. However, while a great deal of sensationalism surrounded the recovery of these special relics, subjecting them to official, scholarly and public scrutiny for study and on display caused persons of concern to voice opposition to this form of crass, commercial treatment.

Another mummy of special significance, while not known at the time, would turn out to be that of Queen Hatshepsut who built her mortuary temple at Deir el Bahari. The queen's mummy, languishing in the by-ways of unidentified persons had one outstanding characteristic no one had paid much attention to. This was a missing tooth. As it turned out, there was a personal toilet cabinet of the queen that was well-regarded. Only recently opened for inspection, it was discovered to contain a missing tooth. Lo and behold, a bee-hive of activity emerged to determine whose tooth it was. Then someone remembered there was a female mummy, languishing in the realm of the unknown that also had a missing tooth. Fired-up interest assembled a scientific team who, through dental science, x-ray technology, a committed objective, and so the scholars were able to determine the tooth fitted the missing space on the unidentified mummy.

BLACK NATIONALISM STILL ALIVE AND WELL

BN PHOTO - Dr. Felder poses in front of a street market as others look on.

BN PHOTO - Dr. Jack Felder congratulates Sonny Carson for keeping the pledge while Bishop Shivers' son looks on to the left.

FREDERICK MONDERSON

Knowing whose tooth it was; that fit exactly where the missing tooth belonged; scholars were able to determine the mummy was actually that of Queen Hatshepsut. This was a remarkable scientific project that correctly identified the mummy as that of Queen Hatshepsut! Without a doubt, this was the second mummy scholars have been able to correctly identify. That is not to say, the other mummies identified are not who they are recognized but theirs is through circumstantial evidence, a coffin, mummy wrappings, a tomb, etc. However, that of the Queen is more uncontroverted.

While this is so, and coming after, Dr. Zahi Hawass had pointedly stated, "Tutankhamon is the only king of whom we are absolutely certain because we found him in a sealed tomb." Now the queen's identification makes this a second such realization.

However, in regards to the discoveries mentioned, the "Deir el Bahari Cache" in particular, upon discovery of the hiding place of this sacred depository and realization the Rasul Brothers, among others at Luxor, were looting the place and releasing valuable artifacts on the market; official scrutiny caught the culprits and had them reveal the location of the valuables. A whole host of mummies and royal paraphernalia were discovered, scattered throughout the floor of the hiding place, perhaps tumbled out as the thieves rummaged coffin after coffin to find marketable pieces. What the discoverers did realize; first, there was an enormous amount of wealth and some of the most important monarchs, particularly of the Eighteenth Dynasty began surfacing on the market. The "mummy cache" seemed placed in this location for safe-keeping; perhaps, in some upheaval facing the nation and the authorities thought this a fitting resting place, even though the place was crowded with artifacts. There was evidence of confusion regarding whether this or that king was in his correct coffin. Even more important, there seemed to be confusion as to who each king really was, even though there was still sufficient markings, mummy cloth and otherwise, to determine the exact names.

BLACK NATIONALISM STILL ALIVE AND WELL

BN PHOTO - Dr. Jack Felder, Funeral Director Dr. Gafney and Bishop Shivers "shake on it" in Ghana, West Africa.

BN PHOTO - Young and old, all enthused and alarmed by the excitement generated "The day the Runaway came home."

FREDERICK MONDERSON

In the flurry of sensationalism surrounding the discovery, authorities and scholars gathered and eventually unrolled the mummies, taking measurements, doing x-ray studies and examining the bandages and other body jewelry placed there in the wrapping. While the studies revealed much in terms of the physical make-up of the kings and others deposited in the hiding place, it seemed the interpretation of the racial identity of these great Africans actually did not properly reflect the true record. Given that much of this was not only being conducted during the emerging science of Egyptology and the attendant disciplines that would eventually be associated with it, there was the question of ever-present nineteenth century "white supremacy ideology" and practice then prevalent around the world and how this shaped interpretation of the data. Thus, this unfolding phenomenon was not without taint perpetuated by representatives who were colonizing the world, exterminating peoples even killing excavators, seizing cultural artifacts, and interpreting history that showed Europeans as morally, culturally and of course militarily superior to, especially non-white people. Thus, this behavior and mindset culminated in much of 19th Century's belief that Africans could not have built Egyptian civilization, the misinterpreted evidence seeming to point to solidifying that the ancient Egyptians were Caucasians. Naturally, closer inspection proved otherwise.

As discovery after discovery reclaimed much of the ancient Egyptian history, artifacts and personnel in the 19th Century, the tomb of the 18th Dynasty king Amenhotep II in 1898 revealed another cache of important persons. This discovery, therefore, added to a great number of known kings and queens whose rule extended through the New Kingdom and later. Again, the same problem that attended the first find applied to this second. Of interest, however, another important revelation became manifest.

BLACK NATIONALISM STILL ALIVE AND WELL

BN PHOTO - Young Ghanaians were very much part of the excitement of the "Runaway Samuel Carson"

FREDERICK MONDERSON

BN PHOTO - Sonny Carson holds a press conference with Dhuruba bin Waheed beside him.

BN PHOTO - Part of the "near gravesite excitement" pays tribute to Samuel Carson.

BLACK NATIONALISM STILL ALIVE AND WELL

BN PHOTO - Professor James Smalls leads a number of Chiefs to the internment gravesite.

Brian Fagan's book *The Rape of the Nile* chronicled how much artifacts were removed from Egypt especially during the 19th Century, the skullduggery involved, who were the principal players and which the museums, institutions and private collectors were beneficiary from the thievery. Imagine as late as 2015, some 815 pieces were acquired by Museums in Britain alone. Imagine this number, perhaps times over, for the duration of the 20th Century across all Europe and America and perhaps this only scratches the surface. That is to say, practically every major European nation had been involved in collecting Egyptian artifacts. Though the Cairo museum was host it was not until the discovery of the "Deir el Bahari Cache" was it able "to be on par with the Turin Museum," as an example, that had been collecting for the longest. Thus, the "Amenhotep II Cache" added to Egyptian respectability in this regard as it struggled to compete with ill-gotten artificial gains as well as to institute controls on who, what, how, and when of archaeological and anthropological investigation, excavation and removal of artifacts from the country unless sanctioned under official supervision. By the time of the Tutankhamon discovery in 1922, there were sufficient regulation in place as well as the prohibitive nature of sensationalism surrounding something as great as the discovery of an intact 18th Dynasty tomb. Therefore, skullduggery was played down and much of the treasure of the Tutankhamon trove remained accounted for.

Nevertheless, the contradiction associated with the question of 'Who were the ancient Egyptians?' has remained a point of contention to this day. To recap, individuals as John David Wortham in *The Genesis of British Egyptology 1549-1906* (Norman: University of Oklahoma Press, 1971: 9) has written: "Great progress was made during the nineteenth century in the study of Egyptian mummification. Augustus Bozzi Granville, a physician and student of Coptic, undertook the earliest nineteenth century dissection of a mummy at his London home in 1825. From his detailed dissection he correctly concluded that the ancient Egyptians were Caucasian."

This is interesting and misleading because the statement and publication came 146 years after the dissection. However, four "epoch," at least, erupted in proximity to Wortham's statement as reflective of the prevailing view that questions the objectivity of this position all such as articulated and held to be the standard today. These are, essentially, (1) The 1820 *Gentleman's Magazine* article; (2) The discovery of the "Deir el Bahari Cache" and the mummies of Amenhotep II's tomb as explained in Gaston Maspero's *The Royal Mummies*; (3) The 1965 Cairo Publication of H.S.K. Bakry's *A Brief Study of Mummies and Mummification*; and (4) William Arnett's statement in *Evidence for the Development of Evidence of Hieroglyphics in Southern Upper Egypt* in response to Cheikh Anta Diop's principal position in *African Origins of Civilization: Myth or Reality*.

BLACK NATIONALISM STILL ALIVE AND WELL

BN PHOTO - Beside and in the river at Assin Manso, near the place of internment.

BN PHOTO - The famous river at Assin Manso where enslaved Africans were allowed to have their last bath, confined in nearby "Slave Castle" before passage through the "Door of No Return."

FREDERICK MONDERSON

28. JITU WEUSI "MOUNTAIN OF A MAN"
By
Dr. Fred Monderson

Jitu Weusi, Mountain of a Man, born Les Campbell, we mourn your passing but we rejoice for your presence and lasting contributions and we honor you as we have honored Malcolm X, Martin Luther King, Jr., Marcus Garvey, Rosa Parks and Sonny Carson! Quintessential leader who would not accept the "thirty pieces of silver," who could not be bribed, you stood tall and firm as a resolute fighter for justice and social upliftment of Black African people, irrespective! You made your presence felt in many an arena. Educational activist, social critic and strategist confronting life's many challenges, your contributions to your people's march of progress earned you the "living legend" award and because of your vision our people will not perish!

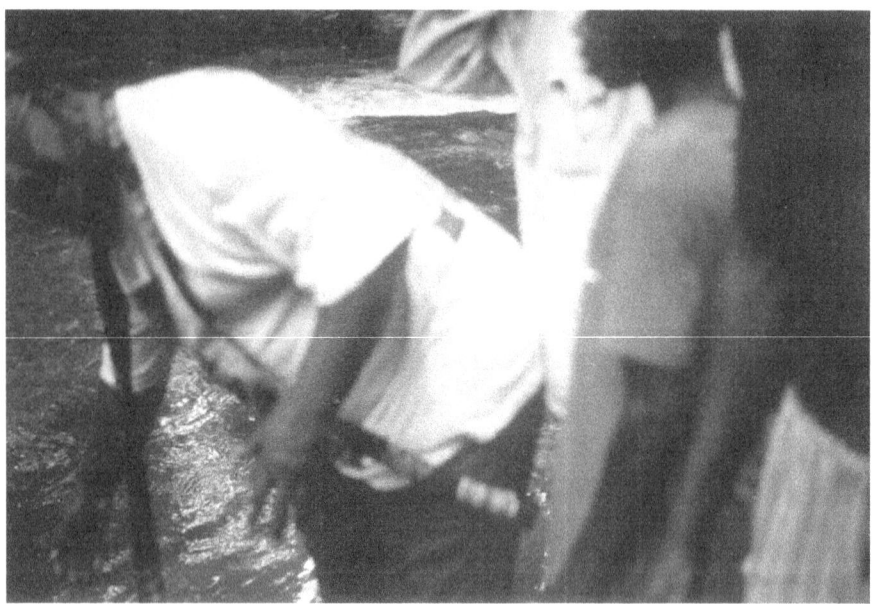

BN PHOTO - Dr. Jack Felder "tastes the waters" of the river at Assin Manso, Ghana.

BLACK NATIONALISM STILL ALIVE AND WELL

Indomitable spirit, leader in education, man of unbounded integrity and insightful thinking, we honor you because you fought the good fight, you kept the faith, and in this you were a perpetual light of social conscience. Creative genius of "The East" who innovated the African Street Festival now the International African Arts Festival among many other creations, your place among revered ancestors assured, the pantheon of black champions now have a new star!

Brooklyn Icon, fearless and from "The East" to Attica and Ocean-Hill-Brownsville Decentralization to the Franklin Avenue Shuttle struggle, as well as from the public school classroom to the college campus and back to the public school, your unmatched contributions for educational excellence and social justice are too numerous to mention. With the desire for quality education as watchword and hallmark of your work of upliftment, educator, activist, headmaster, advocate, administrator, your strivings established the highest standards for intellectual development of our youth.

Guiding light, visionary with clear sightedness, the influence of your creative classroom educational activities matched the brilliance of the brightest day, inspiring many to develop skills to achieve success. Resolute nationalist, Pan-African stalwart, your aspirations for your people's progress were seldom surpassed; and your equally untiring efforts as member of the "Bones Committee" helped assure "the Runaway" Samuel Carson successful passage for internment in Ghana, West Africa, opening the "Door of Return."

FREDERICK MONDERSON

BN PHOTO - A young woman does the same "Taste the waters" of Assin Manso.

 Master organizer, unquestionably in education and in Black Solidarity Day activism, politics and jazz organization, your name resounds as an effective and successful strategist of exceptional note. Son of Brooklyn, man of integrity, fortitude and resilience, allow us to clone your image, persona and strategic thinking abilities as an effective tool in our ongoing struggle for social, political and economic empowerment for advancement of our people.

Man of action and boundless vision, though sorrowful at your passing, we celebrate your creative spirit with sweet melodic sounds similarly played by the Jazz Consortium you orchestrated and forever memories of you will be remembered through the African Street Festival, a contribution of immense proportions.

Revered leader, man of many seasons, it is our especial hope, your righteous memory, image and name will forever be a part of the history of struggle to uplift all people, particularly Black people. We also hope the children will remember you because we honor you as father, husband, tactician and community leader for your unrelenting

BLACK NATIONALISM STILL ALIVE AND WELL

struggle to advance our cause and make Brooklyn a better place for them and all other residents.

BN PHOTO - Part of the excitement surrounding the arrival of "Runaway Samuel Carson" to Assin Manso, for internment.

BN PHOTO - Women were instrumental in reception of the "Bones of Runaway Samuel Carson."

FREDERICK MONDERSON

BN PHOTO - The place of final repose for the "Runaway Samuel Carson" so he can stop "Running" in Ghana.

BLACK NATIONALISM STILL ALIVE AND WELL

BN PHOTO - The "Bones of Runaway Samuel Carson" finally finds rest (left); and Professor James Smalls, perennially on guard in interest of African people, watches as Samuel Carson probably offers his "Thank you."

Brother we salute you, we praise you, we honor you, and we thank you for a brilliant, lengthy, constructive and successful life of meaningful service to the Brooklyn Community and African people worldwide. We are grateful you inspired us to persevere in the manner of Jitu Weusi's Way of integrity, stability, farsightedness and constructive service. This is the name Claver Place, the place of your origins, should be named, for your life has been an effective beacon that reflected the highest illumination, standards and aspirations of the Borough of Brooklyn and the best example of black manhood.

FREDERICK MONDERSON

BN PHOTO - Another look at the "Decorated Final Resting Place of Samuel Carson."

BN PHOTO - That "Pan-Africanism Lives On!!!" is the title of this Forum and Dr. Len Jeffries (extreme left) sits in support.

BLACK NATIONALISM STILL ALIVE AND WELL

Dominic Carter stands alongside Emma and Luis before Rev. Al Sharpton's portrait at the 25th **National Action Network** Anniversary.

FREDERICK MONDERSON

Portrait of Rev. Al Sharpton unveiled at national Action Network's 25th Anniversary celebration, April 16, 2016.

BLACK NATIONALISM STILL ALIVE AND WELL

29.   HAPPY MOTHERS' DAY
By
Dr. Fred Monderson

As a dutiful and loving son, I'm apt to say my mother, Mitta, has been the "Best Mother." Now as we celebrate this time of recognition for the wonderful work, particularly African-American, mothers have accomplished in the task of motherhood, in rural, urban and all over sub-urban America and elsewhere, we need to give special praise for their unselfish efforts. Their love, concern, caring and commitment deserve our unending adulation and support. Such a greeting comes from their sons and daughters, husbands and brothers and all well-wishers. This becomes even more real with the cards, perfume, gifts, candy, flowers, dinner, entertainment, theater, etc., they so rightly deserve! Such then, are affectionate sentiments extended to those loving, compassionate, uncritical, understanding, pleasant and forgiving mothers, stalwarts of the African-American community, families in general and the family institution so crucial to our very survival.

BN PHOTO - The Ladies of Alpha Kappa Alpha Sorority, Inc. were there for the 50th Anniversary "March on Washington."

FREDERICK MONDERSON

BN PHOTO - Boots (right) and a friend came out for "Obama at Sharpton's Affair."

For this Mothers' Day in the land of Red, White and Blue, an interesting connection can be established, when viewing the historical landscape of Africa for evidence of creative accomplishments of African motherhood.

Lucy at 3.2 million years in the Hadar region of Ethiopia is an early ancestor of the African experience. Later, the "Scientific Eve" had been identified as an African female who roamed the East African plains 150,000 years ago. Through DNA reconstruction she has been credited with being the mother of all existing humans on earth.

The Great Mother of Kemetic/Egyptian cosmogony, Nut was married to Geb and they produced children Osiris, Isis, Seth, Nephthys, and Horus. From this age of deity through the last prehistoric times, males being interred in shallow graves, besides other artifacts, had included carved figurines of these earliest African "mothers."

BLACK NATIONALISM STILL ALIVE AND WELL

BN PHOTO - There is a "Message in the Message" of this sign about Incarceration.

However, the first great dynastic mother was Neith-hotep, wife of Narmer and mother of Aha, his successor. The "Narmer Macehead" depicts this African queen seated beside her husband atop a flight of stairs as part of some celebratory occasion, as an example of equality. At the end of the first dynasty Mer-Neith was both Queen and Pharaoh. Hetepheres, wife of Snefru, founder of the fourth dynasty, was mother of Khufu, grandmother of Khafre and great-grandmother of Menkaure, builders of the 3 great pyramids at Giza. What an illustrious progeny to which she gave life, courage and ingenuity as such attested by the greatest form of architectural accomplishments, mountains of splendidly constructed stone, defying time in all their majestic beauty.

Von Bissing, a German Egyptologist, writing in *American Journal of Archaeology* recounts an incident in the war in between Heracleopolis and Thebes during the 11th Dynasty. Intef of Heracleopolis began the consolidation of Upper Kemet/Egypt after the collapse of the Old Kingdom and the resulting First Intermediate

FREDERICK MONDERSON

Period, which led to establishment of the Middle Kingdom. Having mobilized his forces, finally Intef took the field of battle against Mentuhotep, the Theban. However, coming out of the pass on the "Plains of Thebes" he encountered Mentuhotep's superior army ready and waiting.

BN PHOTO - This couple proudly stands on the Great Lawn with other brothers in rear and further on the Washington Monument all attesting to Minister Farrakhan's insistence, "Justice or Else."

Thereupon, Intef called upon his mother Queen Achtothes to broker a peace with Mentuhotep's mother Queen Aam to save the day's fighting between these two African forces. These mothers then presided over the peace as preparatory to challenge the Memphite prominence, and unify the nation to usher in one of the greatest periods of intellectual, literary and imperial expansion, consolidation and reorganization. Such honor indicates the high esteem of the well-respected African mother. Such a mother, whose son is pictured "with black flesh" and very instrumental in establishing the continuity of Old and Middle Kingdom cultural, religious and scientific development in ancient Africa, has a special place in the iconography of African historical reconstruction.

BLACK NATIONALISM STILL ALIVE AND WELL

The Middle Kingdom came to an end and gave way to the Second Intermediate Period that brought the Hyksos invaders who held the northern land of Kemet captive for over a century. Sekenenra Tao I and his wife Tetisheri, "great royal wife and king's mother," saw her husband fall in the protracted war of liberation against northern domination that ultimately freed the land from the foreign invaders. After her husband died, a palace coup broke out. Flinders Petrie credits this Seventeenth Dynasty as "Coming from Nubia and holding Thebes as its Capital." Tetisheri rallied the loyalists and put down the uprising. She became regent to her son Sekenenra Tao II who married his full sister Ahotep but was also felled by an axe blow to the head. She then supported his son Kamose who fought the Hyksos but his brother Aahmose completed their expulsion and established the Eighteenth Dynasty and New Kingdom. Then Aahmose married his sister, Aahmes-Nefertari.

BN PHOTO - Tutankhamon and his wife in the Temple of Luxor. It is a travesty how their faces have been disfigured because they look so African!

FREDERICK MONDERSON

BN PHOTO - Young Mother Kashida Maloney of Brooklyn, New York, stands between two statues of King Tut as an Egyptian native looks on.

The sister marriage now seems justified, for, having now won the country back, whom would grandmother Tetisheri have approved to support her grand-son in the difficult tasks ahead. None but the loyal Nefertari, his sister! Aahmes-Nefertari became a distinguished ancestress of the Eighteenth dynasty and she and her son Amenhotep I were later deified with a temple built in their honor at Thebes. Her grandson Tuthmose I overran Palestine and provided strength, stability and wealth to Kemet. Much later in the Tuthmoside dispute between Tuthmose II, Hatshepsut and Tuthmose III, the woman who dared to seize power and rule for two decades, built the wonderful Deir el-Bahari temple modeled after Mentuhotep's 500 year old nearby masterpiece, she would later boast of her blood ties to the ancestress of the Eighteenth Dynasty, Aahmes-Nefertari.

Another and even more important observation about Aahmes-Nefertari is her portrait in the British Museum. The bejeweled Aahmes-Nefertari, whose name is in a cartouche signaling royalty, is depicted as "painted black" and wearing the fashion of the times, a long flowing robe of red, white and blue. Imagine! The first time

BLACK NATIONALISM STILL ALIVE AND WELL

the tri-colors red, white and blue are pictured together in history, we see then on a Black African Queen, 1500 years Before Christ!

Amenhotep III built a palace, Malcata, for his wife, the Nubian Queen Tiy. Their son Amenhotep IV married the daughter of Dushrata, Thadukippa of Syria, whose name the Africans changed to Nefertiti the "fair one cometh." Aahmes-Nefertari, on the other hand, was called "the most beautiful one cometh." Notwithstanding and throughout it all, Amon reigned supreme as deity with his wife Mut, and their son Khonsu, forming the Theban Triad.

Rameses II of the next and powerful Nineteenth Dynasty, built his magnificent worship temple at Abu Simbel and right next to it he carved another temple to his beloved Nubian wife, Nefertari, signaling the great love and respect he held for her.

During the "Golden Age" of West Africa, Ibn Battuta, Islamic traveler in that region, tells of the hospitality mothers extended to the visitor who arrived at their village. Interestingly enough, Queen Nzinga may not have been a mother for she was too busy fighting the Portuguese who enslaved her people. Her resistance nevertheless symbolized an in-clandestine abhorrence to degradation of the African mother during the horrendous Middle Passage, slave trade and slavery. Unfortunately she had no counterpart in America where the enslaved African mother was often abused by the oppressor. However, Yaa Asantewaa was the Ghanaian Queen mother who fought the British. On the other hand, Harriet Tubman, as mother of the Underground Railroad was very busy, heading north with brothers and sisters on the way to freedom and thus etched her name in the annals of Black female revolutionary consciousness.

FREDERICK MONDERSON

BN PHOTO - While one sign emphasizes economics, the other shows the strength of the first **Million Man March**, both point to the potential power of the African-American, especially his "One Trillion Dollars" annual spending habit.

The Educator Mary McLeod Bethune gave much so that Blacks would become educated to hurdle barriers in American scientific, industrial, educational, artistic, political and economic enterprises. Amy Jacques Garvey resolutely supported her husband Marcus Garvey. Mitta Mary Monderson, who on March 6, 1957, dressed in the colors of the Ghanaian flag on the day of their independence and sent a clear and conscientious message of Pan-African nationalist consciousness. Rosa Parks, "mother of the Civil Rights Movement," Coretta Scott King, Myrlie Evers and Betty Shabaaz, "Mothers of Martyrdom," were "first nationalist mothers" and "elder statespersons," who have all been pillars of monumental resoluteness in defense of rights and human dignity for African Americans and women of all persuasions and ethnicities. In process they assisted America to move towards living out the true meaning of its creed.

BLACK NATIONALISM STILL ALIVE AND WELL

Also, let us never forget the wives of W.E.B. Dubois, Booker T. Washington, Paul Robeson, Dr. Ben's Gertrude, Dr. John H. Clarke's wife, Sister Cybil Williams-Clarke, Dr. Leonard James' Marilyn, and Dr. Leonard Monroe' Nellie and we must give kudos to Bishop Chess' wife Martha Chess.

BN PHOTO - Former Councilwoman Una Clarke, mother of Congresswoman Yvette Clarke, surrounded by and listening to her constituents.

So on this Mothers Day let us salute the many mothers, including Fannie Lou Hamer, Queen Mother Moore, Marcus Garvey's Black Cross Nurses, Winnie Mandela "Queen of the Black World" and those as Enid Forde, Marjorie Matthews, and Hazel Dukes who brought sunshine to board rooms; Mrs. Francis Hagler's concern about educating the young; also Lou Ann Dyer, Mrs. Taylor, the PTA mothers; Cherise Preville, "Mother Olga," Cherise Maloney, Carmen Monderson, Audrey Monderson, Keisha Johnson. Those mothers are holding it down in the best way, among the beautiful ones such as Sister Barbara, Claudia, and Fina as well as Connie Lesold. Then there are the "Mothers gone to heavenly glory" Ms. Maude Holloway, Elsie Richardson, Margaret Vinson, and Ruth Goring in Crown Heights. We can add Debra Souvenir-Tyndale, Debra Lesane, Hope Mason of Kings County Hospital Center, as well as LaRay Brown of Health and Hospitals Corporation, and Jean Leon and Yolanda Lezama-Clarke, as well as Una Clarke who did very well as mother to Congresswoman Yvette Clarke. Neville

FREDERICK MONDERSON

Norville's Claire, Gloria Brown, Michelle Obama, Estelle Brown, Delores Brown, Pat Richardson, Pamela Covington, Rasheedah Nasir, Martha Chess, Njonji Granville, Michelle George, Adele Flateau, Princess Esty and Dejanne Taylor, Sister Barbara, "Miss Pearl" Weatherspoon, Enid Graham, Mavis Hill, and "Aunty" are all stalwart mothers. Joycelyn Loncke and her sister Loncke-Waithe are doing wonderful things as "Pan African Mothers" in Guyana. This greeting also goes out to all the other mothers who vote, go to school, are in business and administration, cook, sew, teach, comfort, go to church, shop, wash, work, offer guidance to the young, and doctor and support their Black men. Have a Glorious and Happy Mothers' Day! You have stood long and hard in struggle, challenges, trials and tribulation. Now stand tall and receive your richly deserved "bouquet of recognition and respect" as the quintessential essence of a race, for your ancestors have been mothers of the human race.

BN PHOTO - "Mothers on an Educational Tour to Egypt," join Cherise Maloney of Brooklyn (fourth from right) along with a gentleman, Dr. Leonard Monroe of Ypsilanti, Michigan.

BLACK NATIONALISM STILL ALIVE AND WELL

BN PHOTO - This is certainly one way to enjoy the **Million Man March** just "cooling it!"

30. THE POWER OF WOMAN!
By
Dr. Fred Monderson

Recently, the decision to remove the Confederate Flag from the South Carolina State Capitol grounds by Governor Nikki Haley signaled "a great day in South Carolina." But seriously, it is difficult to find another day of such significance in the South where the universal soul of humanity could class this as a joyous occasion. Nevertheless, the flag has now been taken down along with its pole, given due honors, and deposited in a South Carolina military history museum where the Civil War conflict's end 150-years ago will be most adequately remembered. However, we must never forget Malcolm X did remind us, "History is a good teacher," not simply because it focuses on a single event but most important it can reflect the span and flow of time for purposes of constructive study.

FREDERICK MONDERSON

BN PHOTO - Jesse Jackson and Marc Morial of the National Urban League lead marchers at the 50th Anniversary of the "1963 March on Washington."

Speaking of history, we need be reminded also, that while today Governor Nikki Haley is a hero, that new found fame is recent making her "born again" because from her lips, more than a year ago, this action would not have been possible and certainly not from her efforts. Nonetheless, in signing the new bill the governor paid tribute to the "Martyred 9," and reserved a "Pen from the signing" for each of the victims of Charleston's "Mother Emanuel" Baptist Church whose catastrophic end proved the catalyst to begin the consideration and debate that, at times proved contentious with many lawmakers voicing the historical significance and "heritage" of the flag as southern resistance to "tyranny." On the other hand, some lawmakers received oral and written death threats because the light in their humanity, especially in commiseration with the massacred victims, condemned the repugnance of the symbolism of South Carolina flying the Confederate flag. For example, an article in *The New York Times* entitled "State House Oratory Reflects South Carolina's Division Over Rebel Flag," Thursday, July 9, 2015, p. 1, 15, in quoting Weldon Hammond, 76, a Black South Carolinian who

BLACK NATIONALISM STILL ALIVE AND WELL

was "involved in anti-segregation protests in the early 1960s, and spent hours Wednesday in the front row of the House gallery with his wife, Loretta, hoping to see a change that to him was too long in coming," explained: "'It is an insult and a hurt, especially when they say that flag is about heritage. It is definitely something that for all my life we've been trying to disinherit.'" Equally significant, Jerry Govan (D) a South Carolina State Representative saw the flag as a symbol of "hate, viciousness, racism and white supremacy."

The Black residents of that state, long the victims of slavery and resulting racial discrimination, have always felt victimized by this symbol of "white supremacy" they see flying proudly on lands belonging to all the citizens of the state. However, one voice in opposition that stood out remarkably well, a descendant of the Confederate President Jefferson Davis rose to the occasion in that august chamber and made a profound and impassioned plea for removal of the flag, identifying it as a symbol of "hate" and "racism." That is, correctly critical of "heritage" in this instance, Representative Jenny Anderson Horne, a Republican, emotionally exhorted the body as opposition and delaying tactics took hold, by saying "The people of Charleston deserve swift and immediate removal of that flag from these grounds. I cannot believe that we do not have the heart in this body to do something meaningful." Still, as the man said, "It was long in coming."

FREDERICK MONDERSON

BN PHOTO - "Biggie" and the Missus were there to add their support for the **Million Man March's** mantra of "**Justice or Else**!"

That emotional filled voice, "speaking truth to power" may have made the difference in swaying the vote, but it also signaled the awesome "Power of Woman" committed to "bringing effective change for good into the world." But, truly speaking that profound expression of conscience on behalf of advancing the cause of humanity is not germane to a single race. In many respects, the Black Woman has been so engaged, whether as mother, divinity, ruler or religious worshipper. That powerful significance of womanhood from ancient times first exemplified in Eve, of the African Plains some 250,000 years ago, then as the ancient Egyptians reminded us, the species not only carried the divine essence but were also goddesses who enabled and empowered females of royal blood to transmit that special divine spark unto the Pharaoh as king, certainly contributed to himself being a divinity on earth. This phenomenon weighed significantly when, in his critique of a "Caucasian ancient Egyptian," Cheikh Anta Diop in *African*

BLACK NATIONALISM STILL ALIVE AND WELL

Origins of Civilization: *Myth or Reality* argued for matriarchy over patriarchy, and also dictating matrilineal over patrilineal descent. Equally and important, these Black and indispensible human specimens have been victimized through death, harsh treatment, the indignity of economic peonage and unemployment, social ostracism while experiencing the horrors of having loved ones subject to the terror of beatings, hangings, tar and feathers, and even murder. They have been restrained by mechanical devices, even having their elderly men called "boy," and having to defer to others because of their race and untold times been victimized within New World Slavery. Many met untimely death over the centuries of slavery, even after freedom and guarantees of the Civil War Amendments to the Constitution. Nonetheless, while Governor Haley and Representative Horne must be remembered for their bold and courageous stance in face of racial bigotry masquerading as historic and cultural pride, the future needs to know how we got to this epoch making moment and the role the Black Woman of yesteryear played in that continuously unfolding historical drama often named the American experience.

BN PHOTO - Beauty in the shade, sits next to posters of Michelle Obama and her daughters.

FREDERICK MONDERSON

From the foundation of America the Black Woman has been an essential lynchpin in the growth and development of this nation. After all, she had equal representation aboard slave ships bound for plantation servitude in the New World and America. It stands to reason she fought kidnappers on the African coast; endured the stench and humiliation in the Cape Coast castles; been sexually and otherwise assaulted in those dungeons and aboard slave ships; been psychologically abused, disrespected and even more so, to see her man physically and emotionally abused and psychologically disfigured as they both endured the Middle Passage's and Triangular Trade's unbelievable horrors. As Malcolm X, that veritable fount of modern wisdom, put it: "We did not land on Plymouth Rock, Plymouth Rock landed on us!"

Thus, in the entirety of that long train of abuse, the Black Woman was subject to all the physical and emotional agonies the Black Man was a victim of. Most important, it's on record slave-catchers and slave-dealers mostly took the youngest and most beautiful African Woman of child-bearing age they could find to further their financial and commercial interests. On board slave ships during the Atlantic journey women were sexually and psychologically abused in front of their chained and captive men. Upon arrival, let's not talk about the agonies of family separation; significantly the beautiful Black Woman was victimized through being examined naked in public by licentious traders and perspective buyers; then leering overseers played their part on the plantation; and finally by the masters and their sons whose sexual desires were unrestrained making her a victim of "sex on demand" and the emotional cruelty such a condition created.

BLACK NATIONALISM
STILL ALIVE AND WELL

BN PHOTO - More of Jesse Jackson and Marc Morial leading the "March on Washington," 2013. Notice how Jesse keeps his "Eyes on the Prize!"

Who could countenance the humiliation of Black men having their intended wife "sampled" the night before their wedding? Just as significant, in the TV Series, "Fight Against Slavery" narrated by Ruby Dee in the 1970s during the Bi-Centennial era an interesting scene is vividly remembered. A young Englishwoman had arrived on a plantation in the West Indies. As she was being escorted by a planter, the braggart tried to impress the young woman about his sexual prowess. Essentially stated, he "wanted to de-flower a young slave virgin for every year he lived" and had been true to his word. Modestly, she asked, "Well, how old are you?" In that broad, boastful smile the braggart responded, "I am now 65 years old!" You do the math!

This type of wanton and unrestrained behavior as they made them "Stand in Fear" is a miniscule example of the "cage of sexual tyranny" the African, Black Woman endured throughout the period of both Slave Trade and Slavery. Without question, though this particular instance occurred on the West India Plantations, it was by no means restricted to that region. Following British Abolition of the Slave Trade in 1807, America outlawed the trade in 1808. This important development came after a 20-year period of political contention as lawmakers throughout the Union debated the economic feasibility of this decision. In that 1787-1788 "age of constitutional development" after independence; the slave holding South, and South Carolina as a principal slave owning state, was adamant about political representation for membership in the new Union. Hence the consensus arrived at was the "Three-fifths Clause" or "Three-fifths Compromise" where "5 Black Men were counted for 3 White Men." The Black woman did not count for political representation. Nonetheless and factually speaking, when today, White Women argue they are worth 70 cents to the White Man's dollar, we first of all must wonder how much the Black Women as Harriet, Diana and Sandy are worth. Even more important, there is no way to gauge what the Black Woman was worth in 1808, not as a contributor to society but as property, or more properly, chattel.

Notwithstanding, in outlawing the Atlantic Slave Trade, an "Internal Slave Trade" developed in the "Deep South," very much the "lynching states," where "Slave Farms" subjected the Black Woman to the most inhuman factory-like sexual breeding practices and experience. Many were given a choice, "Make so many children and the master will free you!" One woman is on record of producing 36 children for her master and still she died a slave. Naturally each child represented more wealth for the master on the plantation or in that lucrative "Slave Market" brought there in "Slave Coffles" to be sold at "Slave auctions" especially in such areas as Charleston, South Carolina, one of the biggest slave markets in all the land!

Given every form of mistreatment the Black Man was subject to, the Black woman was a part of; whether in the "House" or in the "Field," the Black Woman was not only engaged in productive laboring but remained an object of admiration and potential seizure by Black men, White men, overseers, owners, or just passing merchants looking to be amused by a defenseless female. However, while the moral suasion of the "Slave Community" was a check on

BLACK NATIONALISM STILL ALIVE AND WELL

the Black Male's sexual appetite, no such checks applied to White lust.

BN PHOTO - One of the strategies of the March was to put the children up front, for they are the future and their well-being is at stake as we move forward, fifty years after "1963."

Nonetheless, and despite the obstacles and psychological trauma endured, the Black woman stood by her man, raised a family, sought an education, struggled to contribute to society whether as cook, domestic nurse, poet, abolitionist, teacher, scientist, doctor, medical nurse, lawyer, judge, revolutionary, Underground Railroad Conductor, and even preacher. In that journey, the faith, fortitude and humanity of the Black woman, especially the praying ones, proved to be a source of strength in an exceptionally drawn out and moving experience. However, what makes the Charleston Massacre so insidiously different, six of the nine were women, slain "On their knees praying to their god!" Throughout history, even the most barbaric conquerors often said to the vanquished, "My god or death!" Never, "Let me kill you while you're praying!" Now, enduring the racist depravity of which the Charleston shooter was

FREDERICK MONDERSON

guilty of, and the racial hatred the South Carolina Representative denounced in the House Chamber for its viciousness and racism; the most profound act was that of the survivors magnanimously forgiving the assailant because they were god fearing, in the divine element when executed and full of love for humanity. In some respects, Murlie Evers, Coretta Scott King and Betty Shabazz experienced that "sudden death" shock Clementa Pinckney's wife experienced but lived on and resolved to work for good. While Fannie Lou Hamer did not experience the Black martyrdom resonating across the South especially in the Civil Rights era; however, representing the "Grassroots" in struggle, her good enlightenment was, like Harriet Tubman, to liberate the enslaved human body, spirit and mind. Still, these exemplary souls, meeting challenge after challenge and tragedy after tragedy, must have been "carried by God" confidently believing the divine plans the destiny of us all.

BN PHOTO - Well, the sign says it all, "I am Still a Man" and the powers that be should not forget this important message and its significance.

BLACK NATIONALISM STILL ALIVE AND WELL

That outpouring of the good side of humanity's behavior so characteristic of the "Power of Woman" is what moved the world to wonder at the "mountain-top human spirit and behavior" of the Black Woman who was often held in scorn and ridicule. This extraordinary conscience of the human spirit inspired by the awesomeness of a benevolent, loving and inspiring god is what President Obama, a man of many words, was able to recognize and expressed so brilliantly in his Eulogy for Reverend Clementa Pinckney. There he recognized and praised that magnanimous gesture of forgiveness on part of the nine but especially those six Black women's families so injured, having lived within the turbulence of the Carolina Teacup. Their forgiving nature in wake of such a calamity not only surprised but gladdened the world of the good while clearing their conscience of the burden of hate as they looked to their god for guidance, comfort and inspiration in trying to soothe their unbelievable and collective grief.

It is interesting, amidst that profound period of grief, those left to carry on, did not at short notice get an epiphany to forgive; it was inbred in their psyche and was an essential part of the armament that brought them and others of similar experience through the long night of "American slave captivity." Given that dark besmirched moment, the power of forgiveness not only shocked, yet impressed, the world community, but this action provided that soothing peace achieved along the stairway heavenward towards the divine, all practicing religions persons go to church, mosque and temple, week after week, seeking, yet few find.

FREDERICK MONDERSON

BN PHOTO - Well, well, well, Erik Michael Dyson poses with Erik Monderson, here for the "March on Washington," so in future he could tell his children "My Dad brought me to Washington to explore and continue the Legacy of Dr. King."

31. OBAMA: UNEASY LIES THE HEAD
....

By
Dr. Fred Monderson

Shakespeare was spot on in saying "Uneasy lies the head that wears the crown" though he referred to physical threats to that head. In other respects, the line may refer to one's job which also depends on performance. In the case of President Obama, all of the above and more could apply to his situation. One thing is sure; the hair on his head has certainly changed as a result of the burdens of the office. Nevertheless, a cursory look at the issue confronting this President can be an indicator of what to expect as the next presidential election approaches and all contenders and their allies make their case to lead the nation at these unfolding and critical times. What is clearly evident, political and ideological lines are beginning to become solidified. In 1941, after the Japanese attack on Pearl Harbor, one of the significant Japanese Naval Commander, though under orders,

BLACK NATIONALISM
STILL ALIVE AND WELL

confessed, "I'm afraid we have awakened a sleeping giant." The rest we know is history. The astute President Obama, playing it cool, allowed every major Republican player to show the true nature of their inner thoughts as they heaped insults, unconscionable demands on his person and office.

1)   From the inception, we applauded President Obama for choosing his team of advisors and support personnel from among the brightest minds America could muster. These people approached their responsibilities with a seriousness of mind, professional intent and began making inroads into the multitudinous problems they were assigned to combat. Under Obama's stewardship of Bernanke at the FEDS and Geithner at Treasury and the significant input from leading economic experts including former FED Chair Paul Volker who advised the President; with rapidity this team began clearing out "Door Number One" through fiscal and financial reform, tackling the loss of jobs, unemployment, housing foreclosure, even rescuing the banking and auto industry and passing meaningful legislation across the board such as Lilly Ledbetter and credit card reform. Having cleaned out "Room Number One," they opened "Room Number Two," not realizing in addition to "Door Number Three" there were also rooms in the basement full of the stuff they had been shoveling in "Room Number One." Notwithstanding, the President remained focused, choosing to make the tough decisions that only extraordinary leaders have the tenacity to make, amidst attack by pseudo-patriots.

FREDERICK MONDERSON

BN PHOTO - Everyone came to express their sentiments in "Justice for Trayvon Martin" slain at the hands of a would-be "cop" Trayvon's mother determined was in fact a murderer and "terrorist."

2) President Obama's foreign policies and relationships bore significant fruit and signaled to the world America had turned onto a different path and now had elected the first African American as its principal spokesman as proof of this new reality. But the President realized; other world players India, China, Japan, Germany and so many others were making significant economic strides. Governor Jennifer Granholm, former governor of Michigan summed up the foreign challenges by saying, particularly in regard to China, "our passivity is their opportunity." Nevertheless, as the opposition continued to play childish games while strongly defending privileges of the privileged, Obama has taken the long view and continues to

BLACK NATIONALISM STILL ALIVE AND WELL

say "No to special interest" in his effort to make the economy work for the Middle Class and all other Americans. At the same time, he kept proposing clean energy, industry and educational reform in initiatives to keep America competitive in a fast changing world. By the end of day one, however, "vultures" began "circling" his proposed "carcass" as the "lepers" also contributed their share.

Under a ruse that Obama would abrogate the Constitution and prohibit the "Right of the people to bear arms," right wing groups in opposition to the democratic establishment and now purported allies of the Republican opposition began stock-piling arsenals of armaments for the coming "race riots" in the now touted "Post-racial America." Imagine! However, nearly seven years after, the "riots" did not come despite horrendous acts designed to precipitate such. Nonetheless, while such "shopping" was good for the economy one important caveat was overlooked. That is, the role of the Black American in the military, having fought in all of America's wars from the Revolution to the present, what they have learned in service and how they would respond to such blowhards!

3) Not only was Crispus Attucks the first authentic martyr whose blood fertilized the soil of the American "tree of liberty" and Salem Po and his boys backed Washington's power play, an unmistaken fact was overlooked in that age. While the French under Napoleon, an enemy of the British, were quick to recognize the young American nation and sent Frenchmen to fight; in the Battle of Savannah, their surrogates were Haitians who performed with commendable excellence. Upon their return to Haiti these veterans were able to launch the Haitian Revolution. However, they did make one confession. "We have learned the ways of the white man!" This meant they had learned how to load and fire the cannon with tremendous accuracy and also how to handle the pistol and rifle with great effect. Distinguished African military service continued in the War of 1812, the Mexican War (1845-46), the Civil War (1860-1865), the effectiveness of the Buffalo Soldiers against the Plains Indians (Native Americans), the War with Spain (1899-1902), World War I (1914-1918), World War II (1939-1945), the Korean Conflict

FREDERICK MONDERSON

(1950-1952), the War on Communism (1947-1990), Viet Nam (1954-1975), Grenada (1987), Gulf War I (1(2003), 991), Gulf War II (2003-Present), Afghanistan (2001-Present), Iraq and the War on Terrorism.

They even fought in the War on Poverty and the War on Drugs. In all this, African Americans learned every facet of military engagement, weaponry, administration, logistics, demolition, aerial flight and even Technological Cyber Warfare. All the while these Blacks who demonstrated exemplary courage, and meritorious patriotism were learning, learning, learning and have been watching, watching....

BN PHOTO - The United States Supreme Court building, in all it legalistic majesty!

James Brown sang, "I don't know Karate but I know Ka-Razor." In the "Age of Apartheid," when South Africa was accused of pursuing nuclear weaponry, Julius Nyerere said, "Let them go ahead, South Africa will be the first Black nuclear nation!" In the case of right wingers thinking, Black leadership offered, "Have your way, do you thing!" However, using old folks folk-lore advice, they had recounted, A blind White man went to "see a heavyweight fight"

BLACK NATIONALISM STILL ALIVE AND WELL

between a black and a white contender. He had a companion at ringside who gave blow-by-blow commentary as the fight unfolded. As the fight moved into the latter rounds and spirits became excited, the blind man asked, "What's happening now?" His companion responded, "The white guy has the black guy down!" The blind man responded in wit and wisdom, "The black man down? Well, keep him down! For when the black man raise, hell raises!" This is excellent wisdom for the arsenaled right-wingers! If their armed over-confidence should precipitate that race riot conflict perhaps the Blacks who kept killing each other will wise up. Let us not forget the Black military veterans, active and retired, who looked, and the role they can play and will play. In the tradition of warrior queens Michelle will also have to step-up to the plate to play her indispensible role as a commander of troops.

4. President Barack Obama is a genuine, visionary, patriotic American leader charged with cleaning out the barn, farming the land and animals with an eye to next season's crops, required to keep an eye on poachers and must negotiate with potential shoppers at home and abroad. He has been a victim of perennial criticism and unrelenting obstructionism. Still, the President's "Catch 22" is to defend the rights of and encourage the progress of the same people mining the fields he must plow, tender and navigate. As such, persons of lesser vision criticize the President' leadership but give a pass to Senator Mitch McConnell whose primary objective from day one has been to "make Obama a one term president;" Senator Jim DeMint has wanted to create his "Waterloo;" the inelegant Joe Wilson's disrespectful "pearl" is "you lie;" a "Minister of the Cloth" whose daily prayer is that "Obama dies;" his misguided disciple, the "black protester with guns" does not realize he is as much a "Nigger" as Obama; not to forget those circus criers who shout "Dick;' "ashamed;" "not like us;" "go for the jugular;" "kill the Nigger;" "socialism;" "where's your birth certificate?" "Show me your College Transcript," etc., and any and all such disgusting sound bites. Yet, as Obama listens to those baited distractions he remains steadfast, focused on the responsibilities of his job description, viz., leading the nation, reforming the financial and economic system,

proposing initiatives for clean energy to make the nation self reliant in this respect, offering benefits to encourage excellence in education, improving conditions of schools and their equipment, passing significant legislation that address the broad masses of the American people and a whole lot more, despite Republican legislative obstructionism.

Because Americans were hoodwinked by Republican smoke screen tactics, as a weapon against the Democratic Obama, the 2010 mid-term national elections brought to power the "Teeth (Tea) Party" component of the anti-Obama Republicans and they have been manipulating the Congress. These House legislators particularly, in their "cart before the horse" mentality and the "tail wagging the dog" syndrome showed their true colors and now as the smoke has cleared onlookers wonder how commentators really missed all this seemingly unpatriotic behavior. Thus, one of the reasons Republican 2016 contenders can make outrageous statements about Washington and that electorate can love them is because of a "dysfunctional Congress;" of course, with Republicans in charge!

5. With pomposity and arrogance gained from their 2010 election victory, Republicans led by the "Tea Party" minority held hostage the American people's aspirations as President Obama attempted to end the Bush tax cuts for the wealthy. In the "Jobs" debate, Obama's performance has been misrepresented to amplify claims he is not producing jobs, forgetting at the onset of his administration, the nation was hemorrhaging 600,000-800,000 jobs per month and his efforts reversed this, adding low hundred thousands of new jobs monthly. In that same "Jobs debate" as the President wrestled with tax relief for the wealthy the claim has been, these are the people who create jobs, but despite the years of the Bush tax cuts, jobs were not created. So, blame the President for not creating jobs even though the Congressional Budget Office gives a figure of more than 10 million jobs created or saved by his administration; thus far, the rich gets the credit but Obama gets the demerits.

BLACK NATIONALISM
STILL ALIVE AND WELL

BN PHOTO - A wonderful family stands beside "Dorrance Brooks Square" in Harlem, New York in honor of a local hero.

After the blow-hard rhetoric of Donald Trump and especially his calling out John McCain, many people were upset. As the President put it: "The same patriotic Americans who are upset about Trump questioning John McCain's hero status, were not upset as was I continually raked over a bed of hot coals!"

FREDERICK MONDERSON

DORRANCE BROOKS SQUARE
.038 acre

Dorrance Brooks (d. 1918) was an African American soldier who died in France shortly before the end of World War I. A native of Harlem and the son of a Civil War veteran, Brooks was a Private First Class in the 15th Infantry. In World War I, African American soldiers served in segregated regiments and were not eligible for aid from the Army Nurse Corps or the American Red Cross. In spite of these discouragements, Brooks distinguished himself as a faithful and patriotic soldier. Brooks was praised for his "signal bravery" in leading the remnants of his company after his superior officers were killed.

When this square was dedicated on June 14, 1925, more than 10,000 people were said to have attended the ceremony, presided over by Mayor John F. Hylan and Colonel William Hayward, commander of the 15th Infantry. The New York Times reported that Dorrance Brooks Square was "the first public square to be named after a Negro soldier." In October 1952, President Truman, who four years earlier had issued an executive order requiring "equality of treatment and opportunity" in the armed forces, addressed an audience of 50,000 from this small square to celebrate the desegregation of the military services.

Dorrance Brooks Square continued its tradition of being central to the fight for racial equality. In the late 1960s, two community leaders helped found an organization in the St. Luke's Episcopal Church across the street from the park. Dr. Mamie Phipps Clark (1917-1983) and Ella Baker (1903-1986) formed "We Care" to reach out to young people in the neighborhood during the height of the civil rights movement, helping area residents obtain employment, job training, health care and legal assistance, as well as publishing City Scene, a community newspaper. These efforts were crucial at a time when the injustice of racial segregation ignited Harlem, challenging individuals and institutions to organize and break down racial barriers.

Dr. Clark dedicated her career to ending racial inequality. She served as director of the Northside Center for Child Development, a facility she founded with her husband, Dr. Kenneth B. Clark, to provide educational and mental health services to youth in Harlem. Baker was one of the country's most important civil rights leaders, serving as a Student Nonviolent Coordinating Committee activist and leading efforts to address segregation in the City's public schools.

Parks acquired the site by condemnation on July 22, 1913. An open triangular space, it is bounded by West 136th and 137th Streets, and St. Nicholas and Edgecombe Avenues. When the square was dedicated, a flagpole and a cannon (later removed) stood at its south end. Today, the square is lined with benches and London plane trees (Platanus x acerifolia). In 2001, two benches and two trees were dedicated to Dr. Mamie Clark and Ella Baker in honor of their contributions to this community. In 2012 the Dorrance Brooks Property Owners and Residents Association partnered with the 369th Historical Society to help assist Parks in its efforts to care for this historically significant site.

City of New York  Michael R. Bloomberg, Mayor
Parks & Recreation   Veronica M. White, Commissioner

www.nyc.gov/parks
June 2012

BN PHOTO - A short Biography describes the man Dorrance Brooks for whom the Square is named after and which served as a rallying place for Black youth when the nation was in turmoil especially after World War I and again in the Post Civil Rights era.

Again, emboldened with this "win" the unreasonable "Tea Party" leadership of the Republican Party continues making exorbitant demands in their face-off with the President in the continuing legislative arena especially now that they control both houses. In

BLACK NATIONALISM STILL ALIVE AND WELL

their childish dreams these people could never countenance the significance of the thoughts of John Kennedy in a Speech given January 9, 1961 in the Massachusetts State Legislature where he boldly asserted: "Today, the eye of all people are truly upon us, and our governments, in every branch, at every level, nation, state, and local, must be a city upon a hill, constructed and inhabited by men aware of their grave trust and their great responsibilities." Still, McConnell played his "mandate card" and John Boehner disrespected the President by not returning his repeated phone calls. As these minions inflated their situation hoping to be viewed as whales, Obama remained concerned about America's aches and pains and so he invoked that long established tradition of compromise to halt the nation's hurried amble towards the gallows of national and international financial default. In good sense as he relented, Speaker Boehner boasted his guys "got 98 percent" of what they wanted in that famous stand-off and McConnell gave the now famous smiling "I got that Nigger" thumbs up. Reflective of this conundrum, an observed Bumper Sticker read "Liberty means defending someone else's right to do what you don't like."

Nevertheless, as Obama continues to take names, is slow to anger and "After a long train of abuses," this "gentleman leader," acting like the adult in the room and in reminiscence of his "If you're listening, lay off my wife" admonition, is justified in spanking his "disagreeable Republican children."

FREDERICK MONDERSON

BN PHOTO - Street-name honoring Rev. Dr. John W. Saunders located at convent Ave and W145 Street, in Harlem.

32. HONORING A GIANT
By
Dr. Fred Monderson

CEMOTAP attracted a tumultuous turnout at the Dr. Robert Johnson Life Center, to honor and celebrate the 72nd birthday of Dr. Leonard Jeffries, historian, scholar, activist, author, healer, on Saturday, January 24, 2009, at 2: 00 pm.

Sister Betty Dobson did the Welcome; Sister Yvonne Hill, the Prayer; Dr. James McIntosh 'Who is this African Man and why do we Honor him?' Brother James Small 'A Tribute from a Spiritual Son;' and Dr. Leonard Jeffries himself, offered a 'Blessing of the Food by the Honoree.'

After the Introductory Music by Mark and the Music Messengers, Birthday tributes were offered by Attorney Alton Maddox, Dr. Adelaide Sanford, Sister Frederica Bey and Brother Gil Noble. After a music interlude, and collection of gift envelopes, Sister Viola

BLACK NATIONALISM
STILL ALIVE AND WELL

Plummer boasted: 'I roasted him five years ago.' Then there were highlights of 'My life with Leonard' by his wife Dr. Rosalind Jeffries, and then the Honoree offered 'Thank you my friends.'

Dr. James Macintosh, Master of Ceremonies, provided a glowing and well-deserved tribute to Dr. Leonard Jeffries that set the stage for a night of great praise and earnest outpouring of love, respect and accolades for a giant and great warrior chieftain. In referring to his subject, he began by saying: "Marcus Garvey said 'Men in earnest are not afraid of consequences.'" Then he quoted Claude McKay's poem "If We Must Die."

BN PHOTO - "Land of the Free" must "Support Trayvon's Law" - because we insist - "Justice or Else!"

This literary classic of the Harlem Renaissance appropriately epitomizes the condition and struggles of the great one who never shied away from great engagements. The poem reads:

"If we must die, let it not be like hogs
Hunted and penned in an inglorious spot
While round us bark the mad and hungry dogs

FREDERICK MONDERSON

Making mock at our accursed lot.

"If we must die, O let us nobly die
So that our precious blood may not be shed
In vain; then even the monsters we defy
Shall be constrained to honor us though dead!

"O kinsmen we must meet the common foe!
Though far outnumbered let us show us brave
And for their thousand blows deal one death blow.

"What though before us lies the open grave
Like men we'll face the murderous, cowardly pack
Pressed to the wall, dying, but fighting back!"

Then Dr. Macintosh quoted the English poet Rudyard Kipling who believed "Even a broken clock is correct two times every day;" before he glowingly synopsized why he was honoring and supporting Dr. Jeffries.

"If you can hear the truth you've spoken
Twisted by knaves to make a trap for fools
Or watch the things you gave your life to broken
And stoop and build 'em up with worn-out tools

"If you can meet with triumph and disaster
And treat those two imposters just the same
If you can fill the unforgiving minute
With sixty seconds' worth of distance run
Yours is the Earth and everything that's in it
And which is more; you'll be a Man my son."

Saying that Kipling and his types have had to recognize Dr. Jeffries was a man, is the reason **CEMOTAP** was honoring this giant, celebrating his 72nd birthday.

BLACK NATIONALISM STILL ALIVE AND WELL

BN PHOTO - These Ladies are "Empowered" while another wants "DC Statehood Now!"

Even more, McIntosh offered some important reasons why Jeffries could be considered for the honor. These are: "Not just because he rose out of the Newark Public School system; not because he became President of his graduation class at Sussex Avenue School; or graduated with honors from Barringer High School; not because he graduated from Lafayette College (in Easton, Pennsylvania), or joined operation crossroads, or lead trips to Senegal; not because he left law school to get the background in Political Science that he would need to serve his life's mission; not because he married **Nana Essie Abibio, Queen Mother of Education, Development and Social Services of the Edina Traditional Area in Elmina**; not because he has travelled back and forth to Africa 40 times (actually 100 times); or has been building a hotel for our people on the motherland; or taught thousands of students in and out of the class room about mother Africa and the greatness of African Civilization. Not because he has nurtured other giants such as Brother James Smalls; not because he has loyally supported U.A.M. Brother Alton and Sister Leola Maddox during their bleakest hours; or helped Dr. John Henrik Clarke establish the African Heritage Studies Association. Or that he has helped set up the Black Studies Program at San Jose; not because he has lectured at Harvard, Yale and First World Alliance. He was being honored, not because he was installed as the Division Chief of Agogo, Ghana; not because he fought to change the curriculum of NYC schools or did so many other great things. But, we honor him

FREDERICK MONDERSON

because he is a man who has stood for African people; because he represents the very best of what it means to be an African man, a complete man with the kindness and humility for his people and possess a fierce warrior spirit for any who would harm his people. This is why we celebrate Dr. Jeffries."

BN PHOTO - These Young Ladies are not only "Empowered" but they certainly subscribe to "My Voice Matters."

Prof. James Smalls confessed about the influence Dr. Jeffries has had on the evolution of his cultural consciousness, from his days as a student at City College and up to today. Prof Smalls said; he learned from Dr. Jeffries the importance of economics, politics and culture. Then he added: "your culture is at the core of your spirituality. African spirituality is its most profound attribute." Looking at the audience, he reminded them as to the reason they were in attendance: "You're here because you see god in him. His spiritual-beingness! True revolutionaries exist in the spirit." Then he admonished them, "You must restore your spiritual religiosity. If you can't kill the African spirit, you can't kill the African revolution."

Next it was Regent Dr. Adelaide Sanford who gave a tremendously glowing tribute emphasizing the gentle, creative, omnipotent power of Dr. Jeffries, the author of a portion of the Curriculum of Inclusion that told the African-American story. He has a nobility of spirit, great magnanimity, majesty, dignity, pride, is an extra-dimension of the creator, centered on the reality of who we are. He is also brilliant, gracious in the face of confusion, steps over the debris, and rises from the ashes. Then she turned to the audience and confessed, "I be loving you!"

BLACK NATIONALISM STILL ALIVE AND WELL

Gil Noble of **Like it Is**, likened Dr. Jeffries to someone mirrored in Dr. Martin Luther King's declaration that, "A man can't ride your back, unless it's bent." He confessed, in his day, no Black History was taught in school so he had to learn Black History from those like Dr. Jeffries. Therefore, he was there to salute the honoree's sojourn on this planet.

Alton Maddox exclaimed Dr. Jeffries "Takes the burden off of us." Thus, "We will celebrate Dr. Jeffries' birthday every month this year, on the 19th." Fredericka Bey, visiting from New Jersey, was equally eloquent in her praise of the man who has given so much. Sister Viola Plummer spoke to Dr. Jeffries of the "African spirit you embody. The African-ness that made you who you are - never to bow down."

Dr. Rosalind Jeffries explained some aspects of her life with Leonard. Upon their marriage, she confessed of not being prepared for sharing her husband with the struggle. She had no preparation for what to expect. Yet, she boasted, "I got a giant, genius, magnanimous man, possessing a tender streak; tender, loving, full of absolute truth. He lives on the cutting edge of things and this is dangerous." Jokingly, she continued, "He did not want to be born. They used forceps to pull him out. He is a genius and godly being."

BN PHOTO - A cross-section of the people who came to celebrate the 50th Anniversary of the "**March on Washington**" for this signals the importance of the idea of demonstrating for social justice.

FREDERICK MONDERSON

Finally, it was Dr. Leonard Jeffries turn to address those who came to acclaim him. He began by pointing to Wade Nobles' dictum: "Power is the ability to define reality and to have other people accept it as if it was their own." Then he opened up, "We are the creation. It was an African victory. African primacy created the evolution of society. The cradle of civilization. There were no Europeans in the origins; no Europeans in evolution; no Europeans in civilization." Then he explained the role of the Ethiopians who comprised the 25th Egyptian dynasty and were the only kings who ruled the entire distance of the Nile Valley. He too took that journey of 1000 miles of glory from Khartoum to Cairo for the "Nourishment of the mind. This is what sustains me," he confessed. Finally, he informed "My wife is my rock and my best friend."

BN PHOTO - "Redeem the Dream" needs more "Jobs to Rebuild America" and at the same time there must be "Justice for Trayvon Martin."

BLACK NATIONALISM STILL ALIVE AND WELL

33. A. PHILIP RANDOLPH MARCH ON WASHINGTON, D.C. 1941
By
Dr. Fred Monderson

Who was A. Philip Randolph? If we read his writings, we would realize he was one of the most brilliant minds of his age, Black or White. Randolph was confronted with the problems facing Black people in the first half of the 20th Century and he ably articulated and effectuated a leadership role that raised the issues and advanced the cause of Black freedoms and quest for equality in the Depression and Post-Depression age. A die-hard advocate of labor, Randolph saw Black salvation in America from a position of labor activism that brought integration in the workplace but more importantly allowed the worker to demand and receive a decent wage to help raise the family. Beyond this milestone, he advocated mass movements and demonstrations to secure equality and social justice, and civil and human rights.

To understand the struggles of A. Philip Randolph, one has to understand the condition of Black people by the time of the Great Depression in 1929 and the significance of the election that followed in 1932.

From the time of Abraham Lincoln's Emancipation Proclamation (1863), and the work of Radical Republicans in Congress who were instrumental in securing the 13th, 14th, and 15th Amendments to the Constitution (1865-1868) and numerous Civil Rights legislation in the 19th Century as a result of Reconstruction (1865-1877), Blacks have voted Republican, the "Party of Lincoln." Yet, substantive issues were not addressed in the age of terror, especially in the South.

FREDERICK MONDERSON

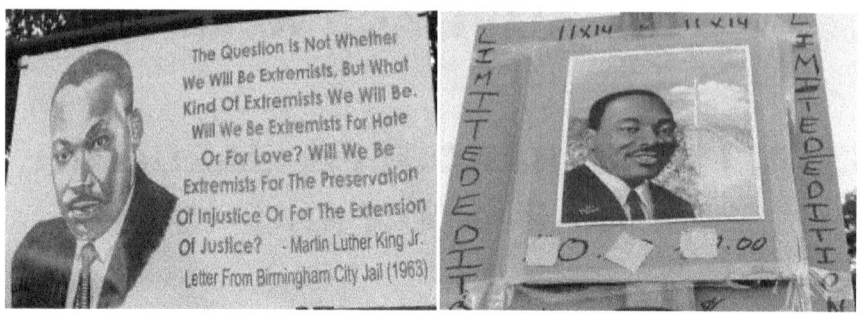

BN PHOTO - A "Man of all Times," Dr. Martin Luther King, more than any other person, epitomizes the "March on Washington."

John P. Davis in *The American Negro Reference Book* (1967: 63) recounts how after disappointments with the Teddy Roosevelt and Howard Taft Administrations, things got no better and Blacks looked for relief. "In 1912 they were willing to turn to any group that promised some hope. To some Negroes, Woodrow Wilson seemed to provide some hope when he said, during his campaign, that he wished to see 'justice done to the colored people in every matter; and not mere grudging justice, but justice executed with liberality and cordial good feeling." Shortly after Wilson's inauguration, it became clear to most Negroes that they could not rely on Wilson or his party for support in their efforts. Soon, segregation was reintroduced in the nation's capital and in the offices of the Federal government."

Still, this political party commitment continued through World War I (1914-1918), the great economic advances of the 1920s and passed the great Stock Market Crash in 1929, which ushered in the Great Depression. Yet, despite their loyalty to the Republican Party that generally won most elections, Blacks were for the most part, ignored and their condition never improved in the "age of terror" which they lived.

In this, the first few years of the **Depression** hit home hard and Blacks were doubly affected, being the last hired and first fired. Therefore, Blacks decided to switch parties in 1932 and voted overwhelmingly for the democrat Franklin Delano Roosevelt, who proclaimed and promised the "New Deal." They repeated this

BLACK NATIONALISM
STILL ALIVE AND WELL

support again in 1936 and again in 1940. As such then, while the "New Deal" sought to seriously confront the wrenching conditions of the Depression with a number of "Alphabet Programs," the issue of the day was jobs. Interestingly enough, as the drums of war in Europe began to beat louder and louder in the minds and hearts of the American people, the war industry of the "home front" geared for the inevitable. In this one place where jobs were in great supply as we fed the "Lend-Lease Program," the ugly face of racism and discrimination sought to exclude the Black man, confining him to a few jobs in the most degrading and dead-end positions of janitor, sweepers and elevator operators. The record seems to show, for example, of the thirty thousand jobs in New York City, only 142 were held by Blacks in the above mentioned positions and this example was indicative of the broader social condition of Blacks in the nation's workforce.

BN PHOTO - Yes, we must "Honor their Memory by Fighting Voter Suppression."

According to Executive Order 8802 issued June 25, 1941: "Whereas there is evidence that available and needed workers have been barred from employment in industries engaged in defense production solely

FREDERICK MONDERSON

because of considerations of race, creed, color, or national origin, to the detriment of workers' morale and of national unity."

Bradford Chambers in *Chronicles of Black Protest* (1968: 174) recounts how: "In the armed forces, segregation was still the official government policy, a carry-over from the Civil War. Black newspapers reported 'race riots at Fort Oswego; discrimination at Fort Devens; Jim Crow Conditions at Camps Blanding and Lee; and the edict - 'Not to shake a Nigger's hand at Camp Upton.' The Baltimore Afro-American called for thousands of Black men to desert rather than serve in army camps in the South."

Into this mix, A. Philip Randolph had been active for more than two decade, primarily as a labor-unionist but more interested in the well-being of Black people, then generally referred to as Negroes. As early as 1935 he became President of the Brotherhood of Sleeping Car Porters on the railroad, but also active in the National Negro Congress, Co-Chairman of The American Committee on Africa, as well as Co-Chairman of The American Negro Leadership Conference on Africa.

Philip Foner in *The Voice of Black America* (1972: 808) tells about A. Philip Randolph. "Born April 15, 1889, in Crescent City, Florida, Randolph finished high school in Florida, worked his way north and subsisted on odd jobs while attending City College of New York. (He never earned a college degree, and was mostly self-taught). Together with Chandler Owen, a young black law student at Columbia University, Randolph became active in the Socialist party, and both edited *The Messenger*, a radical black journal of opinion which endorsed Socialism and was a leading voice of the "New Negro" in the post-World War I period. Randolph was asked by the Pullman Porters to help them organize, and in 1935, after twelve years of hard struggle, the Brotherhood of Sleeping Car Porters, with Randolph as president, forced the Pullman Company to recognize it."

BLACK NATIONALISM STILL ALIVE AND WELL

BN PHOTO - Yes, they came in groups from all over, seeking "Justice for All!"

In his address to the National Negro Congress held in Chicago February 14, 15 and 16, in 1936, of which a pamphlet is in the Schomberg Library in Harlem, New York, and in Foner (1972: 810-811) where after speaking of the problems facing Europe on the eve of World War II Randolph turned to the condition of the Black man in America in that "Depression" and "New Deal" era. To this he stated: "Our contemporary history is a witness to the stark fact that black America is a victim of both class and race prejudice and oppression. Because Negroes are black, they are hated, maligned and spat upon, lynched, mobbed and murdered. Because Negroes are workers, they are browbeaten, bullied, intimidated, robbed, exploited, jailed and shot down. Because they are black they are caught between the nether millstones of discrimination when seeking a job to join a union."

FREDERICK MONDERSON

BN PHOTO - They all came to demand "Justice in the Courts, Justice at the Polls" and as everyone will demand, "We March for Jobs and Freedom."

"Thus, voiceless in thirteen states; politically disregarded and discounted in the others; victims of lynch terror in Dixie, with a Scottsboro frame-up of notorious memory; faced with the label of the white man's job and the white man's union; unequal before the law; Jim-Crowed in schools and colleges throughout the nation; segregated in the slums and ghettos of the urban centers; landless peons of a merciless landlordism; hunted down, harassed and hounded as vagrants in the Southern cities, the Negro people face a hard, deceptive and brutal capitalist order, despite its preachments of Christian love and brotherhood."

Further he indicated, Black progress must come through admission into the industrial and craft unions, to which he opined: "the craft union invariably has a color bar against the Negro worker, but the industrial union in structure renders race discrimination less possible,

BLACK NATIONALISM STILL ALIVE AND WELL

since it embraces all the workers included in the industry, regardless of race, creed, color, or craft, skilled or unskilled. Thus, this congress should seek to broaden and intensify the movement to draw Negro workers into labor organizations and break down the color bar in the trade-unions that now have it. The next instrumentality which the workers must build and employ for their protection against economic exploitation, war and fascism is an independent working-class political party. It should take the form of a farmer-labor political organization. This is indispensable in view of the bankruptcy in principles, courage and vision of the old-line parties, Republican and Democratic."

Randolph says further in Foner (1972: 813-814) pointing out: "The fight for civil and political rights of the Negro peoples can effectively be carried on if only those organizations that are pushing the struggles are broadened and built with a wider mass base. Those organizations that are serving on the civil-rights front effectively for the Negro are the National Association for the Advancement of Colored People and the International Labor Defense. It needs to be definitely understood, however, that the fight in the courts for civil and political rights cannot be effective except when backed by a broad nationwide, if not international, mass protest through demonstrations in the form of parades, mass meetings and publicity."

He cautioned, Foner (1972: 814) continued: "The task of overcoming the enemies of democratic institutions and constitutional liberties is too big for any single organization. It requires the united and formal integrating and coordinating of the various Negro organizations - church, fraternal, civil, trade-union, farmer, professional, college and what not - into the framework of a united front, together with the white groups of workers, lovers of liberty and those whose liberties are similarly menaced for a common attack upon the forces of reaction, backed by the embattled masses of black and white workers. The united front strategy and tactics should be executed through methods of mass demonstration, such as parades, picketing, boycotting, mass protests, the mass distribution of propaganda literature, as well as legal action."

FREDERICK MONDERSON

BN PHOTO - Yes, "We Demand Equality for All," and we are "Against Anti-worker Laws and Voter Suppression."

"The salvation of the Negro like the workers must come from within," he believed. Then he chronicled challenges facing Blacks, particularly during the 1930s. He indicated: "These issues should be obvious, clear and simple, such as prevention of stoppage of relief, cuts in relief allotments, layoffs of relief workers or workers in any industry, discrimination in the giving of relief, exorbitant rents, evictions, rent increases, police brutality, denial of free assembly, freedom of the press, freedom of speech to unpopular groups, denial of civil rights to Negroes, access to public utilities and forms of transportation, such as the Pullman car."

He called on Blacks to be involved and advocated: "Wage struggles around war upon Ethiopia by the fascist dictator Mussolini, strikes and lockouts of black and white workers, the amendment to the federal constitution or the adoption of social legislation such as the Retirement Pension Act for railroad workers, fight for the freedom of Angelo Herndon, the Scottsboro boys, the Wagner-Costigan anti-lynching bill, the violations of the Wagner Labor Disputes bill, the forcing of teachers to take the oath, the goose-stepping of the students in the school system thru the R.O.T.C., the abolition of the color bar in trade-unions, the murder of Shoemaker in Tampa, Florida, exposing the menace of the American Liberty League, William Randolph Hearst and the Ku Klux Klan, and supporting the movement of John L. Lewis for industrial unionism."

BLACK NATIONALISM
STILL ALIVE AND WELL

BN PHOTO - Young and innocent, yet she "Demands an end to Racist Violence" and calls on all to "Unite and Fight Racism."

Such is the task of the Negro people as Randolph outlined them. Nevertheless, continued Randolph: "To meet the task, the Negro peoples, pressed with their backs against the wall, must face the future with heads erect, hearts undaunted and undismayed, ready and willing and determined to pay the price in struggle, sacrifices and suffering that freedom, justice and peace shall share and enjoy a more abundant life."

FREDERICK MONDERSON

In a further speech, upon its 150th anniversary entitled *The Crisis of the Negro and the Constitution* in Foner (1972: 816-817) Randolph stated: "Freedom is never given; it is won. And the Negro people must win their freedom. They must achieve justice. This involves struggle, continuous struggle. True liberation can be acquired and maintained only when the Negro masses possess power; and power is the product and flower of organization - organization of the masses, the masses in the mills and mines, on the farms, in the factories, in churches, in fraternal organizations, in homes, colleges, women's clubs, student groups, trade-unions, tenants' leagues, in co-operative guilds, political organizations and civil-rights associations."

Still, despite the organizing and speech-making, Blacks continued to face major obstacles and difficulties in the society. All this, and despite the sympathetic attitude of the President's wife, Eleanor Roosevelt and even the efforts of the "Black Cabinet" who consulted with President Roosevelt himself. As the war unfolded in Europe, Blacks sought meaningful jobs in the war industries form which they were generally excluded. It was time for action!

In January, 1941, A. Philip Randolph, as head of **The Brotherhood of Sleeping Car Porters Union** issued a call for a "March on Washington, DC.," insisting "Ten, twenty, fifty thousand Negroes" would gather on the White House Lawn on July 1, 1941, to demand the federal government end discrimination in civilian and military job contracts. Importantly, however, if we look to Randolph's activism we get a broader view of the overall condition of Black in the depression years leading to the war, despite their voting record as democrats.

BLACK NATIONALISM STILL ALIVE AND WELL

BN PHOTO - The Message is clear: "We March for Jobs and Civil Rights."

Randolph was joined by other Black leaders Walter White, Adam Clayton Powell, Jr., and Frank Crosswaith to demand, according to Chambers (1968: 175) that the "federal government take action to stop discrimination in the defense industries and the armed forces." Imagine, 9 years later and three significant Democratic victories and Blacks were still waiting for significant changes in the American social and civic order. Chambers (1968: 175) continued: "The idea of a black revolt in a time of crisis threw Washington into a panic.

FREDERICK MONDERSON

President Roosevelt called the March leaders to Washington and tried to persuade them to call it off." They refused! Interesting, for people don't generally refuse the President.

The Program of the March on Washington on July 1, 1941 was as follows:

"1.   We demand, in the interest of national unity, the abrogation of every law which makes a distinction in treatment between citizens based on religion, color, or national origin. This means an end to Jim Crow in education, in housing, in transportation and in every other social, economic, and political privilege; and especially, we demand, in the capital of the nation, an end to all segregation in public places and in public institutions.

2.   We demand legislation to enforce the Fifth and Fourteenth Amendments guaranteeing that no person shall be deprived of life, liberty or property without due process of law, so that the full weight of the national government may be used for the protection of life and thereby may end the disgrace of lynching.

3.   We demand the enforcement of the Fourteenth and Fifteenth Amendments and the enactment of the Pepper Poll Tax bill so that all barriers in the exercise of the suffrage are eliminated.

4.   We demand the abolition of segregation and discrimination in the army, navy, Marine Corps, air corps, and all other branches of national defense.

5.   We demand an end to discrimination in jobs and job training. Further, we demand that the FEPC be made a permanent administrative agency of the U.S. Government and that it be given power to enforce its decisions based on its findings.

6.   We demand that federal funds be withheld from any agency which practices discrimination in the use of such funds.

BLACK NATIONALISM STILL ALIVE AND WELL

7. We demand colored and minority group representation on all administrative agencies so that these groups may have recognition of their democratic rights to participate in formulating policies.

8. We demand representation for the colored and minority racial groups on all missions, political and technical, which will be sent to the peace conference so that the interests of all people everywhere may be truly recognized and justly provided for in the postwar settlement."

The March never happened, because of necessity President Roosevelt signed Executive Order 8802 in June 25, 1941, days before the March date. This Executive Order banned discrimination in the war industries and government training programs, and established a President's Commission on Fair Employment Practices.

Nevertheless, while FEPA (Fair Employment Practices Act) banned selective job discrimination, desegregation of the Armed Forces had to wait until the death of FDR, end of World War II and the new Harry Truman Administration, when the Armed Forces Act officially ended discrimination in the military.

Notwithstanding, most of the other issues mentioned in the program had to be hard won in the late 1940s, the 1950s and well into the Civil Rights struggles of the 1960s and beyond. We can never forget Frederick Douglass' statement: "Power concedes nothing without a struggle."

It was Randolph who actually originated the "1963 March on Washington." Davis (1967: 476) wrote: "The march on Washington originated with A. Philip Randolph, militant head of the Brotherhood of Sleeping Car Porters. It was organized and programmed by Bayard Rustin, former field secretary of CORE, who also organized the New York City school boycott. Every Negro protest organization working for integration was represented, as were a number of white or mixed supporting organizations representing

FREDERICK MONDERSON

labor, churches and civic and various liberal groups. Martin Luther King, Jr., James farmer, Roy Wilkins, A. Philip Randolph and John Lewis were the principal speakers."

BN PHOTO - Yes, "Dr. King's Legacy … Jobs not War" insist we "Unite and Fight against Racism."

Randolph was unquestionably a brilliant mind, consummate activist, jailed for 2 years while editor of the *Messenger* during World War I, his ideas laid the foundation strategies for the later Civil Rights Movement. He initially called for a United Front Movement. Unfortunately Randolph has not gotten the credit he deserves for the pivotal and avante garde role he played as a Civil Rights activist who made a difference. He does have a bust of his image in Union Station, Washington, DC.

BLACK NATIONALISM
STILL ALIVE AND WELL

BN PHOTO - National Association of Social Workers celebrates Civil Rights History and its "Social Workers Join the March on Washington"

34. TALKING POINTS OR COGNITIVE DISSONANCE?
By
Dr. Fred Monderson

In a recent episode in the "Disrespect Obama Saga," as CNN has reported, Lt. Colonel Robert Maginnis, accused the President of not having the "testicular fortitude" to take on ISIL in Syria.

First of all, in his Editorial, "This Light Colonel," has prognosticated about issues above his rank! After all, Mr. Maginnis is a not even a "Full Bird Colonel" and yet he wants to criticize decisions made by the Commander of the United States of America Armed Forces and the Joint Chiefs. Either the President's superior assessment strategy is certainly above this gentleman's, like so many Obama critics, assessment of complex thinking or their gray matter suffers from cognitive dissonance. At a time when Americans are "war weary" and President Obama carefully assesses situations, "war hawks"

FREDERICK MONDERSON

would have the nation engaged in conflicts in Pakistan, North Korea, Somalia, Libya, and Ukraine and on a collision course with Russia; not to mention Iraq and Syria. Thus, 21st Century strategic thinking may very well be a problem for 20th Century "fossils" still perambulating as pedestrians while Mr. Obama is exercising post jet-age thinking strategy speed consonant with his responsibilities as President of the United States and Commander of the Armed forces in a fast changing world.

It is interesting to hear commentators, pundits, and talking heads, weigh in on the President's response to this or that issue as it surfaces in the general public. These experts pontificate on the President's action or inaction as if they are observing his behavior, body movements and thinking from their first row position in the **Situation Room** or any White House locations where such matters are discussed and decisions arrived at.

Riding on Delta Airlines a sign read, "America Invented Aviation." It also invented the movies; so, analogies using movies or video images are not inappropriate. At Ronald Reagan's inauguration ceremony festivities, as Ray Charles sang "America the Beautiful" and the camera drew-back, the singer seemed in a "pit" singing and Reagan in a throne pedestal near the clouds" in that building. From this lofty position the great one seemed to make his decisions and it is also possible where he also took a nap.

In Steven Segal's movie **Under Siege I** about the seizure of the battleship **Missouri**, Commander Rybeck communicated with a room full of top military brass and high ranking civilians where such matters are handled. In the movie **Air Force One** starring Harrison Ford a similar situation is referenced. Thus, these expert commentators seem seated in such locations and importantly portray those proceeding to the public stating the President has not done this or that and give their short-sighted reasons for their belief. Republican opponents of the President are no different as they seek to make "pea-size" inroads to his thinking factory.

BLACK NATIONALISM STILL ALIVE AND WELL

Even an expert like General Wesley Clarke, former Supreme Allied NATO Commander, vacillating in his comments as to what the President did and did not do when it came to surveillance over Syria against ISIL, stated: "We want to get more updated information to add to what we have about ISIL command centers, military displacements, training camps, convoys, etc., to be ready for any bombardment." Again, in case of the newly released journalist Curtis, in his first comments, he expressed thanks "For all that was done to secure my release." Though America does not negotiate with terrorists, it is not-inconceivable to think they were not out of the loop in negotiations especially if there is plausible deniability. Equally, the flawless though unsuccessful mission to rescue Foley and the other hostages proves there is movement even if the prognosticating souls are not privy to it. We must not forget, during the Civil Rights Movement protests, many said, "The FBI is just standing and doing nothing or simply taking notes." No, they were observing and recording events, seemingly preserving names, images and events for later history, whatever the purpose.

BN PHOTO - While "Voting Equals Democracy" we must be concerned about "Black Genocide in 21st Century America." So says **MAAFA 21**.

Republicans who never saw an Obama measure they could like "punted" on every Obama effort of authentication of anti-Assad policies. The "War Hawks" like John McCain and his squadron who wanted to arm the rebels in Kosovo also advocated arming the rebels in Syria. Credible commentators argued the Syrians would have caved as did Iraqi soldiers as in wake of ISIL's advances.

FREDERICK MONDERSON

President Eisenhower laid down the rule, "The strength of American domestic policy is the foundation of its foreign policy." George Bush's failed financial and economic policies; auto industry and Wall Street near collapse; high unemployment; rampant outsourcing of jobs and businesses; infrastructure disrepair; all reflected his failed foreign policies; failure in Iraq and Afghanistan and failure in the world's perception of America.

BN PHOTO - "Dreams not Drones" is the hope of those working for the good for the planet to "Prevent Catastrophic Climate Change."

On the other hand, Mr. Obama's response to the auto industry against Republican protestations; bank bailout and Wall Street rescue; shovel ready strategies for jobs and business incentives to lower unemployment; holding the line against firing first responders; Lilly Ledbetter and encouraging mothers to return to college; bolstering community college roles in technical training for jobs of the future; incentives for more efficient energy sources; emission reduction and better gas mileage for cars; inroads into the immigration debacle; and credit card and student loan rate reduction and more. All were accomplished despite the "Party of No" obstructionism on foreign and domestic policy front, repairing America's perceived image abroad; managing the wars in Iraq and Afghanistan and spanking the Somali pirates; meeting the challenges

BLACK NATIONALISM STILL ALIVE AND WELL

of Cody's Army of God and Boko Harum; even silencing the upstart Kim Il Jung. All this, Mr. Obama was able to accomplish despite Congressional Republican and media obstructionism that gave openings to the likes of America's enemies.

Some commentators have argued the Arab-Israeli conflict is 1000 years in the making. The war on America did not begin in January 2009 and will continue long after Mr. Obama's journey is completed. Given all the players' pros and cons, above and below, even between the lines, he has done a damn good job. His successes, however, are not a single individual's doing. More importantly, when decisions are arrived at, as in the famous Delta Six Mission against Osama bin-Laden picture image with his 1000 yard stare, Mr. Obama is surrounded by and aided by the best advisory aids, military and civilian. This is particularly evident when insiders share information about the President that he is "frightening well prepared on all issues. Mr. Obama's opponents want him to share his strategies and decisions with them before he implements such. Then they block such moves or loud-mouth comment on his plans alerting foreign adversaries. Strange those individuals such as "The light-Colonel" cannot see Obama's forest for the trees strategies though his supporters believe he may be the last great president!

FREDERICK MONDERSON

BN PHOTO - While we recognize "Poverty" has a lot to do with it, we must put an end to a dangerous trend and "Stop Prison Pipeline" but more important "End Poverty."

Despite what many consider the treasonous intent to nullify and obstruct his initiatives and policies the list of positive successful Presidential achievements is a matter of record. The hatred many people harbor for this first African American President despite this, his record as President during arguably the most complex and the most difficult years of any president, his record is credible and worthy of respect.

Mr. Obama's intellectual autonomy and personal integrity are inimical to the negative images and stereotypes of an African male in the most powerful office of this nation and therein is the cause of the Cognitive Dissonance regarding all his professional and personal activities.

BLACK NATIONALISM
STILL ALIVE AND WELL

BN PHOTO - Marchers demand "End Homelessness" and "Raise the Minimum Wage."

35. "FOOLS" ON "ERRANDS"
By
Dr. Fred Monderson

It has been often said, "If you keep doing the same things you will get the same results." Someone should tell the Republicans who now control both Houses of Congress. On the issue of the Keystone Pipeline, President Obama as Chief Executive and Chief Legislator had found fault with the measure and promised to veto it. He even compromised and suggested; if corrected from its present state, he would consider it more seriously. During the State of the Union Address, Mr. Obama urged the New Congress to pass a jobs bill that would, principally, address the problems of the nation's crumbling infrastructure such as schools, rails, roads, bridges, ports, tunnels, etc. He contrasted the benefits of such a bill against "one pipeline" which seem more than reasonable.

FREDERICK MONDERSON

Republicans in Congress, bullied by the emergent "Tea Party" movement had set a list of priorities they would enact if they were successful in the 2014 mid-term election. So fate, perhaps, misguided would have it, Republican "Thumped" Democrats, succeeding to control of both Houses of Congress. Emboldened by their good fortune largesse from the American public "victim" of a sordid portrait of President Obama the Republican propaganda artists had painted, they began sharpening their "long knives" and "checking their list," perhaps more than once.

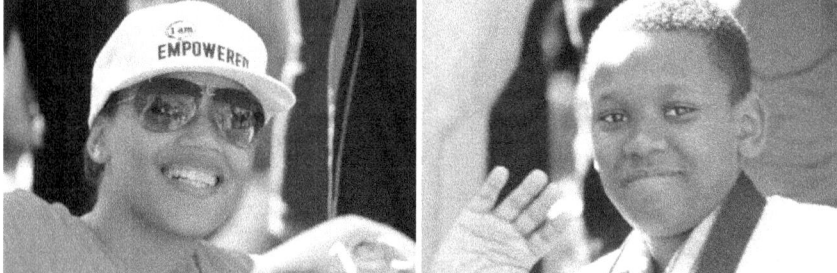

BN PHOTO - Theirs is the future and these young marchers are "On it!"

Unmindful of the President's veto threat, Republicans passed the Keystone Pipeline bill. Their claim, the pipeline as "their jobs bill" would provide "thousands of jobs," while Senator Charles Schumer (D. NY) responded it will provide "only 35 permanent jobs." Thus, it makes one wonder, 'In that "Washington Desert" who is manufacturing that "Snow Job?"' Another question enquiring minds want answered is 'What is the true nature of this new Republican mandate?'

Decrying American voting apathy in past elections and especially in this 2014 mid-term, it's been revealed only 36 percent of the electorate participated. In view of Republican gains and if we give them a 55 to 45 or 60 to 40 advantage, that means their mandate based on the turnout is not that overwhelming, despite Hillary Clinton's wisdom, "A win is a win!" The interesting thing is, Republicans are not for the general welfare only their base and supporters. However, as Executor of the Constitution formed to promote the general welfare, the President's job is to determine what

BLACK NATIONALISM
STILL ALIVE AND WELL

is beneficial to the broad masses of the American people. That is why among the broad repertoire of his tools, the veto is important.

Now, there are two principal types of veto, the "Pocket Veto" and the "Regular Veto." The "Pocket Veto" is a "backdoor" way of saying no to a bill, while the "Regular Veto" is a more confrontational rejection.

The history of Republican behavior towards the Obama administration has been a sordid experiment in American government hypocrisy and chicanery. Powerful individuals from the highest levels of the American government and their allies have prosecuted an offensive climate of disrespect and racial hatred towards Mr. Obama particularly because of his race. What is even more sinister, according to the "father of the Republican Party" Abraham Lincoln, "Silence in the expression of wrong-doing creates culpability on the part of such onlookers!" Because a fundamental tenet of Republican political behavior, "group think" or "law of the pack," no leader of stature has visibly taken a stand against the racial crucifixion of Mr. Obama, especially in the excellent performance of his responsibility as President and Chief Executive. That is to say, persons such as Senator Mitch McConnell, Speaker John Boehner, Sarah Palin, Michele Bachman, Joe Wilson and even Donald Trump have risen not simply to their highest level of incompetence but to their grossest levels of despicable behavior for elected officials and leaders in a nation that aspires to be a moral leader of the world community.

After having passed the Keystone Pipeline bill Republicans announced they will next focus on the **Affordable Care Act**, they have derisively named "Obamacare. The "blind leading the blind," Mitch McConnell and John Boehner, have been shown to be not simply persistent but foolish. The "ship of fools" they are piloting have voted to repeal "Obamacare" just short of 50 times.

They are now trying to achieve the half-century mark. While history will record the Affordable Care Act as Mr. Obama's signature

FREDERICK MONDERSON

legislative accomplishment, those analytic appraisals of the last two Congresses characterizing Mr. Obama's second term will be highlighted by this monumental Republican failure to truly assess Barack Obama as a political opponent but also how the broad masses of the American people view Republican chicanery. Even more important, when "Obamacare" was first rolling-out his program a threshold of seven million registrants was projected to make the system functionally cost effective. Despite the negativity first propagated about the new health care, the supposed economic costs to taxpayers, that it was a government program and not actually private, "Granny's death bed experience," and especially the initial problems in the roll-out, Republican gloom never materialized. Currently, enrollment is fast approaching 17 million. Thus far demonstrated callous Republican behavior is threatening to eviscerate the health care protections of the 17 million Americans, while they line up to drink from the one billion dollars promised in the Koch brother's financial donation.

BN PHOTO - APRI Retirees were out there helping deliver the message of the "March on Washington."

BLACK NATIONALISM STILL ALIVE AND WELL

The sad reality, however, with scalpel in hand, President Obama is waiting in that big White House Oval Office to circumcise the bill once it lands on his desk!

In *American Government* by Robert C. Bone, (New York: Barnes and Noble, 1977: 74-75), he states: "Perhaps the most effective influence the President possesses over legislative actions is not mentioned in Article II. This is the veto power provided by Article I, Section 7, which deals with congressional legislation. Such a power had long been possessed by the British ruler but Hamilton pointed out in *The Federalist* (No. 69), a classic commentary on the Constitution, rather than an "absolute negative" the President has only a "qualified negative" over legislative actions. This is so because Congress, by a two thirds vote in both houses, can pass legislation over a presidential veto."

Jack C. Plano and Milton Greenberg in *The American Political Dictionary* (eighth Edition) (New York: Holt, Rinehart and Winston, Inc., 1989: 183-84) describes the veto as: "A legislative power vested in a chief executive to return a bill unsigned to the legislative body with reasons of his objections. The Constitution provides that every bill, both public and private, that passes the House and the Senate must be sent to the President before it becomes law. When the President receives a bill, he may: (1) sign it, whereupon it becomes law; (2) not sign it, whereupon it becomes law after ten congressional working days; (3) veto it, and send it back to the house of its origin; or (4) not sign it, whereupon if Congress adjourns within ten days the bill is killed (pocket veto). The President vetoes a bill by writing "veto" (I forbid) across the face of the bill; he then sends it back to Congress with a message setting forth his objections. Congress may amend the bill according to the President's demands and then re-pass it, or it may reject the President's objections and override the veto by re-passing the bill with a two-thirds roll-call vote of those present and voting in each house. Finally, the President's veto may be sustained, which occurs more often than a direct override of the veto."

FREDERICK MONDERSON

BN PHOTO - Youth Council - Unit 3870 of the **National Association for the Advancement of Colored People** (**NAACP**).

Again, Plano and Greenberg explained the significance of the veto as: "Presidents employed the veto power infrequently and with great caution until the post-Civil War administration of Andrew Johnson. Since 1865, the veto power has been used with increasing vigor by most presidents; Grover Cleveland, with 414 regular and pocket vetoes, and Franklin Roosevelt, with 631, has been its most persistent users. The scope of the veto power has also expanded since 1865. The earlier view that the veto should be used to block unconstitutional or technically imperfect laws has been supplemented by its employment to express disapproval of any kid. Although the veto is merely suspensive in effect, few vetoes are overridden by Congress, since if one-third plus one of the members voting in either house support the President's view, the veto prevails. The threat of the veto can also be used effectively by a chief executive to shape and change legislation while it is still in the hands of the legislature."

The story is told of a political opposition in the Ivory Coast, West Africa, against President Houphey Boingy. One demonstrating gathering assembled chanting "Down with Boingy," then decided to

BLACK NATIONALISM
STILL ALIVE AND WELL

march on the Presidential Palace. Along the way, exhortations were uttered until they reached their destination massing in front of the gates. They even demanded the President come out and speak. In his brief address to the agitated gathering Mr. Boingy simply said the following: "Say what you want, I am what you have!" In the American political democratic system, until 2016 Mr. Obama is all the Republicans have and thanks to the veto and their inability to override with scalpel in hand he will be "shearing the sheep!"

The sad thing about the Obama-Republican saga, as the Lilliputians struggle to tie-down Gulliver, they remain unmindful of the illuminated record of their behavior towards a decent yet thinking individual. That is, Mr. Obama knows all the players; he has experienced everything including the kitchen sink they threw at him; has effectively out-think their greatest minds; and still hold them to a standstill. Still, as this drama unfolds, the public is forced to enquire, 'What manner of man is this?' For, like the Duracell bunny, Mr. Obama "takes a licking and keeps on ticking" towards 2016 and beyond and never missing a beat in his responsibilities despite unprecedented Republican obstructionism along the way.

BN PHOTO - GMMA in Quoting 1 Samuels, 30: 8 says - "We shall Recover All!"

FREDERICK MONDERSON

BN PHOTO - The Message to Nissan is: "Labor Rights are Civil Rights."

BN PHOTO - The message of Labor is always the same, "Social Justice for All" "Support Trayvon's Law," "Protect Voting Rights."

36.   DEFENDING A MYTH!
By
Dr. Fred Monderson

On Monday June 22, Congressman James Clyburn (D. SC), appearing on Wolf Blitzer's Situation Room was interviewed following Governor Nikki Haley bi-partisan support and statement regarding removal of the Confederate flag from the grounds of the South Carolina State Capitol in which he praised this "idea whose

BLACK NATIONALISM STILL ALIVE AND WELL

time has come!" It is interesting that just prior Mr. Blitzer had interviewed a gentleman of the League of the South in which he went on and on about the virtuous defense of the flag because of the 100,000 South Carolinians who died fighting an invader under that flag. Elderly and mature, he still seemed nervous, "defending the seeming indefensible!"

So, in his response to "Blitz," Mr. Clyburn explained his researched understanding regarding the Confederate flag. First, he reminded this flag did not come from the battlefield at the end of Civil War hostilities. He did indicate the current Confederate Flag was hoisted in opposition and response to progress made during the Civil Rights Movement of the 1960s. Even more significant, he correctly identified the Confederate Flag not as belonging to South Carolina but Tennessee as created by General Forest Beckford, founder of the Ku Klux Klan. The version flying in South Carolina was actually that of West Virginia. Thus, theirs is truly "Defense of a Myth!" He went on to explain the people defending the flag did not even know their own history! Fact is, "they did not know they did not know!"

However, this idea of defense of a myth is not new. In fact, down through recorded history, people, not necessarily misguided, but they have, through circumstances and cultural custom, been inculcated in "Defense of a Myth" and such resulting way of life. And, as "practice makes perfect" and "repetition is the bane of learning," these individuals became psychologically ingrained in believing their myriad bits the whole of reality. As such, if we examine myths in historical perspective we would realize Mr. Clyburn's subjects are subscribing to beliefs in which they stand as the majority of one, or, perhaps a small sum.

FREDERICK MONDERSON

BN PHOTO - "People of Goodwill" always seek to better the lot of society through their actions demanding "Justice in the Courts" and "Justice in the Classroom."

First, even though there are problems of reality as portrayed in the movie **Ten Commandments** starring Charleston Heston and Yul Brynner, a scene in the movie depicts King Seti I of the 19th Dynasty, when confronted with the prospects of a "Messiah" instructed his son and successor Rameses II, "If it is a myth bring it to me in a bottle. If it is a man, bring him in chains!" This admonition began events throughout history where myths have sustained people, led them falsely in beliefs and still been stanchly defended. Sometimes it led the wrong way at the fork in the road!

The story of the **Donation of Constantine** is another of those fascinating but intriguing historical documents involved in an issue of great controversy. Purportedly put to analytic scrutiny because it's an extant historical document justifying certain types of actions, problems were observed in its wording. Accordingly, Roman Emperor Constantine was on the verge of a major battle and the night before he had a dream involving a bishop's miter and other religious symbolism. Successful in the next day's battle, he attributed his success to divine intervention and as a result ended persecution of Christians and accepted Christianity as an official religion within the Roman Empire. In good faith, he convened the Council of Nicea in 325 when a great many bishops were summoned and instructed to prepare the way for the church going forward. As such, to create a unified front and solidify the magnanimous developments, the Emperor ceded great tracts of land to the church and produced a document, a deed that became the "Donation of

BLACK NATIONALISM STILL ALIVE AND WELL

Constantine." Held in great reverence, some 800 years later, linguists and other scholars, examining this prized document were alarmed it was forged, a fake, possessing no legitimacy!

What these sleuths were able to ascertain, there were words and phrases in the document that were not "invented" at the time of its issuance. That is to say, linguistically speaking, new words and phrases are added to language every day and others, by virtue of not being used, are dropped. A good example explaining this phenomenon is best understood in the following analogy. Let us, for argument sake say, we have a document written in 1920 after the Versailles Peace Conference of 1919. Sometime in the 1970s a popular phrase "Where's the beef?" appears in a TV commercial. Given this is a later creation, to have it appear in an earlier document when it was "not yet coined" or in use, tells scholars it's a later insertion and so, the authenticity of the document becomes questionable and it is deemed a forgery. This is what happened in the case of the Donation of Constantine.

BN PHOTO - Many came from all over to show their support, hear the message and return with a deeper understanding of the issues and bring about change from the "Grassroots Community."

FREDERICK MONDERSON

BN PHOTO - The National Urban League affirms: "I am Empowered!"

In the emergence of that "superior, Western, European mental capacity," a great number of historical falsifications were perpetuated to the detriment of many people and cultures. Even more important, science especially was led in the wrong direction for the longest until meticulous scholarship, *al be it* too late to prove the forgery; and, sad to say, the people concerned or benefitting from the hoax remain vociferously committed to proclaiming and defending the stated situation. Hence, we could end up with Mr. Clyburn's "Defense of a Myth!"

In the great religious swindle denying African involvement and playing a significant role in the formative efforts to establish Christianity, untold energy was expended omitting the influence of Africans as church fathers and popes. We know in the classical world, "everything African was African!" However, within the modern mind influenced by the falsity of white supremacy, even when the person, through historical evidence, was proven to be born in Africa, the spurious argument held, "Yes, he was born in Africa but of European parentage!" Undoubtedly, while this denial is more modern than ancient, it's been part of the overall methodology and

BLACK NATIONALISM
STILL ALIVE AND WELL

strategy not only to contribute to the myth of white supremacy; that is, elevating white and denigrating black; but it has caused untold psychological damage on the one hand and fooled many people on the other. The issue with the fathers of the church, notwithstanding, the case of Priscian is another prime example. This North African born individual dominated all forms of western grammatical structure for more than 1200 years. Born in the 7th Century, he wrote and taught in Europe all aspects of grammar with only minor adjustments being made to his method at the end of the 18th Century. Still, little is known of the man as an African and the significance of his work and this is considered a major historical distortion.

The "**Myth of Prester John**" is significant for the African and resources of Africa. It is a well-known fact, just prior to Columbus' voyages of discovery to the New World, Portuguese explorers Bartholomew Dias and Vasco Da Gama began explorations southward along the West African coast. As prospects for riches, trade and otherwise, the "Myth of Prester John" was created possessing end of the rainbow attractions of adventurous integrity and promises of wealth as rewards. The myth held, Prester John was considered a white, Christian, king ruling a kingdom peopled by Africans. Strange, but this white over Black is the argument applied to Egypt. And so, adventurers of every hue and cry set out to find this Prester John. Well they came searching; missionaries wearing religious garb as the first wave of imperialist colonizers, then traders, consuls and soldiers. Before long, while still searching for the king, "spheres of influence" were created, trade encouraged, land concessions secured and consuls sent to protect the missionaries and traders. To aid these, soldiers were sent who recruited locals to form "frontier forces" commanded by white officers whose role was to establish law and order. Naturally, these locals became spies breaking down their own cultural norms and acted as interpreters and so dramatic changes took place. Meanwhile Europeans continued to beat the bushes in search of Pester John.

FREDERICK MONDERSON

BN PHOTO - No matter which group, the message is the same, "Equality for All," "End Racial Profiling," "Support Trayvon's Law."

In all of this, propaganda labeled Africans as "killing and eating the white man." As Prof. John Clarke correctly reminded, "We invited the white man to lunch and we became the meal." Or, even the insight offered by King Menelik II of Ethiopia who defeated the Italians at the Battle of Adowa in 1896. "I know the strategy of European governments," he explained, "first they send missionaries, then consuls, then soldiers to protect them both." Or, even more as Jomo Kenyatta wrote in his book *Facing Mount Kenya*, "When the missionaries came, they taught us to close our eyes and pray. When we opened our eyes we were holding the Bible and they the land." In similar fashion, the Bible Study Group at "Mother Emanuel Church" invited young Dylann Roof into their religious circle and the killer committed the most unspeakable act of racial hatred made tangible in fact! So, some have argued, in as much as Prester John was not found there may very well be individuals still searching the bushes of Africa for him.

The "Myths of the Phantom and Tarzan" got much traction from that astute English mind, where Edgar Rice Burroughs, etc., fabricated superhuman white individuals overcoming and outwitting untold numbers of Africans and as Hollywood got in the act we laughed heartily in movie theaters as Africans, caricatured, reinforced the "Cigar Store African" image and myth. Even Calypsonian Mighty Sparrow sang how British Education Minister Cutridge's curriculum was intended "to create comedians."

BLACK NATIONALISM
STILL ALIVE AND WELL

BN PHOTO - "What happens to a Dream Deferred?" You tell me!

FREDERICK MONDERSON

BN PHOTO - Ask "The Black Institute." They will tell you!

That assiduous European mind, quick to explore and exploit every situation, offered all forms of rationalizations for the Slave Trade. Starting with African culture being different from that of Europe; Noah's curse condemns Africans to "obey your masters;" the Slave Trade was just that, instead widely believed robbery; Africans sold their brothers into slavery; trans-shipment was not that bad, they arrived refreshed and ready for New World sale; to hide the physical and psychological brutalities of the Middle Passage experience they were plied with skin oils and fed a last hot meal; "tight packing" and "loose packing" demands of the Triangle Trade justified expected profit margin; the terror of separation and fears of an unknown future; all in preparation "To Make Them Stand in Fear" of the white man! These were all aspects supporting the myth of white supremacy

A similar not too different case headlined the *News of the World* newspaper some 15 years ago. A By-line read, "Scientists discover the Home of Queen of Sheba, in Nigeria." Lo and behold, the

BLACK NATIONALISM STILL ALIVE AND WELL

centerfold showed the image of a white woman, despite the fact the Queen's famous words were "I am Black and comely!" Ivan Van Sertima argued the Queen's empire may have stretched across the belt of Central Africa, from east to west. This meant her empire was many times the size of Solomon's tiny country. Nevertheless, that an Editor could publish such a false photograph is an equally significant hallmark of distortion to defend a myth.

The "Myth of a Caucasian Egypt" is one of those contemporary issues strangling this aspect of African history because for most of the 19th and 20th Centuries, unchallenged interpretations of the evidence has created a false, ossified belief. Without question fathers of the foundation of Egyptological archaeology, linguistics, and anthropology did exceptional work of reclamation, analysis and identification and interpretation. However, since these were humans, and there was no Diop as critic, mistakes were made in interpretation of the data. But, ideas gone abroad are difficult to recall particularly since they were ingrained in an era of white supremacy chauvinism and imperialism's clamor. That is also why "Moderns" as Derry, Emery, even Wortham could claim "The Egyptians are Caucasians."
That is why, such scholars as Elliot Smith, even C.G. Seligman's *Races of Africa* could claim Caucasian penetration not simply in the Delta but as far as into Nubia. Conversely, while David O'Connor could pronounce, "The Egyptians were not white," William Arnett in *Evidence for the Development of Hieroglyphs in Southern Upper Egypt* could assert, "While Dr. Diop proved the Egyptians were not Caucasians, the bones could not prove they were Negroes." Despite Arnett giving only half a loaf, Diop did provide tremendous evidence to prove "Africa in Egypt" and "Egypt in Africa." Nevertheless, the "Myth" lives on of a "Caucasian Egypt." In the search for early man in the 1930s, after exhausting possible homes of Europeans, despite Raymond dart's insistence scholars should search Southern Africa, Le Gross Clarke, an Englishman, doctored a modern skull and created the "Piltdown Hoax" that mislead palaeo-anthropology science for decades until L.S.B. Leakey discovered Zinjanthropus-Boisie, 1.75 m years old in 1959 and put Clarke's myth to rest.

FREDERICK MONDERSON

BN PHOTO - There are profound messages in these images that go to the heart and conscience of being human.

The "Myth of African contributions to American culture" not only flies in the face of reason but insidiously questions the role of the fundamental pillars of music, sports, even entertainment in this

BLACK NATIONALISM
STILL ALIVE AND WELL

country. More particularly, the importance of religiosity, compassion, healing and the power of prayer on behalf of America and its leaders are without question among this nation's most valuable and cherished resources. Black scientists and inventors and their inventions, mathematicians, and much more are not only undercounted for but were omitted for much of the 19th and 20th Centuries. Even more important, for the last 50 years, school science texts across the curriculum, have totally ignored the Black scientist, underscoring the myth supporting falsity in American education thereby providing justification for a curriculum of inclusion.

BN PHOTO - Doing the "Rice Paddy Dance," Veterans at the Vietnam Veterans Wall.

FREDERICK MONDERSON

BN PHOTO - "Run2theBattle.org" - "I have a dream too;" this child asks us to "End abortion;" "End black genocide;" and much more.

Today the "Myth of the Confederate Flag" seems to be dissipating as smoke in open air. Across the nation, not simply citizens but state houses with links to the flag are now experiencing a groundswell to distance themselves from the odious atmosphere now revealed in association with the flag. A glaring irony pictured on Wednesday, June 24th 2015, when the caisson carrying Reverend Clementa Pinckney to "Lay in State" in the South Carolina State Capital building; it passed the Confederate flag fluttering in the wind. Meanwhile, many gathered nearby chanting, "Take it Down!" However, and because of the legislative maneuvering involved, in a clever ruse, an important South Carolina legislator proposed, for the Reverend's funeral, "We could take the flag down to clean it!"

It is a sad tragedy throughout the continued progress of America, lives were lost, suffering ensued, perpetrators of evil acts have, for the most part, gone unpunished and remain unrepentant having committed untold terrorist acts against Black Americans. Nevertheless, whatever may be said by the nefarious, some have

BLACK NATIONALISM STILL ALIVE AND WELL

branded racist, bigoted, inconsiderate, evil, the magnanimous humanity of African Americans un-measurable commitment to religious tenets of love, forgiveness and commiseration for fellow man are significant anchors proudly buoying the American ship of state boosting the Red, White and Blue flag's image among the many nations comprising the human family.

BN PHOTO - National Association for the Advancement of Colored People" (NAACP) in "full effect."

FREDERICK MONDERSON

BN PHOTO - "We March for Jobs and Freedom" and to "Protect Voting Rights."

BLACK NATIONALISM STILL ALIVE AND WELL

BN PHOTO - "Standing on the Side of Love" and demanding "Close Prisons not Schools," "Justice for Trayvon Martin" and "End New Jim Crow!"

FREDERICK MONDERSON

BN PHOTO - "Civil Rights for Every One" is a reasonable demand for Civility, again and again.

37. "PUTTING THEM AWAY NICELY"
By
Dr. Fred Monderson

Having attended the funerals of Sonny Carson, Jitu Weusi, Elombe Brath, Major Owens, Mary Pinkett, Ollie McClean, Rev. Clarence Norman, Sr., and most of all, the spectacular home-going of Dr. Yosef ben-Jochannan; I'm reminded of when the question of burials of our loved and revered ones was put to Dr. John Henrik Clarke he simply responded, "We Put Them Away Nicely." In the African community, that final going home ceremony is most an affirmation of joy rather than an expression of sadness! Granted, we'll miss the loved one and so some sad remorse is expected, but the joy of having experienced their presence, witnessed their good works and their light illuminating the path of humanity as a part of their earthly existence is what constitutes the joyous moment. With that belief comes even greater expectation that this earthly goodness so wonderfully created will continue to benefit those who shared in the magnanimous life experience.

BLACK NATIONALISM STILL ALIVE AND WELL

While million-year old African fossils many not have revealed any evidence of the beauty of a well-orchestrated burial, this is not the case among Nile Valley dwellers who went to great lengths to dispose of their dead. In that case, the ancient Egyptians left extraordinary evidence of intricate preparation to make the afterlife a truly wonderful and lasting experience. The building of pyramids and tombs, the development of the practice of mummification, the provisioning of the tomb, the religious beliefs and practices conducted, prior to and after depositing of the deceased into his "eternal home," are parts of the big picture that we vigorously discuss their experience today, millennia later, means that immortality they sought was attained.

BN PHOTO - Dr. Jack Felder makes a point at the "After Funeral Forum" in Ghana.

FREDERICK MONDERSON

BN PHOTO - Other participants at the "After Funeral Forum" discussing the significance of Samuel Carson opening the "Door of Return" and also inaugurating the First Emancipation Day Celebration, August 1, 1998.

From as early as the Predynastic Period before 5000 B.C., evidence indicates a belief in an afterlife phenomenon that became formulated, crystallized, and imbedded in a religious practice subscribed to by high and low, that is from king to commoner.

As it came to be articulated in a philosophically enshrined belief system, these ancient Africans believed this earthly existence was a temporary sojourn but the world beyond death is of a more eternal nature. They held that a life guided by the principles of Ma'at, viz., justice, truth, righteousness, with adequate preparation cold attain that justification and immortality. As such, in the evolution of tracing such a belief, the period immediately before the dynasties is divided into three culture sequences labeled Badarian, Amratian, and Gerzean or Naqada I and II. From this early time, c. 4200-3200 B.C., evidence in graves point to an aspiration in an afterlife where individuals hoped to continue their lives, in spirit form essentially, and similarly as they did on earth. The graves reveal the deceased equipped, for example, his tomb with tools of his profession; food, clothing and leisure devices; and even in the case of companionship

BLACK NATIONALISM STILL ALIVE AND WELL

males had miniature effigies of women to accompany them for purposes of pleasure.

BN PHOTO - "Nation of Islam" member on the street in Ghana, at time of the "Bones" returning "home."

Narmer, a Theban from Upper Egypt, mobilized a military force c. 3200 B.C., sailed north to Lower Egypt and defeated a comparative force, as some have argued, because of the emerging and prevailing wealth of the Nile Valley. Then this first king of the first dynasty unified the country under a single administration ushering in the Archaic Period of dynasties 1 and 2. He set in place the social, political and administrative structures that would shape the society for three millennia. By the time of the Old Kingdom, Dynasties 3-6, with the society's fundamental institutions in place, the practices of art and architecture and religious beliefs began to define the manner of disposal of the dead. Whereas in the Predynastic Period burials were simply holes in the ground, by the third and fourth dynasties funeral architecture evolved through the mastaba, Step-Pyramid and finally the True Pyramid forms. By the fifth and sixth dynasties, five pyramids were illustrated with the *Pyramid Texts* that by the Middle Kingdom became the *Coffin Texts* and in the New Kingdom, the

FREDERICK MONDERSON

Book of the Dead. Certainly by this time the art of mummification was evolving in practice

While in the Old Kingdom the *Pyramid Texts* of hieroglyphic symbols nearly a millennium in evolution, represented a collection of social commentary, primarily they represented the religious dogma that defined and regulated the process by which the king was received in the afterlife and where he became a god. In this case, the "big dog" or king with the requisite resources at his disposal left ample evidence of the practical, philosophic and religious drama designed to create the immortality we have become so familiar with. However, all the trappings that go into the pyramids, tombs, the decoration and provisioning of the "eternal house" attracted a "criminal element" that would desecrate the sacred site, assault the blessed dead, and loot the treasures accompanying them into the next life. Thus, "lock and key;" "Watch man" in endowment responsibilities; traps and pitfalls; nothing really stopped the desecration and denial of the ultimate objective. Therefore, the deceased finally resorted to a belief in magic that would protect and transform his preparation of the final objective.

As such, a number of factors contributing to the end result can be enumerated as follows:

(1)   Because the Egyptian believed this earthly existence was temporary and the future life more permanent, he built his domestic residence of perishable material and secured his "eternal home" for more lasting duration, with attendant protections. Conversely, and as an example, the king built his palace of perishable material, and his god's temple of the more permanent material, stone.

(2)   The process of provisioning, that is, making his tomb comfortable for the spirit that would inhabit it, was provided with all manner of luxury items from food to tools and leisurely and recreational items of games, musical instruments to furniture and religious paraphernalia.

(3)   All representations were symbolic and aesthetic conventions expanded and became refined domestic utensils, military equipment,

BLACK NATIONALISM STILL ALIVE AND WELL

industrial implements and other entertainment paraphernalia including evidence of the hunt, the banquet scene of music and joviality, working the fields, making grape juice and wine, even bakery, butchery and statuary to represent the deceased.

To this we add, not simply "reserved' statues of the deceased in case the mummy was destroyed but also servant statues called "Ushabtis" or "answerers" who would do the manual things the deceased was required to do such as working the fields, to preparing his food and toilet, to providing joy, entertainment and protection.

BN PHOTO - Sonny Carson is flanked by Bishop Shivers' son and Dr. Jack Felder after the "Bones Ceremony."

FREDERICK MONDERSON

BN PHOTO - The dynamic scene at Gravesite as local priests struggle to insist Mr. Samuel Carson gets the best burial possible.

38. "UNITY MARCH FOR GRANGER!"
BY
DR. FRED MONDERSON

In a tumultuous outpouring of national pride and fervent patriotism, while flouting the colors, Guyanese from all over flocked to Church and Bedford Avenues in Brooklyn, to "March and Rally" in support of the new government of former army General David Granger. In a strategic coalition David Granger's **ANPU** and Moses Nagamootoo's **AFC** registered a stunning defeat of the incumbent PPP under the leadership of Donald Ramotar backed by Bharrat Jagdeo in election held May 11, 2015.

In many respects, this was a date long awaited since 1992 when the PPP captured the Presidency of the Cooperative Republic of Guyana. The interesting thing about that win was the new leaders instituted a voraciously vicious and corrupt system of government of

BLACK NATIONALISM STILL ALIVE AND WELL

unparalleled nepotism some have characterized as an ethnocracy! In a nation comprising some six races, with the PPP representing some 45 percent people of Indian descent; the opposition representing 40 percent of African heritage; and various ethnicities the remainder; privileged Indians dominated all aspects of the society especially the economy and exerted undue influence on the judiciary amid unparalleled charges of corruption and political party favoritism. In this unprincipled warped political experiment and ignoring all others, the PPP government, beginning with Cheddie Jagan, succeeded by his wife Janet Jagan who trained Bharrat Jagdeo and he was succeeded by Donald Ramotar, all unjustly favored their ethnic base, allowing it to capture some "95 percent of the nation's economic" infrastructure. Not only did they only allow the African element to spend their monies in Indian owned establishments but the government waged a campaign of employee replacements in strategic institutions, prosecuting economic squeezes against African businessmen and turned its back while allies waged a campaign of extra-judicial killings claiming untold numbers of lives no one has answered for. First, the Minister of Home Affairs Gajraj was implicated in nefarious activities; removed, he was re-assigned as Ambassador to India, but the shenanigans continued.

BN PHOTO - The Guyana flag proudly flown at the "March for Granger" on Church Avenue in Brooklyn.

The convicted drug trafficker Roger Khan, among several supporters of the government, acquired large tracks of crown land in unpublished, bid-less, giveaways. The government was moot as several African businessmen were forced from engaging in any meaningful and legal business enterprise that was subsequently taken over by supporters of the PPP. Even more significant, for nearly two decades Guyana was characterized as a drug conduit to America and Europe in the most ingenious methods, whether in exported wood, fish, food packages, by couriers employing American and European airport personnel and who knows what other means. The embarrassment characterized Guyana as a laughing stock among nations while well-meaning Guyanese were embarrassed by the shameful behavior.

Now, having outlasted this catastrophic era in the nation as disgraced history, and after Guyanese constituents had spoken through the ballot box; there was cause for celebration and so, many came to support the new government's call for unity and to party! Given such, the "Unity March," more practically a "March for Granger" was actually a miniature Brooklyn "Labor Day Celebration" many times over. The people were overjoyed and motivated to be free from an "Indian Government Captivity!" They came to celebrate "The Man Granger" who, in an ingenious and well-worked coalition strategy moved the obdurate and malicious mountain of "Indian Fiefdom Control!"

BN PHOTO - The sign says it all, in this "March for Peace," emphasizing "**One People, One Nation, One Destiny**."

BLACK NATIONALISM STILL ALIVE AND WELL

BN PHOTO - Part of the crowd of persons who came to celebrate in this "**March for Granger**."

They came to celebrate General Granger for efforts to focus a new beam of light into the pervaded darkness of Guyana government practices that for more than two decades was amoral and philosophically unethical as it ignored the practical constitutional responsibilities of an elected government to the totality of its citizenry. It is expected the same protections and privileges given foreign visitors, every Guyanese citizen, at home and abroad, is inherently entitled to.

Let us for argument say, any person wrongly victimized sues the government and a court of competent jurisdiction rules in their favor; would the current or ancient regime be held putatively responsible? This is where constitutional guarantees of citizens come into play. Released from such prohibitions and the freedoms to expect such are what the revelers came to celebrate and expect demonstrated in this "March for Granger."

Being removed from under the dark clouds of drug trafficking and money-laundering stigma; the obnoxious stench of official corruption and nepotism; exerting undue influence over the nation's judiciary; challenges to the protections to home and person are what

FREDERICK MONDERSON

participants came to celebrate and expect in this "Walk for Granger!"

BN PHOTO - Another view of the crowd of celebrants who came to celebrate Mr. Granger's victory at the polls in Guyana.

Overseas Guyanese in Brooklyn, New York and others from far away as Connecticut; Washington, DC; Atlanta; Toronto, Canada; and even Guyana itself; revelers representing family members, friends and neighbors in the "Old Country;" all came to celebrate the promises and assurances of a bright, safe, healthy and prosperous future for young, old and yet to be born Guyanese. The fervor and air of joviality seemed to represent the molding of a truly free, independent, joyful and carefree Guyanese personality, resurrected and anew! They came to march for the promise of a sound education, a fair chance at economic success with the ability to raise a family in nation building continuity and relish in the prospect, respect and dignity of being Guyanese at home and abroad. They came to feel being Guyanese means something special and not some estranged individuals whose country was constantly black-listed as a drug-cartel stooge while its government turned its back to the people but offered a friendly face and assisting hand to moneyed interests suspected in all forms of activities evident in their ostentations display of rapid rise in wealth, while it blocked every effort to pass a money laundering bill to check such illegal activities.

BLACK NATIONALISM STILL ALIVE AND WELL

BN PHOTO - One happy celebrant shows the colors and the motto: "A good life for all Guyanese."

FREDERICK MONDERSON

BN PHOTO - Poster showing the various Presidents who have led Guyana in its 50 years of independence.

"Sometimes" and "All true (100%)" Guyanese came to march in expectation of accountability of government workers and the adherence to the rule of law as the "Granger Era" must symbolize and vigorously pursue the idea of "**ONE PEOPLE, ONE NATION, ONE DESTINY**!"

BLACK NATIONALISM STILL ALIVE AND WELL

They came to the "Unity March for Granger" to dance and sing and did; wailing "We ain't giving up No Mountain, We ain't giving up No Tree, We ain't giving up No River, that belong to We!" And they sang, "Not one Rice Grain; Not one Cuirass; Not one Ripe Mango; Not a Blade of Grass!" And they sang, "Not one Blue Saki; Not one Eddoe; "Not one Jackass; Not a Blade of Grass!"

BN PHOTO - Some of the Marchers who came out to celebrate David Granger's victory at the polls in Guyana, defeating the incumbent PPP who led the nation for 23 years.

FREDERICK MONDERSON

BN PHOTO - Head of the parade "March for Granger" on Church Avenue in Brooklyn, New York.

39. "PLAYING THE JAGAN CARD!"
BY
DR. FRED MONDERSON

Now that the election of May 11, 2015 is over and the incumbent government headed by President Donald Romotar has lost while the APNU + AFC coalition has won, the "minions often masquerading as whales" have invoked the **JAGAN CARD** - "We were cheated, not defeated" or "We wuz robbed!"

For twenty-three years the PPP led first by Cheddi Jagan, his wife Janet Jagan, Bharat Jagdeo and then Donald Romotar have ruled Guyana with a callousness and in an arrogantly disgraceful manner, never complaining about losing or being robbed while running the country down to the bottom of the soles of its feet! In a land of many waters, such is a rare and cherished commodity. In 2006 Tony Vieira boasted, "Show me a road the PPP built!" This is thus indicative of dereliction of its responsibility towards the Guyanese people.

BLACK NATIONALISM STILL ALIVE AND WELL

BN PHOTO - "Buxtonians for **APNU + AFC**" is a mighty slogan demonstrated here.

FREDERICK MONDERSON

BN PHOTO - Well, she's all decked out in colors of her nation.

BLACK NATIONALISM STILL ALIVE AND WELL

There are no good losers! All losers are losers, but when losers refuse to accept their loss based on merit or lack thereof, such behaviors underscores their losing underbelly ingloriously camouflaged while freenzily feeding at the public trough; then one has to wonder at their morality and ethical standards as supposed "national statesmen!"

Arriving at Cheddie Jagan International Airport on an American passport, a female immigration officer informed: "Sir, you need a visa which will cost $25.00 US." Her associate, another male immigration officer said, "No! He was born here! He does not need a visa!" *Ipso facto*, when Bharrat Jagdeo especially traveled abroad as the President of the "Cooperative Republic of Guyana," even Donald Romotar, they did so as my President! I was the best serving waiter at the first Independence Dinner serving the Royal table. So good, I was promised a medal but never received one! As such, then if these Presidents did not represent me in the most genuine manner, it is incumbent on me to criticize them. But they did not!!!

Imagine! Jagdeo as "Champion of the Earth," as currently charged, has been sowing poisonous seeds of racial hatred in an attempt to continue winning the support of Indians who constitute the backbone support of his political party. But this man Jagdeo, who has been heralded as the protégé of former President Janet Jagan opened a whole can of worms. Thus, one has to wonder, did he acquire his racist tendencies, as charged, from his association with Mrs. Jagan or did he incubate them on his own. After all, the columnist Freddie Kissoon has constantly questioned the intellectual capacity of PPP theorists of whom Jagdeo is the premier strategist.

Case in point, some years ago disaffected members of the PPP formed a political party and contested the 2012 election of which Jagdeo's party won and formed the government but lost its parliamentary majority. That political party vowed never to collaborate with the PNC opposition. As events unfolded, particularly as characterized in a column written by Freddie Kissoon in which he brilliantly described the deplorable condition the PPP

FREDERICK MONDERSON

led government had run the country into. Everyone knows, in PPP strongholds in Berbice and elsewhere the streets are beautifully paved and the lights are lit, but in Georgetown the gutters are overflowing with dirt and other garbage. The Kokers are also in deplorable condition! To say no more! There was a time when kids playing nearby could retrieve their marbles from the gutters but alas, those days are long gone, thanks to the PPP. However, juxtaposed are economic skyscrapers representing "Indian control of 95% of the nation's economy" which many characterized as funded by drug-laundered money; and thus, it is blatantly obvious why there has been no honest effort on part of the PPP led government to pass a money laundering bill!

BN PHOTO - The White Shirts were part of the detail to ensure safety for the marchers.

BLACK NATIONALISM STILL ALIVE AND WELL

BN PHOTO - Such jubilation could only come from the relief after more than two decades of misguided rule by a political party only interested in "Grabbing."

Now, as circumstances unfolded, political opposition parties merged to form a united front. This, the PPP failed to envision, making manifest their unrelenting efforts of catering to their moneyed supporters manifesting the ethnocracy mentality they demonstrated and effectuated at the expense of the Guyanese people. It is truly strange that their Indian supporters, more than 200,000, did not seem to read Freddie Kissoon's article yet they voted to support an ancient regime wallowing in corruption; unmindful of accountability on part of the rulers towards the people of Guyana. These are the sown seeds of political, moral and historical failures.

This reality has certainly gone abroad! Standing at the airport carousel at JFK International Airport waiting for luggage having arrived on a flight from Guyana; some five years ago, three Indian men were shooting the breeze! The first one said, "Man, Guyana is a joke!" Hearing the word Guyana I listened more intently! The second said, "You don't want to tell people you are from Guyana. Every time the news reports there is a drug bust coming out of

FREDERICK MONDERSON

Guyana, a fellow worker comes to my cubicle and teases me un ending. It is so embarrassing. The world knows Guyana has become a conduit for drugs in the most unimaginable yet seemingly creative manner."

The third man whispered to his colleagues, "I hear the Americans have handed Mr. Jagdeo's government a list of some 42 person who are big time drug dealers but the government has yet to accuse one of them." Silently I thought, that's the "Indian government in Guyana" that is responsible for all the black eyes the country is getting! Thus, from way back there was need for a change. Lest we forget, Malcolm X often reminded, "History is a good teacher" At the height of the French Revolution in 1792, the Englishman Edmund Burke wrote in his *Reflections on the Revolution in France*, "The only thing necessary for evil to triumph is for good men to do or say nothing!"

Who could forget, after the PPP triumph under Bharat Jagdeo at the 2006 election, miscreants defaced several PNC billboards, with black paint! The one in front of the National Theater and another in the industrial area in South, among others, are stark reminders of the racial hatred that pollutes the PPP mindset. Neither Jagdeo, nor Gajraj, nor Rohee had the "testicular fortitude" to condemn this disgraceful display. Thus, as these "good men" stayed silent, evil as racial hatred triumphed! Perhaps this was their intent! Nevertheless, the scuttlebutt holds in that mindset "black is evil" and so these people harbor that evil.

BLACK NATIONALISM STILL ALIVE AND WELL

BN PHOTO - Another segment of the marchers for Granger here to celebrate his victory at the polls, May 11, 2014.

BN PHOTO - More of the "Marchers for Granger" as they paraded on Church Avenue.

FREDERICK MONDERSON

Now, in 2015 modern times, instead of crafting a political campaign based on accomplishments on behalf of the Guyanese people, PPP cadre, of whom Mr. Jagdeo is a principal, fed their people a distorted record and picture of L.F.S. Burnham, former President of Guyana and now dead some three decades! That is, after they have done everything to besmirch his name, image and message and even deprived the indigenous of Timheri as a significant indigenous landmark in naming it for Cheddi Jagan. Meanwhile the opposition campaigned "It's time for change!" "There should be one Guyana;" "no preaching of racial hatred;" "everyone should have equal access to the nation's resources and the ability to pursue business enterprises with the same opportunities." "Down with little Caesars!" A general rule holds, political leaders should be held accountable for their tenure in office and criminal behaviors should be punished to the full extent of the law!"

An insightful Guyanese theoretician once offered, "After the 1964 election, Mr. Jagan did not reach out to the African people. Instead he preached to his Indian base, 'I was cheated, not defeated!'"

Today, history has repeated itself! Decades later, neither Mr. Jagan nor his wife Janet; and neither Mr. Jagdeo nor Mr. Ramotar has reached out to the African people to offer even their discarded potato peelings. Everyone knows "Buxtonians stop train!" When they did not bow down to Janet she attacked Buxton promising a clear view from the main road to Cheddi Jagan International. Nevertheless, and rightfully the Mighty sparrow once sang, "The Age of the Tyrants decline!" Naturally there are a few "Negro 'Soup drinkers' in their midst!" In the new era of accountability, many of these and others must now seek visas to reside abroad. However, who knows how many names were mentioned in "Roger Khan's prison song," while the long arm of American law is "waiting in the slips!"! One local New York newspaper connected the jailed drug trafficker Roger Khan and former President Bharat Jagdeo as associates! And this is the Pied Piper some 200,000 Indian people chose to lead them into the wilderness of an uncertain future.

BLACK NATIONALISM STILL ALIVE AND WELL

BN PHOTO - Still more Marchers for Granger following his victory at the polls.

BN PHOTO - Even more marchers for Granger celebrating his victory at the polls.

Again, like Mr. and Mrs. Jagan and Jagdeo, President Ramotar did not reach out to the African Guyanese people but continued a policy

FREDERICK MONDERSON

of brutal oppression forcing them to pray and hope a "Change is gonna come!" Rightly so, "Change has come!" The rest is history repeating itself as the PPP leadership again echoed the Jagan **pliant**, "We was robbed" or "We were cheated not defeated!" But, as Guyana has shed the poisonous cocoon of the past decades and seeks to soar into the future as the Golden Arrow, even PPP supporters are wailing, "For the party to survive viably **JAGDEO MUST GO**!

BN PHOTO - There seems to be no end of Marchers in support of David Granger.

BN PHOTO - Even more marchers, such enthusiasm, all for Granger!

BLACK NATIONALISM STILL ALIVE AND WELL

BN PHOTO - Erik stands next to the postbox in Sponge Box makeover, in DC.

FREDERICK MONDERSON

40. WHEN MCCONNELL MEETS OBAMA!
By
DR. FRED MONDERSON

It wasn't a beer summit! It wasn't to a fish-fry when President Obama invited Senator Mitch McConnell to the White House to discuss the nation's business. With a number of pressing issues facing the incoming 114th Congress of which Mr. McConnell will now replace Senator Harry Reid as Senate Majority Leader, the meeting promised to be intense, crucial and will mark a new chapter in White House/Congressional cooperation for negotiations of substantive issues. After all, a history of relationships between the two leaders has been marred by party rivalry and much more; but the Senator, while donning his poker face wants to appear defiantly business-like yet conciliatorily cordial, with the nation's future at stake. Thus, Mr. McConnell arrived at the White House door as a myriad of questions began cascading down that percolating waterfall mind of his; without question, he is experienced in the art of the possible! Yet, he remained mindful he is coming up against a big one! He is then ushered into the room where such important and pressing issues are discussed and hammered out. Once there, waiting for the President, however, rather than take a seat, the Senator paces the room, admiring the photographs of great men gracing the walls and for a moment wondered, then dismissed, "Nah!"

Before entering the room, President Obama, on his part, having anxiously worked on the invitation, nervously pondered the encounter. For a moment, he thought of donning his "imperial décor" and making "a grand emperor's" appearance. That is, crown, gown, scepter, jeweled arms, a dagger in is waist, just in case, and accompanied by his fan bearers and entourage! He, however,

BLACK NATIONALISM STILL ALIVE AND WELL

dismissed this form of appearance as too "over the top" and decided to appear just as businesslike as the Senator. Then he entered the room, greeted the Senator with a handshake and advised he take a seat. At table, the President offered, "Coffee or Tea" but thought "he must not get the better of me!" The Senator accepted coffee and both men prepared his own from fixings previously placed.

BN PHOTO - Dr. Martin Luther King, Jr. in whatever representation is still "a man of the people," we celebrate in January of every year.

FREDERICK MONDERSON

BN PHOTO - Duke Ellington, Dr. King and Rosa Parks with another beauty in DC.

There was a deafening silence in the room as each man sipped his java, as the two great minds raced breathtakingly over hill and dale to arrive at ice-breaking consensus getting to negotiations. The President again greeted, "Hello Senator, welcome!" Mr. McConnell replies, "Hello Mr. President, I hope Michelle and the girls are well! Give them my best!" A curt thank you and a smile by Mr. Obama seemed a tremendous ice-breaker. Both men then sit at the sparklingly polished conference table.

Mr. Obama, realizing Mr. McConnell is in a much more powerful position than previously, ponders how he will get him to come aboard and help pass some of his pressing legislation.

BLACK NATIONALISM STILL ALIVE AND WELL

BN PHOTO - Eric and Luis before A. Philip Randolph's bust in Union Station, Washington, DC.

FREDERICK MONDERSON

As Mr. McConnell sipped his coffee, black with two sugars, he peered over the cup's brim, thinking! "What an uncomfortable position I'm in! I laid my cards out early and he trumped me. Now he's here in his second term and though I'm incoming Majority Leader and must work with him in the people's interest, I'm not sure how he feels. I know he's a good guy but my people have not been kind to him. If only we could take back some of what was said! I know there is a lawsuit pending and there is talk of impeachment but I'm sure our people don't want to shut down the government, again."

Mr. Obama, on the other hand, studying Mr. McConnell, thinks, "He's a smooth operator who has thrown everything at me including the kitchen sink. Still, I must avoid letting him have his way with me as he and Speaker Boehner did in our previous encounters."

Mr. Obama then spoke. "Senator you know we must work together for the good of our country. People sent us to Washington to pass laws to benefit the nation."

"I agree, Mr. President!"

"Still," Obama added, "even as some 10.9 million private sector jobs have been added to the work force, your party members in the House have blocked my Jobs Bill. Persons such as Senator Cruz in your House have blocked my Executive and Judicial Nominations. Your party members also refuse to permanently extend tax credits for working families."

"Well Mr. President, it's not like you think" the Senator responded." I know my fellow Republican Representative King from New York labeled Mr. Cruz a 'fraud' but we represent a wide spectrum of Republican thought and if you try hard enough, I will try to work with you."

"Sure" Obama replied, but thought, "You pay more attention to the interest of the one percent."

"Like I said, my constituency is wide ranging."

BLACK NATIONALISM STILL ALIVE AND WELL

"Let us talk about the vote to fund the government." He seemed to touch a sore spot.

Silently, the Senator again thought, "I know we lost favor with the American people when we shut down the government the last time. We cannot afford to act in a similar manner but Mr. President you must give us something." "Mr. President," he continued, "if you scratch my back, I'll scratch yours."

"Ok, Senator. What would be your primary request?"

"How about scaling back Dodd-Frank financial regulations to give banks some relief. To which I would add, environmental regulations that reduce EPA funding and preventing the agency from regulating the lead content of ammunition or fishing tackle and exempting livestock producers from greenhouse gas regulations?"

BN PHOTO - Another view of the Supreme Court of the United States with its motto of "Justice Under Law" and its wonderful Corinthian columns.

FREDERICK MONDERSON

BN PHOTO - Eastern entrance of the Capital Building, Washington, DC.

"That is a really tough request," the President replied. "How about moving forward on my Surgeon General and other nominations and no substantial challenges to my Affordable Care Act? As you know, practical governance in the history of our nation has been the willingness to compromise. I want funding for Homeland Security Department, Medicare payments for doctors and a more vigorous Highway Transit Fund. "

"Mr. President I will have to do a lot of arm twisting but I will push to fund the government until next September, but you must strengthen the military and there should be no funding for the District of Columbia Marijuana legalization effort.

"But I must get funding to fight Ebola at home and abroad and to fight in Iraq, Afghanistan and against ISIL (ISIS) as well as to train Syrian rebels."

"Sir, let us get something done and then we can work on the others."

"Ok!"

Both men parted feeling they had accomplished something through talking and compromise.

BLACK NATIONALISM STILL ALIVE AND WELL

BN PHOTO - Side entrance of the Jefferson Building of the Library of Congress.

BN PHOTO - Front entrance of the Jefferson Building of the Library of Congress.

FREDERICK MONDERSON

41. CALLING OUT OBAMA!
BY
DR. FRED MONDERSON

The "Britisher" who murdered the American hostage Tim Foley, in stating ISIL's message called out Mr. Obama, which in itself is an affront and challenge! It was terrible he committed an unspeakable horror but to specifically direct his invective towards "Obama" was a challenge that has to be met. However, we must first of all recognize the three-fold nature of this situation.

First, ISIL, in seeking attention to their much lamented military action many have characterized as barbaric, needed to respond to American Iraqi bombing pushback enabling humanitarian assistance to Yazdis cornered on that Iraqi mountaintop. As bombings signaled America's repeated resolve in standing good and against tyranny and terrorism, Edmond Burke's universal admonition became more manifest. "The only thing necessary for evil to triumph is for good men to say or do nothing!" Thus, America's response to the siege was to bomb ISIL's targets in the vicinity.

Second, say what you will, but America is synonymous with championing the underdog and oppressed. This has become much more realistic when it comes to guarding and responding to the safety of its citizens facing harm abroad. Jim Foley, an American journalist, was captured by rebels some have labeled terrorists in Syria, more than two years ago. It is understandable, the dangers of being in harm's way in the middle of such a conflict. However, there is international law stating "Prisoners of Wars" should be treated humanely and this was expected regarding Mr. Foley. Well, the ISIL rebel did the unthinkable in beheading Mr. Foley. This unspeakable act sent shudders across the globe that, in this day and age; persons, in this case, terrorists, could act so inhumanly, especially boastful in public.

BLACK NATIONALISM STILL ALIVE AND WELL

BN PHOTO - Garden decoration in Washington, DC at the Enid A. Haupt Garden.

BN PHOTO - Another masterpiece at the Enid A. Haupt Garden, within the Castle Grounds, Washington, DC.

Ok. So the ISIL terrorists have been rampaging across Iraq and Syria, pillaging, killing in murderous swaths and seizing territory. Then they beheaded Mr. Foley. In this final assault and insult, they called Mr. Obama's name as representative of the American people.

FREDERICK MONDERSON

They spoke directly to him in a threatening tone. Reasonable people will acknowledge, Mr. Obama must respond having being called out.

Equally, Lieutenant (Light) Colonel Robert Maginnis wrote an editorial critical of the President. A CNN program anchor asked Mr. Maginnis to explain his statement that "Mr. Obama lacked the testicular fortitude to attack ISIL at their bases in Syria!"

BN PHOTO - Part of the majesty of Washington, undiluted, and serene in its beauty.

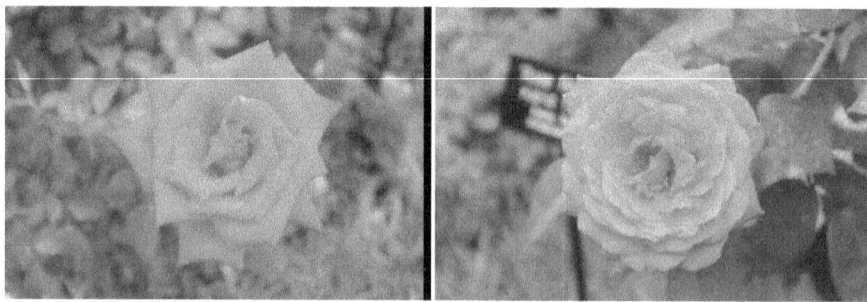

BN PHOTO - Even more beautiful flowers from the National Garden in DC.

BLACK NATIONALISM STILL ALIVE AND WELL

Here again, the wherewithal Mr. Obama brings to the table as President, viz., a wonderfully active intellectual capacity grounded in an effective work ethic associates and assistants have characterized as frighteningly well-prepared on all issues of concern. All this is enhanced by an exceptional team of advisers, military and civilian, who contribute various expert viewpoints on issues that enlighten and encourage Mr. Obama to arrive at the most optimum decision regarding any issue under study.

Mr. Obama has always demonstrated his thinking style is not one to rush to judgment but to deliberate all the pros and cons before arriving at a consensus and then final decision. However, in case of ISIL, as the United States of America Declaration of Independence insists, "After a long train of abuses," and if you add the personal touch the executioner added, the consequences should be expected. Add to this Mr. Maginnis' dare, tons of "bricks" will descend on ISIL!

BN PHOTO - The beauty of nature reflects the inner beauty of man irrespective.

FREDERICK MONDERSON

BN PHOTO - More of the beauty of the National Garden in Washington, DC.

So, the President ordered surveillance over Syria to gather real-time information about ISIL's status. In some of General Clarke's comments, though critical at times, he stated: "The President ordered air reconnaissance to add to existing knowledge about ISIL." Here again is reinforced an aspect of Mr. Obama's thinking strategy. Make sure every step is on a firm foundation by studying all aspects of its ramifications. However, past experiences have taught Mr. Obama a great deal. President George Bush took a "go it alone attitude" against Saddam Hussein in Iraq in 2003 when the world admonished against such recklessness. This damaged the world's perception about America which Mr. Obama had to repair and reverse at the same time enabling him to learn many things.

BLACK NATIONALISM STILL ALIVE AND WELL

Mr. Obama is not simply a passive thinker, for while he contemplates the "Syria scenario," he continues to pound ISIL movements in Iraq. All the while he strategizes to organize a coalition that will represent a broad consensus designed to eviscerate the "cancer" he spoke of. As caution rules his thinking, when pressed on Syria in a News Conference on Thursday August 28, 2914, Mr. Obama insisted he "did not have a strategy, yet!" He insisted this is because many, especially the press, had jumped ahead of him and were practically printing dynamics of his bombing strikes in Syria.

Many quickly sought to characterize Mr. Obama as either weak or ineffective because he did not have a "Syrian strategy," but in clarification it became clear what he actually meant. As explained, his ISIL strategy was based on creation of a unified Iraqi government that was inclusive of significant elements of ethnic Iraqis. Once this is achieved, there would be support for Iraqi forces in armaments and training. He seeks to engage regional governments to become involved because ISIL poses an even greater threat to them in the long run. He was working to engage global allies to support action against ISIL and then once these "ducks were lined up," he would consult Congress to authorize the use of more effective military force against ISIL in Iraq and then possibly in their home base in Syria.

Men of vision reason, the President "does not want to tip his hand" for as many would tend to believe, ISIL are also watching his press conference. However, what the President is showing by his actions are as follows.

1. The humility of the really powerful.

2. The integrity of a human being who respects the sanctity of human life which his critics do not have.

3. In his respect for human life, Mr. Obama is reluctant to risk the life of others without all legitimate consideration.

FREDERICK MONDERSON

4. He recognizes Iraq is a sovereign nation and under international law recognizes America does not preclude the sovereignty of every other nation.

5. When it became clear Osama bin Laden had taken up residence in a sovereign nation he had the "Testicular Fortitude" to order military action that ended the life of the murderous mastermind, a feat which had eluded several presidents before him.

6. The leader of Al Qaeda in Somalia, Al-Shabab, Mr. Ahmed Godane, long on Mr. Obama's radar and his resulting demise says much for planning and strategy, equally Obama's "stick-to-it-iveness" which trumps the Colonel's contention.

Perhaps when this is over, Lt. Colonel Maginnis will have the "testiclar fortitude" to eat crow and admit sending Seal Team Six to pursue Osama bin Laden was indeed a courageous act as did the Somali surgical strike.

Thus, Mr. Obama actions will not only address the Colonel's challenge but will answer the executioner's dare and punish him for his cruelty and upstart arrogance!

BLACK NATIONALISM STILL ALIVE AND WELL

BN PHOTO - Still more of the beauty of nature to be found in the National Garden.

42. OBAMA AND LEADERSHIP
BY
DR. FRED MONDERSON

Of all American presidents demonstrating outstanding leadership in challenging times, perhaps none has faced more difficulties than Barack Obama. Granted each President faced, for example, George Washington and foundation of the nation; Thomas Jefferson and the Louisiana Purchase and Barbary Pirates; James Monroe and his Doctrine; Abraham Lincoln and Secession and Civil War; Franklin

FREDERICK MONDERSON

D. Roosevelt and the New Deal in run-up to World War II; Dwight Eisenhower and the Korean War; Ronald Reagan and the Cold War; and George W. Bush stung by September 11, 2001; but none, in time perspective, has faced the challenges meted out to President Obama. Thus, contrary to misguided belief fed by insidious propaganda, Mr. Obama had demonstrated exemplary leadership. Nevertheless, perhaps only some people, his critics, in need of a Hubble Telescopic vision can see, understand and appreciate his accomplishments and this is what makes his tenure as the 44th President so exceptional.

George Washington and the founding fathers, in establishing the new nation and institutions, the parameters of its survival and sustainability viz., the constitution endowing institutions and a variety of powers to make the system work was indeed a formidable challenge. Yet, with the exception of a few Tory loyalists, everyone was rooting for the success of the President and his men to make the new nation a success. Upon realization that Jefferson's Louisiana Purchase not simply tremendously expanded the physical borders of the nation with the promise of the potential for great economic prosperity in both free and slave sections of the economy, many of the vast majority of movers and shakers lauded and aspiring property owners, hailed Mr. Jefferson for the nation's extraordinary good fortune now that the Haitian Revolution under Toussaint L'Ouverture had forced Napoleon to bequeath that great largess to America for some $15 million, less than the price of some New York City apartments these days. Thus, Jefferson's work in writing the Declaration of Independence and launching the new nation, together with the Louisiana Purchase endeared the nation to support his presidency especially in his challenge to the Barbary Pirates.

BLACK NATIONALISM
STILL ALIVE AND WELL

BN PHOTO - Again, more of nature's beauty found in the Capital's National Garden.

FREDERICK MONDERSON

BN PHOTO - Here's another beauty of nature to be found in the National Garden.

Following cessation of hostilities in Europe ending the aftermath of the French Revolution and Napoleonic Wars; and in America, the War of 1812, classed as the Second War for Independence against Britain that ended in 1815; James Monroe faced the horde of European imperialists seeking to regain their New World recolonization. Again, this bold move that created a lucrative economic market for the US in Latin America was hailed as a great leadership strategy especially since it was backed by the power of the British naval might.

With a nation divided culturally, economically and politically, the beat of the drums of war, secession and actual war, the loyalists supported Mr. Lincoln and hailed his leadership at a time of great distress for the nation. Winning the day, or war, outlining a plan to

BLACK NATIONALISM STILL ALIVE AND WELL

bind the wounds of war and heal the nation then deploy a plan towards a path of economic development, Mr. Lincoln was seen as a genius. Losing his life as he did, his greatness was amplified.

Franklin D. Roosevelt was elected in 1932 on a New Deal promise as the nation swelted under the trials and tribulations of the Great Depression. In a "damn the torpedoes, full speed ahead" attitude, Mr. Roosevelt challenged the nation from "Captain to Cook," to rescue his beloved land initiating untold numbers of programs, in a "If one does not a work, try another" mindset as frame of reference. Ahead of his time in recognizing the aspirations of all Americans, viz., labor, immigrants, power companies, Blacks, women, FDR pressed ahead with his alphabet programs until finally challenged by the "9 old men" of the Supreme Court. Men of vision and tenacity are seldom stopped in their tracks but either walk around or through obstacles. In time, even the Supreme Court came around and with lots of help from being drawn into World War II, Mr. Roosevelt pulled the nation out of the Depression placing it on a path of economic prosperity with untold economic and other safeguards in place.

FREDERICK MONDERSON

BN PHOTO - Here we go again, admiring nature's handiwork in the National Garden.

The size of the Roosevelt Memorial in Washington, DC is indicative of the expansiveness of the man's thinking and actions wherein all people lent their shoulders to his wheel as he rescued his nation from the clutches of its most catastrophic challenge initiated in the Great Depression. His vision and leadership set the stage for unparalleled transformation of the nation. It is no wonder both Presidents Lincoln and Roosevelt proved to be Mr. Obama's greatest role models.

Dwight Eisenhower, a general in World War II became President from 1952-1960 and had to contend with the Korean War and also the communist threat and the Cold War. He was well liked and Americans rallied to his efforts to readjust in wake of the realistic dynamics of the post-World War II and Korean conflicts.

BLACK NATIONALISM
STILL ALIVE AND WELL

President John Kennedy came and left early but he transformed the office of the presidency and the nation and its image on the world stage. In meeting Khrushchev's challenge in the Cuban Missile crisis, not only did President Kennedy diffuse the potential consequences of a nuclear conflict but he exemplified American resolve when all the marbles were at stake. This martyr's death emboldened his successor Lyndon Baines Johnson to masterfully bring into legal fruition Mr. Kennedy's "Great Society's" vision. This work in progress resulted in the *1964 Civil Rights Act* and the *1965 Voting Rights Act* among other substantive measures that changed the nation in the most unimaginable manner.

BN PHOTO - Simple yet profound in its decorative effect, another DC landscape gem.

Though he denied being "a crook," Richard Nixon created foreign policy masterpieces in establishing détente with China and Russia that were significant first steps in Ronald Reagan's path to glory in confronting the Berlin Wall's divide. Nevertheless, Ronald Reagan the actor and governor of California certainly endeared himself in the minds and hearts of the American people though a career that

FREDERICK MONDERSON

spanned several decades. As President, this public capital proved favorable in acceptance of his social and economic policies and his military build-up that resulted in collapse of the Soviet Union as they tried to match his level of military preparedness. So much so, no modern President received as enormous posthumous recognition as Ronald Reagan in his extensive funeral and naming of airports and public buildings in his honor. His 11th Commandment, "Thou shall not criticize a fellow Republican" became enshrined in American and Republican political lore and his aura continues to radiate from the shrine of his memory as Republican "wanna-bes" seek to exploit mileage of his blessings through association with Mrs. Nancy Reagan, identification with the Reagan Library or curry-favoring to Reagan's lieutenants and even exploiting the notion through "I was in the room with Ronald Reagan" and similar sayings.

BN PHOTO - "Beauties in the Park," mother and daughter relax in the shade of nature's bosom, Washington, DC.

BLACK NATIONALISM STILL ALIVE AND WELL

BN PHOTO - Not far from the Castle, a beautiful landscape of many colors.

Pulling all the strings that got him into the White House, George Washington Bush lulled the nation into a false sense of security that Al Qaeda exploited in effectuating their 9/11 plan of an unprecedented attack on the homeland that killed thousands. It was foolish that conspiracy theorists blamed Mr. Bush for concocting the attack. Notwithstanding, he cherished his respect for history given his being named after the first George, Washington that is, and his oath to uphold the office. That he made some faulty decisions, as a human being this is understandable, owing to poor advice and faulty intelligence. Some have argued Sadam Hussein's attempt on the life of the Senior Bush prompted George to invade Iraq after the Afghanistan "Shock and Awe" blitz. Nevertheless, the reality of two wars, the Bush Tax Cuts for his "base," a Prescription Drug Plan that was unpaid for as well as skull-duggery speculation in banking, runaway Wall Street downward spiral speculation and the unchecked housing market as a result of lax regulation brought America to the brink of economic disaster and failed-state status. Now, having laid low at the end of his tenure, Mr. Bush is being rehabilitated through exploitation of his good side. Nonetheless, the goodwill endeared to these great presidents, elected twice, did not include endowing such benefits upon Barack Obama.

FREDERICK MONDERSON

BN PHOTO - Whoever invented flowers this beautiful certainly knew what he was doing.

BN PHOTO - Another of nature's masterpieces, found in the National Garden in DC.

BLACK NATIONALISM STILL ALIVE AND WELL

BN PHOTO - Need I say more on the beautiful make-up of this wonderful flower?

With Mr. Obama, we have "a horse of a different color!" He broke the mold of 43 white-only presidents. None of the former presidents had risen from the humble beginnings of Barack Obama, struggled to acquire that "Million Dollar White man education" from Columbia and Harvard, "done business white but married black" and possessed the tenacity and wherewithal to challenge for, campaign and win the Presidency of the United States, twice. As such, a credible argument can be made; losers wanted to shift the responsibility for the nation's calamity and so acquiesced in Mr. Obama's victory in hopes to benefit from his cleaning out the "messy stables." However, in a nation of contingency planning from day one, if not before, elements probably hatched the plan to create his demise as he first tackled the problems, created constructive solutions and moved the nation from

FREDERICK MONDERSON

the brink of economic collapse and mounting disrespect on the world stage. Then, Mitch McConnell and his "Mandate" happened.

Despite his years in Congress, Mitch McConnell does not seem capable of single-mindedly originating his "I intend to make Barack Obama a one-term President" mantra. He must have had input, followed orders to hatch such a seemingly brilliant yet flawed, outwardly racist, statement and assignment! "Original as it may seem, one has to wonder if he is capable of writing his own material even though he seems to have tried to do a good job executing such!"

BN PHOTO - Another of those wonderful fruits of nature, clothed in flowery dress.

BLACK NATIONALISM STILL ALIVE AND WELL

From that day one seedling planted in the nucleus of the anti-Obama temple, a forest of ill-will germinated as countless off-shoots vied with each other to disrespect, threaten and block Mr. Obama's every legislative initiative designed to aid the broad masses of the American people. Republicans removed their focus from doing the people's business to insuring Mr. Obama's tenure as President is a failure. Connecting the dots, it is evident racial animus has been a catalyst for all such behaviors. The interesting thing about Barack Obama is his demonstrating exemplary leadership as he chooses to see the "boys will be boys" nuisance as just that as he earnestly sought to execute the requirements of his oath of office. One of his errors was to not, very early, "fire on the Rebel Camp" massing on his perimeter. Nevertheless, he has remained relentless in keeping the wolves at bay, struggling to rescue the American economy despite "front and back fires" scorching his path. This unending sabotage is not by "angels with dirty faces" but "devils with clean faces!"

After all, according to a major front-page write-up in *The New York Times*, certainly after the 2012 election but more probably about the 2012 victory, even 2008an influential group of Republicans met and planned to treasonably sabotage Mr. Obama's term in office. However, his extraordinary leadership style successfully navigated the Republican legislative and non-governmental organizations' minefields.

FREDERICK MONDERSON

BN PHOTO - Even more of nature's beauty clothed in flowery dress and found in the National Garden, DC.

Mr. Obama's deliberative style, his tremendous self-preparation and familiarity with all the issues, unrelenting search and dispatch of Osama bin Laden; that Wall Street has tripled its worth and his watch; passage of Lilly Ledbetter; and Obamacare with some 8 million registered for its privileges, 9 million private sectors have been added during his presidency, two wars were ended, the Somali Pirates are unemployed. So much more attests to Mr. Obama's leadership skills and style. Unlike many who shoot first then sort later, Mr. Obama first deliberates in his leadership style. When Senator John McCain thought of military action in Eastern Europe, Senator Obama responded, "I have spoken with my advisors and we need to study the situation some more." This deliberation prevented American military involvement attesting to leadership skills. In Libya Mr. Obama was accused of "leading from behind" but no American lives were lost. Since, many foreign policy issues have and continue to unfold testing Mr. Obama's leadership.

BLACK NATIONALISM STILL ALIVE AND WELL

In the new episode of the downed Malaysian Airliner over the Ukraine Airspace, many persons wanted to instantly blame Russia under Mr. Putin's leadership. Rather than outright accuse Mr. Putin, President Obama had a number of subordinates hint at Russia's complicity as Mr. Obama sorted the intelligence. Rather than come right out, Mr. Obama's deliberative strategy connected the dots before outright laying the blame for the tragedy at Mr. Putin's doorstep. In this and so many ways, Mr. Obama exemplifies extraordinary leadership.

FREDERICK MONDERSON

BN PHOTO - How wonderful to think such beauty can bloom and bloom no more.

BN PHOTO - Nature's beauty comes in many shades and colors.

FREDERICK MONDERSON

BN PHOTO - Nature's beauty can not only demonstrate but inspire and encourage in its magnificence.

43. HOME GROWN RACIAL TERRORISM BY Dr. Fred Monderson

Today the debate rages about the South Carolina flag as symbol, under which the young and ranting madman Dylann Roof; who killed 9 Black people in Charleston's historic "Mother Emanuel Church;" was and is seen hurrying in his descent into racism's nihilistic infernal regions. Given this Confederate symbol emerged in response to hard fought for Civil Rights gains in the 1960s and has remained, instead of a badge of heritage, a symbol of rabid racism and the hallmark of a state viewed as the nucleus and cauldron of an

BLACK NATIONALISM STILL ALIVE AND WELL

odious and unjust system of slavery many have characterized as a crime against humanity. However, while we may applaud the outpouring of commiserate healing, hope and compassion to this repeating tragedy of Black churches bearing the brunt of racial animus, we must never forget, the DNA of South Carolina, Charleston and the Confederate flag is steeped in that vexatious institution of "Chattel Slavery" and the incomprehensible "Internal Slave Trade" with the infamous "Slave Farms growing people" to enrichen slave owners' bankrolls.

Nevertheless, we must realistically recognize racial hatred towards Blacks, African-Americans, is deep-seated and as "Old Ideas Never Die," this nation must seriously address and really seek to heal this cultural cancer before we reach the point of no return. Often political operatives opposed to President Obama speak of financial burdens on young people not realizing the nation's racial heritage and its viable institutional racism is more a nuclear explosion waiting to happen than financial costs that can be managed.

FREDERICK MONDERSON

BN PHOTO - "End Mass Incarceration" and the "New Jim Crow."

In today's age as the nation seeks to combat extremism and terrorism abroad, this exact malady is alive and well fostered by our own homegrown Isis thugs. Even more important, exacerbated racial animosity is deep seated in the American psyche; yet, those who could address this venom simply ignores the issue, sidesteps or offers rationalization that is more a signal of moral bankruptcy. As such, the racially inspired killing manifested in the recent Charleston Mother Emanuel Church shooting is simply traceable to the climate of racial hatred and disrespect leveled against the first Black President. Even more, it is the tip of the deep-seated psychological pathology with implications significantly impacting social behavior.

BLACK NATIONALISM STILL ALIVE AND WELL

The surprising reality of this phenomenon is people who profess a devotion to the Christian faith and experience oftentimes practice the most insidious and barbaric behaviors towards African people unmindful, their religious heritage, their flaunted cultural heritage, are embedded in the Blackman's intellectuality and psychological consciousness. Consider in times past Greece was the fountainhead of the beginnings of Western Culture. Today, Egypt has been coveted, the African denied his heritage therein and every effort made to erase his involvement in that Nile Valley cultural genesis while Europeans boast falsely of "our Egyptian beginnings."

History has shown, the animosity of American racism antedates the founding of the African Methodist Church in 1816 and efforts of Blacks to "Game the Slavery System," by converting to Christianity. More particularly, it antedates 1787 "Three-Fifths Compromise;" the "1619 Jamestown landing;" the "1503 Papal Bull" endorsing slave trade; even the "1492 Columbus adventure;" and the "1485 Fall of Granada." In fact, the "711 invasion of Spain by Blackamoors" and founding of Europe's first, the University of Salamanca, comes closer to a date we can begin to search for the origins of European racial bigotry and hatred. While there is no need to explore "Christianity Before Christ" and the fact Jesus had "wooly hair;" none can deny that Simon of Cyrenaica ably bore the weight of Jesus' cross. From this date, not simply the first martyrs, the African Church Fathers, the intellectual foundations and brilliance of St. Augustine, the unparalleled dedication and sanctity of Benedict of Nursia, Ethiopia as the first Christian nation and the intellectual foundations and moral guideposts found, established and helped sustain the Christian religion were African in nature and are powerful examples that Africans are not simply visiting congregants but the pillars, altars and candlesticks upon which the foundations of western religious beliefs and practices were founded. Dr. Yosef Ben-Jochannan's *African Origins of the Major Western Religions* masterfully examines this issue and credits Africans with being significant lynchpins in the formation of Judaism, Christianity and Islamic modes of worship.

FREDERICK MONDERSON

Perhaps it was Benjamin Ben Jonah, the medieval merchant and traveler, according to J.E. Harris' *Africans and their History* (1972: 15) who exacerbated Noah's curse on Black people that became a significant factor justifying the slave trade and slavery. He wrote, "'There is a people … who, like animals, eat of the herbs that grow on the banks of the Nile, and in the fields. They go about naked and have not the intelligence of ordinary men. They cohabit with their sisters and anyone they find…. These sons of Ham are black slaves." This view was an elaboration of Babylonian Talmudic writings from the 2nd to the 6th Century AD that held, according to Thomas F. Gosset, *Race*: *The History of an Idea in America* (1963: 3) that "The descendants of Ham were cursed by being black." According to J.E. Harris (1972: 14) and quoting Patti and Graves in *Hebrew Myths* New York (1964: 121) even further, "… it must be Canaan, your firstborn, whom they enslave …. Canaan's children shall be born ugly and black! … Your grandchildren's hair shall be twisted into kinks…. [Their lips] shall swell;'… Men of this race are called Negroes; their forefather Canaan commanded them to love theft and fornication, to be banded together in hatred of their masters and never to tell the truth." This "Biblical" derogation helped fuel all subsequent negative characterization of Black Africans worldwide. After all, the Papal Bull sanctioning the slave trade and ultimately slavery was based on the enshrined idea that the African was black and cursed and hence a justification for selling him into slavery with its resulting racism whereby adventurers and "men of the cloth" ventured out to "wash an Ethiopian white!"

Strange, nowhere during Medieval times are Blacks represented nor recorded as slaves nor was the word Negro in use. This word was not used before the 16th Century.

In the article "Color, Racism and Christianity" by Rigger Bastide in **COLOR AND RACE** Edited by John Hope Franklin, Boston: Houghton, Mifflin and Company (1968: 34-49) we are introduced to alarming details about the evolution of white supremacy's degradations of Africans, first in iconography, symbolism, then philosophic argumentation and social practice. Thus we read: "But

BLACK NATIONALISM
STILL ALIVE AND WELL

the greatest Christian two-part division is that of white and black. White is used to express the pure, while black expresses the diabolical. The conflict between Christ and Satan, the spiritual and the carnal, good and evil came finally to be expressed by the conflict between white and black, which underlies and synthesizes all the others. Even the blind, who knows only night, think of a swarm of angels or of devils in association with white and black - for example, "a black soul," "the blackness of an action," "a dark deed," the "innocent whiteness of the lily," "the candor of a child," "to bleach someone of a crime." These are not merely adjectives and nouns. Whiteness brings to mind the light, ascension into the Holy Spirit, and the transparency of limpid air; blackness suggests the infernal streams of the bowels of the earth, the pit of hell, the devil's color." (36-37)

Even further, "Although Christ transcends all questions of race or ethnology, it must not be forgotten that God incarnated himself in a man of the Jewish race. The Aryans and the Gentiles - even the most anti-Semitic - worship their god in a Jewish body. But this Jewish body was not white enough for them. The entire history of Western paintings bears witness to the deliberate whitening or bleaching effort that changed Christ from a Semitic to an Aryan person. The dark hair that Christ was thought to have had came to be rendered as very light-colored, and his big dark eyes as blue. It was necessary that this man, the incarnation of God, be as far removed as possible from everything that could suggest darkness or blackness, even indirectly. His hair and his beard were given the color of sunshine, the brightness of the light above, while his eyes retained the color of the sky from which he descended and to which he returned." (37)

FREDERICK MONDERSON

BN PHOTO - District Leader Jeffrey Davis with Luis (left) and Erik (right).

"References must again be made to a painting. The Three Kings or Three Wise Men who came to worship the newborn child were depicted as white men at first. They later came to represent the three great continents: Europe, Asia, and Africa. Balthazar was the Negro King who came to bring his tribute to the fair-haired child amidst the golden straw. He was pictured behind the other two Magi and even sometimes kneeling closest to the babe, but never between the other two - that would have been equivalent to ignoring his color. Racism subsisted in the disguised form of a patronizing attitude in this first attempt to remove the demoniac symbolism from the black skin." (38) A similar effort can be seen in the creation of colored saints intended for races other than the white race. St. Mauritius, a commander of the Roman legions in Egypt who was martyred there, was originally depicted as white but then as a Moor, and finally in the thirteenth century as a Negro." "Such changes were exploited for purposes of evangelism as the frontiers of the known world extended farther. The church long ignored St. Benedict of Palermo, known as St. Benedict the Moor, but finally officialized him with the development of missions in Africa and of slavery in the Western

BLACK NATIONALISM STILL ALIVE AND WELL

Hemisphere. This case illustrates another rationalization on the part of the church intended to break the nominal chain of symbolism. In order to escape from feminine temptation, St. Benedict prayed god to make him ugly - so god turned his skin black." (38-39)

"To see only symbolism in these cases would, however, be a mistake. Because the symbolism is merely repressed, it returns from another angle. From the mystical, it is converted into the aesthetic. Evil takes the form of ugliness. Above all, the colored saints - St. Mauritius, St. Benedict the Moor, St. Iphigenia the Mulatto, and St Balthazar the Negro King - are only intermediaries, well below the Virgin Mary and Christ, who stayed white. They express more the differences, the abyss, between people of different races than the unity. They stand for stratification in a multiracial society. The color black found only a subordinate place in the hierarchy of condescending from white to black." (39)

So we see, despite what may be said about this incident that the shooter was wearing the Apartheid and Rhodesia emblems as well as the Confederate flag, the climate in which this horrific act took place must be given serious consideration as the insidious process of mischaracterizing and demeaning Black under white was long in coming through official and religious sanction.

Thus, it is not that unusual from the time Barack Obama declared for and won the Presidency the climate of racial hatred and disrespect escalated as evident from the actions of individuals high in government and their allies in private and public walks of life; to this we may add pronouncements of militias and other hate groups fed in the maelstrom of supposed Christian brotherhood. We must never forget what may be said, Malcolm X praised Islam for a true belief in and practice of the fatherhood of god and the brotherhood of man. This does not, however, include those who hijack Islamic teachings for nefarious ends.

FREDERICK MONDERSON

The fact the shooter, not simply said he came to shoot Blacks but stated that Blacks had taken over the country and he wanted it back, such behaviors and statements are traceable to "crosshairs" Sarah Palin and all who galvanized to her "Take our country back" pliant. These people resuscitated and encouraged a climate of racial hatred that any behavior on part of any individual as the "White House Protester" and the Racist Roof is not unexpected and justified. And even when they condemn such carnage as does the Council of Conservative Citizens hate group, they offer false rhetoric supporting an ideology and belief system that polarizes and radicalizes many on a hopeless path as the South Carolina shooter. The fact is, when farmers plant peanuts they cannot expect to get Idaho potatoes. As such, many of these individuals cannot genuinely commiserate with the South Carolina victims for such behaviors would appear hypocritical. The old admonition, "be Careful of what you pray for, you many get it!" applies in this case. Given that as the racial madness directed against Barack Obama unfolded and no individuals of substance spoke against the simmering racial madness, it has become full blown. In as much as mass shooting of innocent individuals is becoming increasingly frequent, then we can only pray and hope the next one may be sometime in the distant future.

BN PHOTO - Legendary Photographer Lem Peterkin strolls at the International African Arts Festival in Brooklyn.

BLACK NATIONALISM STILL ALIVE AND WELL

44. THE SCOURGE OF RACIAL HATRED
By
Dr. Fred Monderson

As a student of the esteemed Professor Dr. Leonard James at New York City Technical College of the City University of New York, Brooklyn, among hundreds, perhaps thousands, we were taught a Methodology of History very different from the usual method. Not foremost the question of when something happened but what happened, how it happened, why it happened and last but not least, when it happened. There were also other variables such as the ability to make Critical Comparative Historical Analyses and the role such factors as Internal and External developments play in creating outcomes that are favorable or unfavorable.

One such ingredient as part of the Methodology, Internal and External, can be applied to a discussion of the question of racism in America, today an issue many believe needs attention but never gets. Many will agree, decisions of great significance need a point, place or time of departure in order to arrive at a satisfactory conclusion or answer to the question under study. In that case, the External and Internal components of the Methodology can be applied to the phenomenon of recent events in Charleston, South Carolina. Interesting, the tragedy of Charleston raised the issue of "heritage" and its dynamics as manifested in history, hate and racism. And purported harmony among citizens, while in fact, deep-seated racism simmers beneath a sheer veneer full of ugly social, economic, political and educational;/ puss, and if pricked can easily explode. That is to say, heritage should truly be considered on both sides of the racial equation.

Sad to say, the Charleston Church martyrs proved a catalyst and drove a number of subsequent developments to the surface, chief of which were the viciousness of the church massacre with intent to incite a race war; the realization, even a "holy place" is not immune from such violence; a profound and true belief in the goodness of God and the forgiving nature of the "victims;" the bold and courageous vision to recognize the existence of prevalent racism and hatred masquerading as "heritage" and the actions to speak out against such harmful negativity; a realization, removal of the Confederate Flag was not only easy but soothing; and most important, this entire phenomena of events is only the "tip of the Iceberg," and must be urgently addressed to help America shed the shackles of this devastating psychological "ball and chain" that stifles its moral compass especially in all its prevalence across the South.

Strange, but this boiling cauldron is not really new and can be easily traced in a series of developments emerging from as late as 2008, even if we, in this respect, not give much attention to the previous age through which the foundation of all this rests. From the time Barack Obama declared for the Presidency, in 2008, the scab of American racism was pricked and slowly but profoundly it began oozing the puss of a psychological and social sin that has long stained the conscience of this nation despite the fact African-Americans have given so much blood, sweat, tears, their lives and free labor to help build this land. Winning the Presidency, all manner of opposition declared in response to a Black man leading the nation. From militias who began arming to the teeth for a race war fabricated in their own minds and belabored to impressionable youth and seasoned racists alike; to Dylann Roof following in this putrid path seven years later who massacred in and stained a holy place, was actually a race-war misfiring dud, unable to spark the mischievous intent; and from an Arizona pastor who prayed for Barack Obama's death to "Daddy Cruz" who wanted to "Send Obama back to Kenya," but when Obama offered him Cuba, he declined. Then we had Mitch McConnell who failed to "make Obama a one-term president" and "Waterloo DeMint" who surrendered his seat, to "You Lie" Wilson and "Stupid" Charles Grassley who could only psychologically languish while Obama won twice in the Supreme Court. We could only conclude across

BLACK NATIONALISM STILL ALIVE AND WELL

that wide spectrum of anti-Obama and anti-Black sentiments many "South Carolina Flag Syndromes" of "hate" and "racism" stands camouflaged in business suits across the nation, drenched in perfumes to cover the stench of the racial hatred they harbor.

In the 2012 Presidential Election all the Southern or "Lynching" states voted for Mitch Romney but ostensibly they voted against the Black guy and lost. These slave owning Confederate or "rebel" states could not countenance, given their history, of being on a Black man's plantation. However, it was more than that and it can be argued, the unforgiving nature of losing the Civil War, giving birth to the Ku Klux Klan ideology and practice of lynching and terrorism of Black folk, denial of due process and the right to vote and hold office in a climate of "Jim Crow" and "separate and unequal," having discrimination and terror as its hallmarks, reflect a fiery hatred not easily quenched even with the passage of time despite claims of Christian brotherhood. Hence, the hatred and racism the South Carolina legislators identified in association with the Confederate flag is a well-camouflaged fact abounding denials, notwithstanding.

Given that ideas and practices masked as beliefs and heritage are extremely difficult to surrender and given all of the above, and the fact a good man such as Mr. Obama could not win a Southern state, then the "Carolina Syndrome" is effectively masked and deep seated as especially represented in the 2012 vote results.

Recently *The New York Times* featured an article about a Southern legal eagle who documented some 3,953 lynchings and racial killings across much of this nation's landmass from 1877 to 1950.

The gentleman vowed to memorialize these "Heritage Sites" with a marker. Equally, and given that such cultural markers will blemish a lily-white topography, resistance in the "Carolina Confederate Mold" is expected but the nation must confront the problem.

FREDERICK MONDERSON

BN PHOTO - People of all persuasions came out answering the call to support "Justice for Eric Garner" in Cadman Plaza Park.

Granted some business entities have raised the issue of divesting from states publicly promoting the "Confederate Brand," the first and most profound question that arises becomes, "Is this an economic epiphany or a moral obligation?" If the first, then it is a strategic decision to forestall the consequences of an economic boycott of such a state. If the later, it is a realization on the part of some to divest of the racial albatross this baggage of heritage brings at a time when the consequences exert a stiff penalty in moral and material payments. Second, "With slave trade and slavery, 19th Century racial terrorism and 20th Century lynchings among other unspeakable acts, do residents who live in the potential marker site states have the courage, strength, conviction even wisdom to forgive, themselves, for that history of unspeakable acts?"

Therefore, still more questions can be posed, given the legacy of slavery and resistance and the prevalence of a Confederate culture across the South, which after all, was a defense of slavery despite claims of "A new South" reborn. Thus, the first question is, "Must there be another horrendous act before hate loses?" Rodney King asked pointedly, "Can we all get along?" Should the old legacy of hatred, terrorism and racism remain in the chest and trotted out ever-so-often? The contradiction is, young people want a united country with equality for all given there are so many, internally and externally, who envy and plot against the goodness of this nation as

BLACK NATIONALISM STILL ALIVE AND WELL

represented by the forgiving nature of the, "Do we have the courage to confront the malady" allowing the force to change to emanate from within our Christian values and institutions? "Can we truly teach multiculturalism in our schools?" "How do our practices and teachings affect the young who long for a tranquil future?" and an accurate description of the past. To address the myriad problems, we must move beyond and address the inequality that has plagued our nation for the longest. That is rich over poor; white over black; man over woman; war hawks over peace doves; rural versus urban; employed and unemployed, for as Abe Lincoln admonished, "A house divided against itself cannot stand." It should not be only when catastrophe strikes does the nation come together for a minute!

BN PHOTO - A Sister representing Nurses speaks in support of Justice for Eric Garner while Rev. Al Sharpton looks on.

Americans are thought to be able to do anything but "Can these physicians heal themselves?" Can racists have an epiphany and like Christ insisted, "Love thy neighbor!"

FREDERICK MONDERSON

Then again, contrary to misguided beliefs that though Africans are a god-fearing, praying and forgiving people they are by no means cowards. Aristotle made the contradictory mistake in ancient times when in his work *Physiognomonica* he declared "Egyptians and Ethiopians are cowards because they are black!" What the great scientist did do, first, is affirm the ancient Egyptians and Ethiopians were Black Africans. Second, and unfortunately he misjudged the martial prowess of the Back man evident from the many wars they fought down through the ages.

Internecine warfare for the burgeoning wealth of the Nile Valley; Old Kingdom pharaohs represented as smiting the Bedouin at Serabit el Khadem; Mentuhotep II pacifying and uniting the land to establish the Middle Kingdom; Senusert establishing his boundary at Egypt's southern border in Nubia during the 12th Dynasty; Sekenenra-Ra unleashing a protracted 50-year war of liberation in the 17th Dynasty and his sons Kamose and Ahmose expelling the Hyksos, finally founding the 18th Dynasty and New Kingdom. Whether Amenhotep I, Thutmose I's efforts or Thutmose III's brilliant military strategy on the Plains of Megiddo; Rameses II dominating at Kadesh; Merenptah, "My country, right or wrong;" Rameses III against the "Peoples of the Sea;" the Ethiopians Khasta, Piankhi, Shabaka, Shabataka and Taharka conquest at Thebes, then all Egypt and in Palestine, all happening before "Alexander the Great." Then there was Hamilcar, Hasdrubal and Hannibal Barca challenging the Roman Empire; the Haitians at the Revolutionary War Battle of Savannah; the Buffalo Soldiers on the American Plains; Samori Toure against the French in West Africa; Yaa Asantewaa against the British in Ghana; Shaka Zulu against the Boers in South Africa; and one could ask the Italians about the Battle of Adowa in 1896. Let us not forget Blaise Diagne recruiting 100,000 West Africans to stem German obliteration of French manhood in World War I; Black Americans Charging up San Juan Hill protecting Teddy Roosevelt's Rough Riders and Black Americans overseas fighting "to save the world for democracy." Haile Selaisse stood against the Second Italian coming; the Tuskegee Airmen fought brilliantly in World War II; the feared Black soldier in Vietnam and our boys in the Gulf,

BLACK NATIONALISM
STILL ALIVE AND WELL

Afghanistan and Iraq are remarkable examples of modern military prowess. We cannot also forget the thousands of Black Veterans buried in the Brooklyn Navy Yard including Samuel Carson who died in the Mexican War and in being repatriated to Ghana, West Africa, opened the "Door of Return" so long closed instead of the "Door of No Return" dating back centuries.

BN PHOTO - Part of the Audience at the First International Friendship Festival at Borough Hall, Brooklyn.

Thus, the malicious should know we would rather pray than fight; remaining fully aware that Machiavelli admonished, "Any man who wishes to make a profession of Goodness must naturally come to grips with many who are not good. Thus, he must learn how to be good and not good and use and not use this knowledge as the situation warrants."

Therefore, Americans must girdle themselves in a forging mold reminiscent of the "Charleston martyrs' families" and work for the betterment of the nation, not their narrow racially motivated and

FREDERICK MONDERSON

stained self-interest. In every respect, the old labor movement's admonition "United We Stand, Divided We Fall" should be our watchword as we face the future particularly in view of the many futuristic policies and practices put in place by President Obama to effectively guide his nation for the benefit and betterment of all in this fast changing world.

45. THE ILLUSTRIOUS QUEEN MOTHER
By
Dr. Fred Monderson

With the passing of Queen Mother Moore, African nationalism suffered a serious setback. This matriarch of African liberation left indelible impressions on the consciousness of those struggling against imperialism, colonialism, de-colonization and racism; whether through Garveyism, Nkrumahism and Afrocentricity as well as what is the future direction of Pan-African identification, strategy and struggle. In reflecting on a life of commitment to African liberation, this climax of her experiences is somewhat reminiscence

BLACK NATIONALISM STILL ALIVE AND WELL

of Marcus Garvey's classic statement: "You have caged the tiger, but the cubs are running loose." For certain, the Queen Mother has led an exemplary life! For sure, she has encouraged, supported, trained, and left cubs and young and old lions and lionesses, who are today committed to ideals, aspirations, and philosophic outlooks that motivate and fuel the efforts and desires of African people worldwide. As a result, she has earned her revered place in ancestral heritage and will be welcomed in the heavenly abode of the pantheon of African heroes and heroines. This state of affairs now forces us to consider the successor to the Queen Mother's august and respected place of leadership.

As an early follower of Marcus Moziah Garvey, Queen Mother Moore was influential in founding, sustaining and leading organizations such as the Universal Association of Ethiopian Women, Inc. She was the Founder of Addis Ababa, Inc; founding Matriarch of the Ethiopian Orthodox Coptic Church; founder and President of the African American Cultural Foundation, Inc.; and Founder and President of the Harriet Tubman Association. She was a Life Member of Negro Women; Member of the Founding Committee 1970 Conference: Congress of African People and she was also the first woman to formally address the Organization of African Unity (OAU) in Addis Ababa, Ethiopia. Several organizations were also formed to aid her or as a result of her influence on others. She was indeed a Great Ancestor!

Though Winnie Mandela has been crowned "Queen of the Black World," candidates for the title of Queen Mother need to be identified, considered, considered, chosen and installed to provide leadership of causes affecting African people worldwide in memory of Queen Mother Moore and to keep her spirit alive and working.

To fully understand the position and significance of the title "Queen Mother," a historical reflection needs to be made of individuals who have filled this post, particularly in Nile Valley and later African culture. As such, one of the most celebrated of the "Queen Mothers" is the ancestress of the Eighteenth Dynasty, Aahmes-Nefertari, whose portrait is in the British Museum. This stately beauty is shown wearing a long flowing gown of red, white and blue, 1500 years Before the Christian Era. In addition, she is bejeweled and wears the Vulture Headdress or the "Queen Mother Crown." This is a golden headdress, with uraeus, sun-disk, and plumed feathers atop a mortar. Another colorful portrait of a queen with the Queen Mother Crown is that of Rameses II's Nefertari. The queen is shown in her tomb in the Valley of the Queens, where she offers two vessels in praise of the deity. However, while pictorial examples of the Queen Mother Crown may be lacking, the spirit and personality has survived in the lives of queens who influenced their husbands, sons, grandsons, families, communities, and been forces of inspiration who in turn were praised and revered.

In the "Myth of Isis and Osiris," the king was killed by his brother Seth, while Isis the faithful his wife, together with her sister Nephthys, set out to recover the body. Having found the badly dismembered body of Osiris, and aided by Thoth and Anubis, she was able to reconstitute the parts and through her divine-powers was impregnated by her dead husband. Finally she bore him a son named Horus. Once grown, Horus was able to avenge his father by capturing the despicable uncle and slew him at the spot where the Temple of Edfu was built to mark the spot. Some versions of the story report Horus made a claim to the gods in their great hall of Judgment where he was defended by Thoth, the god of writing and wisdom. This intervention resulted in the great Judges ruling that Osiris was wrongfully executed and that Horus should be installed in his father's stead as king of Upper and Lower Egypt/Kemet. Through it all, Isis, granddaughter of Nut, stood by her son as she had done with her husband. Her influence, therefore, is traceable as a "Queen Mother" who gained great fame for her compassion, commitment, sincerity and faithfulness. From this mythological experience we can start with the individuals who constitute the human side of the dynastic experience.

BLACK NATIONALISM
STILL ALIVE AND WELL

BN PHOTO - Reverend Al Sharpton addresses the Audience before introducing President Barack Obama.

If we begin with Narmer at the founding of the first dynasty, we first encounter the African queen in a majestic position of respect, within the domain of the husband and son. Narmer's wife was Queen Neithhotep, whom we encounter on the Narmer Macehead, a ceremonial weapon that has provided an enormous amount of factual information enabling scholars to arrive at some firm conclusions about this early period in African history. Narmer and Neithhotep's son was Hor-Aha, who followed his father as king. He built an enormous tomb for his mother, several times that of his father. We are led to believe that the influence of the Queen Mother may have begun to be exercised from this early time. In addition, because of the special role of the Queen in transmitting divine genes, she came to hold a special place in the society, as power behind the throne and when that throne was threatened, she exerted her influence to diminish whatever threats there may have been.

Snefru was probably the last king of the Third Dynasty and his wife was Hetep-Pheres who gave birth to a magnificent dynasty, the 4th with its illustrious kings, Khufu, Khafre, and Menkaure. These three pharaohs of the 4th Dynasty built the great pyramids on the Giza plateau.

When an expedition from the Boston Museum of Fine Arts discovered her tomb in the 1920s, they were soundly impressed with the burial remains of Queen Hetep-Pheres, mother of Khufu. Clearly the influence she enjoyed as "Queen Mother" can be deduced from her remains, including efforts at preservation of her body. This incidentally was one of the earliest examples of the process of mummification being employed.

The First Intermediate Period followed the collapse of the Old Kingdom and power was exercised between Memphis in the North and Assuit in Middle Egypt. This period of internal disunity was comprised of the VIIth-Xth Dynasties. The formative era of the Middle Kingdom was begun with consolidation of power by Theban princes who united the south before attempts were made to march northward to unify the country. The German Archaeologist Von Bissing tells in the *American Journal of Archaeology* of a conflict between two of these Theban princes, Intef and Mentuhotep.

BLACK NATIONALISM STILL ALIVE AND WELL

BN PHOTO - President Obama in turn addresses the Audience at "Sharpton's Affair."

Apparently, Intef had launched an attack on Mentuhotep's forces and as he came out of the pass onto the Plains of Thebes, he encountered Mentuhotep with a superior force awaiting him. Intef had his mother Queen Achtothes intercede with Mentuhotep's mother Queen Aam, to bring about a cessation of hostilities to save the day. Clearly, these "Queen Mothers" were significant political and moral influences on their respective families, for as we know Mentuhotep was particularly successful in his efforts to unite the land. He founded the Eleventh Dynasty, defeated the northern monarchs and their allies, the Princes of Assuit, and again united the land. He consolidated his power, reorganized the domain and expanded the cultural, economic and artistic institutions of the society and founded the Middle

Kingdom. Though not much is subsequently known about his mother after this, we could well imagine the level of influence she exercised.

The next significant "Queen Mother" is considered to be Queen Tetisheri. At the collapse of the Middle Kingdom, the Hyksos, an Asiatic people, invaded Kemet and ruled the land from their stronghold in the Delta. The Princes of Thebes and the Upper Kingdom recognized these conquerors as their overlords and paid tribute to them. As with all such invaders, they were haughty and ruthless. After comprising the Fifteenth and Sixteenth Dynasties, a Hyksos king sent a rather arrogant message to the Theban princes. He claimed the hippos grazing in the Nile at Thebes were making so much noise that the Hyksos rulers in the Delta, nearly 500 miles away, could not sleep at night. Therefore, "Shut up your hippopotamuses!" Such arrogance generated an intense response from the Thebans of the Seventeenth Dynasty, whom Petrie referred to as "coming from Nubia and holding Thebes as its capital." They mobilized their forces and begun a protracted war of liberation that lasted for 50 years and ended with the expulsion of the Hyksos.

Queen Tetisheri's husband was Seqenenra, who was felled in battle. His son too, Sekenenra-Tao, felled in battle by an axe-wound to the head. His mummy is now in the Cairo Museum. While her husband was away fighting in the war of liberation, a palace coup broke out led by "Tety the Handsome." This gallant queen rallied the faithful and put down the rebellion. She saved the throne for her progeny. In that ongoing war of liberation, Kamose her son, continued the struggle and expelled the Hyksos and his brother Ahmose completed the job. This latter founded the XVIIIth Dynasty and New Kingdom. Ahmose or Aahmes married his sister, Aahmes-Nefertari who became ancestress of the Eighteenth Dynasty. Clearly, for her gallantry Tetisheri was rewarded, given the title and exercised the requisite influence as "Queen Mother." We get an early glimpse of the "Queen Mother" or "Vulture Crown" being worn by her daughter Aahmes-Nefertari, whose influence was in itself far reaching. She was a black skinned beauty who gained legendary status. Years later, when Hatshepsut was on the throne of Kemet, and faced with

BLACK NATIONALISM STILL ALIVE AND WELL

questions regarding her legitimacy to rule, she boasted of her heritage that was tied to this queen.

Hatshepsut herself was Queen or should I say "King" of Egypt/Kemet. She had a daughter named Nefru-re, whose tutor was Senmut her architect. She had another daughter named Hatshepsut and this daughter married Thutmose III. As such, Hatshepsut could be considered both "Queen" and "Queen Mother," though her influence as the latter was much curtailed.

The next significant Queen mother was Queen Tiy, wife of Amenhotep III and mother of Amenhotep IV, Ikhnaton, the revolutionary. This Queen, who looked "so Nubian," was thought to be everything but African and credited with having too much power and influence. She held a position of reverence with her husband Amenhotep III, the "Magnificent," who built Luxor Temple, the "Grand Lodge." He also built a palace called Malcata, the "place of rejoicing" for this "Queen Mother." Her influence on her son Amenhotep IV, Ikhnaton, and his religious revolution was significant, though Hayes believed reactions to the Amarna heresy absolved her of any involvement.

On a scarab she is shown wearing the vulture headdress or "Queen Mother Crown." The queen of Tutankhamon, the next king in this dynasty, is shown wearing this crown with a menat and sistrum in a small shrine of her husband.

During the Nineteenth Dynasty, the great pharaoh, military strategist, father, husband, builder, high priest, etc., Rameses II, built the Abu Simbel temple in Nubia. There he was worshipped as a God! Adjacent, he built another temple for his beloved Nefertari, the Nubian. Some thought he built his and her temples to solidify his relations with the people of Nubia after marrying one of their princesses. Nevertheless, despite having several wives and untold numbers of sons, one could well imagine his favorite Nefertari as playing the role of Queen Mother with its attendant responsibilities

FREDERICK MONDERSON

and influences as their nation dominated the ancient world, and left ample evidence of their relationship.

In the time of the empires of the Western Sudanic empires of Ghana, Mali, and Songhay, Ibn Battuta wrote of the equality, freedom and independence of these societies.

Yaa Asantewaa was a respected and significant heroine in Ghanian and West African history. In the heyday of British imperialism in Africa, she was appalled at the performance of her nation's troops against a British army who had sought to desecrate the "Golden Stool," symbol and soul of the Ghanaian people. Following their defeat in one of a series of wars, she motivated and galvanized the warriors who were ultimately victorious against the British. Here is another unique example of Black troops defeating a disciplined and more heavily armed European army. In this case, however, it was commanded by a Queen as in the case of Candace of old Ethiopia and Queen Nzinga against the Portuguese during the days of slave trade and ultimately slavery.

In the American slave experience, those fundamental social institutions as marriage and the family were never respected by the slave holders. Yet still, grandmothers because of their age and "uselessness" to the slave masters were the greatest assets of our people. They were the first "Queen Mothers" of our experience in the New World. My grandmother, Cherise Preville, played that crucial role of "Queen Mother" and then my Mother; Mitta Monderson played a similar role in raising my off-springs. Cherise Maloney is another such "Queen Mother!" So too is Carmen Monderson as well as Marilyn James. And so it had been through the Sixteenth, Seventeenth, Eighteenth and Nineteenth Centuries. This is also the role such notables as Phyllis Wheatley, Harriet Tubman, Sojourner Truth, Mrs. Frederick Douglass, Mrs. Booker T. Washington, and Mrs. George Washington Carver played in bringing us up to the start of the Twentieth Century. We must not forget Bottom Belly and Queen Mary of Jamaica, who led the Maroons.

BLACK NATIONALISM STILL ALIVE AND WELL

Espousing liberation, intellectual advancement, economic empowerment and cultural and historical identification, Mrs. Amy Jacques Marcus Garvey, Mrs. W. E. B. Du Bois, Mrs. Paul Robeson, Mrs. Caseley Hayford, Mrs. Nandi Azikwi, Mrs. Kwame Nkrumah, Mrs. Julius Nyerere, Mrs. Eric Williams, Mrs. Malcolm X, Betty Shabaaz, and a whole host of others including Fannie Lou Hamer, Ethel Waters, Lorraine Hansberry, Ruby Dee, Jackie "Moms" Mabley, Constance Baker Motley, Ella Baker, Margaret Taylor Burroughs, Mary McLeod Bethune, Sisters Bettye Mullings, Melinda Melbourne, Rhonda Mormon, Josephine and Katie, Carmen Rudder, Sasser and Washington, and Jones, Smoke and Griffin, so too Linda Bascombe, Hyacinth Rowe and Mrs. Palmer, Rosa Parks, Mrs. Purdie, Mrs. Harper, Mrs. Woolcock, Mrs. Loncke, Mrs. Browne, Mrs. Estelle Brown and Lorna Brown, Dorothy Dandridge, Ruth Goring, as well as Elsie Richardson and Margaret Vinson, Carol Taylor, Betty Dopson, Adelaide Sanford, "Sistah" Viola Plummer, Ruth Lewis, Harriet McLeod, Mrs. Francis Haggler, Gracelyn Willis, Mable W. Robinson, "Queen Mother of the Middle Passage" Dr. Deloris Blakeley, Barbara Jordan, Camille Yarbrough and Gertrude Ben-Jochannan. Some people would add to this Mrs. Herbert Daughtery, Mrs. Angela Jitu Weusi, and Mrs. Mae (Sonny) Carson, and Mrs. Alton Maddox, who have been significant "Queen Mothers" of our people's struggle!

So as we traverse the Twenty-First Century, we shall go forth with a tenacious feeling of empowerment and resilience, knowing that many "Queen Mothers" have been beacons of inspiration on behalf of African people in the past and in the future. We need remember these noble women and the organizations they founded, sponsored, and supported. We must also recognize these "Queen Mothers," encourage them and support their efforts. In this way, the historic institution of "Queen Mother" will remain functional, vigilant, influential and useful in advocating economic, political, intellectual, cultural and spiritual liberation of our people, now and in the future.

FREDERICK MONDERSON

BN PHOTO - Brooklyn Borough President Eric L. Adams stands with the Guyana Contingent at the International Friendship Festival.

46. QUEEN OF SHEBA IN RACIAL PORTRAL AS HISTORICAL DISTORTION
By
DR. FRED MONDERSON

Standing in the line some time ago for the cashier at a local supermarket, my eye caught one of the customary tabloids with headlines that read "World's Mysteries Solved." Like any enthusiastic of any such esoteric phenomenon, I purchased the paper and took it home. Such topics as a new discovery of Noah Ark's are-occurring historical theme, and "Vatican Confirms the Existence of Angels," were some of the articles in this issue. Turning to the centerfold, my eyes caught the story, "Scientists Discover the Home of the Queen of Sheba." This was a short story, juxtaposed to a large

BLACK NATIONALISM STILL ALIVE AND WELL

picture of the Queen of Sheba. It was a picture of a beautiful woman, white! What's wrong with this picture?

Just then a friend, Rodolfo was visiting my home. When I brought this to his attention and having some familiarity with my work, he admonished: "You should write an article on this distortion." Finally I agreed. Looking at the Article again it read, "British Archaeologists have discovered the home of the Queen of Sheba, located in the southern Nigerian forest region." Often times the general reading public would overlook such a report.

Many times readers have questioned the veracity of the Tabloids to sensationalize their stories that, in a number of instances, are outright distortion of fact. Too often, Gary Byrd on WLIB New York radio has said, "The information you don't have could kill you." Equally too Malcolm X has admonished his listeners to be skillful readers for newspapers have a tendency to put things in a manner that denigrates Blacks, and generally distorts the truth; they also hide important news deep within the paper. For nearly three decades **CEMOTAP** has challenged caricature of Blacks in the media.

Into the second decade of the 21st Century and a new millennium, Blacks in America and hence worldwide, must be concerned about the ever present problems of racism that distorts the image of Blacks whether politically, historically, culturally, psychologically or simply say as human beings.

The fact is, in a general sense, the information presented to Blacks and Whites, pertaining to the same issue are colored differently. Blacks, who have been maligned for centuries, are presented with information by their scholarly researchers based on empirical inductive reasoning. Whereas, Whites are presented with the same information based on deductive reasoning. The end result is, Blacks in the know who trust the reports of serious Black researchers end up knowing the truth. Whereas, whites who are either intentionally misinformed or are unconcerned about the nature of their sources,

FREDERICK MONDERSON

end up being mis-educated about a number of things. I say that to say, even in academia, you sometimes have two classes being taught down the hall from each other and the instructors teach two versions of the same issue.

I use ancient Egypt/Kemet as a good example but the distorted picture is not limited to that subject.

Now to present my case, I will document a few examples to show that historical truths are perennially distorted and to set the record straight, men and women of objective scholarship must constantly challenge distortions.

As a student of Professor Ben-Jochannan, I have often listened to his debates and observed the ink spilled discussing a line in the Bible. Depending on the versions one consults, the question is always did the Queen of Sheba say, 'I am Black and comely.' Or, 'I am Black but comely.' In the first instance she is saying "I'm Black and beautiful" and being proud of it. In the second instance, in saying "I'm Black but beautiful she is, if you will, denigrating her Blackness but affirming her beauty. People on a pejorative bent towards Blacks flaunt the latter affirming she was not proud of her Blackness, though they would concede she was Black and beautiful. Did the editor of the tabloid know this or was he simply uncaring and determined to distort in the belief it would go unnoticed. Of course, if Solomon had married the Queen of Sheba and made an 'honest woman' out of her, this matter would probably have been resolved. Now, in an extension of this argument, a more potent social issue is raised.

BLACK NATIONALISM STILL ALIVE AND WELL

BN PHOTO - The "Guyana Contingent" at the International Friendship Festival.

FREDERICK MONDERSON

There is no need to dwell on the slavery issue in the master, slave, male-female, a la, Jefferson-Hemmings, relationship. Word on the street today is that "Black men marry white women to screw them. White men screw Black women but don't marry them." In most cases, a Black man marries a white woman for her beauty. Seldom, is she a professional. 'Guess who's coming to dinner,' Michael Jackson, Clarence Thomas, Quincy Jones and O.J. Simpson. When they're out in public, more than the customary stares, questions, 'What is she doing?' and 'Why are they here?' When the relationship sours he is still the 'N' word! The white male, on the other hand, marries the Black female, primarily because of her professional standing, perhaps for her beauty. When they're out in public, 'Oh what a beautiful couple.' If they're not married, it is not inconceivable that he would 'Roast her' as in the case with Whoopi Goldberg and the white actor she was seeing, who did just that on national TV. Now to move on!

Historical distortions like forgeries are nothing new. The "Donation of Constantine" is one such example of a forgery.

People with historical consciousness know that after the decline of Egyptian/Kemetic civilization, and the rise of Greece and Rome, Jesus the Christ came, was crucified, died, buried and rose again. In the centuries right after, early Christians were martyred through fear of the Roman rulers that the promised heavenly kingdom was a threat to the Roman Empire. After the games and the maulings by African lions, the martyrdoms, etc., Constantine the Great became Emperor of Rome. On the eve of a major military engagement he had a dream or vision that involved religious matters, priestly paraphernalia, the Bishop's Mitre, and insignia of his vestments, etc. Succeeding in battle the next day, Constantine credited his dream with being part of his good fortune. He declared "We killed enough Christians," "Let's cage the lions," "Stop Christians for lunch," "End the crucifixions." He declared Christianity would be recognized as a legitimate religion in the Roman Empire. Church could get equal footing with state and Christians would be respected. He called the *Council of Nicea* in 325 A.D. and invited all the Bishops of the

BLACK NATIONALISM STILL ALIVE AND WELL

Christian church to hammer out the glitches in the fundamental tenets of Christianity. Constantine was hailed as the first Christian Emperor of the Roman Empire.

A document entitled "The Donation of Constantine" later showed the Emperor had donated extensive tracts of land to the church that was tax-exempt, etc. A thousand years later, an Italian Pico Mirandella, a linguist, while doing research made a remarkable discovery. As anyone familiar with linguistics would know language constantly changes. New words are added and old words dropped. Remember, 'where's the beef?'

Mirandella showed that the document contained words that did not come into the vernacular until centuries after Constantine; therefore, he declared the document 'Donation of Constantine' a forgery. Using the same "Where's the Beef" analogy, a 1920s document purports something of significance and the above line used, when it was not yet "Born" is a useful example. Thus, it is considered historical fraud or misrepresentation.

The search for "Prester John" was one of those monumental failures that were also a perennial success. Perhaps as equally important as the riches of the east, the search for Prester John motivated Portuguese explorers for centuries. Since he was never found, it is not inconceivable that the thought of finding his kingdom is not a moot issue.

Following the decline of the Roman Empire and Rise of Islam, the Moors or Shakespeare's "Blackamoors" invaded Southern Europe. They occupied that land from 711 to 1485 providing the "Arab conduit" of ancient African intellectualism, developed in the Nile Valley. Perhaps in that age the myth of Prester John was born, yet it fueled particularly Portuguese aspirations of exploration and colonization. The notion of Prester John, a White king ruling a Black kingdom in Africa motivated untold numbers of global white

FREDERICK MONDERSON

supremacists searching on that continent. Everyone came, searching, yet to find this individual.

As Professor Clarke liked to say "The Africans invited Europeans for lunch and we became the meal." The result was "naked imperialism" "enlightened imperialism" and then "intellectual imperialism." Of course, the missionaries were a vanguard in colonial strategy. We can thank Jomo Kenyatta for his insightful assessment of this aftermath in *Facing Mount Kenya*. "When the missionaries came they gave us the Bible and taught us to close our eyes and pray. When we opened our eyes, we were holding the Bible and the Europeans the land."

BN PHOTO - Brooklyn Borough President Eric L. Adams leads the **Parade** at the First International Friendship Festival.

As a youngster growing up in Guyana, reading was an enjoyable past-time. However, there was no "Black History," these were not yet "born." Even though they have been manifestly evolving from time immemorial. We were taught English History 1066-1485, from the Norman invasion to the War of the Roses and ascension of the

BLACK NATIONALISM STILL ALIVE AND WELL

Tudors. We read about the Phantom in Africa. He was a masked crusader who single-handedly subdued all comers in the heart of Africa. As if that was not enough, Edgar Rice Burroughs gave us Tarzan and Hollywood had a field day in its systematic and well-choreographed denigration of the African persona. And, we all laughed heart-fully as one white man defeated and made fools of "tribes of Africans" portrayed and degraded as "savages." A recent article indicated there were no Africans in Walt Disney's new movie, Tarzan. That's taking it to the next level!

The Western literary traditions begin with Homer's *Iliad* and *Odyssey*. It is believed he visited Egypt/Kemet. The description of Thebes with its "palaces" and "hundred gates" refers to the City of Thebes in the time of Rameses III of the XXth Dynasty. The erudite Cheek Anta Diop argued: "If Homer visited Egypt and this fact is attested to by Greek tradition-it was probably during the time of the XXVth Sudanese Dynasty, under Piankhi or Shabaka, around 750 B.C." Then again, much controversy surrounds the Greeks in Egypt. Modern scholars have accepted some of these classical writers' views on the Egyptians but they reject salient parts particularly of an ethnological nature. Herodotus visited Egypt around 450 B.C. and in his *Histories* Book II, *Euterpe*, is devoted to that land. Granted he traveled the land seeking information from priests who guarded their history and culture very well. Yet he secured information from them. He also observed much but he was right about their color!

In the era of the 18th century, the American, French and Haitian Revolutions, when men aspired to the nobility of freedom, of spirit and body, Africans in American were enslaved. In that era of *philosophes*' and free thinking, Count Volney wrote his *Ruins of Empire*, wherein he postulated the view, "men and women of sable skin and frizzled hair, then enslaved, founded along the banks of the Nile River, the fundamental laws of science that governed the world, while much of humanity was still in a barbaric stage."

FREDERICK MONDERSON

In 1799, Napoleon's artillery officers discovered the now famous Black basalt tri-lingual inscription called the Rosetta stone. In 1822, this became the basis of Champollion's decipherment of hieroglyphics, *Medu Netcher*. In 1836, Sir Godfrey Higgins published *Anacalypsis* in 2 vols. In this masterful work he identified the ancient races and military, political, spiritual, and religious luminaries who were Black. A powerful work of erudite scholarship, *Anacalypsis*, challenges all comers to contest its revelations.

In the age of political, military and economic imperialism intellectual advantage became an extension of that movement. Archaeological excavation in the Nile Valley got a significant boost in the years 1870-1930. Not only was that discipline placed on a systematic and scientific footing, a number of organs of literary expression were inaugurated to chronicle the constantly unfolding spectacular discoveries. The *American Journal of Archaeology* was a prominent publication among numerous others. In the 1898-99 Archaeological Season the "Mortuary temple of Nebhepetra Mentuhotep II" was discovered at Deir el-Bahari, Thebes. It was cleared in the 1903-04 season. A statue of the king was found wearing his *heb sed* attire. The statue was removed and to this day resides in the Cairo Museum

A phenomenon occurred which is not dissimilar by today's standards, "All the news printed to fit!" All that *American Journal of Archaeology* IX (1905: 98) could say of a physio-ethnological nature was the "thick lips with edges defaced by sharp ridges, the heavy chin and the muscles emphasized round the corners of the mouth and nose, are derived from the mannerisms of the late Sixth Dynasty." It is interesting, however, First, how the pertinent information is scattered and can only be found in bits; Second, that though much information is missing, we see connections between the first and third dynasty; the sixth and eleventh; the twelfth and eighteenth; and the seventh and eighteenth dynasties despite the many claims of a Caucasian Egypt. Again, Malcolm's admonition, "No matter what the man says, you better look into it."

BLACK NATIONALISM STILL ALIVE AND WELL

BN PHOTO - Dr. Fred Monderson and Mrs. Carmen Monderson at the International Friendship Festival.

For Black readers then, in an age of slavery, civil war, and aftermath reconstruction, Jim Crowism, Tenant Farming, Separate but Equal, discrimination, and racism, it was difficult for Black readers who could not analyze *American Journal of Archaeology's* description, having no meaning! No major publishing vehicle in the United States carried it until W. Stephenson Smith in 1959 dared to say Mentuhotep II had "Black flesh.' The statue is in the same place in the museum, but for more than half century Black readers did not know the Theban Mentuhotep II of the XIth Dynasty was a Black king. That is, until Dr. Ben Jochannan began carrying Afro-Americans to Egypt. That too, is why Prof. Monderson, a student of the august elder, intends to continue the tradition of research, writing and publication and carrying our people to Egypt to expose them to the ancient African heritage and legacy. Not simply Mentuhotep's statue in the Cairo Museum but the wonderful temples of Karnak, Luxor, Deir el-Bahari, Abydos, Dendera, Edfu, Esna, Kom Ombo, Philae, and Kalabsha and Beit Wali, and Abu Simbel, beacons all, with their wonderful architectural, spiritual and intellectual enlightenment.

FREDERICK MONDERSON

Tutankhamon, as Prof. Clarke liked to say, "Was a minor king who got a major funeral." In 1922, Howard Carter discovered his tomb in the Valley of the Kings. Two life-like statues of the boy king stood at the entrance to the burial chamber.

Comparative analysis is a potent tool or weapon in dismantling and destroying the myths of distortion. The French scholar Jean Yoyote in Georges Posener's *Dictionary of Egyptian Civilization* (p. 291) speaks of Tutankhamon's treasures: "Everything was there. Nests of sarcophagi, statues of the king, golden jewelry, magical and everyday furniture, golden shrines, and alabaster and faience vases, the whole comprising an unrivalled collection of objects for the study of the arts and ritual ceremonies." Elsewhere (p. 293) he says: "The everyday requirements of a prince were buried with him, including; weapons, chariots, vessels, embroidered garments, chests and other pieces of furniture. The funerary equipment of the glorified dead was always plentiful-Canopic jars, ushabtis of every material and figures of gods, to which must be added portable shrines and the blackened wooden statues which had been used in the funeral rite. Everything was costly and worthy of a king." Again, elsewhere (p. 75) "The Red and Black Land." Red the desert, Black, the plain. Where the Nile "rose to flood the land and replenish it with new soil each year." Or, should I say, "Red equals Death and Black equals Life!"

At the 1998, ASCAC Conference at City College, New York, in a taped interview, Prof. Diop says "Kemet" or "Black Land" referred to the indigenous people and not the land. He said the word does not appear with the derivative for land and that it is for the Black people. Even further, while this may not still be, owing to the reorganization of the Museum, "Blackened wooden statues" of the Kings Amenhotep I and Amenhotep II, among others were observed by this writer. Interestingly enough, juxtaposed in the case was a black wooden statue of a panther. The placement of the panther in the case confronts and contradicts such claims those similar statues as the two from Tutankhamon's burial chamber only had ceremonial uses.

BLACK NATIONALISM STILL ALIVE AND WELL

In 1985 as the nation approached the 50th Anniversary of the celebration of Columbus' discovery of America, this in itself a distortion, Dr. Cheek Ana Diop wrote a letter to the *Journal of African Civilization*. It discussed the finding of tobacco, a New World strain, in the Mummy of Rameses II. This mummy of the New Kingdom monarch, discovered in the late 19th Century, began to decay. It was rushed to Paris to undergo scientific surgery to arrest the decay. The Senegalese scholar Diop was qualified enough to be part of the examination team. The only Black accorded that privilege. Perhaps had he not been there, the manifestation of the discovery and the tenacity to defend its meaning and significance would probably not been made manifest. Diop was mentioned in UNESCO's final report on the "Peopling of the Nile Valley." They commended Cheikh Anta Diop and Theophile Obenga as being the best prepared of all the participants at the conference.

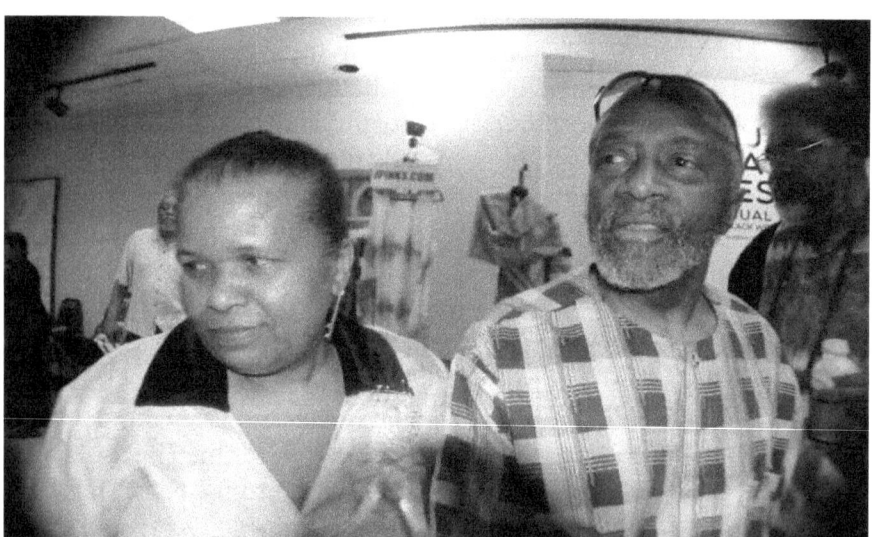

BN PHOTO - Cherise Maloney is one of the "Mothers" beside Michael Hooper at **Roots Revisited** "Mothers Day Honors."

The esteemed multi-disciplinarian deduced that New World tobacco in Rameses' stomach meant he smoked the stuff or consumed some just before death. Even more important however, it meant his

FREDERICK MONDERSON

emissaries visited the New World and returned! This meant Africans were in the New World nearly 3000 years before Columbus! In addition, at the 1992 Temple University Diopian Conference, papers were presented showing the Malian king Abu Bekr and a fleet of ships left for the New World at the start of the fourteenth century nearly 200 years before Columbus. This being so, Africans should be celebrating the 700th year of that adventure. Much of this is not known, though back in 1992 we celebrated 500 years of the exploration, conquest and exploitation and extermination of New World peoples and cultures. Let's not forget, records in the logs of Magellan's ships indicate as they were crossing the Atlantic, 'Africans in long canoes' were observed returning from the New World. Equally too, Dr. Charsee MacIntyre, argued for the arrival of little Africans in the New World as early as 120,000 years ago. Prof. Betancourt cautioned those dates though he did affirm firm dates at "70,000 years" before our era.

Malcolm X looms so large in our history. A student at Temple University once submitted a dissertation request to show that the "Norse Epics" were those of Blacks. Also, that "Eric the Red" was not the white, full red bearded individual so often pictured. He was like, say, Malcolm as "Detroit Red." The rather articulate and well-known Professor responded, "Well, without a lot more documentation, I can't sell this to the Graduate Board." It got the sort of "Let's kill it in Committee" treatment!

Finally, and cut this short, Dr. Cheek Ana Diop, also with an opportunity to examine the Cairo Mummies, in his Magnum Opus, *Civilization or Barbarism: An Authentic Anthropology*, informed us the mummies had their skins peeled like potatoes to hide their blackness! However, the "blackened wooden statue used in the funeral rite: is actually a misrepresentation. In The Roy al Mummies, G. Elliot Smith the atomist mentioned "a black resinous material placed over the mummy" but you could see the "brown skin beneath." A credible argument is they was no need to paint the statue black.

BLACK NATIONALISM STILL ALIVE AND WELL

All this and so much more, distorted, omitted and hidden from Black readers. Thus, these bring us to the old adage: To be properly informed Blacks need critical Black researchers to ferret out the truth as well as the Black Press to keep them well informed.

BN PHOTO - Claudia and Mavis join Cherise Maloney among Mothers honored by **Roots Revisited** on "Mothers' Day."

47. THE POWER OF ECONOMIC BOYCOTT BY DR. FRED MONDERSON

On Tuesday August 6, 2013, the noted radio personality Bob Law, joined by Rev. Calvin Butts, moderated a program at First Church of God in Christ on Kingston Avenue and Park Place in Brooklyn, regarding black earning power, the potentialities of their spending practices and the capabilities of an organized economic effort that

FREDERICK MONDERSON

maximizes this spending potential as well as where to invest with the greatest economic benefit to African people.

Mr. Law pointed out; this new movement is a national effort supported by Rev. Ben Chavis, Conrad Mohammed, Sister Souljah, Rev. Dr. Calvin Butts of Abyssinian Baptist Church and a number of politically and economically conscious individuals across the national spectrum. Reminding that "Jesus came specifically to his own," Bob Law told the nearly three hundred individuals gathered to receive his usually highly informative message; he wanted them to join his effort because a great deal was at stake. He wanted them to assess the situation and redirect their spending habits to really get the most "bank for their buck."

For one thing, a plague has infested the Black community that beyond economic considerations has implications for health concerns with a tremendous impact on the family structure. This is exacerbated because many families, individuals, are struggling in the bowels of our community and they don't even realize the true impact of this "sweet tasting plague." Even more important, they are at a disadvantage because of the inability to control their spending habits, then as an analogy he delved into the impact of the Montgomery Bus Boycott of which Rev. Augustus Jones and Rev. Wyatt Tee Walker were a part and how that strategy undergirded the effectiveness of the Civil Rights Movement within the context of Adam Clayton Powell's admonition, "Don't buy where you do not or cannot work!" As such, Mr. Law spoke to the "preponderance of fast food joints" that "saturate the Black Community" and create a moral and social dilemma of dependence with lasting implications not simply for economic matters of spending, but health and the inability to pay full attention to one's own eating habits, food choices, preparation, etc.

This is especially so because of the lack of fruits and vegetables in the African American diet, because of their unavailability in the Black Community. This in turn has given way to that preponderance of Fast Food establishments that calls into question health issues as diabetes, cancer, heart attacks, strokes plaguing Blacks at a time when health care is more and more expensive and hospitals that

BLACK NATIONALISM STILL ALIVE AND WELL

serve the Black community are being closed en masse. Case in point in Central Brooklyn alone we can show many hospitals are closed or closing. Brooklyn Women's Hospital, Caledonian, Brooklyn Jewish, St. Mary's, and Long College and Interfaith are on life support.

This "Fast Foods state of affairs" prompted this reporter to investigate this matter further. As such, I chose the "Nostrand Avenue Corridor from Fulton Street to Eastern Parkway in Brooklyn." This is a good representative sample, of the Black Community, and while the results are not exactly a duplicate elsewhere, they can, however, serve as a pretty good barometer to assess the significance of the problem posed. Well, what did this inquiry find?

There are "23 Fast Food Establishments" not counting the nearly 12 or so Delis in this 12-block stretch along Nostrand Ave from Fulton Street to Eastern Parkway. There are 4 at Fulton Street and Nostrand Avenue alone and 1 or sometimes up to 3 on each block as you approach Eastern Parkway. As such, in this and other instances, Bob Law wanted to redirect spending habits, because we represent these businesses' "margin of profit." When "they lose that margin of profit" they respond to the demands of the Black Community. One way to get this nation to respond to our concerns is the economic boycott and it becomes more effective if conducted on a national level across city after city, state after state, with religious institutions paying a significant role.

Next Reverend Butts began to elaborate on the problem. Reminding that "We represent the margin of profit" then if "We stop buying a product" the makers suffer and begin to listen to our concerns! This strategy has had the greatest success backed by the Black Church, whether it's the African Methodist Episcopal, the Christian Methodist Episcopalian, or the Church of God In Christ. The Montgomery Bus Boycott led by Rev. Herbert Oliver was effective because of the role of the church! Adam Clayton Powell's mantra, "Don't buy where you can't work" was not "Burn Baby Burn" but

FREDERICK MONDERSON

"Economics Baby Economics." We must remember Marcus Garvey and Elijah Mohammed encouraged our people to "Do for self!" The Black Churches were built by people pooling their money. Bishop McCulloh and Sweet Daddy Jones were able to establish banks, insurance companies, foundations with people pooling their money. "When you begin to amass economic strength you gain respect in this nation. We can focus our economic strength."

"We have the right to read, own property, save our money. We spend crazy with people who really don't care about us. They don't employ us but take our monies out of our community. We can make a difference." Remember, "a little bit of salt changes the flavor of food." When we buy we must ask, "Where are the Black people who work here?" So, we must shop at Black establishments. We must respect ourselves and we must spread the word! We must remember radio stations such as KISS and WLIB do not program in our best interest. TV is not of any substance. We must spread the word through our churches, civic organizations, and fraternities. We must become disciples of an economic gospel that puts our community first." Dr. Butts confessed, "I am a devotee of this methodology. We must remember the effectiveness of the principles of Kwanza. We must Remember Trayvon Martin. Finally, I want you to pay attention to 3 movies; *Fruitvale Station*, *The Butler* and *12 Years a Slave* for these movies chronicle our experiences."

Bob Law again addressed the gathering. He introduced Bishop Jerry Seabrook. The Bishop referenced a recent episode. Today the streets of Detroit looks like a war zone. The City is in default. Yet, poor folks raised $18,000.00 in a free-will offering for a pressing cause. This was pocket money understandably. People protesting and marching were outraged because of Zimmerman, Randy Evans shot by Officer Torsney who was declared not guilty because of a "temporary insanity" plea. Then there was Eleanor Bumpers in the Bronx. These all claimed police feared for their lives when they shot these people. It is clear from Dred Scott's 1857 Decision to now, we are still denied justice! A national coalition is formed around this issue. Let us begin to use the leverage we have in our community which is our economic strength in our spending habits.

BLACK NATIONALISM STILL ALIVE AND WELL

Annually we spend nearly one trillion dollars! Blacks outspend everyone else. We spend more money on everything than everyone else! Revlon! Nobody respects us! Everybody takes us for granted! When the Russian Prime Minister said something derogatory about Gays, these people called in the "Vodka lords" and told them "We will stop buying your Vodka unless you say and do something!" That is clout! "Economics is one of the ways we have power." Remember Emmett Till. It was not stand your ground in St. Louis, New York, Mississippi and Florida. It is the institution of racism. Institutional Racism. "What's in your hand?" "Over One Trillion Dollars!" "Hold on to your dollars! Instead, give to constructive organizations that are working in our best interest." Give your "Burger and Fries" monies to Sankofa Academy or the Learning Tree School.

African Americans consume more fast food than every other group. The location of fast food establishments is determined by race. Racial profiling is conducted on every level. There are 6 times as many fast food restaurants in the Black Community than in any other communities. We must remember 80 percent of processed food in the United States is already banned in other nations because of the preservatives put in them to extend shelf life. Burger King, Wendy, Kentucky Fried Chicken all take out money from our community but don't support anything we do for social justice. The Fast Food industry depends on our money! We must push back and not allow our community to be systematically pulled from under us. We must never forget police lynch mobs murder our people and are acquitted. The Cola industry and Craft and Mac and Cheese are making millions. We must be a part of this national movement. Remember, John Killins, Lorraine Hansberry, James Baldwin all, for the longest, spoke out against this issue. Yet, we are still denied justice and freedom.

FREDERICK MONDERSON

BN PHOTO - Erik and Luis speak from the Podium at Boro Hall.

Then Mr. Law mentioned Rev. Leon Sullivan in Detroit. He was trying to get to some big wig in the auto industry to say we need jobs. The man outright said "I don't have time to speak with you." That was Wednesday afternoon. Rev. Sullivan got the word out to 72 pastors. On Sunday morning word went out from these church pulpits "Don't Buy his product!" By Tuesday morning, the man called Rev. Sullivan stating, "When are you available to meet with me!" This shows leadership has traditionally come from the church. Systemic racism is condoning and supporting institutional racism. They are closing hospitals, close over one hundred schools. So, "We Must Stand Our Ground: Turn Black Spending into Political Power!" We must use our money to influence policy! We must have an intelligent policy that is used effectively.

We don't have to stop all Black folks from buying fast food. Just 8 percent need stop buying fast food. This is indeed a national movement. Chukwu Lumumba in Mississippi and Maulana Karenga in Los Angeles are part of this movement. Then he admonished, "Can you hold back some of your Fast Food Spending. Your Burger and Fries Money."

Bishop Seabrook called for a self-assessment. These fast food establishments are not hiring anyone from our community. Chinese, Hispanics, Koreans not hiring anyone from our community!

BLACK NATIONALISM STILL ALIVE AND WELL

Someone offered, "Have you seen a Chinese restaurant go out of business?" Then he addressed Black on Black crime.

"We rally around other people killing us but not rally around us killing us. If we come together in unity we could stop some of this injustice. Burger King is a Florida Based Fast Food company."

We must remember we spend between 900 billion and one trillion dollars. 321 billion on books, 714 billion on beauty and hair products. All the while 24 schools were closed with 19 more are on the block; 34 schools must be replaced; 23 Schools closed in Philadelphia alone. All the while 420 billion are spent on prisons.

Ollie McClean, Founder and principal of the Sankofa Academy, nearly 30 years in existence, sadly now departed, next related the positive curriculum taught in that school. She delved into some of the activities the young people are a part of and the percentage who go on to college. This, then, is a good example why Bob Law suggested, "Hold Back the Burger and Fries" small change and give to such positive organizations as Sankofa and the Learning Tree. Meanwhile we will continue to coordinate economic strategy boycott across the country!

FREDERICK MONDERSON

BN PHOTO - Carmen makes her statement from the Podium at Boro Hall.

48. SONNY CARSON MAKING OF A REVOLUTIONARY
By
Dr. Fred Monderson

Revolutionaries are people, often called reformers, who struggle to change inequities, whether political, social, artistic, economic or educational, in social systems, institutions or society. Conditions that motivate individuals are generally ripe with oppression necessitating extended activism, much negotiation and even armed struggle. The process involves blood, sweat, tears, isolation, character assassination, and sometimes even death and dishonor. However, because those sincere individuals oftentimes have right

BLACK NATIONALISM STILL ALIVE AND WELL

and truth on their sides, history's pendulum of equity eventually swings in their direction justifying their efforts and crowning their richly deserved, hard earned glory. I should add, in today's world with its technological developments, armed struggle is not as viable an option particularly in societal context. As within the United States, organize, organize, organize, join organizations and effectuate unending creative protests are some of the best strategies! However, since persistence and consistency are mandatory, remember Lerone Bennett said: "Don't expect to win by Monday afternoon." The more potent and effective tool is that used by Dr. Martin Luther King in non-violence, civil disobedience and active activism. Surely they took his life but he brought our people a long way.

We could equally assign the term to religious reformers of which Akhenaton, the 18th Dynasty pharaoh (Amenhotep) is considered a religious revolutionary who also introduced new ideas in science, art and architecture. Imhotep was a genius and architectural revolutionary who built the Step Pyramid at Sakkara for the Pharaoh Zoser, 3rd Dynasty, 2600 B.C., that still stands today which is a triumph of his innovative building techniques. Mentuhotep II of the 11th Dynasty was certainly revolutionary in enclosing mortuary structural paraphernalia in his worship temple building at Deir el Bahari. Queen Hatshepsut of the 18th Dynasty told the world the Sun God descended and impregnated her mother so she was sired by divine intervention. This was certainly revolution in its conception which recognized the Queen as early thinker. Senmut the architect who helped Hatshepsut seize pharaonic power in a male dominated world and ruled for two decades was obviously involved in a revolutionary process. His building of the Queen's temple at Deir el Bahari, next to and 500 years after Mentuhotep's Middle Kingdom structure, that he innovated with so many new features, classifies him as revolutionary in thinking and architectural construction. However, this essay attempts to focus on revolutionary action that addresses oppression and people's attempts to change their societal norms and the political landscape of their nation.

FREDERICK MONDERSON

Equally and significantly, for the Black African race, the first revolutionary struggle against injustice has been the one to combat the "Curse of Ham" in the Bible. There is no other people on earth who has been cursed and despite the passage of time, the notions of the ages of "political" and even "religious correction," this problem has not been addressed. So that struggle must continue unless some people accept the merits of the situation and live in perpetuity in the belief that Blacks are cursed! Imagine all the unspeakable atrocities committed by other peoples and races, yet they are not cursed! However, but a Black man, actually a white man turned Black, who looked at his drunk and naked father must bear the animosity of that degradation for all time. While this notion is alien to Africa, imagine what form of cruelty this, myth made tangible in fact, really is?

Significantly, and in particular regard to slavery and other forms of injustice, we first learn of large scale and systematic resistance to tyranny and oppression in the tale of a Roman slave named Spartacus who led a great force against that mighty Empire. But, though crushed, the memory of his actions put tyrants on notice. Slaves will rebel, causing great economic damage and dislocation to society's order as they seek to right the wrongs of their conditions and set their people free. The African-American historian Herbert Aptheker chronicled more than 100 slave rebellions in the Americas, and though many did not succeed and get positive press, they remain on the books and have been inspirational to many revolutionaries.

The enslaved Cuffy led a rebellion in Guyana as early as 1763, a date which incidentally set in motion conditions that led to the American Revolution when that Great American statesman Patrick Henry proclaimed: "Give me liberty or give me death!" However, it was Crispus Attucks who has been the first revolutionary to lay down his life, the first authentic American hero Was a Black man; and also Peter Salem and Salem Po who were out there with George Washington and the "Green Mountain boys." Cuffe's struggle and aims were inspirational in the fight for Guyana's independence two centuries later in 1966. In the early 1800s, a Black-American ship captain of the same name, Paul Cuffe, repatriated Blacks back to

BLACK NATIONALISM STILL ALIVE AND WELL

Africa in his own vessel so they would escape the challenges and miseries facing free and enslaved Blacks in early 19th Century America.

The American people's revolutionary fight for freedom against tyranny, oppression, taxation without representation and the unjust nature of colonialism did several significant things with long-lasting impacts on history. First, it produced the **Declaration of Independence**, **Articles of Confederation** and **US Constitution** that challenged and inspired the French, Haitian and Latin American revolutionaries, as well as later peoples to be successful in their struggles for independence. At that time, Benjamin Banneker's intellectual and architectural contributions in planning America's foundation were equally revolutionary. Sad, however, the day he was being buried arsonists fire-bombed his home destroying all his papers and life's work. On the other hand, the actions of Toussaint L'Ouverture, Henry Christophe and Jacques Dessalines were certainly revolutionary, emerging from slavery to struggle, free and found the First Black Republic in the New World in the state of Haiti. Unfortunately, the pressure brought on Haiti by slave holding nations discouraged these great leaders' progeny from remaining true to the revolutionary spirit and this has helped contribute to the mess poor Haiti experiences today.

The second important thing about that American spirit, it exposed the underbelly of the horrible institution of slavery that not only later tore this nation apart but ingrained its tentacles and ugliness in an institutionalized system in *de jure* and *de facto* injustice. This in turn gave birth to Jim Crowism, lynchings, racial discrimination, economic disparity, and the workings and essential features of the second generation offsprings in James Crow, Jr. Esq., and his *modus operandi*. The end result is racial profiling, police brutality and so much more, and despair feeding an ingrained self-hatred on the part of the victims of the cruel malady.

FREDERICK MONDERSON

Jean Baptiste Pointe du Sable and the founding of the site that became the City of Chicago was certainly revolutionary! This pioneering spirit followed in the footsteps of Estanvanico who challenged the wilderness and blazed a trail across this country.

Nonetheless, in the dictum of a majority of one, Black and white American men and women have risen up to challenge that system of oppression, defusing it in all its institutionalized rancor and odiousness. In this quest, they were bruised and battered, giving and even having their lives taken by unjust and inhumane, heartless individuals. John Brown is a good example. The seeds of that resistance began on the shores of Africa resisting the slave catchers. It continued aboard the slaving vessels resisting the cruelty and inhuman conditions and made manifest in the likes of the Amistad and Gabriel Prosser's revolt. Yet, the truly revolutionary struggle began in earnest on the spiritual front when Revs. Absalom Jones and Richard Allen walked out on their Methodist Episcopal Church Christian brothers and sisters and founded their own African Methodist Episcopalian Church in 1816. Equally too, Christian slave owners quickly and strategically closed the "salvation route" to African emancipation. Nonetheless, the use of the word African was revolutionary in itself for it kept the light shining in those dark days! In fact, the tenacious cement-like nature of that African spirituality, to this day, has meant salvation even to those who have not been or are in the revolutionary struggle challenging the spiritual warfare directed against the sons and daughters of Africa.

Gabriel Prosser and Jack Bowler led a revolt in 1800 and this response sent a strong and significant warning to the bastions of oppression. Captured and bound, in his challenge in face of this tyranny, Prosser compared himself to George Washington. He said, essentially, according to Norman Hodges' *Black History*, Monarch Notes, (1974: 77), "I have nothing more to offer than what General Washington would have had to offer, had he been taken by the British officers and put to trial by them. I have ventured my life in endeavoring to obtain the liberty of my countrymen, and am willing to sacrifice to their cause …. I beg as a favor that I may be immediately led to execution. I know that you have predetermined

BLACK NATIONALISM
STILL ALIVE AND WELL

to shed my blood. Why, then, all this mockery of a trial?" Again, revolutionary action was followed in 1822 by the Denmark Vesey conspiracy in Charleston, South Carolina. Vesey's insurrection, however, was betrayed by a "house (Negro) slave," in the Escariot Syndrome mode. This was Malcolm X's "We sick boss recognition." Nevertheless, the message keeps being sent.

Significantly, resistance triumphed in the literary masterpiece of David Walker's *Appeal to Colored Men* in 1826 to rise up and overthrow oppression as a God given right. A few years later, Nat Turner's 1831 blitzkrieg Slave Rebellion with its bone chilling seriousness that killed 45 whites was a rude wake up call, even though he was betrayed and executed. This action also sent a powerful message.

Strange enough, oppression is its own enemy for it gives birth to fearless individuals who emerge and challenge the system. A decade after Nat Turner, Samuel Carson ("The Runaway") ran away from slavery, joined the US Navy, fought and died in the Mexican War and was buried in the Brooklyn Navy Yard, to be resurrected with a significant impact a century and a half later. Henry Highland Garnett, a great abolitionist gave voice to activism and resistance about mid-Nineteenth Century. In his own right, Dred Scott stood up and allowed Chief Justice Roger Taney to use the power of the state, the US Constitution and the Supreme Court in the most oppressive and humiliating manner to sit him down.

Conversely, a century later, in an age of passionate activism, when Rosa Parks sat down, the Supreme Court stood up having done so a decade earlier in the *Brown v. Board* ruling. From here on in, the courts followed a "Domino Theory" reversing many previous rulings, standing up for the Blackman.

Interestingly enough, Roger Taney's historic ruling actually exposed and expressed the inherent contradiction of the **Declaration of**

FREDERICK MONDERSON

Independence, enforcing it in law. The **Declaration of Independence** affirmed: "We hold these truths to be self evident that all men are created equal and are endowed by their creator with the inalienable rights to life, liberty and the pursuit of happiness," meaning right to own property.

At that time Blacks were enslaved and they had none of those rights. One hundred years later Chief Justice Taney so emphatically pointed it out! "Blacks were property and neither men nor citizens of the United States." This came about because, upon capture in Africa and trans-shipment across the Atlantic for purposes of transforming the "New World," colonialism used the force and power of law to deprive Africans of their humanity, reversing the process of evolution, depriving them of their manhood, and making them less than a man! The 3/5 Compromise Law of the U.S. Constitution reversed this making him 3/5 of a man! Imagine being a man from the feet up to just below the shoulders; headless, therefore brainless! The "Super-masculine menial!" is what Blacks were reduced to being. Equally, slavery was so cruel it never permitted or recognized the institution of marriage among the enslaved. Thus, it never permitted families that basic, human, nurturing social unit.

Therefore, when Coleman Sharpton was sent from South Carolina to Florida to pay a debt of the Thurmond family it was some feat to keep his wife and two kids together. He could not complain. The law did not protect him. He had no guarantees of life, liberty or pursuit of happiness. He was chattel, same as a sheep, a bale of cotton, a pig, goat, horse, property! This state of affairs is what tore the Union apart in the Civil War. It's what John Brown rose up against and gave his life to end. It's the same issue represented, or "Old wines in new wineskins," of the new oppressive strategy.

It's the same issues abolitionists like Frederick Douglass, Harriet Tubman, Martin Delaney, Sojourner Truth and the Black regiments in the Civil War fought, worked against and hoped to change, yet saw it slow in coming. But there were other Black Abolitionists in the struggle as indicated in Benjamin Quarles' book by the same

BLACK NATIONALISM STILL ALIVE AND WELL

name that maintained William Wells Brown, Charles Lenox Remond, James Forten, Lensford Land and Prince Saunders were very active as abolitionists. Their white counterparts in the abolitionist struggle included William Lloyd Garrison, Arthur and Lewis Tappan, Theodore Weld, and James G. Burney who put their money and effort into the struggle against this form of oppression. Theirs was a continuation of the struggle begun by the English abolitionists Granville Sharpe, Wilberforce, Buxton, Clarkson and so many others who worked to end the Slave Trade in Africans as the first step to eradicate that institutionalized "crime against humanity" represented by internal and external slave trade, slave farms in the deep south, the "home of prolific lynchings," and slavery. The Underground Railroad and its agents were also part of the radical revolutionary spirit transforming America, when Harriet Tubman (1820-1913) declared: "I never lost a passenger and I never ran my train off the tracks." "I must live free or die!"

The rights, privileges and advantages gained in Reconstruction following the Civil War produced significant Black southern political power in the persons of Robert Smalls and Blanche K. Bruce as Senators from Mississippi and a number of Congressmen including Robert Smalls of South Carolina; John W. Maynard, Louisiana; John R. Lynch of Mississippi; Benjamin Turner of Alabama; Robert C. DeLarge, South Carolina; Josiah T. Walls, Florida; and Joseph H. Rainey and Robert Brown Elliot of South Carolina. Their white allies Thaddeus Stevens and Charles Sumner soon passed on after their work on the *Reconstruction Acts* of 1865-1868 and the *Civil Rights Act* of 1875. Important also, betrayal in the shameful and political sell-out in the Election of 1876 spelt doom for Blacks in the south and nationwide.

In this new reality, Black gains were snatched by the "Elder Crow" and the Ku Klux Klan, Knights of the White Camelia, Knights of the Rising Sun, the White Line, The Palefaces, all with their intimidation of Blacks through lynchings, tar and feathers and as co-conspirators enforcing poll taxes, property taxes, literacy tests and the "Grand

FREDERICK MONDERSON

Father Clause," all with devastating ramifications. Later "White Citizens" groups equally tried to stop Black progress. But the way forward was already established and such terrorism did not stop churchmen from Republican activism during the age of Reconstruction, Rev. Hiram H. Wells of Mississippi; Rev. Richard R. Cain of South Carolina; and Bishop Henry M. Turner of Georgia who played major roles in unfolding 19th Century politics in the United States. In the southern white backlash, Congressman George A. White of North Carolina remained a single voice against spreading Jim Crow.

Out of this mayhem emerged Booker T. Washington whose contemporary George Washington Carver began revolutionizing farming techniques and the southern economy from his base at Tuskegee Institute. In this nightmarish age for Black people, Booker T. preached "Do for Self," and founded Tuskegee Institute to teach Blacks industrial skills in a "Tuskegee model." Elijah McCoy, the "real McCoy," and Granville woods were industrial engineers as well as Machinist Frank J. Farrell in the Knights of Labor, whose pathways were followed by such eminent scientists as Charles Richard Drew, Ernest Everett Just, James Latimore and Percy Julien. Nevertheless, "men of devil like aspirations" later infiltrated Tuskegee Institute and perpetrated the Tuskegee Syphilis Experiment that maimed and disfigured many Blacks for decades. By the last two decades of the 19th Century, 3 Blacks were being lynched per week! This forced women like Ida B. Wells, a protest leader in the 1890s, to tell Pres. William McKinley: "We refuse to believe this country, so powerful to defend its citizens abroad, is unable to protect its citizens at home."

In those days of unspeakable horrors perpetrated against Blacks, two revolutionary giants emerged. Much like the tides, strong Black men keep coming! W.E.B. DuBois was a literary and intellectual giant whose writings, activism and pronouncements dominated the 20th Century, long after his death in Ghana in 1963. The first Black Harvard University PHD in 1896, author of *Reconstruction*, *The Slave Trade - 1638 to 1888*, *The Negro*, *Souls of Black Folks*, *The Gift of Black Folks*, *The World and Africa* and more, his interests

BLACK NATIONALISM STILL ALIVE AND WELL

were manifold, for he was the "Father of Pan-Africanism" and a vocal voice for the oppressed. He edited *The Crisis* newspaper. His counterpart in the first decades of the 20th Century, though they differed in strategy, was Marcus Moziah Garvey whose mass movement under the banner of the Red, Black and Green's Universal Negro Improvement Association and African Communities League mobilized millions of Blacks worldwide and essentially foreshadowed James Brown's 'Say it Loud, I'm Black and Proud' shibboleth. Garvey made the Black man believe in himself! His saying "Up you mighty Race, You can accomplish what you will" almost has cultural status with James Weldon Johnson's "Lift Every Voice and Sing" the Black National Anthem. A third revolutionary was William Monroe Trotter, who at the turn of the 20th Century demanded "Full equality in all things governmental, political, civil and judicial." J. Thomas Fortune advocated and set up "Protection Leagues" in many states. Booker T. Washington was never given his full recognition as a Pan-Africanist of note.

BN PHOTO - Borough President Eric L. Adams poses with the Dominican contingent at the International Friendship Festival as the young lady sleeps through it all.

FREDERICK MONDERSON

Paralleling DuBois' activism and literary expression, Drusilla Dungee, John Huggins, Arthur Schomberg and Carter G. Woodson opened an intellectual front. Woodson, a journalist for Garvey's newspaper, the *Negro World* Published *The Mis-Education of the Negro* and *The Education of the Negro*. He is considered the "Father of Black History Month" celebrations. Thank God, this has had long lasting and positive ramifications!

It's reasonable to assume these intellectual revolutionaries operating within the minefield of American social injustice influenced Paul Robeson as they probably influenced the educator Mary McLeod Bethune. In that age as the world shrank by events of the devastation of World War I and World War II, Langston Hughes carried the torch in the Harlem Renaissance while Claude McKay's powerful poem "If We Must Die" was really far reaching in its implications. Equally too, the emergence of unionization in the colonies of Africa and the West Indies, trans-Atlantic travels, Blacks coming of age and recognizing their limitations and potentials, decolonization in the colonies, all fueled a new movement to put human rights and civil liberties on the crucible of America's conscience. This was the Civil Rights Movement! It gave birth of "Sit-ins," formation of the Southern Christian Leadership Council (SCLC), "Freedom Rides," creative protests and other forms of activism that led to the "March on Washington" in 1963, the deaths of 3 civil rights workers, Andrew Goodman, James Chaney, and Michael Schwerner and the Birmingham church bombings that took the lives of 4 young girls. Then there were assassinations of Black leaders in the persons of Malcolm X, Martin Luther King, Medgar Evers, James Meredith, and several others. These events of martyrdom helped bring about significant civil rights and voting rights legislation at national and state levels.

Men with military service, an eye opener for Harry Belafonte, Rev Shuttlesworth, Thurgood Marshall as legal counsel for the NAACP and his victorious *Brown v. Board of Education of Topeka, Kansas* in 1954 decision had fueled the challenges to white supremacy, racial segregation and discrimination, with the audacity to tell Bull Connor and his type, "Bring it on!" Don't get me started with Huey

BLACK NATIONALISM STILL ALIVE AND WELL

Newton, Bobby Seale, Eldridge Cleaver before salvation and Fred Hampton of the Black Panther Party and their efforts and challenges.

As these events unfolded revolutionary Black men and women began to spring up in the States, in Africa and the Caribbean. The persons of Martin Luther King, Malcolm X, Stokely Carmichael (Kwame Ture), Elijah Mohammed and the Black Muslims, James Meredith and Medgar Evers, Andrew Young, Rosa Parks, Rev. Joseph Lowery, Jesse Jackson, and Fannie Lou Hamer, that staunch Civil Rights activist in the U.S.; in Africa, Kwame Nkrumah, Namdi Azikwe, Tafawa Balewa, Julius Nyerere, Chief Luthuli, Patrice Lumumba, Sekou Toure, and Nelson and Winnie Mandela all followed in the footsteps of Bishop Crowder, the West African missionary and activist; and, in the Caribbean Forbes Burnham; in Jamaica, Norman then Michael Manley; and in Trinidad and Tobago George Padmore, Jeremiah Butler and Eric Williams. This latter personage particularly, who blended political insight and acumen with intellectual fervor and academic excellence began chronicling many significant events in the African experience including *Capitalism and Slavery* and *From Columbus to Castro*.

Joel A. Rogers opened new intellectual frontiers with his books *Sex and Race* and *World's Great Men of Color*; George G.M. James in *Stolen Legacy*, and Chancellor Williams in *Destruction of Black Civilization: Great Issues of a Race*, while Dr. John Henry Clarke, Dr. John Jackson, and Dr. Yosef Ben-Jochannan in the United States challenged literary backwaters and became prolific speakers and authors emphasizing roles of African people in creating historical accomplishments. Dr. Clarke emphasized the US role of Blacks and Africa particularly, Dr. Jackson explained about African Civilizations, and Dr. Yosef Ben-Jochannan researched Nile Valley cultural history. Chief Anta Diop and his associate Theophile Obenga deconstructed and reconstructed the role of Blacks in ancient Egypt, publishing several important works including *African Origins of Civilization: Myth or Reality*, *Cultural Unity of Black Africa*,

FREDERICK MONDERSON

Civilization or Barbarism and *The Peopling of Ancient Egypt and the Decipherment of the Meroitic Script.*

By this time, the great Black revolutionaries in the fields of science, agriculture, stage and screen, education, literary and intellectual output had beat back the specter of Black illiteracy and fear. They secured and cleared new ground upon which they built citadels of Black integrity, industriousness, artistic creativity and intellectual and educational daring. They were the dynamos of their people's social and human progress along the right path of human development, experimentation advancement and continuity.

On another front, the political struggle was hard fought, sometimes bitter but it had sweet results in the election of Black mayors Richard Hatcher, in Gary, Indiana; Coleman Young, in Detroit, Michigan; Charles Evers in Fayette, Mississippi; Carl Stokes in Cleveland, Ohio, and later Andrew Young and Maynard in Atlanta, Georgia. Such progress was the result of Black enfranchisement granted by the Civil Rights Acts and the Voting Rights Acts passed because of the fearlessness of creative protests with a revolutionary fervor.

These fathers and mothers paved the way for revolutionary progress of Blacks in music, business, screen and television and in medicine and administration. Louis Satchmo Armstrong, Nat King Cole, The Drifters, Ben E. King, Otis Redding and Carla Thomas, Dizzy Gillespie, Charlie Byrd Parker, James Brown, Marvin Gaye and the Motown sounds began to sing away the veils of the blues. Lorraine Hansberry's *A Raisin in the Sun*; James Baldwin's prolific pen wrote *Nobody Knows My Name* and *The Fire Next Time*; Richard Wright *Black Boy*; Ralph Ellison *Invisible Man*, Claude Brown *Manchild in the Promised Land*; and Leroi Jones (Amiri Baraka) *The Dutchman* and *The Slave*. C.L.R. James chronicled the Haitian Revolution making us aware of the events of this historic development and thus he is considered revolutionary. The suave of Sidney Poitier and Harry Belafonte aided every civil rights cause in their own low key manner. Equally, such revolutionary groups as The Last Poets, the multi-talented Rashan Roland Kirk, and Dick Gregory coupled their

BLACK NATIONALISM STILL ALIVE AND WELL

musical expressions and comic performances with messages of social consciousness and political activism. A street player as Jonathon Clarke considers himself a revolutionary jazz musician who plays his music on a soprano saxophone in the streets. Let us not forget James Farmer of **CORE** as well as W.E.B. Dubois' role in founding the **Niagara Movement** and the **NAACP** in the early days of the 20th Century and Whitney Young of the National Urban League. We must recount the contributions of A. Philip Randolph, Jackie Robinson, Satchel Paige, Jack Johnson and Jessie Owens who were all blazing trails in their respective fields. As such, they not simply helped to raise the people's consciousness but had begun to challenge and beat back the citadels of Jim Crowism in its many guises, racism, overt and covert and institutional, and began opening doors and paving the way for the next generation of activists.

Out of this legacy emerged Sonny "Abubadika" Carson, Jitu Weusi, Maulana Karenga, Dr. Jacob Carruthers, Conrad Worrill, Chief James Parker, Rev. Herbert Daughtry, Rev. William Jones, Attorneys Alton Maddox, Mason and Colin Moore, Michael Warren and Michael Hardy and even such icons as Jeanette Gadsen and Carlos Lezama who added the carnival cultural flavor to Black expression. Jimmy Cliff, Mighty Sparrow and Lord Kitchener certainly lent their share of partying to make the suffering go down more easily.

The new revelation that the Rev. Al Sharpton's ancestors were enslaved by the ancestors of the most vocal and intractable racist and slavery apologist, Strom Thurmond, who incidentally loved Black women as did Thomas Jefferson, underscored the view that people who probably abhorred slavery produced progeny who were/are foremost revolutionaries and activists. Samuel Carson ran away from slavery, and serving his time in the U.S. Navy added to the myth of "The Runaway" until discovered by the Navy in 1996. Then resurrected and galvanized he was buried in Ghana by his

FREDERICK MONDERSON

revolutionary great-nephew Sonny Carson to serve as a point of pilgrimage for African-Americans seeking their roots in Africa. His "going home to Africa" was certainly revolutionary for it was the first time that any African who came through the "Door of No Return" ever returned to the mother continent, thereby opening the "Door of Return."

The moral of this story is that though many spurious and misleading allegations were made about the benefits of slavery, a rather accurate realization that some descendants of the slaves became revolutionaries in their own right and in different fields fighting the powers that be. After all, in the heyday of the French Revolution, the Englishman Edmund Burke's *Reflections on the French Revolution in France* affirmed: "The only thing necessary for evil to triumph is for good men to say nothing." In our case, not that there is an exception to the rule but that the exception proves the rule in that good people will rise up to challenge oppression and injustice. Martin Luther King in his "I have a Dream" speech spoke of hewing a 'stone of hope from a mountain of despair' and while Jesus, who incidentally was a Black man, spoke of a 'mustard seed of faith,' we recognize there were millions of slaves lost to Africa. W.E.B. Dubois gave a figure of 100 million. Nevertheless, the few, yet significant revolutionaries mentioned here have shouldered the burden and advanced the cause of their people, for the benefit of all humanity. We know without question any gains made by Blacks benefits all Americans and America as well.

BLACK NATIONALISM STILL ALIVE AND WELL

BN PHOTO - A wall mural opposite Abyssinian Baptist Church in Harlem.

49. PERSPECTIVES ON SONNY (AB) CARSON
By
DR. FRED MONDERSON

The roles of historical figures who impact on their community, nation and in an extra-national manner are sometimes not readily discernible to the general public but with time things have a tendency to come to the fore. One such character, who has had a similar impact on American history with afore mentioned repercussions, is Sonny Robert Carson. Paradoxically, while the general public has not recognized this important historical person, his immediate community with whom he interacted and impacted upon wanted to make sure that he was not forgotten.

Upon his death the Black community, from diverse parts of the states came to pay last respects to Sonny Abubadika "He who leads his

FREDERICK MONDERSON

people" (A.B.) Carson. This is a title given him by a Ghana Chieftain who visited America in the early 1970s. While not as extravagant a send-off as that given to U.S. President Ronald Reagan, this President of the **Committee to Honor Black Heroes**, the community in a manner reminiscent of the Biblical story of the individual who would not let the angel depart until he had blest him, insisted that Sonny get all the "trimmings" accorded his due respect. Like Prof. John H. Clarke has often said, "We put him away nicely." In that, with ceremonies at The House of the Lord Church, Friendship Baptist Church, Brown Memorial Baptist Church, gatherings in the Restoration Plaza and a tour de force march with funeral cortege from the Brooklyn Bridge, down Flatbush Avenue, up Fulton Street and across Troop Avenue to Gates Avenue then down Gates to Brown Memorial Baptist Church on Washington and Gates Avenue. A week later, dancers from Ghana gathered with the community at the Malcolm X School in Bed-Stuy to give more due to Sonny.
Anyone not familiar with the man could easily ask, "Why all this?"

The answer is simple.

Sonny Carson was an extraordinary individual. A man of vision, courage, fortitude, daring and with a big heart; he emerged from a poor upbringing, was involved with drugs and crime, a gang-leader; he went to jail and saw first-hand the debilitating experiences of that institution. The Book and Movie, **The Education of Sonny Carson** chronicles his early years, the dynamic challenges facing urban Black youth in the post-World War II decades, as a Korean War veteran, his time in jail, and how events set the stage for the ultimate transformation he would experience upon his release from prison.

Almost instantly Sonny Carson became concerned about people, their problems and the aspirations and required tenacity to meet those challenges. As he rendered assistance he used guile, all the while, with a big and beautiful smile. However, it was never misunderstood that beneath that broad smile was a serious,

BLACK NATIONALISM
STILL ALIVE AND WELL

determined and courageous leader who was well respected for his commitment and consistency in the Black community when facing challenges.

Upon his return from prison Sonny became aware of social and psychological inequities facing Blacks within that prison industrial complex frame work, not only in New York but across the nation as a whole. This is why he dedicated his life to offering assistance to persons caught within the perilous web of that emasculating experience. But he did not stop there. He saw social disparities in economic opportunities and employment practices, education, housing as well as in locations where Blacks spent their hard earned dollars.

In this latter respect, Sonny realized many stores operating in the Black community were white owned and staffed. He organized economic resistance. He said if we could shop here we could work here. He faced opposition at first but gradually doors were opened, Blacks were hired leading eventually to recognition of Black ownership. Hence was born the notion of the economic boycott. But Sonny did not stop there. His activist mojo was working. He became involved in education, was a member of CORE and all this was happening within the context of the national Civil Rights Movement, the Black Muslims and emergence of Malcolm X, the Black Panther Party, the Anti-Viet Nam War, resistance on college campuses and all forms of movements for change across the American political, human and civil rights landscape. By the 1970s Sonny Carson had come of age as a fully fledged activist of national standing tremendously aggrieved at the loss of Malcolm X and Martin Luther King. Similarly in the 1990s that compassionate side of him would be further aggrieved in loss of Biggie Smalls and Tupac Shakur.

Sonny became a member of **The Republic of New Africa** and was elevated to status of a Judge before his untimely passing. This group wanted southern states set aside for Black independence

FREDERICK MONDERSON

contending that they would never have equal status in America. However, realistically considering the social, political and military history of this nation that is a difficult proposition. Perhaps he knew this and thus he maintained his anti-white beliefs because of how that group had treated his people in America. The walls of his office were plastered with pictures of "hanging Black Men" to serve as a reminder of the history of this heinous experience. Still, he was a principled man and was never satisfied with the explanation of the implications of Black Muslim murder of Malcolm X. However, while respecting the principles and program of Kwanza, which he incidentally made a special effort to participate in, he was later incensed that the leader would allow the flag to be changed or rearranged so the government could issue a postage stamp for Kwanza.

His constantly working incisive and analytic mind, a profound understanding of the change agents acting across the national landscape, political assassinations, murders, jailings, the infusion of drugs into the Black community, his travels abroad in Africa and elsewhere, by the mid-1990s Sonny Carson had come of age again. He had grown from a mere hill to a mountain of a man.

Sonny Carson's enlarged status was manifest when in 1995 his activism took him to the Brooklyn Navy Yard where coincidentally the US Navy discovered they had buried Samuel Carson "The Runaway" and turned his remains over to this grand-nephew Sonny Carson. There were several hundred names of Black Veterans also handed over to Mr. Carson. These were published in the New York *Afro Times* newspaper and are included in the book, *Sonny Carson: The Final Triumph*. Sonny equally wanted living relatives to trace their heritage to these veterans and come forward with proof of their relationship to the Black veterans who were buried in the Navy Yard.

BLACK NATIONALISM
STILL ALIVE AND WELL

BN PHOTO - On one of its "College Tours" **Roots Revisited** visited the **University of Maryland at the Eastern Shore** and noticed this logo.

Forthwith Sonny formed the "Bones Committee" and began planning how best to dispose of the body. For nearly two years the Committee met two and three times per week and considered Arlington National Cemetery but settled on Ghana in West Africa as the final resting place for "the Runaway." Inasmuch as millions of Africans were shipped through "The Door of No Return" by his choice Sonny had opened "The Door of Return." This is the first time this was ever done, returning a former slave to Africa. The significant historical occurrence highlighted the First Emancipation Day Ceremony inaugurated by Ghanaian President Jerry Rawlings on August 1, 1998. The site chosen for Samuel Carson's internment was Assin Manso, an area near the river where captured Africans were permitted their last bath before being shipped through the "Door of No Return" to the Americas to become slaves helping to transform these two continents. He was buried alongside Crystal, a Jamaican slave and as Sonny envisioned, the site has become a place of pilgrimage for African Americans seeking to reconnect with their roots in Africa.

Sonny went to great lengths in outreach to relatives of Black servicemen buried in the Brooklyn Navy Yard so that they could claim their ancestors' remains, re-establish their familial connections as well as feeling a sense of pride in being linked to service to this nation. He even wrote President Clinton imploring the Chief Executive and Commander-In-Chief to issue an Executive Order recognizing the service of these Black veterans whose service dates to 1801, before the time of his ancestor Samuel Carson killed in the war with Mexico in 1844.

Equally, recognizing the shenanigans going on at the Brooklyn Navy Yard during the Giuliani administration, as the United States Navy sought to divest itself of that property, Sonny insisted Blacks be issued business opportunities there. His rationale is that as a burial site of great depth in this nation's military history, great portions of the Navy Yard was segregated, but more important it was "Black sacred ground." Therefore, to begin, a Black Memorial was in order and equally, opportunities also for Black involvement in the economic development of the Navy Yard were in order. Unfortunately with the passing of Sonny Carson this idea lost its most forceful proponent and seems to have died.

Further, as an activist and non-believer in the American political process, yet incensed at the loathing and disrespect the 'Monarch at Gracie Mansion' Mayor Rudy Giuliani held towards Blacks, Sonny became political amidst the successes of Million Movement, viz., Man, Woman, Youth, Family, Mom, he called for a "Million Voter Registration" of unregistered Blacks and Latinos in New York City, so as to oust the Mayor. At that time Giuliani was on the ropes because of his attitudes of contempt for Blacks and Latinos. The later catastrophe of September 11, 2001, provided him the opportunity to rise to leadership of unparalleled management. Some of the Mayor's critics, somewhat rightly, claim the terrorist attack was such a ghastly act any of us patriots given the resources of New

BLACK NATIONALISM STILL ALIVE AND WELL

York City leadership would have responded in equally magnanimous management methods.

Notwithstanding, Sonny Carson was a busy man. He continued his activism, advocating for enfranchisement of ex-convicts, attending hearings against police brutality, engaging in demonstrations against Koreans on Fulton Street and Church Avenue, in the Crown Heights debacle, offering advice to incarcerated persons and those charged with crimes, penning his letter to the people, attending funerals, championing causes of tenants whose landlord were recalcitrant, speaking out against government agencies such as child welfare who were hurting rather than helping families, answering the phones, hundreds of calls from across the US and Africa daily and staying abreast and championing parents and children's rights in educational issues. He took on Rudy Crew and the Board of Education, had his finger on the pulse of Medgar Evers College and Restoration Corporation. All this and more as he chaired the Committee to Honor Black Heroes successfully naming Marcus Garvey and Malcolm X Boulevards in Brooklyn, creating the name Malcolm X School in Bed-Stuy, influencing the name of Toussaint L'Ouverture School on Empire Blvd and laying the foundation for replacing Fulton Street with Harriet Tubman Blvd.

Yet, all these involvements seem not central to his desire to respectfully intern the remains of his ancestor Samuel Carson, the "Runaway." Sonny formed the Bones Committee that met two or three times per week for nearly two years at McDonnell's Restaurant on Macon Street, at the Patterson Residence, in Restoration, the church on Adelphi Street, anyplace where there could be a sit-down. On Black Solidarity Day, first Monday in November in 1997, he rolled out the coffin in care of Dr. Gaffney and led a march down Fulton Street. In July 1998, a ceremony was held at the Seaside in Queens and later that month a ceremony was held 'Brooklyn Remembers Runaway Samuel Carson' in Prospect Park that was well attended and publicized in the *Daily Challenge* and *Afro Times*.

FREDERICK MONDERSON

Then it was off to Ghana for the heralded internment during the First Emancipation Day Ceremony August 1, 19998.

Back from his successful and Final Triumph, Sonny Carson continued his busy schedule of activism, working until his health failed him. He was hospitalized and then himself became an ancestor.

This chronicle of the later life and times of Sonny Carson is to complement all that has been said and written about the man. More importantly, however, it is an insider's testimony of someone who had the privilege, for a short time, of being juxtaposed to the events surrounding a Great Black American champion's life and legacy.

BN PHOTO - Another beauty from the National Garden in Washington.

BLACK NATIONALISM STILL ALIVE AND WELL

50. ROSA PARKS
BY
DR. FRED MONDERSON

Sitting on the bus from Washington to New York, the traffic was stopped to allow a motorcade carrying the hearse of Rosa Parks about 11:00 am, Monday October 31, 2005. Just then I thought, no one knows or can predict the final events of their departure from this world. The ripple effect of one's actions can set in motion intractable events that can have long lasting local, national and even international implications. As such then, the events Rosa Parks set in motion were so cataclysmic, the forces she unleashed forced the President and the United States government to honor her in the most unimagined manner, lying in state in the Capitol Rotunda. Ms. Parks was the first woman to have this distinctive honor bestowed and the second Black person to be so honored. The first was a DC policeman killed in the line of duty. Unthinkable that a black girl could grow up and have such a profound impact on the American psyche and social and political process, is unimaginable. One wonders then, who fits the bill as a leader and can a quiet and soft spoken person fit that bill.

But who was Rosa Parks?

Now, to understand the progress of Blacks in America that Rosa Parks helped to significantly further, we could look at the last 200 years at the start of the century or even the first decade of the century. We could also look at the first decade after mid-century. Thus, we could examine 1800-1810; 1850-1860; 1900-1910; 1950-1960; and 2008-2010. However, since we're midway through the latter decade 2005 will do.

FREDERICK MONDERSON

1800-1810 - Thomas Jefferson's tenure as President; Louisiana Purchase; Haitian Revolution; Britain outlaws the Slave Trade; America outlaws the Slave Trade.

1850-1860 - The Compromise of 1850; Lincoln Douglas Debates; Dred Scott Decision 1857.

1900-1910 - Jim Crowism; Separate and unequal educational opportunities; founding of Civil Rights organizations.

1950-1960 - Nascent Civil Rights Movement; Brown v. Board of Education; Rosa Parks and the Montgomery Bus Boycott; Civil Rights Revolution

2000-2005 - Black Political Muscle; Economic powerhouse.

BN PHOTO - Roots Revisited Mothers' Day Program at Restoration Center.

BLACK NATIONALISM STILL ALIVE AND WELL

51. "CHICKENS COMING HOME TO ROOST" BY DR. FRED MONDERSON

The colonial climate that followed the Berlin Conference of 1884-85 Partitioning Africa on Paper, set the stage for an active Partition on Land campaign unleashing a thunderous military strategy to remove all forms of African resistance, contributed to the highest stage of imperialism resulting from Africa not simply being conquered and made prostate, but ultimately entangled in a number of events that led to World War I and the known "classic fascism" leading to Italian invasion of Ethiopia. In 1936, Haile Selaisse, Emperor of Ethiopia, appeared before and appealed to the League of Nations denouncing Italian aggression and insisting the body must condemn such imperialist adventurism. In summing up his address, the Emperor prophetically reminded, "Today for me, tomorrow for You!" As such, in three years World War II broke out engulfing the world in the most cataclysmic devastation that threatened the very survival of nations and people. In present circumspect reflection, we must be careful not to allow history to be repeated as elements posture on the brink of such devastatingly threatening developments.

For nearly eight years Republicans from the highest leadership to rank and file have allowed, engaged in callously and meticulously pilloried President Obama, staining the "Republican brand" and in the process the United States Presidency, the same position their contenders aspire to today. From the 43 percent who voted against the Black man, unending character assassination from "Nigger in the White House" to being unpatriotic, socialist, Muslim and "Palling around with terrorist," to lacking "testicular fortitude," "Poisoning the Well" and running a "Gangster Government" as well as the child-like charade of the "Birther Movement," such actions reveal an insidious and dangerously vindictive Republican underbelly. Even more, such unbridled "oral diarrhea" on part of Republicans Donald

FREDERICK MONDERSON

Trump, Michele Bachmann, Rick Santorum, "stupid" Senator Grassley, and "You Lie" Wilson in company of "Waterloo" DeMint and "Obamacare is worse than Slavery" Ben Carson, have now opened the gates for the "Chickens to come home." Only this time their bite is worse than those of Carson's "rabid dogs" and this casts a negative view on the nation as a whole.

BN PHOTO - Creative Art on the grounds of the University of Maryland at the Eastern Shore.

First, the New York *Daily News* labeled Donald Trump a "clown" perhaps because of his "Birther charade;" one local paper recently labeled him "chump;" much of this due to his newly minted insulting callousness characterizing Mexicans as rapists, criminals and drug dealers; that he would "build a wall;" mockingly attacked Carly Fiorina's face; blowing hard that "Iowans are stupid" for voting for Ben Carson; to his newest "Lulu" of "excluding Muslims" all seems rescued fresh from the "dark strain of American conscience." Yet, many of the 30 percent see him as worth an applause, standing ovation, giving unquestioned support much of which Alan

BLACK NATIONALISM STILL ALIVE AND WELL

Dershowitz explained as being "inconsistent with the character of this country." Even more, and not surprising, as the verbal mayhem unfolded, the world watched and wondered, isn't the "ugly American" abroad or is he now at home?

That designation and the active anti-Obama vituperative accusations with resultant threats to the President and his family, earned Republicans the designation "Party of No" particularly because they blocked every legislative initiative President Obama proposed; vociferously and vituperatively attacked his Affordable Care Act law; eviscerated his Jobs Bill; challenged the Asian Trade Deal he crafted; sought to block his immigration initiative; criticized his Cuban embargo breakout with establishment of mutual embassies all the while invoking a stale Republican pliant "Obama is Soft on Terror!" Equally they "try to make hay" that he is pursuing a failed policy on Iraq and Syria. In fact, as a thinker, President Obama has applied an analytically meticulous mindset in a new age of modern warfare and is not falling for Isis and Al Qaeda "Hokey Dokey," while seeking to garner an active and effective Middle Eastern Coalition as he pounds their terrorist encampments proclaiming no significant "Boots on the Ground" is the way to go.

Keen observers notice how statesmanlike President Obama appeared to be at the recent Global Climate Change conference. Espousing that presidential demeanor without question, observers believe none of the 16 Republican contenders would probably have been perceived as resolute American ambassadors as President Obama appeared.

Nonetheless, recent developments point to, some believe, one frightening specter Donald Trump represents to the Republican Party and the facetious representative of the American brand particularly as a potential Commander-in-Chief. This is not only unsettling but can be more dangerous than America's most virulent enemies hope to be. Reason reveals, because over the last several years Americans

FREDERICK MONDERSON

did not turn off the Trump spigot, his bigotry is now full blown. Guess what? He needs to stop spewing such pathological and deep-seated polluted beliefs for such bigotry goes against and will pose a serious problem for the American brand going forward.

Trump's most vocal supporters need to take note, Fareed Zakaria spoke of the "Rise of the Rest" and President Obama recognized America's approach to the world and its challenges cannot be in the mold of Roosevelt's "big stick," but more of a "smart heart" being mindful of President Clinton's dictum, "America's greatness lies in its moral not military might." As such, current Republican "fools rush in where wise men fail to tread" strategy is more appropriate to the "horse and buggy" age rather than today's analectic post jet-age speed. Now, in view of such realities, while Republicans disagree with President Obama's incremental progression in economic and financial policy, the reality is job growth increased tremendously, housing starts have increased, the auto industry is booming, research and development in education and science is very encouraging, and unemployment declined towards the 5 percent historic lows; Wall Street DOW is beginning to bang the door at 18,000 up from 6500 when Obama began, and prevailing belief is many of Trump's supporters and associates are laughing all the way to the bank from this financial windfall; college enrollment is up and also Affordable Care Act registration has topped the 16 million mark. In his studied and sure-footed approach, Mr. Obama has achieved a great deal despite Republican obstructionism and he has masterfully represented the nation in presenting a climate change proposal whose acceptance is practically a fait accompli; while real-politik dictates, the Iran Deal is in full-swing and the strange bedfellows of Mullahs, Assad, Obama and Putin must lay in bed with Hollande, Merkel and Cameron to effectively bring Middle Eastern states into coalition to defeat Isis. Taking the long view in a more sophisticated military strategy, in his policies Mr. Obama has remained actively and intelligently involved and must get credit for reducing American military casualties.

BLACK NATIONALISM STILL ALIVE AND WELL

However, as the "Pied Piper" keeps thundering towards the cliffs of oblivion carrying his loyal supporters into that chasm, we wonder where are the Republican men of substance demonstrating "testicular fortitude" to stand and condemn this new and dangerous foray.

Selassie's "Tomorrow for you" is now and as the old adage holds "when the enemy begins to self-destruct, stay quiet," so President Obama remains mum! Today some Republicans finally thinking about the predicament, including Dick Chaney, Paul Ryan, Jeb Bush, Nikki Haley, even Presidential historian Douglas Brinkley, have all come to realize, "We've let the dogs out, but they're biting left and right." But, as old ideas die hard and thanks to Donald Trump's insensitivities many project a possible Clinton occupancy of the White House again. More important, however, America's enemies have been handed tremendous propaganda ammunition and after he is "fired" Mr. Trump will have to explain his anti-Muslim statements to Middle Eastern Arabs and Muslim partners and business associates.

It is interesting, a CNN anchor recently hosted a focus group and a two-term New Hampshire representative, a trump supporter, went on ad nausea that President Obama is a "liar" and "when he spoke last Sunday he was lying to the nation." Turns out this woman was an active "Birther" advocate allied with Donald Trump's fool's errand.

Now, like a spoiled child, Donald Trump is threatening to run as an independent candidate and as his action will not only make the next president's job more difficult, Mr. Trump will go on to make more money in his business ventures. In this, he may forget the poor people who supported him and his notoriety in not only proposing impractical and hardly attainable but equally unconstitutional machinations and promises that "glitter but is not golden" which will continue to stain perceptions regarding this great nation.

And as such, thanks to Mr. Trump the voters may "throw out the Republican bums" at the next election. Say what anyone will,

FREDERICK MONDERSON

President Obama's legacy as per Paul Krugman's "Greatest President ever" assessment may ever further materialize because there is still much more to come and Obama continues to build up accomplishments, despite the actions of the "Party of No."

BN PHOTO - Reverend Al Sharpton poses with an interesting young lady, perhaps thinking of being his future replacement.

52. THE "SOUTHERN FIREWALL" BY DR. FRED MONDERSON

A new classification, not a new concept or reality, has emerged in the current political debate, namely the "African-American firewall" and it has never been truer. The iconic Malcolm X, waxing philosophically and realistically, pointed out the national electorate

BLACK NATIONALISM
STILL ALIVE AND WELL

is so evenly divided, the African-American vote makes the difference and determines "who go to the White House and who goes to the Dog House." In the current scenario, as the Democratic contenders Bernie Sanders and Hillary Clinton vie, and he Mr. Sanders projected a potential winner in both Iowa and New Hampshire, pundits have begun pointing to Hillary's "African-American Southern Firewall" in South Carolina, Georgia and Mississippi especially. This is certainly interesting that the Clinton camp recognizes the importance of the African-American vote and is, first of all, weighing heavily on South Carolina's "Firewall" where the African-American constituency does not have the same appreciation for Bernie Sanders. It is also strange that an African-American, Ben Carson, is also on the 2016 Presidential landscape but ironically cannot "drink from this important political fountain." So, what then is the Quid Pro Quo? Is there a Quid Pro Quo? How do we benefit from this scenario?

Certainly, we must first distinguish between Henry Kissinger and Richard Nixon's "Southern Strategy" and the current "Southern Firewall" strategy. The former was a master stroke to undergird a ticket and secure votes in the southern states, while the latter is a defensive mechanism to block a surging candidate, bolstering another and placing much faith in the African-American constituency's Democratic Party loyalty to reinforce former Secretary of State Hillary Clinton's "Grassroots" inclusion program. South Carolina is thus early and pivotal in this unfolding political drama and it should be noticed the Clinton camp seems all "wrapped up in the Obama colors" because the President is a "favorite son," not simply here but throughout the South to which the Democratic primary now focuses. However, this demonstrated loyalty is never handsomely repaid and any concessions and privileges are only provided under duress and hard won circumstances.

Nevertheless, we need carefully examine the American political landscape to understand how the African-American constituency has risen from "King's footstool to King maker." As such, it has been a

FREDERICK MONDERSON

slug-fest, fighting for every inch of territory from the time the United States Constitution recognized the enslaved African as $3/5^{th}$ of a man to the *1965 Voting Rights Act* and the subsequent coming of age of the Black vote in persons such as Representative Charles Rangel and the gentleman from Michigan. Thus, a quick perusal of the American political landscape demonstrates:

1. The 1787 Compromise or the $3/5^{th}$ Clause - recognized and counted 5 Africans for 3 whites for political representation purposes and to secure southern support to ratify the Constitution.

2. The 1793 Cotton Gin of Eli Whitney - made stripping the cotton seed easier thereby increasing produce and facilitating a greater demand for Africans to plant and pick cotton.

3. The Fugitive Slave Acts empowered Slave Catchers to return runaways in which free Blacks were also entrapped and re-enslaved.

4. The 1808 outlawing of the Slave Trade - after a 20-year wait from 1787-1807, the British first outlawing the Slave Trade in 1807 and the Americans followed the next year in 1808. However, this prohibition led to an internal slave trade practiced in the "deep south" in which "coffles" of hapless Africans were observed being taken to market to be sold.

5. General Andrew Jackson's 1819 foray into Florida to punish Native American Seminoles for aiding and giving sanctuary to enslaved Africans who ran away from slavery and made it to their territory.

6. The Missouri Compromise of 1820 banned slavery in that part of the Louisiana Purchase north of a set latitude.

BLACK NATIONALISM STILL ALIVE AND WELL

BN PHOTO - Legendary radio personality Bob Law makes a point at **CEMOTAP**.

7. David Walker's 1826 "Appeal" to enslaved-Africans - "Throw off your chains, resist your enslavement and help overthrow the evil institution of chattel slavery."

8. South Carolina Nullification Act of 1832 and attempts to secede from the Union were severely rejected by President Andrew Jackson.

FREDERICK MONDERSON

BN PHOTO - Brooklyn Borough President Eric L. Adams and his beautiful Deputy Borough President Ms. Reyna attending the First International Friendship Festival in Brooklyn, 2014.

9. The Compromise of 1850 encouraged the later Lincoln/Douglas Debates of 1858 at the time of "a house divided." It

BLACK NATIONALISM
STILL ALIVE AND WELL

specifically enabled California to enter the union as a free state, strengthened the Fugitive Slave Acts and by popular sovereignty allowed people to determine if the Mexican Cession territory was to be free or slave.

10. The 1857 Dred Scott Decision, in denying the humanity and political status of the African person on the eve of the Civil War, helped underscore the brilliance of President Abraham Lincoln. In the Supreme Court decision Chief Justice Roger Taney essentially ruled "a master did not lose his right to property regardless" and that "Blacks were not citizens and could not bring suit in Court" and Blacks "had no rights a white man was bound to respect."

11. At Civil War's end, the "Party of Lincoln," the Radical Republicans won unanimous support of the Freedman through their championing the 13th Amendment that freed the slaves; 14th Amendment which gave citizenship to persons born in the United States of America; and the 15th Amendment gave the right to vote to all such Americans. The Freedman's Bureau doled out support in food, clothing, fuel and health services to the destitute regardless of race. Land was given to create some of the famous Black Colleges and Universities such as Fisk University (the Black Harvard), Howard University, Atlanta University and Hampton Institute that were all beneficiaries of land grants.

FREDERICK MONDERSON

BN PHOTO - Brooklyn Borough President Eric L. Adams poses with some beauties from Kenya at the First International Friendship Festival, 2014.

12.   While Reconstruction sought to level the playing field, the 1877 "Betrayal" that brought the Southerner Rutherford B. Hayes to the Presidency, unintentionally, perhaps intentionally, gave "official" support to terror groups as the Knights of the Ku Klux Klan, Knights of the White Camelia, White Brotherhood, The Jayhawkers, Black Horse Cavalry, etc., who terrorized the Freedman with beatings, tarring and feathering, mutilations, threats, lynchings, and more while the White Citizens' Councils conducted and regulated "White Primaries," etc., undergirded by Jim Crow's *De jure* and *De facto* legislation and practice. When, during slavery Blacks were economic property they were protected by the master; freed and lacking such protections, they were terrorized, lynched, held in economic peonage and other forms of servitude and in an orchestrated fashion kept from the polls. In this era, the racist South Carolina Senator Bill Tillman said in Congress, "We have done our level best. We have scratched our heads to find out how we could eliminate the last one of them (the Black voters). We stuffed ballot boxes. We shot them. We are not ashamed of it."

BLACK NATIONALISM
STILL ALIVE AND WELL

13. The 1896 *Plessey v. Ferguson* decision of the Supreme Court gave legal sanction to "Jim Crow" segregation and racial discrimination under cover of "Separate but Equal" which was in fact, "Separate and Unequal," in both social and economic standing, and especially in education.

BN PHOTO - The "Garifuna Ladies" were in full effect at the First International Friendship Festival.

FREDERICK MONDERSON

14. Overturning the "Grandfather Clause" in 1915, the Supreme Court slowly began to chip away at the mountain of oppression built up especially in the half century from 1865 to 1915, which was a continuation of centuries of ghastly Slave Trade and Slavery in which the masters created a racial hierarchy among "House Slaves" and "Free Slaves." In that relationship, the House Slaves served the master in the capacity of maids, cooks, butler, footmen, coachmen, grooms, valet, nurse and launderers. Equally, a skilled group of Blacks functioned as gardeners, brick-makers, weavers, carpenters, shoemakers, blacksmiths, and masons. Some slaves had mastered their skills and when hired out their master got the praise and money they earned and doled out pittance to the workers. Even more important, from the demonstrated skills, many patents were made by Blacks, registered by owners and these cheated the creators out of the benefits.

The Field Slaves did the main work of staple crop production. They worked from dusk to dawn. Men and women worked the same hours. Let's not discuss personal abuse of the African woman by masters, their sons, overseers and even fellow slaves because of lack of respect and protections.

After winning the vote from 1868 to 1928, Blacks voted, those who could, for a single party, the Republicans. Though promises made were never kept, lynchings escalated and forced waves of migration northward began seeking to escape the climax of 19th and 20th Century American terrorism. However, while Teddy Roosevelt promised a "Fair Deal" and Woodrow Wilson betrayed his promises, Franklin D. Roosevelt promised a "New Deal" which encouraged Blacks to flock to the Democratic ticket in 1932. However, it was FDR's wife Eleanor who helped bring about some relief by listening to and seeking to address Black concerns of inequality.

15. Whatever may be said of A. Philip Randolph, as a quintessential and resolute leader of his age, he proposed the 1941 "March on Washington," because, 9 years after the Black vote solidified FDR's 1932 win and again in 1936 and 1940, Blacks fared dismally in securing jobs especially in the expanding war industry.

BLACK NATIONALISM STILL ALIVE AND WELL

Only fear of such an untimely show of coordinated Black force and the political impact it represented did President Roosevelt adequately address this issue. Issuing an Executive Action he banned discrimination in the war industry job recruitment program. Seventy five years later Black leaders can learn from this master stroke as a political demand especially as the "Southern Firewall" begins to manifest.

16.   While Harry Truman desegregated the military at the end World War II, it took another decade of legal and civil rights agitation before passage of the 1954 landmark *Brown v. Board of Education of Topeka, Kansas* case championed by the later Supreme Court Justice Thurgood Marshall. Yet, Blacks still had to wait another decade for the *1964 Civil Rights Act* and the *1965 Voting Rights Act* and their universal application. However, while these laws were now enacted, enforcement became another matter and in every election since shenanigans has characterized Republican attempts to eviscerate the Black vote. This was particularly so as late as in the 2008 effort to derail Senator Obama's successful run for the presidency. In Republican controlled statehouses across the nation, efforts were made to erect roadblocks through Gerrymandering and other measures to nullify the Black vote.

FREDERICK MONDERSON

BN PHOTO - Mayor David Dinkins came out to be a part of "Al Sharpton's Affair" welcoming President Barack Obama.

In conjunction, the Republican playbook was repeated in the 2012 "Stop Obama" effort and conspiracy that revealed both Republicans and Democrats tied President Obama's hands especially when Republicans swept to legislative control in the 2010 and again 2014 mid-term elections. Then, in control of Congressional funds, they not only continued to block the President's every initiative, it turned out the tremendous effort against President Obama was fueled by a treasonous gathering of high level Republicans going back to January, 2009 if not sooner, who plotted to block the legally constituted government from functioning under President Obama's leadership. While only 20 Republican funded Non-governmental Organizations were named along with former Attorney General Ed Meese in *The New York Times* October 6, 2013 "big write up" article, it stands to reason anyone in the Republican high-echelon

BLACK NATIONALISM STILL ALIVE AND WELL

"Who's Who," especially those publically vocal against President Obama were involved in the treasonous conspiracy. We can't exclude Donald Trump, "the Birther King," whom some have described as fascist (Hitler and Goebbels), recognizing the White establishment is letting him get away with; for as Lincoln reminded; "To be silent in face of wrongdoing is to be culpable of such evil." Even more, Edmund Burke had echoed the same sentiment, "The only thing necessary for triumph is for good men to say or do nothing." Thus, Ben Carson, remindful of Herman Cain, J.C. Watts, Allen, etc., should realize, swimming in dangerous waters can be costly.

BN PHOTO - Former New York State Governor David Patterson and Mrs. Patterson at "Sharpton's Affair" welcoming President Obama.

FREDERICK MONDERSON

All this brings us to the present situation and as we watch these events unfold, we are forced to ask, 'What are Black leaders doing to represent their constituencies?' 'Is the Black vote taken for granted or are Black political operatives only interested in their own re-election?' 'Can they create leverage against the contenders seeking the Black vote?' Whatever, Black voters must recognize the significance of their hard won right to vote, harness and exercise the power of the franchise, and make demands on people who seek their support.

BN PHOTO - Martin Luther King, Jr. in beautiful company at "Sharpton's Obama Affair."

BLACK NATIONALISM STILL ALIVE AND WELL

BN PHOTO - Marc Morial of the National Urban League, at Sharpton's "Obama Affair."

53. THE TRIPARTITE PAN-AFRICANISTS BY DR. FRED MONDERSON

At the start of the 20th Century three great Africans stood up and made a statement that has had long lasting influence and implications for years during and after their transition to memorable ancestorship. Booker T. Washington, W.E.B. DuBois and Marcus Moziah Garvey were each a leader in his own right, they were contemporary and had their differences with each other as well as various approaches to the challenges facing their constituencies, the African people, at home and abroad. Nevertheless, the fundamental issues have always been what did they do and what did they leave beyond their earthly existence and how has this impacted on the African and African-American constituencies they were a part of. In the Case of Booker T. Washington, born a slave he "pulled himself

FREDERICK MONDERSON

up by his own bootstraps" while W.E.B. DuBois, "born of privilege," made a name for himself as the "Greatest African-American intellectual of the 20th Century." Marcus Garvey proved to be the greatest organizer of African people in a single organization. However, while Washington died in 1915 and Garvey died in 1940, DuBois lived until 1963. Interesting, though the Mecca of their struggles and fights was in the United States, Washington died at Tuskegee, Garvey died in London and DuBois died in Accra, Ghana. Nevertheless, in those memorable life experiences, Washington created Tuskegee Institute; Garvey organized the Universal Negro Improvement Association, while DuBois, the intellectual who began penning the *Encyclopedia of Africa*, left a legacy as the "Father of Pan-Africanism."

BN PHOTO - The Hearse carrying Dr. Ben-Jochannan begins to make its way to the Cemetery.

However, and whereas, DuBois earned the title as "Father of Pan-Africanism," and Garvey, by virtue of his universal appeal and organization of the UNIA with chapters in different countries, is recognized as a "Pan-Africanist;" Washington, on the other hand, is not similarly connected even though he is one of the most studied African-American leaders. In this scrutiny, many question his Pan-African credentials. That is, he never gets credit for being a member of this leadership club. Fact is, DuBois was a theorist, an intellectual

BLACK NATIONALISM STILL ALIVE AND WELL

with an activist pen; Marcus Garvey was an organizer, an institution builder whose skill as a printer helped spread his ideas and reached far and wide among oppressed African people in Africa, the Caribbean, Central and South America and here at home in the United States. However, because he powerfully promoted the cause of Africa and Africans his (foreign, Jamaican) nationality did not prejudice the people attracted to his message and concern about the condition, improving it and went to great lengths to get his ideas across. Washington, for his part, though born a slave and rose to extraordinary heights because of inherent ability especially his strategic planning, was characterized as an "Accommodationist" because he accepted money from wealthy philanthropists. Unknowingly, however, as Tyrene Wright, in *Booker T. Washington and Africa: The Making of a Pan Africanist* (2015) explained, Washington's personal papers reveal a different story. They show a man with a profound interest in Africa and the cause of African people; one who "emphasized practice over rhetoric and theory. Clearly his was a profound Pan-Africanist organizational strategy that involved the Tuskegee-man in important developments impacting Africa in his day."

Nevertheless, regarding the negativity of the "Accommodationist" characterization, the question that is most credible is, 'Which African leader of substance who left a substantial legacy of accomplishment, did not seek to accommodate the issues he faced?' As Prof. John H. Clarke once opined, after reading his Atlanta Speech, "Washington did a little 'Toming' but look at what he bequeathed posterity."

Despite what has been said or written, Washington and DuBois were essentially two sides of the same coin which was advancing the cause of African people in America, and to the extent they cast a vision beyond the borders, they became Pan-Africanists, members of a movement concerned about the political, cultural, economic and spiritual welfare of African people wherever they may be on the face of the planet. That is whether they be in America, Africa, the

FREDERICK MONDERSON

Caribbean or Central and South America, even Europe, Asia and certainly Australia, the same level of concern and activist organization characterized their effort as Pan-Africanists. There were friends at first but ideological differences and approaches, strategy wise, caused them to distance themselves. However, the differences were overblown in public and Dubois would later confess this much.

Garvey on the other hand, considered himself the ideological son of Washington, and after Washington's death, "his father's" positions, by virtue of "inheritance" remained ideologically opposed to DuBois. And so, while we cannot disregard the provocative nature of the press and other outside forces, not to forget the role of "infiltrated Blacks who sabotaged Garvey's movement" as well as others who fanned the flames of Black leadership differences, history has shown there was much being done by all three of these great Africans here in America and worldwide. Nevertheless, the most important realization for African posterity is what have these remarkable men done and faced with the many challenges posed with Africa and its progeny lying prostrate, victimized and exploited; how they addressed the issues and what type of a legacy they created and left. How has their efforts survived the destructive nature of time and oftentimes hostile humans and how are their efforts proved beneficial to African people today. Such, therefore, form the issues of concern that had caused **CEMOTAP** to invite two distinguished scholars to shed some light on.

We first look to Tyrene Wright (2015: 17) who characterizes the time in which the drama that linked these leaders unfolded: "The social climate and consciousness of the African Diaspora in the western hemisphere and throughout the world produced two of the most prolific Pan Africanists: W.E.B. DuBois and Marcus Garvey. Each of these men had important relationships and exchanges with Booker T. Washington. Marcus Garvey's relationship with Washington would open the door both literally and figuratively to the first mass organization of the African world through the Universal Negro Improvement Association (UNIA). However, Washington's relationship with DuBois would be inconsequential to

BLACK NATIONALISM STILL ALIVE AND WELL

the progress of Pan Africanism. The relationship between Washington the apparent Accommodationist, and DuBois the Pan Africanist, scholar-activist, has shaped African (American) social and political history in the US for at least a century. Booker Washington, W.E.B. DuBois, and Marcus Garvey would all function differently as Pan Africanists. The methods they employed varied, but like previous Pan Africanists, they all had one singular objective beyond unity, which was to advance the plight of African people in the face of oppression."

BN PHOTO - Another look at the throngs of people who came out to have "one last look" and to say "Thank You" Dr. Ben-Jochannan.

A week ago this enormously gifted and fearless organization and its leadership invited Dr. Raymond Dugay and Dr. Threne Wright to discuss, shed light on and educate its listening audience about the impact Marcus Garvey has had in this country and abroad as he sought to mobilize "four hundred million" Africans across the globe and the resistance, internal and external, he faced, yet he was able to light a fire of intellectual, nationalist, and Pan-African consciousness across the African world that, a century later, still resonates because his ideas, ideals, and motifs were genuine.

In her book, *Booker T. Washington*: *The Making of a Pan-Africanist* (2015: 12) Tyrene Wright recognized Marcus Garvey, as the "son of

FREDERICK MONDERSON

Washington" who saw and experienced the same Pan-African connection as did his mentor. For, as the author writes about Washington, "It was clear to him that there was a common experience and connection that bound the 'American Negro to the African Negro; which unites the Black man of Brazil and the Black man of Liberia; which is constantly drawing into closer relations all the scattered African peoples whether they are in the old world or the new.'"

Dr. Wright characterized the three men in the following manner: "DuBois, as a Pan Africanist, would have a significant impact on the African world, particularly on the continent of Africa. Eventually the congresses would develop into the platform through which African leadership laid the ideological foundations for independence struggles on the continent. DuBois was one of the Pan Africanists who facilitated this ideological development through the Pan African Congresses. He advanced the expression of Pan Africanism that saw the liberation of Africa and its people as the ultimate objective. Marcus Garvey, also a Pan Africanist, promoted nationhood for African people on the continent and abroad. However, his position was rooted in the philosophy of race price, self-sufficiency and the belief that African people throughout the world should unite in an effort to eradicate oppression."

She goes on to describe, "Marcus Moziah Garvey, one of the most prolific Pan Africanists to emerge in the world belonged to the 20th Century. Garvey, without dispute, was able to momentarily organize and unify the African world through the Universal Negro Improvement Association (UNIA) and his newspaper *The Negro World*. The organizations, movements, and transformative leaders that the UNIA produced have had a long-term effect on the African world. Nevertheless, few knew or recognized the deep historical and ideological connection between Marcus Garvey and Booker T. Washington. The Tuskegee model and Washington's philosophy of race pride and self-sufficiency inspired Garvey and motivated him to eventually visit the US, and attempt to duplicate the Tuskegee model as outlined in the 1912 International Conference on the Negro resolutions."

BLACK NATIONALISM STILL ALIVE AND WELL

BN PHOTO - Kathy Sharpton certainly retains that magnificent smile.

BN PHOTO - Dr. Fred Monderson at "Sharpton's Affair" welcoming President Barack Obama.

54. "WE BE MARCHING" BY DR. FRED MONDERSON

I. African people have marched and marched and marched for a whole lot of reasons. In recent years, however, Africans have marched for unity, to demonstrate solidarity, to call attention to iniquitous behavior, senseless killings of Black men, and to address and right wrongs within the social parameters of American society, and, by extension, the world. More recently, we have marched for justice, more especially because of the killing of Black men by Police Officers in New York; even Black men killing Black men. However, this behavior is not germane to New York City for we see it play out in Ferguson, a suburb of St. Louis, Missouri in the death of Michael Brown, shot dead by an officer. Equally this type of behavior generated a similar response in Baltimore with the death of Freddie Gray. This came just weeks after the death of Eric Garner, who, when placed in a "choke hold" by a New York City police officer expired wherein the coroner ruled the action a homicide and even the Commissioner determined this was an illegal action. As the Black world mourned these two deaths, another Black man was shot dead by two Missouri police officers in what was determined a justified action because he had a knife and posed a threat! As we marched for Eric Garner in solidarity with Michael Brown then Freddie Gray the call has consistently been for a fair and impartial investigation that only a Special Prosecutor could provide. In these cases, the Federal investigation is generally more impartial because "They don't have a dog in the fight" and the question of civil rights violation is a significant issue. However, marching for death is not the only reason but there are others for which organizers could get persons to come out. Recently, in 2013, on August 23, perhaps two million converged on Washington DC to mark the 50th Anniversary of the 1963 "March on Washington" in which Dr. King gave his famous "I have a dream speech."

Nevertheless, while we must thank Minister Louis Farrakhan for the clear and farsightedness of organizing the phenomenon of the

Million Marches, alas, the bright intention of that inspiring point of light, in retrospect has taken on even more meaning when we reflect on its significance following the recent 20th anniversary of the 1995 phenomenal mobilization. Like all great ideas, follow-through is important and while the underpinnings may very well be progressing slowly, the outward manifestations are that the movement has certainly picked up due to prevailing and challenging conditions across the nation. Nonetheless, disciples of the marching philosophy have continued despite seeming slowing perceptions because it's always one way to call attention to injustice and bigotry.

BN PHOTO - The incomparable Gil Noble, architect of **Like It Is**, shown here in a Harlem ceremony celebration of being on Television for 30 years and hosted by Elombe Brath.

II. Early Marching set in motion an idea whose time has come and resulted in long lasting ramifications. Another way of looking at it, humorously some have wondered "if the person who invented marching had registered it as a US Patent he or she would have been wealthy."

a. Early Man marched out of Africa

Science has show early man emerged in East Africa and migrated or marched south, north, west and finally east. These efforts were for exploration, to secure food and shelter and progressively people the globe. In the process, early man made discoveries, experimented and manufactured a wide repertoire of tools and established conventions and practice later called culture. He developed language, used fire, established sites for resting, cooking, making tools, cutting up animals, ceremonial sites and even burial sites or graves. And, still he marched. He created units of culture and invented painting. Early man continued his trek heading east until he reached the tip of Asia and finally crossed the Bering Straits reaching what became the Americas. He kept marching all over the twin continents and by this time, some scholars believe, early man had marched to people the world.

One thing was certain, while injustice per se was not conceived, the "justice" in early man's forays was to fulfill the later Biblical admonition, "multiply and populate the earth." The success of this adventure is measured in the domestication of plants and animals, the development of technology for hunting, farming, fishing, navigating waterways, fighting, for domestic use and personal and cultural adornment. The said technology helped develop the practice of building for domestic, civic, religious, mortuary and festive purposes. All these structures needed decoration and thus he perfected the art of painting, sculpture and equally the fine arts of making jewelry for personal purposes and other uses. Therefore, it is easily evident, the "first marchers," who left Africa, achieved the "justice" they unknowingly set out to achieve for they bequeathed to humanity the utility of the march and all the benefits, as indicated, and attendant thereto.

BN PHOTO - The Sign says much about gratitude on behalf of an informed community.

BN PHOTO - The famous drummer Olatunji greets the revered Dr. Ben-Jochannan sitting beside Mrs. and Mr. Gil Noble at the ceremony celebrating Gil's longevity on TV's **Like It Is**.

b. Ancient Man marched down the Nile

The rudiments of ancient Egyptian civilization were long in the making as the dynamics so characteristic of the culture emerged and laid the foundations that sustained pharaonic existence. However, as these unfolded, trade patterns and dynamics developed, internecine conflict emerged, generated by the success of the emerging wealth. Nevertheless, moving forward and into Egypt many have reasoned civilization had its origins in Central Africa. Dr. John Clarke reasoned, like any stage play, Egyptian civilization was rehearsed in Ethiopia and played out down the Nile in Egypt. Now with the discovery of a "paint factory" in South Africa dated to c. 107,000 years ago, the "find" shifted "complex thinking far back in time." Such cerebral thinking certainly lends greater credence to the characteristics of civilization being developed in inner Africa more so than the argument "Asiatic Caucasians" "for some unknown reason" marched across the desert to Egypt bringing "a superior mental attitude." Let's not forget, Africans pioneered and were pushing "complex thinking" as far back as 100,000 years. So one has to question where were the Asiatic Caucasians at that time.

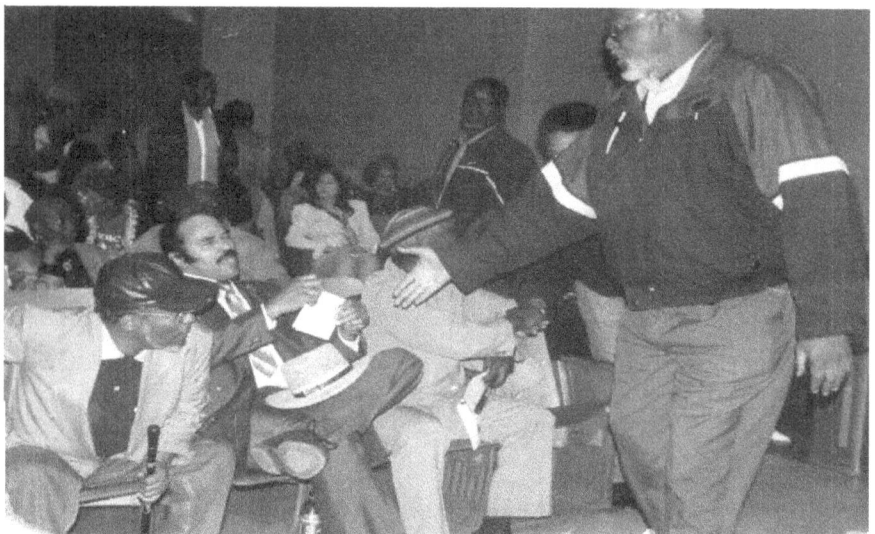

BN PHOTO - Jitu Weusi extends a hand to Tom Watkins Publisher of *The Daily Challenge* as he sits between Sonny Carson (right) and Atiim Ferguson (left).

BN PHOTO - Brothers lay the venerated Red, Black and Green on the Caisson that will carry the coffin of Sonny Carson for his memorable, final march through Bed-Stuy, "Abubadikaville."

While authorities differ, around 3100 B.C.E., the Theban Narmer or Menes mobilized a military force and marched north from Thebes to conquer and unify his country. Perhaps some marched overland. By all conventions he probably descended the Nile River by boat; nevertheless, from then on, marching was a principal means of a military machine that was active not simply in unifying but also in pacifying, consolidating, maintaining and defending the state from internal and external enemies. We see this in the efforts to create and sustain the Middle Kingdom by Thebans, after the travails of the First Intermediate Period following the Old Kingdom collapse.

c.   Imperial Egypt marched to conquer

Regarding the War of *Liberation* in response to Hyksos invaders who marched into Egypt, conquered and spread destruction and instability, they then founded the 15th and 16th Dynasties. As Flinders Petrie in "Egyptian Religion" published in The

Encyclopedia of Religion and Ethics (Edinburgh, 1912), has written, "The 17th Dynasty from Nubia, holding Thebes as its capital..." these Africans mobilized their military apparatus to deal with this foreign impudence. As these Thebans marched forward down the Nile conquering, incorporating and driving the invaders further northward, they finally expelled the despoilers from their sacred land.

Thus, the 18th Dynasty was an extension of the 17th Dynasty and they continued to march to an emerged imperial tune. Not only did Kamose and Ahmose then Thutmose I expel then pursue the invaders, but Thutmose III marched into South-western Asia for 18 annual campaigns to pursue imperial exploits. The famed Battle of Megiddo was the first and most memorable of his military marches. In these campaigns he established Egyptian suzerainty over an enormous area of South-west Asia. Subsequently, the threat of the Egyptian army on the "March" was sufficient to quell ambitions, aspirations of vassal rulers of that region and lands to the south of Egypt.

BN PHOTO - Sonny Carson sits surrounded by members of his entourage, Atiim Ferguson (left) and Rasheed Allah (right) with Chief Parker standing at the rear.

Nevertheless, aspirants of rebellious intent were ever-present and opportunistic and, thus, the script had to be re-written by Amenhotep III, Horemhab, Rameses I, Seti I and with grater fanfare by Rameses II at the Battle of Kadesh, during the 19th Dynasty. The same challenges faced Ramesses III of the 20th Dynasty as he recounted on the walls of his Mortuary Temple at Medinet Habu efforts to counter invasion by the "Peoples of the Sea."

From the 20th Dynasty into the 24th Dynasty internecine fighting among aspirants to the throne of Egypt, forced Piankhi the Ethiopian, in the tradition of the "ancestors" to march northward, set things straight and found the 25th Dynasty. Taharka marched into Palestine to challenge and check Sennacherib. Significantly, with all the attendant challenges, this dynasty ruled a century and was followed by one more, 26th, the last native Dynasty. After this, Egyptian power and control collapsed and it was almost 25 centuries later before native Egyptians would rule their country again. In the meantime, all manner of armies marched into Egypt wreaking destruction, sometimes building and repairing and finally settling down as conquerors. The Assyrians, the Persians, Greeks, Romans, Christians, and finally Arabs all marched into Egypt and left evidence of their being there. The French and British came in modern times and left an indelible imprint especially in relations regarding views on the ancient people and culture of Egypt. Therefore, in this period, only foreign rulers marched in and on behalf of Egypt.

BN PHOTO - Sonny Carson greets Harlem Congressman Charles Rangel in attendance to honor Gil Noble for his monumental efforts to educate the Black Community through the medium of **Like It Is**, the TV show.

d. Inner Africa to the Rescue

Many an argument has been made that as the invaders began to attack Egypt after the 25th Dynasty retreat to Ethiopia, the fundamentals of the culture "marched back up the Nile" and sought refuge in inner Africa. After ruling the entire Nile Valley, from the headwaters of the Nile to the Mediterranean, the Ethiopians retreated or were forced to retreat to their capital at Napata. They returned with much Egyptian culture and professional administrators, who were gainfully employed at Napata. Within two centuries of this move, the Ethiopians relocated their capital from Napata to Meroe and ushered in a new lifestyle with the exploitation of iron as evidence from the "slagheaps of Meroe." With this new and more durable weapon and domestic instrument, many scholars believe the Ethiopian marched across the Sudan to settle in West Africa, and there are oral traditions and cultural technology to support this contention.

Nevertheless, as the ingenuity of human aspirations would dictate, the Medieval West African Empires of Ghana, Mali and Songhay emerged and provided civilizational stability in the age of Middle African history. The hallmarks of their success was the availability of gold, effective administration of a trade pattern that brought merchants from great distances, sound government administration of justice and bureaucracy, agricultural exploitation of the Niger River Valley as a source of water through irrigation, an extensive fishing industry and a security ensured commercial route. This proved important because a large army marched throughout the Western Sudanic savanna region to maintain security and stability for government to function effectively protecting the trans-Saharan trade and enforcing the law, resulting in various kings trying to effectuate them with reforms and policies in the peoples' best interest.

BN PHOTO - Sonny sits beside Tom Watkins and between Atiim Ferguson and Rasheed Allah of the "Five Percenters."

III. West African Experiences

Marching through the western Sudan, the armies of Ghana, Mali and Songhay were able to preserve the integrity of the state and the lucrative Trans-Saharan trade. By providing security for, first the "silent trade" and then the more extensive Trans-Saharan Trade at International, National and Local levels of markets, the governments and nationals of these states prospered. Technology, arts and crafts, agriculture and literacy flourished. Islam made great inroads, first by destroying Ghana, and helping Mali then destroying Songhay. Nevertheless, Islamic scholars helped in adding to the architectural landscape, aiding in government administration and also writing extensively on the history and culture of the region.

Fortunately, the literary tradition they found and intermingled with has enabled modern research to unearth a wealth of Sudanic science and intellectual activity. The work of Islamic travelers, merchants and scholars recorded a rich cultural history of the Western Sudan, often described as *Bilal al-Sudan* (land of the Blacks). We now know the administration of justice was foremost in these states. Intellectual activity flourished at Djenne and Timbuktu Universities where African scholars lectured to foreign and local students. The also wrote historical, scientific and philosophic treatises. Much of this has survived, buried and the scholar Louis Henry Gates of Harvard University, who first unearthed them, is in the process of having them published.

BN PHOTO - Elombe Brathe presents to Sonny Carson flanked by Atiim Ferguson and Rasheed Allah.

The book trade as part of Sudanic commerce was especially important. Scholars and wealthy families prided themselves in possessing extensive libraries of local and imported manuscripts. The famous scholar Ahmed Baba possessed a library of 5,000 volumes which was extremely extensive as a personal possession in this early time. The periodicals *Tarik al-Fattah* and *Tarik al-Sudan* contained rich extracts of the history, culture, mores and folklores of the peoples, their activities, states and monarchs.

When, around 1591, Al Mansour of Morocco, marched across the Sahara with an army equipped with firearms and attacked Songhay, much as his predecessors, the Almoravids did to Ghana c. 1076, though not with firearms; the death knell was sounded for the last of the Western Sudanic Empires. Agriculture was interrupted as farmers were diverted to fight the invaders. The Trans-Saharan trade was interrupted and its security affected. The revenue foundations it provided for government and military administration was lost and thereby destroyed the effectiveness of the state. Learning, literacy and intellectual activity was stamped out. Many scholars were exiled to Morocco. Some libraries were destroyed. Ahmed Baba's library was made to accompany him to Morocco as a captive prize. Any good Islam may have done in West Africa was overshadowed by the vile actions of Al Mansour and his marauders.

Thus, with the Western Sudanic armies defeated and crushed by the superior firearms of the invaders, their governments destroyed, agriculture halted, the Trans-Saharan "Golden Trade of the Moors" dried-up, intellectual activity no longer encouraged and so the "Golden Age" of West Africa came to an end. All economic activity shifted to the West African coast where a new enterprise was beginning with the arrival of European merchants. Alas, a new and more horrible chapter in the march of African people was about to be written.

BN PHOTO - Harlem Congressman Charles Rangel greets Gil Noble sitting beside Mrs. Noble, an enthused Reverend Dr. Calvin Butts of Abyssinian Baptist Church and Councilwoman Una Clarke.

BN PHOTO - Rev. Dr. Calvin Butts seems to be basking in the attention of Councilwoman Una Clarke, and Mr. and Mrs. Gil Noble.

a. Slavers marched their captives to the sea

As the extensive and lucrative nature of New World possessions became more manifest, a new frontier for forced labor was opened. Apparently, the missionary Bishop Bartholomew de Las Casas came to the New World in wake of the Conquistadors destruction of the native population. Seeing the death, devastation and despair created by Europeans in the "New World," he appealed to the then Pope in Rome to act to save the Native Americans; yet he remained mindful of the need for laborers to transform the rich and lucrative tracts of land now given to the conquerors. Thus, the cry became "Let's bring in the Africans who were non-Christian, unfamiliar with the local terrain, and could not blend in, were agricultural workers and could work for long hours in the hot sun." In response to Bartholomew de Las Casas' request, the Pope did issue an edict authorizing the transportation of Africans to provide the needed labor for the *Haciendas* and plantation system then developing in the Americas.

Thereafter, from as early as 1503 to 1888 approximately the great nations of Europe and even America having devastated and depopulated the African coastal areas, then ventured inland and marched captured s to the coast, trans-shipped Them across the Atlantic Ocean and on to the plantations to work, build new societies in the Americas without pay and under the most horrible and inhuman conditions.

While each nation, viz., England, France, Spain, the Netherlands, Germany (Brandenburg), Portugal, America, et al., were involved at different levels and duration, every-body benefited from Slave Trade and Slavery. That is, all but the Africans! And so, for centuries, African people languished under the yoke of "naked Imperialism." With the new reality came the denial of the Africans' humanity and then the right to learn and be educated. When his humanity was finally recognized and the right to learning finally acquired, a system of mis-education was instituted that narrated him out of the order and process of human achievement under the false notion that God and cultural and scientific achievements were European or of European making and extraction. The African was taught the falsity, "Africa and Africans were outside the realms of history." That is, god is white and the European man was made in his image. Thus, in the natural order the European man was superior, the African man was inferior. So the natural order, so the social and political order, this false reasoning was used to justify unspeakable horrors perpetuated against Africans in slave trade and slavery institution practices with their horrendous outcome of racism, discrimination, joblessness, the Prison Industrial Complex, and all manner of unspeakable behaviors meted out to the Black man.

BN PHOTO - The "Big Guns" Atiim Ferguson, Tom Watkins, Sonny Carson, Gil Noble, and Rasheed Allah who all came out to honor the **Like It is** host.

History is replete with anomalies and the one apropos to the Americas occurred in 1492. Following the awakening or rebirth of Europe from the "Dark Ages," "Renaissance" and "Reformation, two Atlantic states, Portugal and Spain emerged as the first two seafaring nations. As such they came to spearhead Atlantic travel for adventure and commercial gain.

BN PHOTO - Gil Noble, architect of **Like It Is** basking in the recognition that his show has been tremendously educational and informative towards Black people for 30 years.

In fact, the Portuguese had been gradually encroaching along the West African coast from around 1440 A.D. or C.E. In 1441, Portuguese sea-farers captured a parcel of West Africans and took them to Lisbon, Portugal. And, thus began European slave trade in Africans more appropriately the Atlantic Slave Trade, often misnomered the African Slave Trade. It is interesting how use of words can create images and ideas in the minds of people that one group wishes to portray to another.

Nevertheless, following Columbus' discovery in 1492, Rome divided "the world" between Portugal and Spain in the Treaty of Tordesillas of that year. Portugal got all of Africa, and to the east, while Spain received everything "overseas," that is, all of the "New World." Portugal protested this, and as a good Christian nation, and "Defender of the faith," the division was corrected by moving the "Line of Demarcation 300 Leagues to the West." As a result, Portugal received a foothold on the South American mainland, Brazil, while Spain retained the rest. In this arrangement, later enshrined in the *Hacienda Treaty* of 1714, Spain was prohibited from capturing Africans in Africa and "marching" them across the seas. This activity, a heinous crime was committed not simply against Africans but humanity in general as the later United Nations would legally declare such conduct "a crime against humanity."

Notwithstanding, for the duration of the Slave Trade millions of souls were lost to Africa. With today's hindsight and in view of Western, European and American "dis-information" techniques we cannot trust conservative figures even from the best intentioned writers, that Africa lost 15 million people in the Slave trade. After all, these are the writers of the same hue that subscribe to the farcical claim "Africa is not a part of world history;" "There is no history of Africa, only a history of Europeans in Africa;" "the ancient Egyptians were Europeans;" "The Nilotic monuments demonstrate Negroes (Africans) were nothing but slaves in Ancient Egypt from time immemorial," and so on.

The disparity in recording is gross. The quintessential African American scholar W.E.B. DuBois was pretty accurate in his comprehensive researches, analyses and assessment that show, "Africa lost 100 million" men, women and children in the horrific crime against the human spirit. DuBois listed all the nations involved in rape, murder, cheating, kidnappings, unethical behaviors, etc., mis-nomered "Trade" where no equal exchanges were practiced. It was not really trade but robbery! He listed the duration of the trade; ships named and not named; lists of enslaved persons exported; persons killed in resisting their captors; the numbers who died and littered the pathways in marches to the coast; and the dying and dead thrown overboard, all in a more accurate accounting. One could also take into consideration the possibility since we're dealing with unethical people, the existence of two sets of books, under-counting, ghost ships, people dying in the holding centers, and the private

"African dealers" tricked once aboard to sell their captives and who were perhaps never counted. Hence, we arrive at figures grossly devoid of undercounting.

BN PHOTO - Chief Parker looks over a slowly rising Sonny Carson who came to recognize Gil Noble for his work at **Like It Is**.

When President Barack Obama visited Ghana on a trip to Africa he visited Cape Coast Castle. The CNN Reporter Anderson Cooper did a special showing, preserved over the centuries some 2 feet of human feces in the dungeon where the Africans were held. Given a bath in the Assin Manso River, they were then marched through the Castle's "Door of No Return" never to see their homes again but, if they survived the perilous Atlantic journey, forced to work to transform the New World in plantation farming. It took the courageous Sonny Carson to repatriate his ancestor Samuel Carson, "The Runaway," back to Ghana to open the "Door of Return."

Thus, with the counting over, the Africans left their native land, and were "marched" across the Atlantic in ships as they faced the tempestuous nature of the seas, the vicissitudes of coffin-like confinement, bad food, poor medical treatment, improper disposal facilities, putrid air, cruelty of the seamen, all this exposure having a devastating psychological impact on the African physical, spiritual and psychic persona. This was part of the Middle Passage where the African spirit and humanity was debased, dislocated, de-centered, disconnected and left in dis-repair.

BN PHOTO - Dr. Yosef Ben-Jochannan sits beside Mr. and Mrs. Gil Noble who sit alongside Sister Sybil Williams-Clarke.

Softened-up in the Trans-Atlantic voyage, "fighting upon arrival," as Bob Marley further sang, "fighting for survival," they were paraded, oftentimes naked, before lecherous, yet "Good natured" Christian persons who "examined" their inner privates in public before purchase. This further completed the psychological emasculation that, coupled with legal sanction, the "Negro" was now "a beast." So much so, the millions of years of science determined physical evolution were now completely reversed and there stood the African, naked on the shores of America, a newly transformed Christian land. After this, he was marched off to till and transform the plantation lands, fearful of the overseer's whip, cruelty of the master and fear and intimidation of the oftentimes, self-appointed, policeman and slave catchers. All working "to make them stand in fear." There the African woman was abused by the master, his sons, the overseer and even other Africans because the African man was rendered helpless and not able to protect his woman.

Now, here's the African, captured, marched to the sea, transported through the "door of no return," exposed to the natural and unnatural cruelty of the Atlantic voyage, dispersed in America, victimized through legal sanction, his family torn apart, separated, then marched off to the fields, the African now faced the created future reality. Captured, he was transported from his natural surroundings, stripped of his name, his culture, his history, his manhood; the African now began his long march for survival, then human and later civil and social as well as educational rights. Only the Lord knows how he made it through. Perhaps it was the resilience of the indomitable African spirit in collaboration of the watchful eye and help of the ancestors who would not allow their progeny to succumb strengthening his resolve against the cruelty of the institution of slavery and the co-adjutants KKK, Knights of the White Camelia, Black Shirts, etc.

BN PHOTO - Jitu Weusi greets Gil Noble while the audience shares the moment on this special day for the TV personality and educator who was quite informative on the air for 30 years.

As time took its toll over the centuries of time and the Slave Trade was finally outlawed, first by the Britain in 1807, and then America in 1808, the "Internal Slave Trade" unfolded. From the depths of the South, viz., Mississippi, Alabama, Tennessee, Georgia, "slave farms" were raised and Black men and women were consigned to unimaginable depths of despair to procreate and enhance the wealth of vicious masters. In this disgusting dynamic, slave coffels could be seen shackled, "marching to market," not to purchase goods but to be sold as chattel alongside cattle and vegetable! Interesting, while later the designation "White slavery" was illegal, "Black slavery" was legal!

In the long march forward, generations after generation, after generation, after generation, the whip, the sub-human living conditions withered the urge to run away, more often than not falling victim to slave catchers, "putting on ole Massa," and finally being in spirit with Crispus Attucks as he marched into martyrdom to free a nation of people from a system that refused to recognize his right of humanity and entitled to freedom. Then a phrase in the Declaration of Independence offered a glimmer of hope before it was lined out to be replaced by the more "generous" offer of a "Three-Fifth Compromise." Still he marched in the Revolutionary War, Salem Po and others, to support the Articles of Confederation, and, victorious, the Constitution of the United States. There being no change, the African again marched and fought in the War of 1812 and were at the Battle of New Orleans in 1815.

BN PHOTO - Una Clarke and Mrs. Gil Noble sit, while a standing Minister Benjamin Chavis is surrounded by Dr. Calving Butts and Gil Noble, among others.

survived A stubborn lot, Blacks were, for, while some of them ran away to Florida and were sheltered by the Native Seminoles, the rest kept marching and fighting right through Andrew Jackson 1818 incursions to punish the Seminoles for their acts of mercy! But alas, Gabriel Prosser (1900) and Denmark Vesey (1822) said "Let's fight for us!" David Walker said, Wait a minute, let's "Appeal" this thing, while Nat Turner equally affirmed, as Patrick Henry did, "Give me liberty or give me death" as he dispatched many before his time. Sure Patrick Henry coined the phrase in the halls of American liberty. He, however, was already free but did not die, while Nat Turner was never free and died, paying the ultimate price, while paying the price of liberty. Still, Blacks continued to march and die for American liberty, equality and justice.

The "Runaway Slave" Samuel Carson marched and died in the Mexican War of 1844. Some believe it was all in vain for nearly a dozen years later, Chief Justice Taney clarified things in the Dred Scott Decision of 1857, which declared, "Slaves were not citizens and could not bring suit in American courts." Even further, the good Chief Justice added, "A black man has no right which a white man

was bound to respect!" Some believe, 150 years later, in some respects, this belief is unchanged! Still, in between Blacks marched in the War Between the States or Civil War, and were victimized by both sides. Yet, the North was more amenable, more liberal, and more supportive, though places as New York early eased their slave restrictions.
\

BN PHOTO - Dr. Ben Chavis has a word with the Program's organizer Elombe Brathe.

The Radical Republicans articulated an agenda that brought the 13th, 14th and 15th Amendments, Civil Rights Acts, even Land Grants to establish Black Colleges but fell short on the "40 acres and a mule" promised by President Abe Lincoln. Still, these Congressional milestones became effete in face of the Ku Klux Klan (KKK),

Knights of the White Camelia, the lynchings, intimidation, the conundrums of share-cropping, Jim Crow laws and practices together with the implications of *Plessey V. Ferguson* (1896) upholding its odious "separate but equal" which was really "separate and unequal" and the later White Citizen's Council holding "White Primaries" which excluded Black voting or holding office.

Despite the hourly challenges, daily battles and yearly wars for self-preservation, human-dignity, actual survival, while some Black marched to escape the South, some marched up San Juan Hill to save Teddy Roosevelt in the Spanish-American War, but never got credit. In wake of the "Tar and featherings," the lynchings, rampant racial discrimination, Booker T. Washington founded Tuskegee Institute in 1881, with its wonderful legacy of Black self-advancement. This "Tuskegee Model" echoing Washington's doctrine, insisted, according to Tyrene Wright in describing the great man as a Pan-African leader of effectiveness, "There can be no liberty without intelligence, no independence without industry, and no power for man and charm for woman without character. Next, Marcus Garvey founded the Universal Negro Improvement Association (1917) that enjoyed tremendous successes in the late teens and early 1920s. More important, however, Garvey claimed to speak for some 400 million Africans worldwide seeking or to organize and instill dignity and independence among those at home and abroad. W.E.B. DuBois and other leaders formed the **Niagara Movement**, **National Association for the Advancement of Colored People** (1909) and the **National Urban League** (1910).

Then, when the implications of African colonization or imperialism, militarism, with associated nationalism hit home to be followed by the murder of Arch-Duke Ferdinand in Sarajevo, such behaviors led to the outbreak of World War I. Then Black Americans were marched overseas "To help save the world for Democracy." Later, as DuBois put it, "We left fighting, we fought and now we return fighting" to challenge Jim Crow and all forms of odious American practices.

BN PHOTO - With Jitu Weusi looking over his shoulder, Ben Chavis offers a hand of friendship.

b. European incursions marched Africans as beasts of burden,

Eric Williams in his book *Capitalism and Slavery* argued, "The abolition of the Slave Trade and ultimately Slavery was an economic necessity rather than a humanitarian venture." To support his view, he chronicled the lucrative gains from the Slave Trade accrued to Britain, one of the principals in the forced removal of Africans to support plantation agriculture and derivative industries in the New World economy.

Williams argued the "Triangular Trade" transformed Britain and equally Europe economically, technologically, militarily, commercially, politically, socially and even intellectually. He showed how banking, insurance, textile industry, boat-building and ancillary trades, expansion of Wharfage, excise taxes, metal works, sugar refineries and rum distillation and a whole lot more gained immensely from the Slave Trade. Seaport towns such as Liverpool,

Bristol and London expanded tremendously as merchants built grand and extensive mansions and increased local and excise taxes.

Nevertheless, despite naysayers, abolitionists Clarkson, Granville Sharpe, Wilberforce, Buxton, Et. Al. waged their humanitarian campaign as a "friend of the enslaved African." Clarkson especially noted how specifically the trade was taking a toll on British seamen whose mortality rate was also high. Many of these same seamen were shanghaied into slave trade service. When one considers how the seamen were treated, then consider what happened to the cargo. Equally the seamen, impressed into Slave trade service, had no compassion on their less fortunate "brethren."

Some defenders of the trade argued and petitioned Parliament regarding the indispensable nature of the economic aspects of the trade on their lives. They also agreed the trade was a "Nursery" for British seamen to be ready for war at sea. Clarkson, however, was able to show investigative Committees of Parliament, many seamen aboard the Slavers were shanghaied and forcefully recruited, them punished for runaway or jumping ships or refusing to serve. When Parliament finally saw fit to outlaw the Slave Trade in 1807, after Clarkson had forced the measure's presentation for some 20 years, Britain deployed a squadron of the Royal Navy to Sierra Leone colony with the specific mission of patrolling the waters off West Africa. They then set out to board Slavers, rescue enslaved cargoes and repatriate them to the West Africa colony. Unfortunately, when a slaver spotted a naval vessel in the distance, they would march their slaves on deck and then toss them overboard. By the time the Navy got there, they could boast: "See, we have no slaves."

BN PHOTO - Dr. Ben Chavis greets Harlem Congressman Charles Rangel.

However, on March 9, 1732, a ghastly experience unfolded and became documented regarding the Slaver **ZONG** under the Captaincy of Master Collingwood who "Threw 132 Africans overboard" because he thought he did not have enough water to make port. The sad part, upon returning to England he filed for insurance under a clause "perils of the sea." Of course this is in stark contrast with Africans who defied their monstrous captors and chose "Revolutionary suicide" by jumping overboard to courageously die rather than be slaves. Taking death, their action mocked Patrick Henry's hollow exclamations!

Nevertheless, the lucky ones encountered by the British Navy were rescued. They were resettled in Sierra Leone, the abolitionist colony, established in 1787 after the 1772 Somersett case ruling by Chief Justice Mansfield that "English soil is too sacred to allow slavery."

Thereafter, all English enslaved Africans were rounded up, along with a few undesirable white females and marched off to Sierra Leone. Therefore the four elements of the Sierra Leone population consisted of English freed slaves, enslaved person rescued on the high seas, the native population and the Blacks who served with the British in the Revolutionary War against America. These were marched to Canada at war's end and later repatriated to create the most diverse population in West Africa. It also raised another question as to why the British did not want them in Canada as sparsely populated that area was at the time.

Meanwhile as these efforts unfolded, a new onslaught faced Africa. Gone were the days of "Naked Imperialism." The new strategy became "Enlightened Imperialism." That is, we'll help the Africans, at a price! Thereafter the continent began to be opened by explorers, adventurers, settlers, merchants, and missionaries, among others who sought to stamp out slave trade and implant agriculture and Christianity in West Africa. But there were other movements afoot.

The Boers in South Africa since 1652 began to march inland after the British secured the Cape of Good Hope in 1814. By the mid-1820s, **Shaka the Zulu Chieftain** had begun his march to build a Zulu nation. Untouched by western military strategy; he innovated a number of techniques including the creation of the Assegai, a short stabbing sword that required his soldiers to engage the enemy in close combat. He pioneered a standing army in Africa, created barracks to house them and also innovated age-grade regiments rather than encourage tribal loyalties. His expansion threatened the Boers' inland trek, so they conspired with his brother, Mpande, to literally stab or spear Shaka in the back in 1828. They promised him the kingship of the Zulu nation if he was successful. Within 8 years, by 1836, the Boers successfully captured the Zulu land and tamed the Zulu spirit.

BN PHOTO - In a relaxed mood, Sonny Carson's mind is still actively planning his next engagement.

In North Africa, Mohammed Ali, a Turkish general, sought to separate Egypt from the Turkish Empire and consolidate his power there. He, however, had to deal with the Mamelukes, the traditional rulers of Egypt, under the suzerainty of the Turkish Sultan. Once assigned to Egypt, after a successful year of agriculture, he sponsored a state banquet and invited the *Who's Who* in Mameluke society.

The Protocol was no weapons were permitted in the main banquet hall. As events unfolded, and everyone was well-fed and drunk, Mohammed Ali moved his assassins in who slaughtered the Mamelukes and he now established complete control of Egypt. The first thing Mohammed Ali did upon seizing control was to promote the native Egyptians to the highest echelons of the military. Next he gave them a role in their government. He made land reforms. Bright young people were sent abroad to western educational institutions to study medicine, science, technology, business in its effort to transform his nation. Much of this he was able to do, including establishing a hereditary dynasty to follow him, without borrowing money from western nations.

In East Africa, the Ethiopian dynastic line traceable back to the union between Solomon and Sheba, Ra Mangasha, Johannes IV, Menelik and lastly Haile Selaisse maintained all efforts to keep their nation free of colonialism at the end of the 19th Century. To wit, in 1896, Menelik II marched his army and defeated the Italians at the **Battle of Adowa** demonstrating military prowess and diplomatic ingenuity in subsequent negotiations despite Africa the subject of Berlin Conference balkanization agreements.

A special detour needs be added here because of continuing historical distortion of a recurring theme. Dr. ben-Jochannan commented on this in his works.

Weigall, an English Egyptologist, wrote colorfully about Egypt after the discovery of Tutankhamon's tomb in 1922 and had great influence in Europe and America. In his book *Flights into Antiquity* (1920) he had presented a photograph of the Queen of Sheba which shows her as white, a European by all standards. Back in 1999, this writer commented on an article produced in *News of the World*. It featured an article entitled "Scientist discovers the home of the Queen of Sheba." The story goes on to say: "British archaeologists have discovered the home of the Queen of Sheba, located in the Southern Nigerian forest region." Again, the photograph presented is that of a white woman! The question is: What does this tell us? As such, a number of truths are evident to the erudite and critical scholar.

First, for eons the Queen of Sheba was thought to be Ethiopian. Ethiopian holy men today claim they possess and are guardians of the "Ark of the Covenant" now in Ethiopia and that it was brought back by the Queen of Sheba after her visit to King Solomon. Now based on the above article, are we to believe the Ethiopian kingdom extended from West Africa across the entire continent from

BN PHOTO - Dr. Calvin Butts and Gil Noble engage Dr. Ben Chavis in the most cordial manner.

West to East? Lines of communication must have been very clear and open for her to hear about Solomon in Israel, and then decide to visit him. Therefore, she had to march across the continent, then march up to Israel to visit the King. On the way back, why then did she leave the Ark of Covenant in Ethiopia and schlep back to Southern Nigeria. Equally, Nigeria 1,000 years before Christ, the seat of a kingdom, must have certainly been a robust economic and social entity to be the subject of such glaring descriptions. This was at a time when even Greece was in its egg. Thus, we must be vigilant in what we read.

Second, what is a white woman doing ruling a kingdom in the heart of Africa? This smells of the Edgar Rice Burroughs creation of "The Phantom" and the likes of "Tarzan," mythical Englishmen with extraordinary powers to outwit Africans that Hollywood carried to the most absurd lengths. The Mighty Sparrow, Calypsonian King of Trinidad, sang of the British Education Officer, in creating curriculum programs for its colonies in the West Indies and Guyana, and how he wanted to "create comedians" and "Keep us in Ignorance." He created learning modules such as "Tom, Tom, the Piper's son, Stole a Pig and Away he ran," and "The Cow Jump over the Moon." This is a modicum of how far-fetched the English mind did go to mis-educate.

Third, we know she was not white because Sheba has often been mis-quoted as saying: "I am black, but comely." In fact, what she actually said was: "I am black and comely." The Queen was not apologizing for her blackness, but praising it. After all, she ruled over a kingdom of black men and women. Are we to imply that all those African people, in a powerful kingdom in Africa, before Greece and Rome came out of the egg, certainly Western Europe, were ashamed of their Blackness when according to their belief system, their god created them in his own likeness!

We know she was a beauty. We also know Solomon had many wives but she upset the applecart. Perhaps Sheba brought out the best in him. This legendary wise man for that one time was a hit. We hear no more about the wives of Solomon, only about the Black Beauty from Ethiopia. Ivan Van Sertima has argued, rightly so, the Queen of Sheba's Kingdom was vastly greater than Solomon and his interest was beyond her beauty but considerations of political and economic alliances. Now imagine this big woman apologizing to a little man! So he won a "piece," underscoring the power of the African woman and woman in general for their ability to intrigue the male, and send him a message in so many ways.

BN PHOTO - As Sonny Carson and Dr. Ben Chavis exchange a powerful handshake, Tom Watkins and Atiim Ferguson look on with Jitu Weusi in the background.

Four, we know the Ethiopians are black, still, writers continue trying "to wash this Ethiopian white." The stereotype of the Queen saying "I'm black but comely" is constantly trotted or marched out when dubious scholarship is presented or a racial type is reinforced. Let's not forget, "Black is Beautiful" has a long progeny.

Elsewhere in West Africa, the Nok Culture was sophisticated well before the Christian era. So much was going on throughout the continent, to quote Teshlone Keto, regarding his outlandish statement that "Africa was outside the realm of history;" he affirmed: "Hegel should have said he did not know African history.'

Just prior to Mohammed Ali's rise to power, in the aftermath of the French Revolution and subsequent War in Europe, the British Admiral Lord Nelson pursued Napoleon to Egypt and fought the "Battle the Nile," which in fact, was not fought on the Nile but on the Mediterranean Sea. Nevertheless, in Napoleon's sojourn in Egypt, besides his military, he took linguists, artists, architects, and other scientists or savants. They made systematic studies of all the existing temples and published a monumental work, now a classic, The *Description of Egypt*. Officers in Napoleon's artillery regiment discovered, at a place called Rosetta, a tri-lingual inscribed stone, later called the Rosetta Stone. Within just over two decades linguists led by Champollion deciphered the hieroglyphic script, laying the foundation for the later discipline of Egyptology. It should be pointed out, later in the 19th Century, Flinders Petrie, the English archaeologist and Egyptologist described Egyptology as comprising an understanding of history, geography and linguistics or language.

By mid-century, all manner of people began converging on Africa from the north, south, east and west. While in the north interest in Egyptian antiquities attracted many types, they also created a climate Brian Fagan later described as "The Rape of the Nile." In West Africa it was March for Timbuktu and to discover the source of the Niger. What is significant, however, all over, missionaries, merchants, explorers, adventurers, scientists, agriculturalists, imperialists, colonialists, butterfly-enthusiasts, writers, settlers, all Europeans, all converged on Africa. All made African march as beasts of burden to tote their possessions, materials and comfort while in the heart of Africa.

BN PHOTO - Councilwoman Una Clarke meets Dr. Ben Chavis at Gil Noble's affair.

c. Leopold marched and decimated millions for balata and rubber in the Congo. Booker T. Washington was actively critical of King Leopold for his atrocious actions in the Congo and that of other Europeans elsewhere in Africa. All this while Booker T. was trying to export the "Tuskegee model" of self reliance, agricultural practices and efforts towards economic and other forms of independence here in Africa and in the Diaspora.

As the various interests converged, explored and made discoveries in Africa, they created what later became "spheres of influence" for their governments. In this undertaking, merchants devised and created trade patterns and markets; missionaries sought to replace the Slave Trade with agricultural produce; scientists; botanists, mineralogists, agriculturalists, all did scientific explorations to determine Africa's economic potential.

As the Industrial Revolution unfolded in Europe, Africa's economic potential in developing world commerce made her an important prize. The "spheres of interests" created in stamping out the slave trade and planting Christianity in Africa gradually merged into *de facto* pre-colonial holdings. Notwithstanding, conflict began to develop between European nationals over, what belonged to whom. As a result, the German Chancellor called the Berlin Congress lasting from 1884-1885, to, in effect, Partition Africa on Paper, along the general lines established in the "Spheres of Interest" configuration. By the end, Africa was partitioned between basically the same slave trading nations.

Not trade but murder, kidnapping, rape, robbery, and injustice, organized and sustained systematic mayhem against a people for the duration of centuries. Na'im Akbar refused to equate the Holocaust with the Slave Trade. He argued, persons lived through the Holocaust but no one lived through the institutions of Slave Trade and Slavery. The beginnings of colonialism through implementation of partition were in many ways similar to the experiences of the Slave Trade. Naturally, after the Berlin Congress, the European powers had to convince the Africans that they, Europeans owned

African lands, and much of this was done through the barrel of a gun aided by Africans who were co-opted to serve as soldiers in such armies as the West African Frontier Force. Knowing the language, the culture and the geography, these soldiers betrayed their people for the "Man."

BN PHOTO - Sonny Carson embraces Dr. Ben Chavis while Tom Watkins looks on.

I guess the best person who could explain this conundrum would be the Comedian Dick Gregory. He would probably put it over this way.

Imagine me and "my old lady" sitting on the sofa in our living room watching Television. A stranger walks up, opens the door, sits on the couch and nudges us to move over. Next he takes the remote and changes the channel. When I say "What the heck you're doing" he says, "I'm the new owner. Yes! We met last year and I took possession of your property." All I could say is, "You're kidding, right?" "No, I'm not," he replied.

Imagine, Slave Trade and Slavery, "Naked Imperialism," expropriation of land, wars of pacification, colonialism and its "Direct" and "Indirect Rule, "Enlightened Imperialism," and "Intellectual Imperialism" as it related to acquisition of Egyptian and other cultures' precious artifacts all having a bearing on the travails and dynamics of the proximate presence of "Direct" and "Indirect Rule." These then were the seed germs that bred and nurtured racism, discrimination, unequal treatment Africans worldwide have been victims of.

While the French got big chunks of Africa in North, West, and Central regions of the continent, Britain received equally large shares in West, South, Central East and North Africa. The Portuguese got Angola, Mozambique, Guinea-Bissau; Germany, South-West Africa (Namibia), Cameroons, Togo and Tanganyika (Tanzania and Zanzibar); Italy got Libya and Somalia; Belgium, the Congo; etc. The best example of colonial exploitation occurred in the Congo under King Leopold's administration. Belgian hunger for rubber exemplified the problem of African raw resources as a principal cause of World War I.

BN PHOTO - Dr. Calvin Butts and Gil Noble share a laugh with Dr. Ben Chavis.

BN PHOTO - Una Clarke, Dr. Calvin Butts, Mrs. and Mr. Gil Noble, Sister Sybil Williams-Clarke and Dr. John Clarke in the Chair beside Tom Watkins and Sonny Carson.

BN PHOTO - Dr. Lewis the Harlem Ophthalmologist and Mrs. Lewis were there for Gil Noble.

d. Africans Marched to Protest Colonization in Africa

The principal causes of World War I include nationalism, militarism, imperialism, all heavily influenced by the "Scramble for African raw materials," and ultimately the murder of the Austrian arch-Duke Ferdinand in Sarajevo tipped the scale. As the war waged, the French Premier Clemenceau sent the French Parliament Deputy Blaise Diagne to French West Africa where he recruited more than 100,000 African soldiers in their cause to stem the German onslaught. The British did the same in Africa and the Caribbean.

BN PHOTO - Cherise Maloney alongside Chief James Parker outside the diner on McDonough Avenue in Bed-Stuy.

There was a direct relationship between World War I and World War II. The players were essentially the same on the same sides. Africans were again marched into this second conflict. However, the minds of Black men in the Black World began to change in unimaginary ways through the efforts of great African minds and courageous actions particularly the Pan-African groundswell.

At the start of the 20th Century three great African began to coalesce in an unfolding historic drama concerned with the condition of Africa and Africans globally. The outcome of this fortuitous series of events that began to unfold; that is, actions especially emanating from the active and collective minds of Booker T. Washington, Marcus Garvey and W.E.B. DuBois would, through a number of circumstances, forever change the Black man and his relationship with fellow Africans and also the world in general, never to be the same.

The first significant such even occurred when a number of Africans including Sylvester Williams of Trinidad and W.E.B. DuBois of the United States called for the First Pan-African Congress in 1900. This bold move attracted Black intellects that began to pay attention and articulate concerns of African people, particularly those in Africa. The second was the emergence of Marcus Garvey and the Universal Negro Improvement Association and the African Communities League. The third was Booker T. Washington creation of the "Tuskegee Institute Model" that had reached significantly functionally successful levels coupled with his behind the scenes work as a Pan-Africanist which began to be fruitful. The fourth most important such development was Dubois' call for a second First Pan-African Congress at war's end in 1919. The major problem this important gathering faced, however, was where would the venue be? The British, Americans and initially the French as well as several European Powers balked at the notion of Black men meeting to discuss Black issues on their territory, controlled by Europeans.

The "Father of Pan-Africanism" DuBois played his hole-card which was Diagne, the French Deputy, who recruited untold numbers of Africans for Clemenceau. Finally, the French Premier recanted and told him to go ahead but keep the gathering in a low-key manner. DuBois figured since the world would gather in Paris in 1919 to discuss the terms of the Versailles Peace Treaty ending world War I, this was the appropriate venue to raise the issues of African real-estate and human dignity.

The knowledge gained here and the other Pan-African Congresses between the two wars. Tyrene Wright, in *Booker T. Washington and Africa*: *The making of a Pan-Africanist* (New York: Global Africa, 2015: 220) identifies the dates of these gatherings. She writes: "The first congress took place in Paris in 1919. The Second Pan African Congress in 1921, held meetings in London, Brussels, and Paris. In attendance were representatives from various African nations. The Third Pan African Congress was held in Lisbon in 1923, and the Fourth Pan African Congress was held in New York in 1927. The Fifth Pan African Congress, arguably the most important meeting, known as the Manchester Conference, was held in Manchester, England. George Padmore, H. Mekonnen, Kwame Nkrumah, Jomo Kenyatta, and Peter Abrahams led the congress. It was a high point of the congresses because for the first time African leadership made a unanimous demand for total liberation and independence of the African continent from imperial domination."

BN PHOTO - Sonny Carson is flanked by his Chief of Staff Atiim Ferguson and Chief Barkim Parker in the Drummers' Grove on eve of Samuel Carson being flown to Ghana, in 1998.

In the emerging dynamics of unionization as a political force in Africa; the experience gained in both wars proved the white man's blood was red not blue; and points of Black intellectual lights from various areas particularly those influenced by Marcus Garvey, articulating in part Washington's model as the son of the great man proved effective. DuBois, an old man in 1945, handed over leadership of the Pan-African Movement to the younger and more vigorous Kwame Nkrumah of Ghana, himself influenced by Garvey's *Philosophy and Opinions*. Chairing this Fifth Pan-African Congress at Manchester in 1945 after World War II, Africans with brain power from the Diaspora especially that of George Padmore, resolved to be more actively press the cause in the march for independence. Many of the great African minds of the 20th Century were there and resolved they would return home, form unions and advocate unionization, decolonization, and self-government and strive for independence elsewhere in the Caribbean and South America. Their successes were evident where, by the 1960's, nearly two dozen African states and several in the Caribbean including Jamaica, Trinidad and Guyana became independent.

An interesting conundrum is recounted here. In 1976 as a student at Oxford University, Exeter College, this writer was privy to a tutorial discussion wherein an Oxford Don pointedly stated: "If in 1900 we (the British) had realized how wealthy Africa truly is, we would have put in place provisions that it would never revert to the Africans." Nevertheless, though much of Africa was granted independence, the European powers put in place what Kwame Nkrumah called Neo-Colonialism where they were still able to wield considerable influence over African economies and the viability of these states.

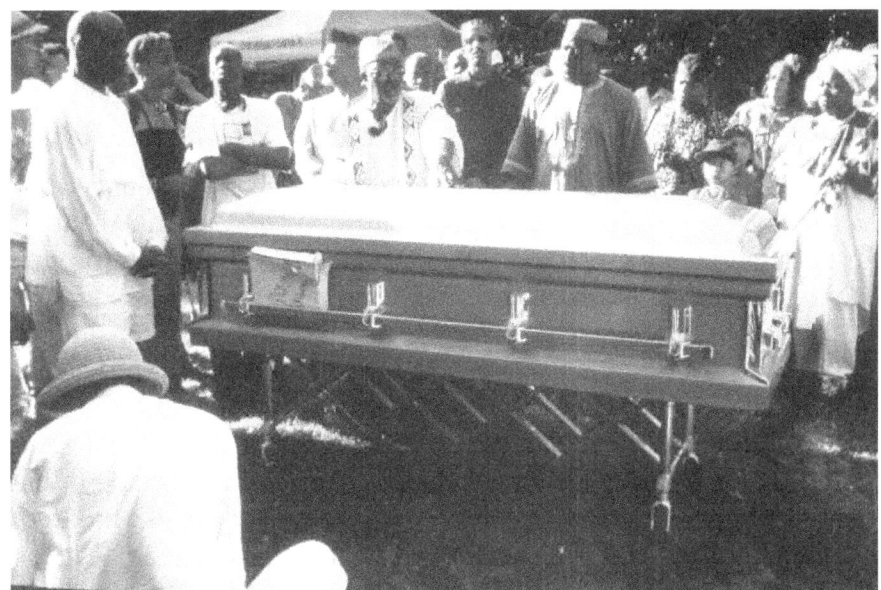

BN PHOTO - While Sonny Carson touches the Coffin of Samuel Carson, Bishop Shivers prepares to bless the "Bones" as Queen Mother Dr. Blakely looks on.

IV. In the United States I.

Because of the nature of the United States of America, the condition and mentality of the Black man there was different to all other Blacks worldwide. More things happened to the Black man in America than anywhere else African people were located. There was more brutality meted out to the Black man of Africa, he fought in more American wars than all others, he had more opportunities than other African peoples and today he wields more influence and economic, academic, political and intellectual power than most people on the globe. However, all the gains he made can be compared to a regiment fighting and having to slug it out for every inch of territory gained. Except, notwithstanding, the regiment would one day "Stand down," this has not been so with the Black man in America where he has faced challenges every minute, "fought battles every day and wars every year," so to speak.

a. Marcus Garvey marched in the streets of Harlem

The Black phenomenon in America during the first quarter of the 20th Century was Marcus Garvey, the Jamaican born. He founded the UNIA that at one time boasted a membership of 400,000,000 Africans world-wide. Garvey arrived in New York in 1916 to meet Booker T. Washington, who died a few months earlier in November, 1915. He was impressed with Washington's philosophy of acquiring technical skills to hold industrial jobs and the founding of his school Tuskegee Institute. Garvey and Washington communicated and Booker T. invited him to come to these shores, but alas, when he did his mentor had passed on to ancestorship. However, the death of his idol did not dissuade Garvey and he settled in Harlem. In no time, he established the UNIA and African Communities League and was holding conventions, rivaling the political movements of the time.

In his Magnum Opus, *The Philosophy and Opinions of Marcus Garvey*, he tells how he dismayed at the condition of the Blackman at the start of the 20th Century; so he set about to remedy it. Accordingly, he wrote: "I looked around for our men of big affairs and could find none." So, he created titles to reflect the emerging consciousness of Black upliftment. Garvey became Provisional President-General of Africa. He created titles as Duke of the Nile and Count of the Congo. Recognizing the impending struggle to "Free Mother Africa" from the grips of colonialists and imperialists, he created the regiments of soldiers and the Black Cross Nurses as their Combat Medics. He personally designed the form of uniform to be worn. He founded the Black Star Line to conduct trade within the Black World. Then he created the Red, Black and Green flag which is the Black man's flag. represented as the blood of the Black man to free the green land of "Mother Africa." He also composed the "Black National Anthem" which the *UNIA* today sings at any of its current gatherings. This is not to be confused with the now functional Black National Anthem, Lift Every Voice and Sing composed by James Weldon Johnson.

BN PHOTO - Professor Patterson, Sonny Carson, Mr. Douglas and Professor James Smalls beneath the Institutional Church, examining a "Station along the Underground Railroad" on Adelphi Street in Brooklyn.

After this Garvey held his conventions with magnificent parades displaying the most splendid colors, uniformity, discipline, all in a respectable and orderly manner that reflected the dignity of the Black man. Considering where he came from; from the depths of despair in the horribly inhuman institution of Slavery, Garvey had Black men and women flying high without touching a drop of anything. Perhaps that mood is comparable to the feeling felt by the millions of Black men and women who descended on Washington, DC, October 16, 1995.

Garvey's people marched with pride and dignity in great expectation of the future upliftment of the race. Little did he or they realize success breeds contempt and ill-will. Perhaps they did. The "powers that be" were threatened! A printer by trade, he published his own newspaper, *The Negro World*. In addition, his speeches and writing cover the full gambit of human relations. As such, he was teacher, preacher, philosopher, leader, businessman, organizer and much more. Since Garvey claimed to represent more than 400,000,000 Black men and women, he was "the most dangerous man in America." There is no question Garvey made mistakes but these were miniscule compared to his good intentions and the pride he instilled and still instills and inspires. A full-blooded Jamaican Black, he distrusted mulattos based on experiences in his native Jamaica. He never understood color within the context of American history, culture and social process. This was one of his mistakes.

The label of "The most dangerous man in America" was leveled against President Barack Obama but unfortunately they could not send him away, as "Daddy Cruz" wanted to "Send Obama back to Kenya."

That distrust of color caused Garvey to be at odds with W.E.B. DuBois, an ardent advocate for Black progress, who incidentally had broken his friendship with Garvey's mentor Booker T. Washington. This meant Garvey was at odds with DuBois who later confessed Garvey's ideas were sound. Garvey's enemies exploited this distrust and plotted with other "coloreds" to bring him down, accusing Garvey of mail fraud. The Black Star Line was a great idea with many flaws. It was a "great alligator that gnawed" at the economic viability of the organization Garvey administered. Another of Garvey's faults is he "trusted without verifying," and the captain of the Black star line bilked him. However, because of what the shipping line meant in terms of potential trade and Black prestige, he poured more and more funds to keep it afloat. This contributed to charges of fiscal mismanagement. Soon Garvey was arrested, charged with fraud for using the mails to solicit funds, tried, convicted, imprisoned, later pardoned and then deported. There is no question there was a political witch-hunt designed to derail the movement he founded and set in motion.

After Garvey was convicted and being led, handcuffed, to Atlanta Federal Prison he raised his manacled arms and made one last prophetic statement that was full of true intent and sweet irony. He said: "You have caged the lion but the cubs are running free out there. So you must look for me in the whirlwind." How right he was for the cubs have grown and their cubs have had cubs, never to forget the experiences and intent of Marcus Garvey. Even more important, the pride and significance of the Red, Black and Green is alive and well and enjoys more meaning and significance today, and will continue because of the historic significance of this motif.

All this notwithstanding, Garvey marched us into history with an ardent and fervent activist intent and demeanor that until we are truly free, there's no stopping us. That is why we view August 17, (1887) Garvey's birthday, as a day of national consciousness for truly, ours is and must always be One God, One Aim, One Destiny.

b.   Blacks marched for jobs in the New Deal and to fight fascism and later communism

Perhaps the tailwind of Garvey's downfall hooked America and the Western World contributing to the calamity of the Great Depression. In fact, while World War I damaged Europe, America was unscathed and her industry mobilized to feed the needs of the war. The take off at war's end was rapid and America especially enjoyed unprecedented prosperity especially in material possessions. Houses, cars, intangibles, mostly on credit, fueled a bubble that ultimately collapsed by 1929. The Federal Reserve System created in 1913 had not evolved to today's standards of tracking the economy, making adjustments along the way and thus the consequences of the exorbitant and rapid growth of the economy resulted in the catastrophe of stock market crash and the resultant depression.

Well, if white America sneezed and then caught a cold, imagine perhaps a virulent case of the flu struck Black America! Six decades out of slavery, Southern "nullification" of the fundamentals of the 13th, 14th, and 15th Amendments and Reconstruction, physical assault of Charles Sumner on the floor of the House of Representatives, attacks on Black rights through disfranchisement, poll taxes, literacy tests, land taxes, grandfather clause, Jim Crowism, peonage tenant farming, the consequences of the 1896 *Plessey V. Ferguson's* Separate but Equal" ruling of the Supreme Court, amidst lynchings, tar and feathers, Ku Klux Klan, Knights of the White Camelia, White Citizen's Council, riots, discrimination, the works; but like Maya Angelou's beautiful poem affirmed, "Still I Rise," the Black experience in America has been one unforgettable experience!

In retrospect, perhaps it was the motivating pride, dignity and self-respect that the great minds of the early 20th Century in the persons of Booker T. Washington, W.E.B. DuBois and Marcus Garvey Tri-Party alliance which spawned and galvanized the Harlem Renaissance is what pulled us through! Then again, perhaps we could also add the experiences gained from our boys being marched off to fight and "save the world for democracy."

Fact is, whether others disagree or not, having served in the military and fought under the colors, Blacks gained insights into fighting for themselves. We must never forget, as Claude McKay reminded, in his *If We Must Die* poem we may be "pressed to the wall, dying, but fighting back."

All this, notwithstanding, the intellectual consciousness gained from expanding total Black experiences forced them to view political realities differently. While some have argued Lincoln was initially ambivalent towards Blacks, his party led by Radical Republicans championed their cause and thus for six-decades Blacks voted Republican. That is, despite the compromising betrayal that brought Rutherford B. Hayes to the Presidency after Ulysses S. Grant, ending Reconstruction as well as denying Blacks the "40 acres and a mule." Seriously, considering all that happened from the end of the Civil War to the Depression, yet Blacks still stayed loyal to a Republican Party that no longer championed their interests, was cause for concern.

While Teddy Roosevelt's "Fair Deal" argued in 1910: "When I say I believe in a fair deal, I don't mean give every man the best hand, All I mean is …that there shall be no crookedness in the dealings" perhaps, in his view, Blacks were not in the game or at the table. However, when his counterpart and cousin, Franklin Delano Roosevelt promised in 1932 a "New Deal" with "a chicken in every pot," thanks to his wife Eleanor, some consideration was given to

Blacks. As such, Blacks then marched in great numbers into the Democratic camp and primarily remained Democrats to this day.

Yet, for the next two decades, the march through the American social order was a bit easier, however, still challenging. It is reasonable to argue, Black marching shoes were more firmly fastened at the boot-straps owing to the Democratic F.R.D. Administration being more sympathetic to their concerns. This can be argued as because of the new found and significant constituency in their voting strength. FDR's wife Eleanor made the First Lady position more meaningful. She helped organize a "Kitchen Cabinet" of Blacks.

BN PHOTO - Sonny Carson, in a very reflective mood as he watches onlooker appreciation for the "Runaway Samuel Carson."

While the "New Deal" addressed the plight of the nation's whites, Blacks received a small share of the largesse. They marched and received some jobs, were able to work and own farms, purchase houses, Black artists painted murals in the WPA Program and Black Americans provided the musical beat to which the nation marched, "swing" and danced. As the impending danger of World War II approached, Blacks signed up to serve in the military even though they were restricted to segregated units.

The Pan-Africanist world-view made them more acutely aware and sympathetic to the injustice of Italian aggression in Ethiopia in 1936. Nevertheless, segregated units did very well in World War II and the Black Activist Sonny Carson has told the story of how his uncle was among one of the first soldiers to liberate one of the Holocaust Death Camps where so many Jews perished. Equally too, the Tuskegee Airmen gained fame as aerial aces whether as solo fighters or fighter escorts. They seem to have taken a page from the book of "the Underground Railroad" Conductor Harriet Ross Tubman who boasted "I never lost a passenger."

All this notwithstanding, A. Philip Randolph challenging President Roosevelt with a "March on Washington" July 4, 1941 forced him to concede and pass Executive Action 8802 allowing employment of Blacks in the War Industries machinery. Yet, there were a whole lot more heroes who served with distinction in the war. Harry Belafonte the actor and singer, recounted how at the end of World War II he became an activist. We are often told Audie Murphy was the most decorated World War II veteran. This is not so, argued Belafonte. It was a Black veteran like himself. Returning home from service in Europe, in his military uniform, the Black veteran chose to ride the front of the bus in the segregated South in 1945-46. The driver called the cops to remove him. They marched or dragged him off the bus, screaming, he hollered, "I'm a veteran, just home from Europe, fighting 'to save the world for Democracy.'" The racist southern cops beat him to death, right there on Main Street, shouting "This is not Europe, this is America." Here then, came of age one of Garvey's "Cubs" who, like his "siblings" spawned their own cubs, echoing an old African philosophical admonition, "Let the circle be unbroken" or more appropriately, "Let the struggle continue" as we march forward.

From that battlefield emerged the Pre-civil Rights era that equally began a close identification with Africa and its assertion to challenge colonialism.

F.D.R. is the only President elected more than twice, in fact, four times, owing to World War II. He died in the first year of his fourth term and was succeeded by his Vice-President Harry Truman. Truman did two significant things when coming to the Presidency. The first was his 1948 desegregating the military. Several things led to this realistic development. To the Black combat veteran the invincibility of the white man was a myth. A straight shot could take him out and many Black veterans were returning home with lots of combat experience. With the emergence of the Soviet Union and its allies pursuing the expansionist philosophy of communism, the struggle came to retain a world-wide state of belligerence. Thus, the American military had to operate within the outward appearance of equality.

BN PHOTO - A devotee kneels before the coffin of Samuel Carson as the Drummers play on.

The second significant act of President Truman was to issue the Truman Doctrine which stated "We will do anything and go anywhere to combat communism." This policy, therefore, guided and drove the anti-communist challenge for the next half century and Blacks had become a permanent and significant component of the military machine that would challenge communists.

Meanwhile, in the aftermath of *Plessey V. Ferguson* (1896) and its "Separate but Equal" philosophy, in reality, "Separate but Unequal," Black legal eagles and their white allies, having perennially challenged the legal system and were able to overthrow the "Grandfather Clause" in 1915, continued the fight to make headway in the legal system. For the next 38 years a number of small legal victories emboldened Black legal eagles in preparation for the historic *Brown V. Board of Topeka, Kansas* in 1954.

BN PHOTO - Sonny Carson, Atiim Ferguson and Bishop Shivers and another mull over the "Runaway's coffin."

V.   In the United States II: The Civil Rights Era

Reverend Herbert L. Oliver, longtime associate of Ollie McClean takes great pride in telling the story of how effective the economic boycott in Birmingham, Alabama, had been changing the economic landscape of that city.

a. **March for the City of Montgomery Bus-boycott** - Following Rosa Parks courageous stance, coupled with Dr. Martin Luther King's leadership, the people of Selma put in place a Bus-Boycott that lasted for a year to protest the iniquities of the transportation system such as Blacks riding at the back of the bus. They were successful because of a tenacious resolve that was everywhere infecting the Civil Rights Movement across the nation, which incidentally was contemporary with and very much influenced with the global decolonization struggles of Africans at home and in the United Nations.

b. **Selma to Montgomery March** - Taking the struggle to a next level, the architects of the movement chose to march from Selma to Montgomery, in a historic show of force and collaboration amongst people of goodwill. The highpoint came at the Edmund Pettis Bridge of which now Congressman John Lewis was abused and emerged as an unbreakable Civil Rights icon along with Jesse Jackson. The movie **Selma**, in graphic form, in which President Barack Obama and Mrs. Obama; former President George Bush and Mrs. Laura Bush; shown on the front page of the New York based *Amsterdam News*, Dr. Adelaide Sanford in wheelchair crossed the Pettis Bridge to mark the 50th Anniversary of that historic march. Yet, perhaps through divine inspiration, at the first attempt to cross the Bridge, Dr. King balked. The Sheriff had set a trap perhaps to slaughter the marchers. However, as more marchers joined the march and the then President Johnson intervened, the next day the march proceeded successfully to lay their case at the state Montgomery capital.

c. **March on Washington 1963** - In many respects, A. Philip Randolph's 1941 threat influenced the **1963 Poor People's March** on Washington. Randolph was there in the organizing committee. However, Dr. King's memorable "I have a dream" speech carried the day and would remain a forceful and remarkable demand for justice across the American political, social and economic landscape.

BN PHOTO - Women did their share of blessing and spiritual transference to prepare "Runaway Samuel Carson" for his historic return to Ghana, West Africa.

d.   March in Vigil to protest Assassination of Malcolm X and Martin Luther King, Jr. - We lost two great fighters and today Black Americans never let the nation forget this tragedy. While January 15th, of each year is celebrated for Dr. Martin Luther King, in Harlem especially nearly 40 years ago, the activist Herman Ferguson had held a vigil-march in Harlem, forcing merchants to close for a few hours to honor Malcolm X, "Our Shining Black Prince." This protest march and pilgrimage to his burial site along his beloved wife sister Dr. Betty Shabaaz keeps growing every year.

VI.   In the United States III - Modern marchers under the leadership of the iconic Minister Louis Farrakhan have set in motion a most potent form of protest, the idea of "Million Marches."

a.   Million Man March - Beginning with the call for One Million men to converge on the nation's capital on October 16, 1995, two million came pledging to be united and work for the advancement of not simply the idea of Blackness but to begin to organize on a micro scale in their local communities.

b.   Day of Atonement - Following up on the successes of the first gathering, the Minister called for a Day of Atonement so not simply Black men and women, but more importantly the American government housed in Washington, DC, would atone for injustices against the African people.

c.   Million Woman March - Not to be outdone, the women got in the act calling for a similar gather of solidarity with the objectives and aspirations of the previous gatherings. This occurred on October 25, 1998 in the City of Philadelphia. This writer was first approached by the iconic activist and educator Jitu Weusi (formerly Les Campbell) to attend the Million Woman March. Queried as to why should a man attend the Million Woman March? He responded, "I'm not going to let one million Black women gather and not be there to provide security." I then said, "I'm going" and was proud to be part of that historic gathering. After all, I was marching for my mother, wife, sister, daughters, aunts, and a whole lot more women I respected as indicated in my articles in praise of the Black Woman." Check it out!

d.   Million Youth March I - Well, I was in Harlem for the Million Mouth March down Malcolm X Boulevard. The two principals grabbing the headlines were Congressman Charles Rangel who accused Khalid Mohammed of spewing hate, but "not in my Harlem." Nevertheless, the march went off without a hitch and photographs recount how the police lined rooftops with cameras and firearms in the event of any on-toward behaviors.

BN PHOTO - Cherise Maloney of Brooklyn, New York, stands center among those admiring and appreciating the Drummers' Grove musicians in support of the "Runaway Samuel Carson."

e.   Million Youth March II - The Second Youth March was held on Fulton Street in Brooklyn, between Nostrand and New York Avenues in 2003. Many speakers including "The Warrior Woman" from the Dakotas make their statements critical of the government and private entities who had been unfair not only to Native Americans but minorities in general.

f.   Million Family March - There was Minister Farrakhan again sounding the clarion call not simply to march for justice but to show the forgiving nature and the resilience of the African Family confronted with all sort of challenges.

g.   Queens Million Man March - Coming home after the Million Man March in DC, Professor James Black of Queens, head of the Queens Million Man March Committee, sponsored a somewhat similar though smaller march that ended in Roy Wilkins Park. Ever since, the Professor and his associates have kept alive the idea of the original Million Man March.

h.   Million Mom March - Well, Moms were tired of seeing their children killed in senseless violence, lack of opportunities for their families, women being paid less than 70 cents for every dollar men made, decided to get out there. They marched against gun violence and called attention to the plague that has continued unabated to this day where gun violence is taking a heavy toll.

i.   Tenth Anniversary of Million Man March - This tenth anniversary of the **Million Man March** in 2005 was a time for quiet reflection but more important to assess how far we had come.

j.   The Brooklyn March for Sonny Carson - Upon the passing of Brooklyn Icon, Sonny Carson, a march was organized beginning at Brooklyn Bridge, down Flatbush Avenue and across Fulton Street to Bedford Stuyvesant (Abubadikaville) in tribute to the Mayor of Bed-Stuy whose long efforts to improve the condition of Blacks has remained consistent, whether in economics or education, and especially for his magnanimous repatriation of his uncle Samuel Carson back to Ghana, opening the "Door of Return."

VII.   In the United States IV

a.   Rev. Al Sharpton's New York City March "Shopping for Justice" December 16, 2006, in wake of Sean Bell senseless shooting on eve of his wedding, was conducted in the "Heart of Christmas" on Fifth Avenue, passing 50th Street and Rockefeller Center. The thousands who came in response to the Reverend's call emphasized, "We're not against the Police but against "police brutality." This outpouring of sentiments for Sean Bell's widow echoed the sentiments expressed for Kadiatou Diallo after the 41 shots fired at her son Amadou Diallo. Officer Weatherspoon explained he found two other bullets making the number actually 43.

BN PHOTO - Sonny Carson stands atop the Red, Black and Green with his book *The Education of Sonny Carson*.

c.   Harlem March for Elombe Brathe - When Harlem nationalist Icon, Elombe Brathe Founder of the Patrice Lumumba Coalition passed, he was honored with a march from the Apollo to Abyssinian Baptist Church for a wonderful "Home Going Service." There too the nationalist cadre poured out in record numbers as they did for Dr. Yosef A.A. Ben-Jochannan.

d.   Staten Island March for Eric Garner - After Eric Garner was killed in an "illegal choke-hold" by Detective Panatela concerned citizens gathered in Staten Island to draw attention to another senseless killing, the Medical Examiner ruled a homicide. The message was clear, stop the nonsense but more important, the purveyors of guns and weapons of mass killings must be held accountable for their behaviors, especially when it's observed a pattern of the senseless killing of Black men. In the rally one year after the death of Eric Garner held in Cadman Plaza Park a clear message was sent to the nearby Federal Courthouse institution "Justice for Eric Garner" is the way to go.

VIII. Conclusions - Thus it can be seen, African people are determined to bring about social and economic justice peacefully through the medium of marching as they have for the longest. The message is clear, as the United States Constitution guarantees the right; "we will keep marching until justice rolls down like a mighty stream."

IX. Another Look at Marching for Justice - All across this nation, people have marched for justice and to redress some senseless loss of life. This response has been due to the callousness of individuals who possess guns, legal or otherwise, who senselessly use their firearms to maim and kill with impunity. The interesting thing is, though Black Lives has been a principal target, across the nation and globally people of goodwill have staged mass demonstrations, marching to call attention as "Our Brother's Keepers" demanding an end to such violence and that governments must uphold their responsibility to protect the people over whom they rule.

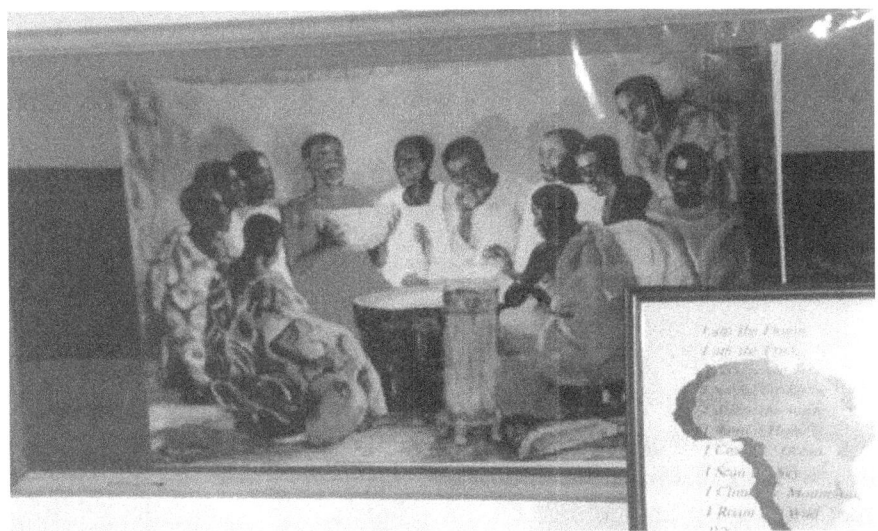

BN PHOTO - A Gathering of Elders, singing: "I am the Flower, I am the Fruit...."

BN PHOTO - Elombe Brathe, Supreme Nationalist, speaks with "Sonny Carson's Lieutenants" Abdul Haqq, Abubaca, Atiim Ferguson, etc. at a ceremony honoring the great man after his passing onto the "Glory of Ancestorship."

55. PRESIDENT OBAMA IN AFRICA I
By
Dr. Fred Monderson

After successfully attending a Summit establishing a new chapter in American-Russian relations, then on to Italy for a G-8 Economic Conference where he and the First Family had an audience with Pope Benedict, President Obama arrived in Ghana, West Africa, for a one-day visit charged with more significance and electricity than that of all past Presidents combined who have visited Africa. To recall, as a Senator from Illinois, Barack Obama visited Kenya, his father's homeland, which provided a tremendous welcome to this "son of a son." In glaring appreciation, Elders dressed Obama in the traditional garb and this provided a firestorm of accusations in the 2008 Presidential Elections at home as opponents sought to paint him as Muslim among many things. However, this time as the first

African American President, rather than return to his "roots" in Kenya, President Obama chose Ghana because of its symbolism as a thriving and vibrant democracy, evident from a recent election and peaceful transfer of power.

In a historic address to the Ghanaian Parliament, carried by CNN and equally broadcast across the African continent, Mr. Obama was pragmatic, stuck to his guns and delivered a tough love speech outlining America's new relationship with African nations. He emphasized the simple and unmistakable fact, "we must start with the simple premise that Africa's future is up to Africans" and recognizing Europe's imperial role on the continent insisted, "a colonial map that made little sense bred conflict and the West has often approached Africa as a patron, rather than a partner, but the West is not responsible for the destruction of the Zimbabwean economy over the last decade, or wars in which children are enlisted as combatants." No, but the West was responsible for centuries of rape and pillage of the African landmass, population and minerals and other resources.

Five hundred years after the discovery of the Americas and the subsequent efforts to conquer this hemisphere, the European Slave Trade in Africans, and plantation slavery with psychological and physical emasculation of the victims of such barbarism, we see the legacy of slavery still functioning institutionally in many guises even though we have crossed the bridge to the next century. This forces us to remember that (in this emerging great nation of America, the English colonials under Britain fought the French, in the *French and Indian Wars* (1756-1763) and fought the British in the *War of Independence* (1776-1783). Runaway Slave Samuel Carson fought in the Mexican War of (1844-45). This new nation then fought the British in the *War of 1812*. Then we fought the Spanish in the *Spanish American War* (1898-1900); the Germans and their allies in *World War I* (1914-1918) though we practically entered the conflict in 1917; again, the Germans, Italians and Japan in *World War II* (1939) entering that conflict on December 7, 1941; the *Korean War* (1950-1953); and against the Chinese, Russians and their allies in the anti-*Communist Cold War*. Yet again, particularly the Russians, who have atomic weapons, probably still aimed at us that can devastate this nation, these people can all come to these shores, "blend in with the population" and with some effort particularly aided by their cultural organizations, begin moving up the social ladder towards realization of the "American Dream." However, the ravages and devastation of slavery and its legacy still identifies sons and daughters of Africa in America and make us victims of racism that was born out of this dehumanizing experience.

Therefore, we need to never forget as we ended the Twentieth Century and crossed the bridge to the Twenty-First Century; it was W.E.B. DuBois who said the question of the "color bar" would dominate these past hundred years of the twentieth Century. All people must move away from this odious conception and practice that is very much alive and well in the world in today's 21st Century! Fordham in *Geography of African Affairs* (1965: 58-59) recounting how Africans worldwide are viewed in the most disdainful manner, supplied an example that indicated, "As late as 1928 a distinguished Englishman" could write, "The Negroes of Tropical Africa specialized in their isolation and stagnation in utter savagery. They may even have been drifting away from the human standard back towards the brute when migratory impulses drew the Caucasian, the world's redeemer, to enter Tropical Africa ... mingle his blood with that of the pristine negroes and raise the mental status of these dark skinned, wooly haired, prognathous retrograded men ...."

He continued (1965: 59) that: "Echoes of this attitude were still to be heard in the British House of Lords in 1961" when he quoted Lord Barbizon of Tara, on March 23, 1961, in *Hansard* Vol. 229, No. 57, Cols. 1277-9. "As I went to it [the United Nations] I really got the impression that there was a convention of nigger minstrels going on ... the Commonwealth is a piebald set-up, and a pie-bald set-up is a poor form of organization that will never last." Of course, that is not to say, some of our people have not progressed despite difficult odds among purposely orchestrated restraints, as they struggled with and without bootstraps.

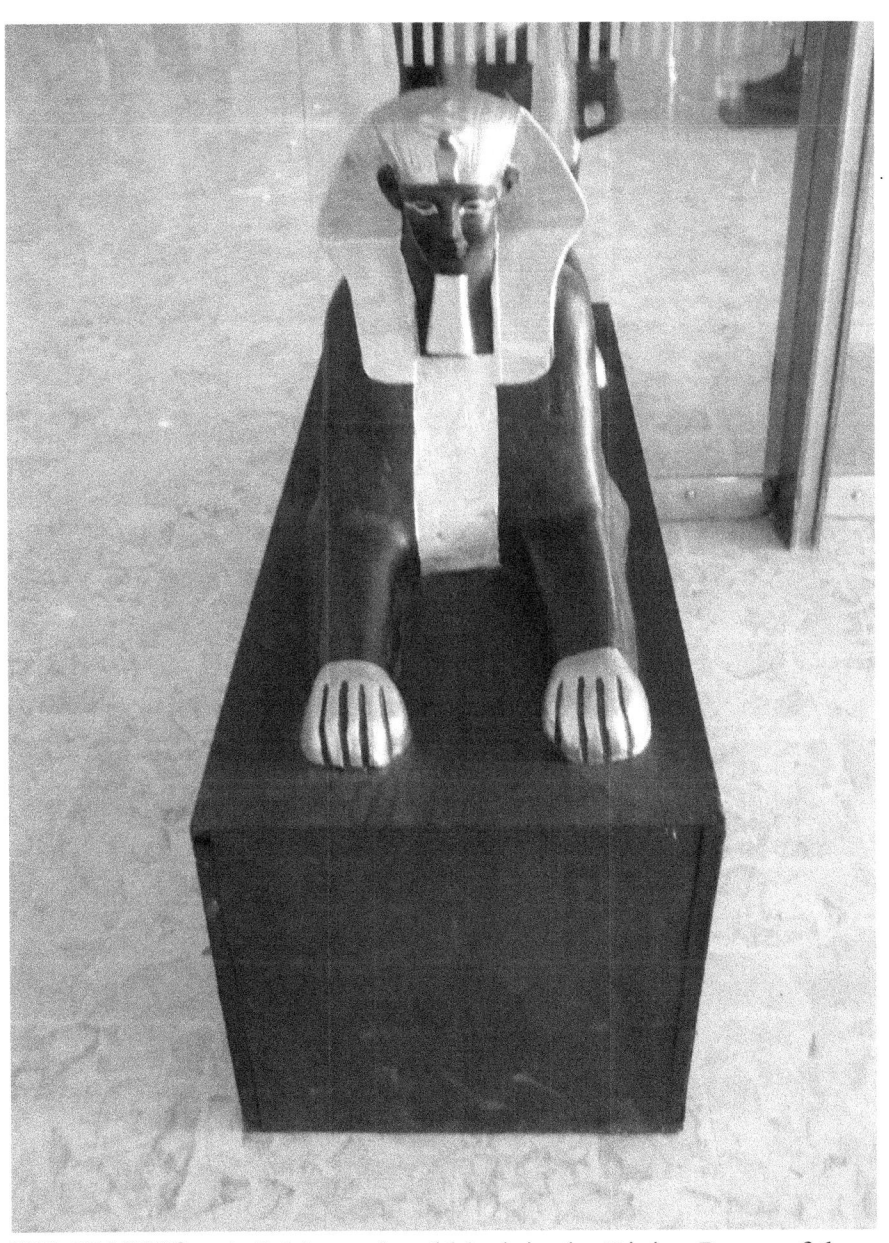

BN PHOTO - A Sphinx painted black in the Dining Room of the Oberoi Hotel, now renamed Movenpick, at Aswan, Egypt.

BN PHOTO - The pathway beside the Old Cataract Garden, one of the most beautiful at Aswan.

BN PHOTO - Another view of the beautiful garden at Old Cataract Hotel.

However, as we celebrated another Martin Luther King Birthday and head towards Black History Month in February, 1998, the voices of such commentators as Julian Bond, Kwame Mfume, Leonard Jeffries, Tony Martin, Sonny Carson and a whole host of others, all pointed to the disparities and difficulties of high unemployment, police brutality, racial discrimination, poverty, lack of proper medical care, drug infestation, crime, poor education, etc., that plague Black and other minority communities. Such an odious legacy is principally because of the African heritage of Black people that seems anathema to many in this nation. Even though we now have a Black President whose term in office is winding down, many people still harbor odious sentiments towards him and other blacks, perhaps it is particularly because of the color of their skin. But it must be remembered, Black people paid the ultimate sacrifice to build America, and we intend to earn our place at the table of this nation, under the philosophic and humanistic banner believing in the fatherhood of God and the brotherhood of man. However, in the current political climate as Donald Trump and his fanatical followers subscribe to an ever-increasing climate of racial hatred particularly cultivated in Mr. Trump's "Birther" movement escapade, African people in America must reflect on their history especially in this nation drawing resolve from the most positive experiences to meet the challenges of the next several projected lean years.

With that, we need to understand the social and psychological dynamics of the forced removal of Africans, called the Atlantic Slave Trade, began soon after the Portuguese landed in West Africa in 1441. That year, a trickle of Africans was first taken to Lisbon, Portugal. Lloyd (1972: 51) has shown how early contacts by the Portuguese along the West African coast was beginning to clear the way for the later onslaught. "In 1434 Portuguese ships passed Cape Bojador in Mauretania; by 1475 Fernando Po had been reached, and in 1483 Portuguese sailors visited the capital of Benin, probably the most highly organized coastal kingdom at this period. The Portuguese were impressed by it and established a trading port at Ughoton (Gwatto) in 1486, but their main attention was directed to the Gold Coast with its more valuable exports; the castle of San Jorge da Mina was erected at Elmina in 1482. Gold apart, the West African coast offered little to attract European trade until the discovery of the Americas provided a demand for slaves."

However, from 1485 onward we witness a number of significant events in Europe. First there was the unification of Spain and the defeat of the Moors at the fall of Granada and in 1492 Columbus' expedition was underway. Decades thereafter, Africans began to be shipped to the Americas to cultivate plantations. By the end of the century, plantations were producing sugar cane and derivative products; particularly in the British West Indies, e.g., Barbados, Trinidad; Slavery came after 1814 in Cape Town, South Africa; and after the Dutch in Guiana now Guyana, enslaved Africans were harnessed to exploit this sweet product with its derivative industries, strange enough, that began to transform industry through jobs in Europe.

Iliffe (1995: 127-128) tells how: "The Atlantic slave trade began in 1441 when a young Portuguese sea-captain Antam Goncalvez, kidnapped a man and woman on the Western Saharan coast to please his employer, Prince Henry-the-Navigator-successfully, for Goncalvez was knighted. Four years later the Portuguese built a fort on Arguin Island, off the Mauritanian coast, from which to purchase slaves and, more particularly, gold, which was especially scarce at this time. After failing in 1415 to capture the gold trade by occupying Ceuta on the Moroccan coast, Portuguese mariners groped down the West African coast towards the gold sources. Arguin was designed to lure gold caravans away from the journey to Morocco. Yet slaves were not merely by-products, for a lively market in African slaves had existed since the mid-fourteenth century in southern Europe, where labor was scarce after the Black Death and slavery had survived since Roman times in domestic service and pockets of intensive agriculture, especially the production of sugar, which Europeans had learned from Muslims during the Crusade. As sugar plantation spread westwards through the Mediterranean to Atlantic islands like Maderia and eventually to the Americas, they depended increasingly on slave labor. The Atlantic slave trade was largely a response to their demand."

Significantly, by 1505 or thereabouts, exploration of the newly discovered "new world" had become ingrained. The result was systematic and widespread destruction of indigenous cultures, viz., the Incas, Mayas, Aztecs, Tainos, etc., that were flourishing in this hemisphere. Commenting on the people who followed Columbus into North, Central and South America at the end of Fifteenth Century, Davidson (1996: 202) wrote: "These others, who were Spanish soldiers and adventurers, ruined the [native] American peoples whom they found. Their intention was not trade, but loot; not peace, but war; not partnership, but enslavement. They fell upon these lands with greed and the fury of destruction. And the [native] American peoples, unlike the Africans, were unable to defend themselves. Being at an earlier stage of social and technical development than the Africans, they fell easy victims to Spanish violence. Along the coast of Guinea, the Portuguese and other Europeans had begun by trying their hand at violence. But they had given that up. The Africans they met were too strong for them. In the Americas it was different."

Even further, Davidson (1996: 203) continued: "There was terrible destruction of the 'Indians,' the name that was mistakenly given by these raiders to the native-born American people. A Spanish report of 1518, only twenty-six years after the first voyage of Columbus across the Atlantic, says that when the island of Cuba was discovered it was reckoned to contain more than a million 'Indians,' but today their number does not exceed 11,000. And judging from what has happened, there will be none of them left in three or four years' time, unless some remedy is applied."

That unfortunate state of affairs, forced Bishop Bartholomew De Las Casas to petition the Papacy in Rome. He requested that Africans be brought into the Americas for labor purposes, to replace the rapidly disappearing indigenous population. Losing the battle to "save the Indians," he unleashed an even greater tragedy that lasted for centuries, and claimed many, many more lives. This stain on humanity's integrity was Europe's Slave Trade in Africans to America.

The Age of Exploration created new opportunities for discovery and transformation of the new lands introduced by Columbus and the other explorers, for which they sought official sanction. The Papal division of the world in 1492 gave half to Portugal and the other half to Spain, Christian nations and ardent defenders of their religion and the Papacy. Two years later in 1494, the demarcation was enshrined in the Treaty of Tordesillas, moving the boundary line 300-leagues to the West. The new official pronouncement gave most of the New World to Spain. This was changed once Portugal complained in which they were awarded a foothold in South America that became Brazil that is today the largest country in South America. As such, this Papal beneficence prohibited the Spanish from involvement in the trade in enslaved persons from Africa. The Portuguese, however, did have a free hand there. Iliffe (1995: 130) continued, recounting: "The first West African slaves went mainly to Portugal, then to Maderia, and then to Sao Tome. Direct shipments from Africa to the Americas began in 1532. As European and African diseases destroyed the Amerindian peoples, African slaves replaced them, because Africans alone were available in the required numbers, and then were cheaper than white indentured laborers, and they had the unique degree of immunity to both European and African diseases which came from living in the tropical periphery of the Old World."

By the late sixteenth century nearly 80 per cent of all exported West African slaves went to the Americas, especially to Brazil, where plantation sugar took root during the 1540s.

The Spanish *Haciento Treaty* was agreed to. Whom-so-ever held it had permission to supply the Spanish possessions in America with enslaved persons from Africa. In fact, Moore and Dunbar (1968: 110) have written: "The British took a leading part in this trade from the middle of the seventeenth century, with the development of the plantation colonies. New impetus was given when at the Peace of Utrecht in 1713 [Britain] obtained the Asiento." This Spanish contract was to supply cargo to and from the New World. For the African victims involved, this dreaded official instrument, yet, provoked many wars at sea among slaving European nations. Dreaded, in the sense that, the Spanish could not get slaves in Africa, so they had them brought to their New World plantation. For Africans, it provided death and hopelessness of Slave Trade and supplying an institution of Slavery. Oliver and Fage (1970: 120) have argued that Spanish territory was very lucrative; and, "The early Spanish colonies there had been supplied with African slaves, mainly through the Portuguese, from about 1510. But it was not until the competitive irruption into the West Indies of the Dutch, French and English in the seventeenth century, when there was a rapidly growing European demand for sugar - a crop making heavy demands on labor - that the transatlantic slave trade began to dominate European activities in West Africa. Compared with an estimate of some *275,000 Negro slaves landed overseas by 1600* [Author's italics], the seventeenth-century figure is thought to be about 1,340,000; the figures of the eighteenth and nineteenth centuries seem to have been about 6,050,000 and 1,900,000 respectively. The new development ousted the Portuguese from the Gold Coast. For a short time the trans-Atlantic trade was almost a Dutch monopoly, but their success provoked English and French hostility, and by the eighteenth century it was the traders of these two nations who were the principal competitors in the international trade, thought the Portuguese continued with a private slave trade of their own, from Angola and San Thome to Brazil. In terms of the trade alone, victory went to Britain. By the end of the eighteenth century her ships were carrying nearly half the slaves taken to America." Two things can be deduced from the above quote. The first is "Negro slaves landed overseas by 1600." The most important term is LANDED and this did not terminate then but continued throughout the duration. Second, a more accurate figure of the totality of the Salve Trade's cost to Africa, according to W.E.B. Dubois was 100 million souls lost!

And so it continued for centuries until the trade and institution was ended in Brazil in 1888. But that is not to say, though scholars have mentioned the Portuguese, English, French and Dutch, that these were the only nations involved. We must remember colonial America was also an active participant in Slave Trade development. This systematic and undeniable holocaust, which Merimba Ani termed the **GREAT MAAFA**, provided an inexhaustible supply of free labor required by slave trading nations then transforming the American landscape. Those other nations involved included the Brandenbergers or Germans, the Danes, and Swedes. Still, though not involved in carrying Africans to the "new world," the Spanish, because of the needs of empire, helped maintain a system of slavery in America, for three centuries after Columbus, that encouraged the perpetuation of this ghastly freed and cruel labor-supply phenomenon.

BN PHOTO - Image of God Bes in the Hathor Chapel at the Temple of Isis.

From the Atlantic Slave Trade's inception, it would appear that few of the traders worried or were concerned about carrying capacity conditions aboard their ships. As a result, the terms "tight packers" and "loose packers" came to characterize how enslaved Africans were transported to the Americas.

As Malcolm X said, "We did not land on Plymouth Rock, Plymouth Rock landed on us." This unfolding and escalated drama and resulting treatment promised nothing but death, hopeless melancholy and despair.

BN PHOTO - These T-Shirts certainly convey a message of love for "Black Hair."

Relative to mortality and in view of this situation, in 1788 and again in 1792, the House of Commons of the British Parliament conducted inquiries regarding the Slave Trade. They found that "persons transported from Africa to the West Indies are kidnapped, solely for the purpose of selling them to the traders." Alexander Falconbridge (1788: 13), a surgeon in the Slave Trade, had written there is "great reason to believe that most of the Negroes shipped from the coast of Africa are kidnapped." Sold to European slavers, the enslaved Africans faced a difficult journey. It took some fifty-two days to cross the Atlantic from Africa to America. At times the voyage was longer. However, it was seldom shorter!

In this harrowing experience, a constant problem of the Slave Trade was overcrowding. The famous slave ship BROOKES, out of Liverpool, sailed to the West Coast of Africa in 1783. This 320-ton frigate was built without forecastle and pierced for 20 guns yet enabled every available square foot of the vessel to be used to store its human cargo. **Minutes of the Evidence on the Slave Trade to Parliament** (1789: 43) indicated calculations were made of the men's room, boys' room, women's room, the gun-room, cabin, half-deck and a number of platforms.

BN PHOTO - Memnon, the twin sentinels, survivors from the Temple of Amenhotep III of the 18th Dynasty.

A. Stuart-Brown (1932: 48-49) described some carrying logistics of this famous vessel: "The slaves were lodged on the lower deck, the men in a room 46 feet by 25 feet 4 inches and 5 feet 8 inches high, the women in a smaller room 28 feet 6 inches by 23 feet 6 inches and the boy's room was 13 feet 9 inches by 25 feet."

In one instance, this slaving ship spent 10 months on the coast and collected 609 captive Africans. Those who boarded first experienced the horrors of "holding" before the "Middle Passage" began.

Dr. Thomas Trotter, the BROOKES' surgeon, according to Evidence of Robert Stokes Esq., Before the **Select Committee of the House of Lords** in 1948, reported seeing Africans all over the ship. In testimony to the **Committee of Parliament**, Stokes (1849: 5) describing his observations, on the ship states the "slaves in the passage was so crowded below, it is impossible to walk through them without treading on them." These conditions existed in the "pre-regulation period" when "tight packers" was the rule.

"Tight packers" meant purchase and carry as many enslaved persons without concern about safety and mortality. Some ships carried as many as 800 persons. Imagine! In the Frontispiece of this same source, Charles Fox, an abolitionist had insisted: "True humanity consists not in a squeamish ear; it consists not in staring or shrinking at tales such as these, but in a disposition of heart to relieve misery. True humanity appertains rather to the mind than to the nerves, and prompts men to use real and active endeavors to execute the measures which it suggests."

After regulation in 1789, BROOKES was restricted to carry only 454 enslaved Africans. The ship was still crowded with 450 aboard. One could only wonder how it managed to transport 609. After regulation, "loose packing" or carry fewer based on ship's tonnage, helped reduce the mortality rate of captives and crew aboard this and many other British slavers. While in this essay the British example is often used, the practice applies for colonial America and other slave-trading European nations, making Britain the "best of a bad lot." Some have disagreed and believe they were the worst during the 1700s-1800s. Fact is, while the British ultimately sought regulation this was not a pre-requisite of other nations. Generally, business operated on the conscience of the monetary unit whether pound, frank, mark, or dollar and as such, the stark inhumanity of the trade victimized and physically dehumanized the African man, woman and child.

According to *An Historical Account of the Liverpool African Slave Trade* (1884: iii) there was an old saying in the City of Liverpool: "Get slaves honestly, if you can, and if you cannot get them honestly, get them!" Of course, a colleague of mine, Stanley Simpson, reviewing this comment asked: "What is meant by the term 'honestly' in this context during the 1700s?" Does it mean pay first for the merchandise? Or, pay a good price for what you got. If so, what would be the true value of a human being? That is the question. In fact, it forces one to wonder what is the true value of an African man, woman or child, then as well as what it is today? When objective observers and commentators apply this context to the present state of relations among victimized people, it does not matter if persons are killed by their own or by others, a human life should not be regarded as being without value. That is why for the last 30 years an underlying theme of every Black Solidarity Day has been: "No (Black) one should die at the hands of another." This was Sonny Carson's idea and should apply equally today across this nation, whether in Chicago, New York, or Los Angeles!

In those Atlantic slave trade times, in the principal British trading city of Liverpool and elsewhere, it was a popular belief, notes *Historical Account....* (1884: 14) that: "Slavery was right; it was supported by the Bible, and strenuously advocated by the clergy of the time; as well as the politicians. They asserted it was divine right that the blacks were of an inferior race and were to be bought and sold by the white man, with his brand on them.... How many crimes have been committed in the name of the book?" Perhaps, however, it was not in the name of the Book but in the name of profits! Nevertheless, though the mentality of that time has changed, its operational handle in today's environment has evolved, for example, from a "Jump Suit" to a "Business Suit."

We are told further in the same source (1884: 16) of George Franklin Cook, tragedian, who was born April 17, 1756 and died September 26, 1812. While drunk at a performance in the Liverpool Theater, he is quoted as saying to his critics: "I have not come here to be insulted by a set of wretches, of which every brick in your infernal town is cemented with an African's blood." We are also informed in *Edinburgh Review* (1908: 26) that the "chief center of the African trade Liverpool, [was] remarkable in the commercial history of the United Kingdom." Even further, the same source, *Edinburgh Review* (1908: 33) states: "Of all English communities, Liverpool derived the most wealth from the debasing trade." More, in the *Illustrated London News* (1957: 18), we are again reminded of descriptions of the city's investment in the Slave Trade as an "impressive array of commercial institutions, banking houses, insurance companies, trading associations and produce exchanges." In addition, *Illustrated London News* (1957: 18) informs further, "Liverpool merchants performed a variety of economic functions incorporating the means for financing and insuring the commodities they bought and sold, and controlling the ships which carried the commodities overseas." Still more, that the "Liverpool merchant body exerted a powerful influence over Parliament through the Liverpool Parliamentary Office." This was probably because the prosperity of the port was tied to the import of raw cotton, sugar, wheat, flour, rum, and tobacco, and to the export of cotton piece goods, woolens, salt, coal, iron products, chemicals, glass and soap. However, this profit motive notwithstanding, things have an uncanny way of working themselves out, for there were individuals whose conscience and high moral standards dictated that they resist and challenge this plague perpetuated by their countrymen. One such instance can be cited of James Fox, an abolitionist quoted as saying during the English Parliament's attempt to regulate the Slave Trade, that: "There can be no regulation of robbery and murder."

We know the Atlantic Slave Trade began after Bishop De Las Casas sought papal approval to ship Africans to the Americas to save lives of Amerindians. Foxburn (1932: 56) has argued: "Las Casas, ... saw no harm in subjecting African Negroes to the treatment from which he sought earnestly to save the aborigines of the new world." However, some have equally held de Las Casas thought this the lesser of two evils. Perhaps he never thought it would escalate as it did. Yet, and arguably so, the trade was continued under religious sanction through the belief that Africans were not Christians, not Europeans, had an "exotic culture" and easily definable by skin color. Therefore, official policy held it was okay to enslave them. Thereafter, in 1562-63, Sir John Hawkins, the first Englishman to trade in enslaved Africans, sailed to Africa in the slave ship *Solomon*. Two years later in 1564-65, he sailed in the slave ship *Jesus*, blazing a trail for his countrymen.

BN PHOTO - The beauty of New York as partly reflected in its flowers, is a wonderful sight to behold.

Harris (1972: 72-73) has argued, "it was a combination of European attitudes about blacks and the demand for cheap labor that sired the Atlantic slave trade and New World black slavery." When the Portuguese arrived in Africa they began seizing Africans to take to Europe as 'curiosity pieces,' at which time it was confirmed, a "new land had been reached." The early African victims were honored in Portugal, taught Portuguese, and used as informants and guides for future Portuguese voyages to Africa.

BN PHOTO - Luxor Temple's Eastern Obelisk still in place while the other's base depicts the missing Western Obelisk that is now in Paris, France.

However, as the number of Africans increased in Lisbon they gradually were relegated to menial tasks, and by the middle of the fifteenth century, a lively trade in African labor (slaves) evolved. Thus, even before the Americas were settled by Europeans, Europe witnessed the development of black slavery, especially in Portugal, Spain, Italy, and Sicily. It has been estimated, for example, that between 1458 and 1460, from 700 to 800 slaves were exported annually from Africa to Europe, with an estimate of 35,000 for 1450-1500.

Some authorities have calculated that from 50,000 to 100,000 Africans were taken to Europe during the whole course of the trade. Whatever the numbers, the point to emphasize here is that a half century prior to their settlement in the Americas, many Europeans (especially the inhabitants of Spain and Portugal, the two countries that spearheaded American settlement) had become accustomed to the enslavement of the Africans.

Yet, and conversely, from the middle of the 18th century, a religious conviction motivated men of good will to lead the fight to outlaw the slave trade. In Britain, many important abolitionists were involved including Granville Sharpe, Thomas Clarkson, Charles Fox, Wilberforce, Macaulay, and the Reverend John Newton, a reformed slave dealer. Reverend Newton authored the hymn "How Sweet the Name of Jesus Sounds," after a religious conversion, while aboard a slave ship he operated off the coast of West Africa.

In 1849, evidence was presented by Robert Stokes before the Committee of the House of Lords, as previously stated. This body, following inquiries of six decades earlier, reflected on the high mortality rate of English seamen in the trade before regulation. Their results revealed the following percentage of mortality rates: 50, 20, 20, 30, 33, 25, 30 and 50. This showed an average of 32 per cent death rate for seamen on board some English slavers. Well, if the slavers were experiencing such high rates of mortality given they had the ability to be mobile, a chance for exercise, fresh air and perhaps better food, imagine what it was among their cargo denied the above and exposed to other unimaginable horrors below deck!

John Latimer (1893: 474-75) in *The Annals of Bristol in the 18th Century* recounted the view of "one captain from the port of the slave trade who did not deserve long ago to be hanged."

BN PHOTO - Bust of Rameses II stands before the Entrance Pylon at Luxor Temple.

Slaving methods of procuring sailors were notorious. In the slaving business, these seamen were: "Dreadfully ill-treated .... drugged with liquor until impotent to offer resistance... sailors ... encouraged to run into debt, and then offered the alternative of a slaving voyage or a goal [jail] ... never permitted to read the articles they signed on entering a ship, and by the insertion in these documents of iniquitous clauses.... wages in the slave trade (30 s per month) though nominally higher, were actually higher in other trades."

Nonetheless, in his *Essay on the Impolicy of the Slave Trade*, Thomas Clarkson (1785: 35) mentioned the "difficulty of procuring seamen for the slave trade is well known at the ports where it is carried on." Again, Clarkson (1788: 57) notes, "in the year 1786, 1,125 seamen will be found upon the dead list in consequence of this execrable trade." That same year, recalled Clarkson (1788: 60) among West India Seamen, "1470 deserted or were discharged .... Only 610 seamen out of the whole number deserted or were discharged yet found their way out of the colonies; ... that 860 yet remain to be accounted for in the expenditure of the year 1786." These figures, reinforced the view that mortality rates were high aboard these "frigates of death," and, once tricked, sailors seemed to want to get out of the business themselves. Still, and also important, not all sailors were shanghaied and money was being made by the investors, whose mantra was "Buy low, sell high!" Imagine!

More importantly, however, was the high incidence of deaths among the Africans, victimized in this Atlantic Slave Trade's forced migration, being the subject of centuries of psychological and physical assaults that was transmitted through the emotional and DNA gene pool for generation after generation. In 1788, Clarkson called for "Efficiency of Regulation of the Slave Trade" because of its effects on both victims in the trade, Africans and Europeans. He supplied particularly interesting data on the subject of mortality. In his evidence, sailors' testimony show regarding slaving escapades, "we purchased 350 slaves and buried 61; in a second voyage, in the same ship, we purchased 350, and buried 200; and in ... we purchased 370 and buried 100 .... We purchased 700 slaves and lost 250 ... we purchased 300, out of which we buried 17 ... 350 were purchased, and 25 were lost as before.... about 500 were purchased, and 150 buried."

Most deaths were due to overcrowding and the inhumanly intolerable conditions of the voyage. Practically, the physical, emotional and psychological cruelty of slavers was significant factors Africans had to reckon with. Victimizers also became victims of conditions they themselves created.

In the end, the African personality, emotional, physical, psychological, was denuded and broken from this horrible experience. Or, as the Afrocentrists would say, the Africans were "detached, isolated, and de-centered." Arriving in the West Indies the African was again debased. There, a final merciless legislative act transformed him into chattel or property. For example, *Report of the Lords' Committee of Council* ... 1789, Part III, in Jamaica, slaves were considered as property as indicated Anno 1696 Act 38: XL.... "That no slave shall be free by becoming Christian; and for payment of debts and legacies, all slaves shall be deemed and taken as all other goods and chattels are in the hands of executors or administrators; ... all children of slaves, born in the possession of tenant for life or years, shall remain or revert."

Again, in Jamaica, *Anno* 1719, Act 67: V..., "no Negro, mulatto, or Indian slave shall hire themselves out to work, either ashore or on board any ship or vessel, boat, ferry, canoe...every such slave so offending, shall be whipped at the discretion of any magistrate in the parish or precinct where such slave or slaves shall offer themselves for hire."

In Barbados, slaves were also considered as property, for according to Act No. 94 of April 29, 1668, the "Negro slaves of this island shall be real estate .... all Negro slaves, in all courts of judicature and other places within this island, shall be held, taken, and adjudged to be estate real ... and shall descend unto the heirs and widow of any person dying intestate."

Again, in Barbados, January 1672, Act No. 178 was considered, "A declarative Act upon the act making Negroes real estate" and "that Negroes shall be deemed real estate and not chattels ... Negroes may be sued for and recovered by action personal ... Negroes continue chattel for the payment of debts."

Even further, on August 8, 1688, Act No. 329 states, "where any Negro or other slave ... shall suffer death then shall such justices and freeholders, colonels and field officers who adjudged such Negro or other slave to suffer death, immediately after sentence thereof given inquire by the best means they are able of the value of such Negro or other slave, in which value they shall not exceed the sum of five and twenty pound sterling .... tempt or persuade any Negroes or other slaves to leave their masters and mistresses ... adjudged to pay the master of the said Negro or other slave five and twenty pounds.'

On November 28, 1705, Act No. 516 read, "... for all Negroes and other slaves that shall be imported to this island and landed there, an importation or duty shall be paid, that the merchant or merchants ... pay into the treasurer of this island ... five shillings current money for each and every Negro or other slave imported, whether male or female, young or old ...."

Finally, a Supplemental Act was passed on February 7, 1715, No. 593 that read as follows: "Be it therefore enacted ... that no Negroes or other slaves whatsoever, which shall for the future be once imported into this island shall be exempted from paying the duty of five shillings a head, but such only which shall be within 48 hours exported in the same ship or vessel."

Therefore, the psycho-social ramifications of the centuries' old experience seemed to, and still, so significantly plague the survivors of the greatest of all tragedies, that Prof. Donna Richards Merimba Ani of Hunter College called The Maafa or "Great Enslavement" as "the basis of the Western World's Economic Development on the Backs of African people!"

Now, when President Obama referred to "mismanagement of the Zimbabwean economy" let us not forget the history that underlay the independence of that nation and the resistance to its independence that were instrumental in forcing President Mugabe into that direction of Zimbabwean financial hopelessness.

BN PHOTO - "PUSH!" "The Brothers" choose the youngest and "Push him" to carry the baton of survival of our people.

56. PRESIDENT OBAMA IN AFRICA II
BY
Dr. Fred Monderson

It is interesting how President Barack Obama visited Africa at different times to make two of his most significant addresses outside of the Continental United States. His Address in Egypt at Cairo University was designed to start a conversation, open a dialogue of mutual respect, mutual dignity "with the Muslim world." His speech at the Ghanaian Parliament in Accra was crafted to send a message to Africa and the world of America's intent to more closely engage the continent of his ancestral heritage. More particularly, to the African nations and their rulers, he insisted the will, interests and future of their people, their greatest resources, must be paramount if Africa is to emerge and play the significant role in world events that it is truly capable of. Recognizing China and other nations are making trade and investment headway in Africa, last year again Mr. Obama visited his father's homeland, Kenya; this time as President; and then on to Ethiopia, acknowledging the ancient nation state and its strategic east African location as an ally in the Middle Eastern conundrum and also reinforced America's ties with Egypt.

Yes, Egypt is in North Africa, it has always been there. Importantly, of all African nations, Egypt benefits most from the potency of the geographical detritus impregnated in the life giving Nile River flowing from inner Africa. The potentialities of cultural effluence from time immemorial has enriched, energized and revitalized that nation and its people in all aspects of their existence.

Ghana, in West Africa, is pivotal in the historical development of modern Africa for a number of reasons, and thus, was an ideal location for President Obama to make his first trip and historic address. The name Ghana piggybacks on the first of three medieval empires of Ghana, Mali and Songhai, which dominated Middle African history. This name was also significant in influencing modern Ghana's march to independence in 1957 and the symbolism it represented in Kwame Nkrumah's vision of an independent and united continental economic, cultural and social African government, shedding the shackles of colonialism.

BN PHOTO - Michael Hooper sits in "Good Company" at the **Roots Revisited** Table at the International African Arts Festival.

In the dreaded Slave Trade, Ghana became a principal transshipment point for enslaved Africans being forcefully embarked to New World plantation slavery. Elmira Castle, in Ghana, is one of many lining the West African coast where European marauders, in the age of "naked Imperialism" used their enormous canon power to fight off Atlantic competitors and when turned around, terrorized the surrounding countryside in their insidious effort to marshal, accumulate, house, and ship Africans through the "Door of No Return," to a life of unknown, yet unspeakable horrors far away.

It is interesting that President Clinton visited Ghana in the last years of his tenure and was shown in a photograph looking through the "Door of No Return." The same may be said for President Obama. The important question, however, is whether the guides informed these two Presidents "an American activist named Sonny 'Abubadika' Carson" reinterred his ancestor Samuel Carson, a US Navy Veteran of the War with Mexico (1845) here in Ghana, August 1, 1998, creating the "Door of Return." Now he is buried alongside a Jamaican slave named Crystal at Assin Manso, beside the river where the captives took their last bath before being shipped through the same and infamous "Door of No Return." In a significant and historic move, Mr. Carson opened the "Door of Return" so African Americans can visit the site for pilgrimage and connect with their ancestral roots in Ghana, as springboard to similar searches elsewhere in Africa. The guide's follow up question to Mr. Obama then should have been, 'Would you like to see the site of African American Pilgrimage at Assin Manso?' Naturally this never materialized particularly for security reasons.

America was essentially founded as a Christian nation and in that searing crucible, many un-Christian acts, such as the Slave Trade and Institution of Slavery were perpetuated against African people for centuries. In an age when people struggled with government to declare the Rights of Man and issue the Declaration of Independence, boasting of life, liberty and the pursuit of happiness as god given rights African people were denied much these universal principles were intended to achieve. Yet, in the religious contradiction in its founding principles, America struggled to evolve a level of tolerance so that through good works the American "melting pot" came to accept in its mix, Baptists, African Zionists, Moravians, Anglicans, Jehovah's Witnesses, Catholics, Jews, Muslims and atheists, all being allowed to practice their beliefs or non-beliefs, peacefully, in a society allowing religious tolerance.

BN PHOTO - The "Monderson Clan" gathered to celebrate the birthday of one of their own.

BN PHOTO - The "Cake" says much and so was very quickly dispatched.

Upon his arrival in Cairo, Egypt, Mr. Obama, true to his campaign promises, wanted to dispel the myth that America was at war with Islam, Muslims. This is because of the recent history of events that led to the war on terrorism and subsequent developments that saw Americans fighting in Iraq and Afghanistan, and equally, seeming to ignore the fundamentals of the Arab-Israeli conflict which is fueled by the Palestinian-Israeli issue. Currently Americans are fighting in Iraq and Syria, advising in Somali against Al-Shabab; in Nigeria against Boko Haram; and in search of the elusive Army of God in Central Africa. So, therefore, in his initial greeting to the audience at the Cairo University and to Muslims worldwide tuned in to the young American President who promised fundamental change in American relations with Islam and the world; he therefore began with the greeting "Salaam-Wali-Kom" to which the response was "Wali-Kom-Salaam," not only from the live audience, but one could imagine hearing it through the TV sets and radios emanating from the worldwide listening audience. He had struck a positively sensitive nerve in this initial and fundamental show of respect. Thus, he could say, "I bring you peace from Muslims in my country" and, having Muslim forebears himself, he had broken the ice! Today Donald Trump's calling card, to which he has recounted many, is "No Muslim Adherents Welcome" to these shores. Foolishly, the sweet music and fine wine served by this Pied Piper has drunken many who may in return be banned from the territories with one quarter of the world's population whether for trade, tourism or even to visit family "back home"

Seeking to defuse the time of tension, and being "proud to carry the good will of the American people," he reflected on the "historical conflict" rather than cooperation colonialism had generated between the Arab/Muslim world and the West, and particularly America. Thus, Mr. Obama wanted to create a new beginning in America's relations. Significantly, as a student of history he emphasized that Islam has always been a part of American history and that American Muslims have enriched American history. Then he went on to boast of "civilization's debt to Islam."

Here Mr. Obama spoke of a "partnership based on what Islam is, not what it isn't." He also sought to make it clear "America is not the crude stereotype of a self-interested empire" and that it's been shaped by events and people who contributed much to shape its creed, "Out of Many One."

BN PHOTO - Manny and Josh (left); and Josh and Aunty Mavis (right).

Here again he emphasized, "Let there be no doubt, Islam is a part of America," and that "words alone cannot meet the needs of our people." Equally, with that astute historical perception, he stated clearly as a remindful warning to so many, at home and abroad, "Any world order that elevates one nation or group over another will inevitably fail." Perhaps the Trumps will learn a thing or two. Here he particularly referenced and spoke against the issue of "violent extremism in all its forms" and that "America will relentlessly confront all extremism which poses a grave threat to our security." It can be reasoned he meant domestic and foreign terrorism. Reiterating the now known fact, President Obama pointed out, "Al Qaeda killed over 3000 people on 9/11" and America in response "partnered with a coalition of 46 nations" to which "Afghanistan demonstrates America's goals and our need for better relationship." However, unlike the rapid withdrawal from Iraq and the devastating consequences, Mr. Obama has promised to retain a significant American military presence in Afghanistan.

Next Mr. Obama dealt with the "Palestinian-Israeli issue" and emphasized his early dispatch of an envoy to the region, the recognition of a "two state' solution "and the need to end the construction of settlements," all while reiterating and reassuring "America's commitment to Israel" and the need to guarantee its "safe and inviolate borders." This issue, however, has been an intractable one; given so many forces impact the conflict between two peoples, Israeli and Palestinian.

BN PHOTO - Always the "Ladies Man," Michael Hooper sports "Stolen From Africa" T-Shirt (above); and again Mr. Hooper shakes hand with a friend.

By the time he ended, commentators agreed this was the "most powerful and most persuasive speech of any President to the Muslim world." They further pointed to Mr. Obama's "emphasis on soft power rather than hard power," and that this represented an "important shift in America's relations with the Muslim world." Commentators again believed, in this respect he had gained "enormous political capital around the world."

President Obama treated, "any attempt to deny the Holocaust ever occurred as criminal behavior." He cited his great uncle, Charles Payne of the 89th Infantry Division, who was an eyewitness in liberating one of the death camps, Again, like Mr. Obama, "the New York activist Sonny Carson's uncle was a member of one of the first Black units to liberate one of the death camps." At a later date, after a visit to Russia, the President arrived in Ghana, West Africa, and addressed the Ghanaian Parliament in a message carried continent-wide. The essential message of his address is that Africa's future is in Africa's hands. "Africa does not need a strong man; it needs strong institutions;" and that Africa's "ruling elites have not thought of reinvesting in the well-being of the masses" of its people, its greatest asset.

Critics wondered why the President chose Ghana instead of Kenya, land of his paternal heritage. Clearly, as Secretary of State Hillary Clinton would later indicate, corruption is rife in Kenya and thus this would have been an unlikely venue for the President to have given such an important speech. However, the stated reason why Ghana was chosen is that it has a functioning democracy with easy transfer of power as evident recently following the last election. Notwithstanding this reality, the role of the military cannot be overlooked, some scholars have argued with "foreign interference" in overthrow of Prime Minister Kwame Nkrumah, Ghana's first elected leader and the names Adjai, Achaempong, and finally Jerry Rawlins, who, incidentally was in the audience, as part of Ghana's troubling past image of "Neo-colonialist" activism. Mr. Obama, in is ultimate visit to Kenya before moving on to Ethiopia decried the "Myth of the Strong man" who is the only one who could keep the nation safe. To this he reminded; Africa needs strong institutions not strong men!" To many long-in-service politicians he implored, "Retire, you're already rich," referring to their "raiding the cookie jar" of the national treasury, rather than training young leadership to move the nation forward.

President Obama, nevertheless, seemed to be building upon the little publicized initiatives in Africa begun by Presidents Clinton and Bush. In America's catch up in Africa, President Obama hoped to challenge major nations such as China who have been making investment inroads on the continent rich in natural resources. China, for its part, has a significant head start since the days of building the Tan-Zam railroad free of charge and having been an active supporter in the struggles against Apartheid in South Africa, Rhodesia and South-West Africa (Namibia.) Mr. Obama, on the other hand, because of his African American heritage, this appears helpful for his new initiatives of bringing Africa into the hub of global commerce. In addition, terrorist infiltration of the African continent and East African ports as naval operational points for military action in the Middle East and Pacific, are issues that drives America's new interest in the long neglected Africa continent. However, he could not emphasize this new involvement without speaking out against corruption, nepotism, mismanagement and inefficiency in Africa as well as the disruptive nature of civil wars and lack of fundamental respect for the rights of Africa's citizens. It is a conundrum that Africa is a resource powerhouse, yet its people are economically impoverished and not well served. This is the theme he emphasized when he later visited both Kenya and Ethiopia.

The practical and diplomatic side of his visit over, the President began an emotional tour of the slave dungeons of West Africa with his wife, children and mother-in-law, as Anderson Cooper of CNN reported on July 18, 2009. The President thought this was a "powerful moment for myself, Michelle and the girls." As he toured the slave castle dungeons and looked through the "Door of No Return," he equated it with his trip with Eli Wiesel to Buchenwald, a Holocaust site and felt "as if the walls could talk" creating a profound, shocking experience.

Acknowledging his wife Michelle as a descendant of slaves, Mr. Obama declared "people were willing to degrade others if they appeared different." Realizing a church was in the castle's yard, President Obama reflected, "Slave merchants may have loved their children and gone to that church above the dungeon."

Taken below to the "Door of No Return," he muttered, "Through this door the journey of the African American began" and expressed "profound sorrow must have been felt as people were hauled off to the great unknown." Dr. DeGruy in commentary reiterated this and revealed, these African victims "experienced profound emotional feelings from sorrow to rage."

The CNN Program's Host, Anderson Cooper of AC 360, mentioned "12-40 million people were forced to make the Middle Passage." This is somewhat inconsistent with conservative traditional doctrinal beliefs that 12-15 million were actually transshipped. In fact, W.E.B. DuBois in his 1896 Harvard PHD Thesis *The African Slave Trade to America - 1638-1888* gives a figure of "100 million souls lost to Africa."

These figures included dead and dying in the kidnappings and march to the shore, on shore in the holding pens and those thrown overboard in the trans-shipment. Let us not forget, March 9, 1732 when 132 slaves were thrown alive overboard in three sets and the ship's owners had the audacity to file for insurance coverage under a clause as "perils of the sea."

The dead and dying on shore was a significant factor in the equation. First of all, we were reminded by President Obama that the slave trade was "very, very big business controlled by royal families of Europe." Let us not also forget, New England merchants built ships and their seamen provided slaves for southern plantation owners. Also, New England merchants established a price of "140 gallons of rum for 1 male African; 120 gallons of rum for 1 female African; and 90 gallons of Rum for 1 pre-puberty female." We could also add the employment opportunities in boat building and ancillary trades as painters, barrel makers, makers of metal hoops that bind barrels, etc.

Not to omit the metal fetters that binds the African captive en-route to be slaves on "New World" plantations.

It is clear, profit motives required strict rules and punishments that were harsh and deadly; all designed to make examples of slaves; or as Terence Stampp in *The Peculiar Institution* indicated in a chapter "To Make Them Stand in Fear!" All manner of owner actions were designed to instill fear and trepidation among the slave lot. Among the many tools of intimidation used by perpetrators of the system in addition to a wide range of restraining devices, in vicinity of the "Door of No Return" were female slave dungeons and punishment cells in the slave castles. In the female slave dungeons, 150 women were packed in a single room. This was really eerie. The punishment cell was a death sentence for those about to die. With no ventilation, lighting, or relief facilities, the room contained a "foot thick of feces." The dungeon's odor coupled with the odor of feces, two centuries later is debilitating, imagine the psychological and emotional impact in the "fresh state" as the enslaved endured, some praying for death or "escape" through the "Door of No Return."

BN PHOTO - Congressman Hakeem Jeffries poses with a constituent.

From these horrible beginnings stem the historical disadvantages and misadventures African people in the Americas were victims of, for a long period of time. Yet, in the centuries long voyage of human degradation the African was forgiving same as the victims of historic Mother Emanuel Church in South Carolina who forgave the killer Dylan Roof, the executioner of 9 parishioners during a Bible Study session.

Out of the dungeon's hole, in the courtyard, President Obama reflected on his wife Michelle's slave roots. He spoke of her great, great, grand-father and great, great grand-mother Jim and Louisa Robinson who started in sprawling South Carolina, about 1850. These people were victims of, according to President Obama, "a terrible labor regime that was oppressive and created deep wound in our nation."

For much of his presidency, descendants of these Bible thumping Christians have been less than kind to President Obama. Essentially, from Ghana on the West African Coast, to Slave Street in Georgetown, South Carolina, the slave experience and its legacy of racial discrimination has imprinted with long lasting emasculating implications on the psychological and emotional well-being of slavery's institutional victims, African Americans. South Carolina, home of "Waterloo" Jim DeMint and "You Lie" Joe Wilson, was not only the largest slave port and market during the hey-day of the horrible trade and institution, right there in the middle of Jim Crow's shenanigans; and as late as recently Jesse Jackson criticized the state for having 36 state prisons and 1 state college. Nevertheless, as the 2016 presidential primary has taken off, South Carolina was projected to play a major role as a "Southern Firewall" and it did. However, many will admit, Donald Trump seems to be going down that same vicious path and carrying many of similar disposition staining America's hard won moral fiber.

BN PHOTO - Ms. LaRay Brown, Tony Martin, HHC Vice President, Jeromane Gaskin, the Honoree, Ms. Bolus, and Mr. George Proctor at 2015 Marje Matthews Health Care Activist Honors.

BN PHOTO - More Honorees at the 2015 Marje Matthews Health Care Activist Honors.

Yet, when all is said and done, President Barack Obama's trip to North and West Africa was a double pointed stroke of genius. In Egypt he was able to deliver a strong message designed to improve America's relationship with the Muslim world and in Ghana, critique Africa's leadership, while outlining preconditions for American assistance and partnership were key. At the same time, he shined the light on a dark chapter on Western and American slave history experience. While this article does not seek to examine the relations of foreign companies in ownership, extraction and price setting for Africa's natural resources and raw materials, suffice to say Europe, America and the West still undermines that area's economic structure. In his trip to Kenya and Ethiopia the President not simply talked about security issues but he brought entrepreneurs, businessman and engineers to talk about helping develop Africa's hydroelectric and other forms of potential all with promises to encourage our economic investment across the continent. One thing is unmistaken; President Obama created tremendous goodwill for American investors in Africa. However, and let us not forget Obama has railed against the role of corruption among African leadership that facilitates that resulting process of "under-development." Therefore, as a good faith broker, President Obama has focused on helping to help level the playing field in Africa's relationships to create a reliable partnership that will be able to extend dependable cooperation as world events become more complex and America seeks more "true friends."

BLACK NATIONALISM STILL ALIVE AND WELL

57. BOATING ON THE NILE
BY
DR. FRED MONDERSON

Boating on the Nile is one of the most exhilarating experiences I have ever had and the one at Aswan, Egypt, Monday October 5, 2015, is no different. The breeze for sailing was exquisite and the sail to photograph the feluccas, motor boats, cruise ships, docked and sailing, the Nubian villages, Movenpick Hotel (formerly Oberoi), the Old and New Cataract Hotels, even the "elephants grazing" at waterside and cartouches on the rocks as well as buildings along the Cornice and tombs of the Nobles and the Mausoleum of Aga Khan in the distance are all parts of a truly heavenly experience. Someone once remarked, "You will never believe what heaven looks like until you get there!" For visitors to Egypt, this is a new, sometimes even relived experience, but for the Nubians who ply the river in their sailing and engine crafts, this is a lived experience.

Come with me to Egypt on an Educational Tour, August 5-August 19, 2016 you will experience all the wonder, knowledge of an Educational Tour, a cultural excursion, a historical experience, a religious and spiritual epiphany and a photographic adventure beyond the wildest imagination to boast about, now until your grandchildren are aged.

Come, have and enjoy this wonderful experience with Dr. Fred Monderson **August 3-August 17, 2016**. Contact Orleane Brooks Williams at **Nostrand Travel Agency**, 718 Nostrand Avenue, Brooklyn, New York 11216. (718) 675-5300.

FREDERICK MONDERSON

BN PHOTO - Sonny Carson seems to be pondering his next move; and Chief Parker giving Sonny that memorable walk into the "Drummers' Grove" at Prospect Park where "Runaway Samuel Carson" was honored before departing for Ghana, West Africa.

One of this writer's professors always insisted begin at the beginning, remembering his "Cotton picking days," otherwise you end up double-backing on your efforts.

According to ancient Egyptian belief, when God Ra, the "Sun-God" was finished making the world the first thing he did was to make Nubians, Black people! He made those blessed Africans before he made Egyptians and most certainly before he made Caucasians and other Asians. Nevertheless, in his daily rounds across the celestial Nile, he sailed the "Boat of the Gods" with his companions and the two fishes as "Outriders" to thwart the designs of the evil god Apep who sought to impede Ra's passage through the underworld to arise on the horizon the next day. In as much as he continued to pour

BLACK NATIONALISM STILL ALIVE AND WELL

forth beautiful rays the god's security team continued to be proven successful. However, in the most ancient of days, the god perhaps rode on a "Ford Model-T," while today he probably upgraded to a "Cadillac with the Norstar system."

In the ongoing struggle to determining rightfully who exactly the ancient Egyptians were, among the many theories, mostly false, we were told the "Egyptians were a boat people." Suffice it to say, they have and still live on the Nile and as such, boats have been their principal means of transportation. However, while this argument is essentially; the others that Caucasians "for some unknown reason" "left their homes to settle a new fatherland" and "bringing a superior mental attitude;" confronted by reason, such falsity is nothing more than "Defense of a myth."

Nonetheless, and looking at this argument more realistically, one can easily reason:

1. These Caucasian migrants, much more than likely, did not know of Egypt, not know its location for as the old African proverb has held, "If you do not know where you are going, any road will take you there."

2. Nevertheless, to imagine these immigrants dragged boats across the desert is inconceivable. More so, to just navigate the desert then begin cutting down sparse Egyptian trees is actually unbelievable.

3. To cross the desert and arrive in Egypt, these individuals would have probably been thirsty, "desert whipped" and hardly be in a position to become white rulers and nobles lording it over a black population who did all the menial work which incidentally was creative!

FREDERICK MONDERSON

BN PHOTO - Eric stands before a beautiful patch of flowers representing "The Big Red One."

BLACK NATIONALISM STILL ALIVE AND WELL

BN PHOTO - The Message delivered, Reverend Al Sharpton departs Cadman Plaza Park after calling for Justice for Eric Garner.

4.   Notwithstanding, as Toby Wilkinson has shown in *Origins of the Pharaohs*, the earliest Nile Boats, certainly the boat of the gods were inscribed on the high rocks/wadis in the Eastern Desert of Upper Egypt in resting places between the Nile and the Red Sea. The most likely scenario is that these desert inhabitants, Africans, were pastoralists who moved their cattle back and forth to available watering holes at a time when rainfall was plentiful, the grass and agricultural produce bountiful until its source dried up and they eventually migrated into the Valley along the banks of the Nile between Abu Simbel and Aswan. The interesting thing is, while these earliest images were inscribed on walls in rest areas in the Eastern Desert, nowhere along the route, either in their places of origin in South West Asia along the passage is any such similar images. Are we to believe these "superior" visitors only thought of the idea of such images when they arrived in Africa and nowhere else?

The Petroglyphs in these cool, elevated rest areas, depict various forms of boats in the same shape we see in the mythology and plying the Nile with their Lotus bow and stern in pharaonic times, and some with replicas carrying individuals as a company of the gods, others with cabins and sometimes a colossal figure or two of some importance. Most important, Wilkinson dates these to at least "One thousand years before Winkler's Mesopotamians!"

5.   On the other hand, or should I say other shore, that is, the Western Desert, Bauval and Brophy discovered at Nabta Playa, a population of people who did essentially what their Eastern Desert counterparts did. In approximate opposite locations in Upper Egypt, at least one group possessed sailing boats, means it is not unreasonable they not simply plied the Nile but crossed over to visit their cousins. However, while the Eastern occupants left evidence of boats, their Western counterparts left scientific evidence of very early mapping the heavens, creating a calendar, pursuing pastoral

and agricultural endeavors, religiously worshipping a "Mother Goddess," and left evidence of migrating back and forth with their cattle same as did their counterparts across the river did. Even though it was a tremendous task to reach their location in the Western Desert, the authors discovered at least one Old Kingdom cartouche inscribed among rocks in their location and reasoned, because they determined and labeled these occupants of the Western Desert the precursors of the pharaohs, it was a case of migrants reaching back to their place of origin seeking their "roots!" No such counterpart exists from whence the Caucasians came!

Strange that the Egyptians have no knowledge of their Caucasian or Asiatic origin which is actually a figment of the 19th Century, racist, imperialist, colonialist mind, again as "Defense of a Myth" perpetuated by bigots who claim to be experts on Egypt but never fully answer Dr. Diop's contentions and conclusions in *African Origin of Civilization*: *Myth or Reality*. Nevertheless, as the argument holds, when the Western Desert began to dry up and could no longer sustain their lifestyle of agriculture and pastoralism, the occupants migrated east and settled in the Aswan vicinity of the First Cataract. This geographical designation in itself is a falsity because numbering the Cataract along the flow of the Nile; the First Cataract should in fact be the Sixth Cataract. An inherent problem of the European mentality concerns its propensity to name things and people. This came about as Europeans ascended the Nile they named the Cataracts as they encountered them with the first being at Aswan and the sixth nearer the source. It is not altogether difficult to envision the Nile God setting out from his source and encountering the first area with rocks in the water, exclaiming, "I will name you the Sixth Cataract." Next he encounters the other and again states, "I will name you the Fifth Cataract, until he gets to the Aswan Area and says "I will name you the First Cataract." So, whose numbering system one has to believe, the European numbering system as they ascended the Nile River or the god and the cultural flow descending the river. Thus, no one speaks to this and the many other contradictions that seek to dispossess the

BLACK NATIONALISM
STILL ALIVE AND WELL

Africans and helps Europe kidnap Egypt and Africa as they did through imperial and colonial machinations.

Pardon the digression but the problem is not as simple as it sounds for it re-occurs at Karnak temple with the numbering of the pylons. Follow me on this!

The First Pylon is actually the last pylon. The Fourth Pylon is actually the First Pylon and the Fifth Pylon is the Second Pylon, while the Seventh is the Third and the Sixth the Fourth. The Eighth Pylon is the fifth. The Third Pylon is the sixth and the Second is the seventh. The Ninth and Tenth Pylons are actually Eighth and Ninth, while the first is actually the tenth. This confusion stems from the European ascent into the temple for as he encountered them he named the pylons. The same phenomenon occurred in determining "The King's Chamber" and "The Queen's Chamber" in the Great Pyramid. We see the same scenario at Amarna, only this time, "The Master Bedroom" turned out to be "The Queen's Bedroom."

FREDERICK MONDERSON

BN PHOTO - District Leader of the 43rd Assembly District, Honorable Jeffrey Davis and his mother exit First Baptist Church of Crown Heights after paying respects and extolling Clarence Norman, Sr., iconic pastor in Crown Heights for many decades.

Standing at Abu Simbel Temple of Rameses II and looking out at the magnificent Lake Nasser, one is reminded of the circumstances surrounding construction of the Aswan Dam when UNESCO appealed to nations with a history of Nile valley archaeological excavation to participate in the Nubian Rescue operations to save Nubian temples that would be lost with the creation of the lake. While other nations sent their representatives to so engage, the University of Chicago's team under Keith C. Seele, suffices to say, discovered at Qustol and secreted in the University Museum's basement, what the Graduate student Bruce Williams revealed was evidence, as printed in *The New York Times* newspaper in 1971, of "The World's Earliest Monarchy found in Nubia."

Hence we are left with the scenario that either the people of the Eastern Desert who left evidence of boats "A thousand years before Winkler's Mesopotamians" or those of the Western Desert who settled the Cataract area, are the ones who created the Ta-Seti kingdom and its pharaonic iconography c. 3400 B.C. that appears some 200 years later in Egypt manifesting as either Toby Wilkinson's title states, *Origin of the Pharaohs* or Brophy and Bauval's *Black Genesis* that dubs the Nabta Playa inhabitants, "Precursors to the Pharaohs."

1.   Narmer's armada descended the Nile from Thebes to conquer and unify the land.

2.   Every other conqueror, Mentuhotep II, Sekenenra-Tao, Kamose, Ahmose, Amenhotep I, Thutmose I, Thutmose III, Seti I, Rameses II, Hatshepsut's emissaries to Punt and Senmut's descent of the Nile with the Queen's obelisk, Amenhotep IV moving to Amarna, Tutankhamon's return to Thebes, Horemhab's ascending the Nile to Karnak to be crowned, Rameses I to build his pylon, Seti I to campaign and return victorious with captives to Karnak.

BLACK NATIONALISM STILL ALIVE AND WELL

Rameses II from the Delta to Abu Simbel and Rameses III battling the "People of the Sea."

Piankhy's descent of the Nile to be crowned at Heliopolis; Shabaka, Taharka, even the reverse of Assyrians, Persians and again Assyrians to sack Thebes.

Greek and Roman conquerors.

The Arabs, Napoleon, the British, Belzoni, Champollion.

Dr. Ben-Jochannan and Dr. Fred Monderson.

Voyage of Hathor from Dendera to Edfu and back.

Voyage for the Opet Festival from Karnak to Luxor and back.

Voyage to celebrate "Feast of the Valley" across the Nile at Thebes.

Voyage of the deceased to Abydos to symbolically be buried near the "Great God."

Hatshepsut's Punt expedition returning laden with produce.

Obelisks being transported down the Nile from Aswan.

Transporting stone for large scale building projects at high tide of Inundation.

All used boats as forms of transportation, so why can't the Africans, but instead migrants across the desert gets this credit.

So come go on an Educational Tour of Egypt on August 5-August 19, 2016 and not simply enjoy the joys of the temple and tombs, partake of the wonderful fare of food, enjoy the ambiance but more importantly, cross the Nile and boat in joyous splendor aboard feluccas, certainly at Aswan but also at Luxor, and if possible at Cairo.

BN PHOTO - Baskets and other forms of creative art that appeals to the many-sidedness of art lovers.

58. PO BEN CARSON!
By
Dr. Fred Monderson

The Republican presidential contender Ben Carson has been fading fast into oblivion which forces campaign watchers to question whether it's the man, his policies or lack thereof, or the other contenders, even the political party and its causes he so adamantly supports. At one point recently, he so challenged the Republican front-runner Donald Trump, almost eclipsing his lead in Iowa, Mr. Trump remarked flamboyantly, "The people of Iowa must be stupid to vote for Ben Carson." Now, a serious problem of Donald Trump, he utters controversial statements that encourage equally controversial analyses to determine beyond the braggadocio and

BLACK NATIONALISM STILL ALIVE AND WELL

brinksmanship he projects, how insidious is his meaning and to whom is he sublimely speaking. However, the problem with Ben Carson on the other hand, is medically he is a genius; street wise he is an idiot. There was another Carson, Sonny; medically he was an idiot; street wise, he was a genius. In none of these categories Ben matched up to Sonny; but given his other baggage, one can easily recognize this comet as it fades into the oblivion in the great politic cosmic void.

In his new political career, the retired Neurosurgeon Ben Carson came out like a new penny, but once in circulation, he became tarnished and quickly lost his "spring chicken" luster. Mr. Carson first took the stage speaking out on Republican issues and soon earned spokesman status. Caught up in the vortex of conservative, Republican and Tea Party stone-throwing, Mr. Carson attacked President Obama, criticizing his Affordable Care Act law facetiously nicknamed "Obamacare," because that was the "flavor of the months." For such a bold move, calling "Obamacare worse than slavery," Mr. Carson had "arrived" and he was truly elevated by having his photograph engraved front page on the Heritage Foundation website. The next step was to declare for the Presidency as a Republican candidate. Unfortunately, there were 16 other candidates and there stood Dr. Carson among the contenders, proudly, as a fly in buttermilk, and uttering the "right wing party line."

FREDERICK MONDERSON

BN PHOTO - Cherise Maloney of Brooklyn, there to be a part of the celebration in remembrance of Sonny Carson.

The cold, callous and calculated attack on President Obama's health care law was like burning one of the bridges to his cultural heritage as a Black man. However, thinking Blacks were in synchrony with Jesse Jackson, when back in 2009 at Mr. Obama's Inauguration the Reverend declared, Mr. Obama is, "The best the Civil Rights movement has to offer." Now, imagine individuals as Donald Trump burning the airwaves with a distorted pliant, "Obama has not done anything for the Blacks!" Conversely, one of his adamantly supporting converts, blurted "Obama has done too much for the Blacks!" What a contradiction and one wonders whether the vast majority of this Pied Piper's followers can untangle this complex yet distorted thought. However, astute Blacks never subscribed to the panacea that electing a Black man to the Presidency would solve many of the problems facing Black people in this country, since it never did with the 43 preceding white men who held the office. These same observers, analysts and commentators, from the inception have examined the spiritual and psychological warfare waged by the people Mr. Carson is now curled up in bed with, especially given they way-laid the first African-American President of this great Republic.

Again, objective observers have taken note of and applauded Mr. Obama's many efforts to help Americans, not particularly Blacks, in various forms as a jobs bill; rescuing the auto industry to maintain American market share and equally save American jobs; bailing out banks tottering on the brink of bankruptcy; lending a hand to Wall Street financial wizards; seeking to infuse life into the housing industry drowning in foreclosure and stalled building construction starts; encouraging Silicon Valley to continue its creative breakthroughs; breaking ground in Research and Development in new and clean energy sources of a renewable nature; being more concerned about climate change; even encouraging mothers to return to college and seeking to emphasize community colleges as a vehicle to generate a more technically

BLACK NATIONALISM STILL ALIVE AND WELL

trained workforce to meet future needs and expectation of the nation. In all these initiatives, "The Blacks" benefitted relative to their proportion in the population as did the greater percentage even though the "Party of No" not only mined the field but blocked every initiative of the President. Fact is, Blacks were so far behind in job acquisition no matter how they fared in the new setting they still remained behind. Nevertheless, only Mr. Obama's vastly superior intellect, his tremendously focused and effective work ethic, aided perhaps through divine intervention on behalf of the American people because Barack Obama stood at the helm of the ship of state enabled America to still progress. Nevertheless, this is the same god Republicans pray to; but as he listens he does not seem to hear the pliant, nor prayer of Republican hypocrites who make every effort to derail the many benefits Blacks were to be given and received from an Obama Presidency empowered as his efforts benefitted the nation.

Notwithstanding, as all this unfolded, not once did Mr. Carson raise a voice or finger in protest or in ethical condemnation as men of questionable aims and intent lambasted the President; some agree much of this was because of his race and tenacity to run, win, stand up and be counted, make policy, deliver the State of the Union Address, command the troops and represent the nation abroad alongside his beautiful wife and partner, the "Mighty Michelle."

As the various factions of the Republican Party labeled Mr. Obama, "Nigger," "Nigger in the White House," and given they associate blackness with such degradation, not only did Mr. Carson not stand up for Mr. Obama, he probably felt, "He's a Nigger, but I'm not!"

However, the Ethiopian Emperor Haile Selassie's 1936 dictum, "Today for me, Tomorrow for you!" may very well materialize in regard this particular Washington, DC political and racial scenario. In the current contest, while Mr. Carson may have started out as a cultural "nice boy" many soon realized he did not have the street smarts and the propensity for treachery proving so indispensible in the unfolding presidential and political party dynamics.

FREDERICK MONDERSON

There is something about the Republican Party that seems to proffer an anti-Black posture that despite the camouflaged masquerade, "sinister pies" are baking in the inner chambers. A credible argument can be made if *The New York Times* article of October 6, 2013 is used as a penetrating example. Mr. Carson's love affair with the Heritage Foundation did not spring to life yesterday and considered "a soldier," one wonders was he in the loop of the "Stop Obama" "treasonous gathering" in which some 20 NGOs including his Heritage Foundation as well as former Ronald Reagan Attorney General Ed Meese were mentioned as participants in planning and dispensing disinformation about Obamacare and other Obama policies. Was he preview to this "treasonous gathering" that sought to thwart the policies of the legally constituted U.S. government under an Obama Administration? As a legal and law enforcement issue, was Dr. Carson involved, was he knowledgeable of the action and intent, and if so, why did he not speak out or advocate for arrest and incarceration of those involved rather than encourage an "under the rug" solution.

Mr. Carson needs be reminded about the history of his political party. That is, from its Post-Civil War "Radical Republican" nomenclature; it's championing of the 13th, 14th, 15th Amendments as protections for the Freedmen; despite Black wholesale "Party of Lincoln" voting until 1932 Blacks languished under "Jim Crow" laws that aided the KKK as an American institution. All helped facilitate Public lynchings, lack of jobs and even economic peonage under sharecropping tenant farming. From 1932 with Blacks bolting the Republican Party to remain loyal Democrats to this day; in response practically every conceivable "trick" and action has been used to disfranchise Blacks at the Ballot box aided by escalating incarceration wherein Blacks and other minorities comprise the greatest number of the US prison population. Yet, Dr. Carson said or did nothing in this respect. We must always remember as Edmund Burke believed, "The only thing necessary for evil to triumph is for good men to do or say nothing." By these precepts, given his deafening silence, the question then become, 'Is Dr. Carson a good man?'

BLACK NATIONALISM
STILL ALIVE AND WELL

As such then, and having served his purpose as a Republican "hit man" who failed miserably in denting President Obama's Teflon armor, Mr. Carson will probably go by way of the "Do Do Bird," but more especially like Michael Steele, Allen West, J.C. Watts, Alan Keyes, all hired "hatchet men" who failed miserably at their tasks and were fired or allowed to fade into the "black hole of Republican Party oblivion." The interesting realization, however, is the potency and leadership President Obama brought to his responsibility that not simply has aided America across the national landscape but equally vanquished so many Republicans of statue, he forced them into retirement or simply to have them "change their call numbers." In all this, Dr. Ben Carson simply stands in line to be another victim of the Obama political skill apparatus.

BN PHOTO - The iconic "Black Mother," who from time immemorial has been nursing the divine child.

FREDERICK MONDERSON

59. THAT OBAMA LEGACY
By
Dr. Fred Monderson

Fresh from the significant agreement at the recent Climate Change Conference, reality dictates observers and history commentators consider Barack Obama's legacy constantly and positively unfolding as his presidential term winds down. No time in American history has the nation been more challenged than when Barack Obama captured the Presidency in 2008! Since, in assessing the times and the man, Noble Economic Laureate Paul Krugman, writing in *The New York Times* declared Barack Obama "The Greatest President Ever!" Naturally, both Mr. Krugman and President Obama were the subject of enormous "pushback" especially from Republicans, viz., right wing and media conservatives; Tea Party operatives in and out of Congress; political operatives on a mission in the persons of then Senate Minority Leader Mitch McConnell and House Speaker John Boehner; ex-Alaska Governor Sarah Palin; Representative Michele Bachmann; former Senator Jim DeMint; the disrespectful South Carolina Representative Joe Wilson, who, in the House during the President's State of the Union Address, in response to a statement blurted out, "You lie;" the Arizona Pastor "Praying for Obama's Death" and his misguided parishioner, the "Black Protester with Guns," himself unable to understand the full dynamics of the issue and his role; to this we may add the late comers "Daddy Cruz" and his erstwhile son Senator Ted Cruz and of course the never to be forgotten Heritage Foundation's "Poster Son" Dr. Benjamin Carson, the retired neurosurgeon.

As the subject of the assessment that Mr. Obama was, like Mohammed Ali, "the Greatest Ever," Mr. Krugman called it as he saw the reality and projection of the man, the burden of the office and how intellectually skillful he effectively carried forth his responsibilities accomplishing success after success. After all, to

BLACK NATIONALISM STILL ALIVE AND WELL

win a Noble prize means the individual possesses an extraordinary intellectual capacity and potential to assess fully the highest and most complex issues and what is higher than the responsibilities given the Presidency of the United States. President Obama, on the other hand, was vilified for more insidious reasons than piloting the ship of state successfully through the perilous waters in which he inherited the nation's mantle and into the calm seas and overhead blue skies wherein he sailed his craft. Yes! Today, when we observe the bigotry and racism spewing from lips such as Donald Trump, regarding Muslims, immigrants, Mexicans, how he views President Obama, Secretary of State John Kerry, Mrs. Hillary Clinton, etc., the manner in which not simply Trump's supporters among Republican Evangelical Christians and others, we ask, 'Are they Christians?' 'Do they speak for Jesus?' Or, 'are Trump and that brand of his supporters hypocritical opportunists?'

BN PHOTO - Art, as beauty, is in the eyes of the beholder, and whether for decorative or adornment purposes, African Art can take its place among the best of all such human creations.

It is interesting, how none of the Republican candidates for the Presidency in 2016 has uttered a word regarding the unfolding

FREDERICK MONDERSON

Black social situation the **Black Lives Matter** movement keeps emphasizing across the nation. Mr. Carson has not uttered a word for or against, nor has the insulting Donald Trump. Perhaps it is because they have no intention to help, perhaps can't do anything about it; or, even more important, as the great visionary Malcolm X once recognized, "The nation is so evenly divided, polarized, the Black vote can make the difference between who goes to the White House and who goes to the dog house!" Therefore, "don't disturb the Black waters; perhaps they may not rise!" For, remember the story of the "blind white guy who went to see a championship boxing match!" He was accompanied by a guide who gave him blow-by-blow commentary as the fight unfolded. As the event waged into the late rounds, the blind man asked, "What's happening now." His commentator responded, "The White guy has the Black guy down!" "The Black guy down? Keep him down, for when the Black man raises, hell raises!" However, with all the publicity Republicans are currently generating, this is hardly likely and the next election will certainly have to contend with the influence of the Obama legacy because the genii is now out of the bottle.

Very early Mr. Obama took the high road in stride regarding attacks on his person, simply exclaiming, "I know politics is a contact sport." However, when it came to attacks on his wife, he stared boldly into the camera and warned, "If you're watching, lay off my wife!" As with addressing all unconscionable bullies, the message was well received. Important, instead of wilting under the huge climate of disrespect and racial hatred generated towards him because of his race, he continued to strategize and effectively continued to rack up "wins" in areas benefitting the American people.

First he proposed women, especially moms, return to college to develop skills needed in a changing economic environment he was moving the country towards. Then he emphasized a more upgraded role for community colleges. Recognizing that student loan is a problem for students and graduates, Mr. Obama directed efforts to help alleviate some of the burdens that keep accumulating. Financial and economic policies eased the job situation with many

BLACK NATIONALISM STILL ALIVE AND WELL

millions of new job hires impacting areas as Wall Street, empowering citizen's purchase of automobiles thereby increasing the industry's market share with the strategies carrying over into strengthening the President's position in securing favorable terms in the Asian Trade Agreement deal. In wake of the immigration reform issue for long stalled, President Obama issued an Executive Order easing the burden on undocumented youth brought to these shores when young by parents themselves undocumented, giving them an opportunity to serve the nation in the military and the promises this patriotic act represented.

BN PHOTO - Well, take your pick, for they all convey art and spirituality in the creative hand of a master craftsman.

60. RALLY AROUND BARACK!
By
Dr. Fred Monderson

"Time will tell" is full of merit and without a doubt; we must now "Rally around Barack" because he has proved he has earned the credits to certainly be considered one of the great Presidents of the United States of America, certainly for this new century. Such a view is credible for a number of reasons including Mr. Obama's full-fledged grasping and grappling with the economic and domestic issues and handling the international conditions facing the nation. Unquestionably, despite all the negativism, he seems to be prevailing in his vision. However, unlike the woman at his town hall meeting who publicly criticized the President and he took it smiling while the *New York Post* and such ilks gave her unprecedented coverage, front page and all, because as an African American she dared to call out the President; many supporters who understood the big picture never wavered in their support and such loyalty now seems to be paying just deserved rewards, as the merits of Barack Obama's strategy and unrelenting hard work ethic continues to unfold. As a matter of fact, while this appeal was first issued during the early years of his presidency, it is just as relevant today as he winds down his tenure. It is just as relevant for his legacy and the significance of his experience and vigilance beyond his term in office.

Perhaps the farmer with his conception of the agricultural season requiring the process of tilling the field, planting the seeds, watering the ground, weeding the shoots and allowing the plants to bud, grow, develop and mature for the harvest could identify with the genuine efforts demonstrated by Mr. Obama. Opponents, competitors, critics and even "haters," on the other hand, have shown their true colors of contempt in the unrelenting attacks on Barack Obama from the time he demonstrated audacity to run for the Presidency of the United States. This bold move for a Black man to run for the Presidency and serve with distinction called into question a number of factors global observers used as a yardstick to evaluate the presumed state of America in the young century. Through his seven years as Head of State, Chief Legislator, Commander-In-Chief and man of the people, in wake of "opposition scorched earth" methods, the words of Edmund Burke in his *Reflections on the Revolution in France* (1792) that "The only thing necessary for evil to triumph is for good men to say nothing" rings true today, as it related to assaults on the integrity of the Senator and now President Barack Obama and for that matter the Office of the Presidency which he represents and uphold. When we reflect on the inhuman characterization of Barack Obama in the "birth of the Tea Party movement" and the unrelenting assaults on

BLACK NATIONALISM STILL ALIVE AND WELL

his human, civic and intellectual personality as represented by the "Birthers Movement" one has to wonder about the deafening silence of those leaders, men of conscience who claim to speak to and for America. Add to this the secretive treasonous gathering of high echelon Republican operatives and the bold and unmistaken confession of then Senate Minority leader Mitch McConnell, "I intend to make Barack Obama a one-term President," was starkly racist as Morgan Freeman boldly affirmed on Piers Morgan.

Principal among questions stated and unstated were whether America was ready for a Black President? This was answered in the most unquestionable fashion. Could a Black effectively run such a major entity as the United States government? The successes he chalked up, answered in the affirmative. Was he sufficiently experienced to contend on the world stage as a major statesman? Consistently he remained in step with the major players on the world stage. Could his new face and voice change the world's image of America, particularly in view of its perception over the last decade or so? It certainly did, and, even more important could Barack Obama run a credible campaign to be elected President of the United States? This he did twice! As demonstrated to all observers, the answer to the last question was the unleashing of a well-orchestrated surprise machine that snowballed in organizational sophistication as he took his opponents down a "dusty road," and the rest is known re-election history.

FREDERICK MONDERSON

BN PHOTO - Sculpture, whether in wood, stone or metal, has been the backbone of all African Art because it conveys a social and spiritual message.

Pitfalls along the way included that nascent "Tea Party" movement working within the Republican Party that vindictively characterized the intelligent gentleman candidate Barack Obama who, is not only organizationally gifted but has remained glued with his "eyes on the prize," looking "straight ahead" and ignoring "Cat calls" while working feverishly at his task. Yet, as Barack took no action towards such behaviors, some clamored "we want our country back" because he is "not like us." Equally they though he was "inexperienced" and even after being elected, he was soon "challenged" by nation states' "bad boys."

All the while the President set out tackling the problems he inherited. Even more sinister, given the domestic and global mess bequeathed this new Chief Executive and Commander-in-Chief, the "Birthers" kept up their attacks. Black Republicans including Alan Keyes and the much publicized "Black Protester with guns" in Arizona whose church leader was "praying for Obama's death;" these were the most vocally sinister. Notwithstanding the latter state of affairs, in view of the task ahead of impending economic, financial and fiscal collapse desperately in need on monetary regulation, a hemorrhaging job market, foreclosures, etc., and with international ideological competition; to accuse the President of being unsuited for office was a blindsided attack that disrespected the institution of the Presidency and the man who held that office. Let us not forget the older attacks during the campaign of Mr. Obama of "not being a citizen," "unpatriotic," "too black," "not black enough," that he "forgot the name of a solder whose bracelet he wore" and to boot opponents rolled out "Joe the Plumber" who parroted a false notion that "Obama was a socialist." Yet, in time, the *New York Post*, in a political cartoon, showed Obama flushing "Joe the Plumber" down the bowl! Today the electorate seems fickle attracted to socialist Bernie Sanders and bigoted Donald Trump.

BLACK NATIONALISM STILL ALIVE AND WELL

Just as Obama's opponents could not honestly admit to the mess their Republican cohorts had created in the American economic, financial, international and political climate, even Mr. Obama did not, at first, comprehend the size of the mess he inherited. Nevertheless, he set about tracking the problems requiring banking and financial and economic reforms; as well as paying attention to problems of housing starts and foreclosures; expressing concerns about jobs, health care and educational reforms; and touting the need for energy independence through innovative research and development of wind energy, energy from the sun, and new forms of batteries, all designed to reduce the nation's dependence on foreign oil. Couple this with the international situation, and the ramifications of two wars in Iraq and Afghanistan, as well as challenges posed by North Korea, Iran, the Middle East quagmire and the global threats of Al Qaeda and the potential of domestic terrorism, to not aid but tear down the President at this time was truly un-patriotic, un-American. In response Mr. Obama nailed Osama bin-laden.

BN PHOTO - African Art is the "Mother of All Art" because it sees the "Art of God in Man" or "Man as the Art of God."

We cannot forget during and after the campaign, physical threats to Mr. Obama increased manifold as right wing groups stockpiled military hardware to combat a falsely perceived and publicized threat Mr. Obama represented. Still, many American "leaders of repute" said nothing though law enforcement agents tightened their scrutiny so as to ensure the president's safety. Added to this, the *New York Post* printed a political cartoon showing two policemen shooting the President disguised as an ape. This action stirred the irony of particularly Obama's Black supporters and many liberal whites across the nation who never let the *Post* forget. Nevertheless, the President continued his tremendous efforts of fulfilling the functions of the many hats he wore.

Of course, the big assignments come to mind first: historic health insurance reform, even though he lost his biggest ally and champion of this bill, Edward Kennedy. The Affordable Care Act's passage was designed to rein in the insurance companies and help control the cost of care for millions of Americans; Wall Street reform, which put in place the toughest consumer protections ever enacted in Dodd/Frank that enabled the financial powerhouse to recover and prosper; the question of passage of the bill to close Guantanamo Bay prison and the move to begin trials of those incarcerated there experienced much "push and pull;" and bringing an end to combat operations in Iraq, which brought more than 100,000 troops home has in some respects backfired as ISIS rose to prominence. However, while Mr. Obama's opponents often blame him they grossly underestimated the narrow-mindedness and failure of Nuri Alaki, the Iraqi/Iran lackey, who betrayed the high ideals of statesmanship.

And there is so much more the Obama-Biden team helped achieve that is right now improving lives across this country: "The first act Mr. Obama passed as President was the Lilly Ledbetter Act giving women equal pay status as men."

The team passed the Recovery Act, which saved and created more than 3 million jobs at the time, provided the largest middle-class tax cut in a generation, and made landmark investments in clean energy, infrastructure, and education. Today, nearly 15 million private sector jobs were created across the board and more.

The Obama administration made critical investments in General Motors and Chrysler Corporation operational financing saving tens

BLACK NATIONALISM STILL ALIVE AND WELL

of thousands of jobs - and perhaps the companies - and spurring a rebirth of the American car industry which could have gone into oblivion. Instead this resulted in greater market share in the auto industry.

The administration wrote into law student loan reform and credit card reform, which ended the worst abuses of the banking industries and are making lending fair for American families.

BN PHOTO - Africans have always been "A boat People." We came by boat and must never forget our experiences then and now! This was particularly evident especially along the Nile River where water travel was the first mode of transportation.

The Barack Administration put two new Supreme Court justices on the bench - Sonia Sotomayor and Elena Kagan, who bring rich and diverse experiences to the Court and his re-election prepared the way for his Democratic successor as President will be able to add to choices on the Supreme Court. The potential of such an act irks many and has spurred much animosity towards the President and his potential successors.

FREDERICK MONDERSON

The Administration has begun to reset America's relationship with the international community, from the ratification of a new START nuclear arms treaty with Russia to tough new sanctions on Iran to strengthening America's long-term partnership with a unified Iraq and to engaging China to rein in its close ally, North Korea. Mr. Obama set in motion a vigorously negotiated dialogue with Iran backed by a significant coalition of states resulting in concessions in the Iran-Nuclear Dead, the world is satisfied with but Mr. Obama's enemies vigorously oppose.

The very thorny "Don't Ask, Don't Tell" legislation which was the right thing to do - not only because it makes the military stronger at a time when it needs to be the strongest, but because Americans are seeking that military might with an abiding sense of justice. This and more was accomplished in a two-year period. Then Mr. Obama advocated and pushed for the protections and benefits same sex marriages and gay and lesbian unions were entitled to.

BN PHOTO - Image from Rameses II's "Temple of the Hearing Ear" at the rear of Thutmose III's Festival Temple the *Akh Menu*.

BLACK NATIONALISM STILL ALIVE AND WELL

We do recognize the November mid-term election of 2010 and 2014 that saw Republicans regain the House of Representatives sent a strong message to the President and the Democrats that, despite what has been done to turn things around; the country wants to go in a new direction. Still, countering conventional wisdom by applying the great resources of his thinking economic and other forms of advisers particularly Paul Volker, as the economy began to improve, the President was able to wrangle a new tax-cut bill despite the lame-duck status of a Democratic Congress, though some have argued Republicans, despite their rhetoric about deficits are more interested in MONEY for the rich, their base, and for their re-election.

Like everything else, "time does tell" and the nation, like the enormous battleship that it is, has slowly begun to turn and as things unfold, Mr. Obama's numbers are improving. This is because the recession is over, businesses are hiring, unemployment rates have dropped, housing starts have increased, Mr. Obama has insisted, having pulled the economy back from the brink, he wants to put it in overdrive. With such efforts, the prospects of Mr. Obama's re-election were justified. While some have blamed the recent violent murders in Arizona on anti-Obama inspired rhetoric that seemed to motivate an unbalanced individual, the President went to Tucson to pay tribute to those victims and sent a powerful message of healing.

Following the terrorist Paris Attack and that one in San Bernardino he sadly had to again console the nation. Some have hailed his reconciliatory message designed to heal and unite the nation, so much so, one of his harshest critics and credible opponents Senator John McCain, came out and praised Mr. Obama's healing words, while Condoleezza Rice, former Secretary of State on CNN's Piers Morgan's new show remarked "Mr. Obama is a decent man and doing his best for this country." Therefore, it is time to "Rally around Barack" to show his detractors, supporters and the world, Mr. Obama is indeed a good man doing the best he can to turn the nation around and help it recover from the quagmire of the last decade. And, with this we rally and stand behind Barack Obama!

FREDERICK MONDERSON

61. DIVIDING THE COUNTRY
By
Dr. Fred Monderson

In response to a question regarding Marco Rubio's "Stumble" in the recent New Hampshire Republican Debate, Representative Jason Chavetz, (R. Utah) appearing on Wolf Blitzer's **Situation Room** repeated the tired pliant that "Obama is dividing the country." This is the tirade Rubio fixated on in his "stumble." Let's be fair, there is something wrong when every Republican sees Mr. Obama as wrong on every issue. This is "Group Think" mentality and this is a pathology. If Issa, Chavetz, Grassley, as for example, could hate with such passionate vehemence, this "coffee spills" and stains their "Lilly white shirts." Whoever is the plastic surgeon who

BLACK NATIONALISM STILL ALIVE AND WELL

worked over Issa did a very good job because for seven years the man seemed to need a serious facial makeover. But now in the driver's seat his smile rivals that of Donald McDonald. These Republicans won't compromise even when Obama tries to fix things, so who's "dividing the country?"

Certainly within recent memory Republicans have unleashed the most aggressively creative negative attacks on Democratic candidates and office holders from their win-no-matter-what playbooks. Remember Willie Horton and Dukakis being "soft on crime;" or "Swift Boat" of John Kerry. Fast forward to 2012, when the "soft on terror" label could not be leveled against Barack Obama, for he had captured and dispatched Osama bin-Laden. However, everyone is familiar with the numerous accusations unleashed in 2008 before and after Mr. Obama won and assumed the Presidency. These were, that "his policies were socialist;" he was "inexperienced;" could not really respond to the "3:00 AM phone call;" and more. Given the dynamics surrounding his person, the notion of "Dividing the Country" may very well have been in the works as Obama traveled the path to the Presidency. That is, if we consider the reality expressed on October 6, 2013 in *The New York Times* article in which a "treasonous gathering" was discussed as planning to undermine the legally constituted U.S. Government under the leadership of President Obama. In that article, Ed Meese, Ronald Reagan's former Attorney General, and an enumerated list of some 20 Republican NGOs were identified as being part of the planning process to "Stop Obama." One of the prongs of the strategy was to train young Republican operatives to traverse the country and "educate the public" about the negative aspects of the Affordable Care Act maliciously labeled "Obamacare." Many observers later slammed the disingenuous disinformation propagandized in this strategy in which Republicans have voted to repeal some fifty times and the Supreme Court upheld in two rulings making "Obamacare here to stay."

FREDERICK MONDERSON

Eric and Manny are dressed to go in **Times Square** where there is excitement all night.

However, the question remains 'who knew what and when did they know of the campaign?' to "stop Obama" as a strategy to create his "Waterloo." That is, such a massive broadside against the Presidency of the United States more than likely involved those in the highest echelons of the Republican Party, given the unanimous Republican voting record of "NO" against every measure Mr. Obama proposed, legislative or otherwise. Equally given Mr. Obama is quoted as saying, "If we can't compromise, we can't govern." As such, earning the title "Party of No" Republicans won't compromise and thus they can't govern. This means, all the senior "Anti-Obama Players" in and outside government must have known even if they had not "signed on the dotted line." Therefore, not compromising they have been unprecedented obstructionists even and particularly holding up many of the Presidents nominations. Then they blame him for using "Executive Action."

Nevertheless, we must consider, in the history and development of this country Blacks have been in step throughout with their shoulders firmly pressed against the wheel moving the nation forward. In that forward Progress, nonetheless, we have seen 43

BLACK NATIONALISM
STILL ALIVE AND WELL

white men serve as President through which concurrently African-Americans stood mightily among the military ranks, from the beginning, defeating the enemy, being wounded, many died, in every war this nation has fought under the President as Commander-In-Chief. When Barack Obama succeeded to that position, an insidious underbelly of elements, mainly Republicans, began painting him indiscriminately with a broad racist brush. Very probably, every conceivable name and accusation was in place in January 2009 when Mr. Obama took the oath of office.

"Queen Mother of the Slave Trade" Dr. Delores Blakeley greets Luis and Erik at "Sharpton's affair for President Obama."

During the Civil War, when northern recruiters went to North Carolina to recruit Blacks, Abraham Galloway, a Black Abolitionist, said "You want us to fight, here are our demands." Sadly, among others the "40 acres and a mule" were never delivered. Thus, given today's climate Blacks should fully assess the situation and similarly make demands especially for the vote and military service.

Close scrutiny will reveal the consistent claim "Mr. Obama is dividing the nation" but such merchants of disinformation have not been specific. Many wonder whether this division is among the rich and poor, Democrat and Republican, Black and White, or along religious lines. It is interesting, one of the claims leveled against Mr. Obama, to this day, is that he is a Muslim, in addition to not being American born. However, notwithstanding, in the early days of his national prominence he was accused of sitting in the pew for 20 years listening to Rev. Jeremiah Wright, who happens to be a Christian minister. This is just one example of the contradictions in the conundrum of the "Republican Anti-Obama arsenal" that makes him a Muslim worshipping in a Christian setting! Even today, while Chris Christie could point to Marco Rubio's rehearsed 25-second anti-Obama tirade; he too, disingenuously stopped short of "criticizing the message" as he "killed the messenger." The fact is every President and his administration has sought to put their stamp on the time duration of their term. More important, considering what he inherited as a Republican legacy, Mr. Obama has done more for this country than most, even though he does not get the true and full credit his efforts deserve. After all, he inherited a tremendous recession and a broadening economic crisis. Yet, emphasizing these accomplishments, National Committee, "There has been 72-months of job growth" under Obama, consistent efforts at "Gun control Legislation" and with the millions now assured of health care protections, he has strengthened the social "Safety Net." Nevertheless, the keen observation of Paul Krugman that Mr. Obama is probably the "greatest American President" may very well be the truest and most sincere statement ever made about his presidency which is based on accomplishments that are not fully publicized.

Notwithstanding, seeking to assess such accomplishments, who could properly gauge the long reach of the "treasonous gathering," since from day one, Militia groups began escalating arms purchases in preparation for an imminent race war that has not materialized to this day. Examining this poisonous propaganda, we conclude; imagine if you will, "Blacks won the Presidency" and they will still initiate a race war! This is another of those contradictions all Republican aspirants to the high office and their surrogates trumpet that encouraged the militia tirade even further. Observers noted

BLACK NATIONALISM
STILL ALIVE AND WELL

more than 90% of Mr. Obama's cabinet and appointments were white men and women. The totality of the thinking of the 17 Republican candidates in 2016 cannot name half as many qualified Blacks for positions in their administration. Time and time again it is stated, the President's job is to protect the nation from foreign and domestic enemies. This certainly includes "enemies" such as rising unemployment; foreclosures; bank failures; a car industry run into the ditch; crumbling infrastructure; teachers and first responders waiting nervously on the chopping block; the nation choking amidst the fog of air pollution; a world threatened by climate change; gas prices escalating at the pumps; the military stretched to combat two wars in Iraq and Afghanistan and numerous other engagements with terrorism foremost among this endeavor; the need for clean and renewable energy; domestic terrorism; racial discrimination and rampant minority incarceration; transportation fatalities; police brutality; militias threatening the government; domestic terror by lone wolves; and so on. Quite rightly, all people across all spectrums of the nation were affected by these maladies and they equally benefitted from the application of the prescription that Mr. Obama and his team instituted to address these problems.

Just prior to the state of New Hampshire voting, John Kasich recounted his complaints to Arnold Schwarzenegger that he was being "beaten-up by critics" and the Gubernator simply responded, "Love the beatings!" However, Republicans were upset Mr. Obama did not "love the floggings" they unleashed on him. He was more focused on his responsibilities than on the behaviors of racists perennially benefitting from white privilege. Even more, the in-clandestine vehemence in which Donald Trump pursued his "Birther" "fool's errand" and so "Poisoned the well" disaffected persons yet see this "Un-presidential timber" as the "Great White Hope," even though to this day he still believes Mr. Obama is not a citizen. This folly flies in the face of the Supreme Court judgment, but more important yet underscores a putrid underbelly. It also says something of those who say no matter what, Trump is one of us. That is, we like the fact, "Trump is insulting his way to the Presidency."

FREDERICK MONDERSON

Young man displays painted image of Barack Obama breaking through the life and experience of Martin Luther King to capture the White House.

62. BARACK OBAMA RHETORIC AND REALITY BY
Dr. Fred Monderson

Barack Obama never "Loved the beatings" but he publicly admitted, "I know politics is a contact sport" and that "U.S. politics is tough;" but he equally affirmed, "I know America is better off" because of my efforts as President. Surprisingly, however, when we consider the rhetoric spewing in the current Presidential campaign, a number of important deductions become very apparent. First and foremost, the Republican front Runner Donald Trump has been tremendously outrageous in his brinkmanship posturing to quote

BLACK NATIONALISM STILL ALIVE AND WELL

Jeb Bush, former Florida Governor, "Mr. Trump has been insulting his way to the Presidency." However, and equally alarmingly outrageous, his growing and equally outrageous band of followers rather than condemn his vile behavior have consistently been flocking to his clarion call and *Ipso Facto* goading him on. Second and most important, the office to which he now aspires has been so tarnished by Mr. Trump's as well as fellow Republicans' behaviors in recent years, it is certainly questionable as to their level of concern for the future of this nation. After all, these people are campaigning on plans to repeal not simply "Obamacare," but practically every meaningful measure Mr. Obama successfully implemented that did not have Republican approval and support. Thus, in the interest of the American people Mr. Obama asserted his authority and used Executive Action, though not as often as his predecessors. If they repeal everything, "Does the car return to the ditch?"

Most observers would consider the above political posturing but the statement of then Senate Minority leader Mitch McConnell "I intend to make Barack Obama a one term President," showed he had morally crossed the line. Morgan Freeman, the Academy Award winning actor, on CNN's Piers Morgan, blatantly stated it was racist! More important, however, coming as it did from within the halls of government, many agree Mr. McConnell had opened the floodgates of the rapidly escalating racism and disrespect Republicans and their supporters have heaped upon President Obama for the duration of two presidential terms. Many people agree much of this "Presidential flogging" was racially inspired. Much more significant, this seems part of a continuum of the Dred Scott Decision denying the African legal standing in the nation. Chief Justice Roger Taney, considered a slavery apologist, helped legally enshrine the "White Supremacy Ideology" ensuring it remained active from 1857 to even today. This continuity of denial of the Black man's humanity has remained consistent despite his blood, sweat, labor and spiritual force unquestionably infused in the structural pillars of this nation.

FREDERICK MONDERSON

Portrait of President Barack Obama unveiled at "Sharpton's Affair" that welcomed Mr. Obama.

BLACK NATIONALISM STILL ALIVE AND WELL

President Obama congratulates Rev. Al Sharpton for his wonderful and effective work as a civil rights leader.

That is why, we must seek to understand the dynamics wherein, from the time of the original rollout of the Affordable Care Act, the rhetoric was deafening and destructively vocal. Republicans operate from within the prism of "Win" or "Lose." Therefore, the grand strategy has always been, "Block every chance of a win for Obama!" This meant, block every meaningful measure he proposed but most important his signature health care accomplishment the Affordable Care Act. In this particular campaign, the "Long knives" in Jim DeMint's "Waterloo;" Billy Crystal's "Go for the Jugular;" "Lipstick on a pig" Palin then accusing Mr. Obama of "Palling around with terrorists" and now falsely blaming him for her son's PTSD as an excuse for his female abuse, yet she refuses to accept this round of the war malady manifestation is a Republican administration creation. Therefore, every Republican candidate, those with or without a "Daddy" wants to abolish this law unmindful of the more than 17 million who have signed up for the measure's health care protections.

FREDERICK MONDERSON

"Always the Ladies Man" Herb Boyd poses with these young ladies who also came out to welcome President Obama at "Sharpton's Affair."

Now on the verge of an encore performance as the "War Hawks" prepare to re-take the helm of the Presidency, they so abused under Obama rule, who could forget disgraceful "You Lie" Joe Wilson or even "Stupid" Senator Grassley who himself could not recognize a constitutional scholar if he came up to him as E.F. Hutton would say, "Slapped him on the bottom and say, I'm here?" Then there's that "Light Colonel" who stooped so low as to examine and question the President's "testicular fortitude."

Let us not forget "Daddy Cruz," banking on spending at least one night in the Lincoln bedroom and so demanded we "Send Obama back to Kenya," but too bad such a dream seems fading thanks to his son's Canadian citizenship Donald Trump keeps emphasizing.

"Joe the Plumber" and "Queen Birther" have faded into oblivion like an imploding star while the new crop of rhetoricians have coined new shibboleths to continue the "dirty work." Meanwhile, President Obama, like the Teflon penny long in circulation, still retains his luster.

BLACK NATIONALISM STILL ALIVE AND WELL

That "White Silence is Complicity" and "National Action Network - No Justice, No Peace" are messages that resonate.

Who could forget when Mr. Obama referred to a female as "Sweetie" and the press and others had a field day vilifying the man? Now, Donald Trump talks "Pussy;" "Bomb the shit out of ISIS" and much, more yet the people love it. We know of Goldfinger's "Pussy Galore;" on CNN one head of an organization invited Anderson Cooper (AC 360) to visit and be made "King of Pussy Willow," a New York state town of such a name. Now we have "Pussy" Trump who says he is only repeating the vulgarity referring to Ted Cruz. This is the future leadership many on the Republican "ship of fools" want to have sail this nation.

Thus, we have to ask what is acceptable as presidential behavior? Has "President Obama so changed America" Republican followers now settle for less?

FREDERICK MONDERSON

We know Mr. Obama dispatched the "losers" McCain, Palin, Romney, Ryan, Perry, De Mint, Allen, Graham, Joe Wilson, and so many thanks to strategic thinking, planning and execution, hallmarks of his focused and effective work ethic. Today Pataki, Christie and others on the chopping block have failed miserably to measure up to the giant Barack Obama.

BN PHOTO - Iconic Jitu Weusi with Dr. Fred Monderson (right).

BN PHOTO - Red, Black and Green, the African Nationalist Flag, given by Marcus Garvey in 1920 and still going strong with its symbolic message.

www.ingramcontent.com/pod-product-compliance
Lightning Source LLC
Chambersburg PA
CBHW061947300426
44117CB00010B/1246